INFRASTRUCTURES OF DEMOCRACY

Politics and Processes of Road Building in Rural Nepal

INFRASTRUCTURES OF DEMOCRACY

Politics and Processes of Road Building in Rural Nepal

Editors
KATHARINE N. RANKIN | SARA SHNEIDERMAN
MUKTA S. TAMANG

Martin Chautari

INFRASTRUCTURES OF DEMOCRACY
Politics and Processes of Road Building in Rural Nepal

Editors
KATHARINE N. RANKIN | SARA SHNEIDERMAN
MUKTA S. TAMANG

First edition 2026

Publisher
Martin Chautari
27 Jeetjung Marg, Thapathali
GPO Box 13470, Kathmandu, Nepal
Tel: +977-1-5338050/4102027
Email: chautari@mos.com.np
www.martinchautari.org.np
ISBN: 978-9937-594-38-7
Price: NRs. 999/-
Chautari Book Series - 120
Layout & cover design: Kishor Pradhan
Printed in Nepal
Cover photo by Pushpa Hamal

Contents

Acknowledgments vii

Abbreviations xi

Introduction

Road Building, the State, and Everyday Practice in Rural Nepal 1

Katharine N. Rankin, Sara Shneiderman and *Mukta S. Tamang*

Chapter 1

The Politics and Practice of Road Building in Morang: A Paradox of Remoteness and Accessibility 63

Lagan Rai

Chapter 2

The Politics and Practice of Road Building in Dolakha: From Users' Committees to Bulldozers 139

Shyam Kunwar

Chapter 3

The Politics and Practice of Road Building in Mugu: Collusion, Consensus, and Critique in Imaginaries of a Connected Future 215

Pushpa Hamal and *Tulasi Sharan Sigdel*

Conclusion
The Politics of Roads and the Praxis of Planning 285
Katharine N. Rankin

Afterword
Reflections of a Project Coordinator 311
Elsie Lewison

Bibliography 319
Glossary 349
Appendix 353
Notes on Contributors 365
Index 367

Acknowledgments

Thanks go foremost to our community-based colleagues, Durga Hansda, Samjhana Nepali, Yaman Sardar, and Shanta Thapa, who worked closely with the chapter authors to conduct ethnographic research and interpret findings. These colleagues also participated in an extended workshop to develop research design and initiate comparative framings; their insights infuse this book. The research team was frequently hosted and loosely affiliated with Martin Chautari (MC). MC hosted a launch event as part of its regular Research Seminar Series, during which we presented the research design and benefited from generous feedback; team members had access to desk and meeting space there and also benefited from the library, as well as advice and insights from colleagues Pratyoush Onta and Lokranjan Parajuli. Buddha Kumar Shrestha and Dal Bahadur Shrestha helped to scan literature and newspaper archives from the MC library, and Rukh Gurung and Kishor Pradhan shared materials and helped troubleshoot technical issues in archiving collections. We are grateful for all this support, and the opportunity it afforded for all of us to participate in a wider community of scholarly and engaged social science research in Nepal.

The Infrastructures of Democracy (IOD) project benefited as well from colleagues who served as "Collaborators," in the parlance of the Canadian Social Sciences and Humanities Research Council (SSHRC), on whom we called regularly in an advisory capacity. Seira Tamang and Mukta S. Tamang helped to prepare job descriptions for core researchers and interview candidates; they also commented on research design materials. Stacy Pigg intersected with the research team around the conception, research, and analysis for a graphic ethnography project centered on the theme of road development in Dolakha District, and particularly engaged with Shyam Kunwar in this work. Galen Murton reviewed drafts of project documents, including the Introduction of this book, met with the research team during a series of analysis workshops undertaken over zoom, and convened a panel on "Building Roads, Bridging Borders" comprised of core researchers, for the conference on Roadology at the Southern University of Science and Technology in Shenzhen, People's Republic of China, 2018. Dinesh Paudel provided mentorship to research team members particularly through participation in a workshop on "Roads, Political Imaginaries, and State Building" at the Sixth Himalayan Studies Conference (HSC6) in Toronto, Canada, 2022. Ram Krishna Sapkota joined the project as Collaborator while serving in the capacity of Director General of the Government of Nepal's Department of Local Infrastructure Development and Agricultural Roads (DoLIDAR); he advised us at the research design stage, particularly around opportunities to engage with the Ministry of Local Development (MoLD). These colleagues enriched both the process and the outcomes of the research.

Thanks also go to Shushank Shrestha who produced the drawings featured in the cover pages for each chapter, based on photographs provided by the chapter authors. Shushank met with the editors to discuss the significance of the photographs in relation to the chapter arguments, and continued the dialogue as he produced the images. Colleagues Dinesh Lamichhane, Pratik Shrestha and Punam Sherpa at NAXA in Kathmandu produced the maps, also in dialogue with the editors. We are grateful to have been able to collaborate with these colleagues whose visual materials enhance the book.

The Infrastructures of Democracy project was support by the Canadian SSHRC in the form of an Insight Grant (no. 435-2014-1883) to fund research activities and a Connection Grant (no.

611-2019-0620) to fund participation of core researchers in the aforementioned workshop and conference. Production of the book was supported from the outset by editor Kathryn S. White, who helped to refine and relate chapter arguments over several early drafts as well as conceive the project over numerous early discussions. At MC, Pratyoush Onta in his editorial capacity exercised commendable patience as the book slowly took shape; communicated with impeccable reliability; and provided comments on the manuscript. Lokranjan Parajuli and Kishor Pradhan also provided invaluable editorial and technical support for the production of the book. Two peer reviewers, Jagnnath Adhikari and Bandana Gyawali, offered comments that significantly informed final revisions and editorial decisions. We are grateful for all this input while of course remaining responsible for any shortcomings.

Graduate students at the University of Toronto played a critical role throughout the research and writing process. Elsie Lewison served as project manager from 2016–2021. She undertook a wide range of leadership roles, from budget management, to web development, to communications within the team, to leading a summer abroad opportunity for Canadian undergraduate students in one of our research sites. Courtney Balaz-Munn and Elsie Lewison input interview transcripts and other data into NVIVO and developed theme-based archives. Helen Loghrin, Hannelore Yager and Ashwini Gadtaula analyzed grey-literature sources and photos. Adrian Khan assisted at the research design phase. We also acknowledge the foundational support of the Department of Geography and Planning at the University of Toronto and the Department of Anthropology and School of Public Policy & Global Affairs at the University of British Columbia. And at home, we are grateful to our families, who have been present through it all: Mark, Sam, and Nina Turin; Nhima Bhuti Gurung; Peter and Niku Zimmerman; Sam Rankin; and Bhakti Maya, Roshana Dolmo, Salina Dolmo and Sheran Tamang.

Finally we would like to end where the project began by acknowledging the ethnographic scholarship of Lagan Rai, Shyam

Kunwar, Pushpa Hamal, and Tulasi Sigdel. Pushpa and Tulasi first proposed that we see roads as a contested political field through which to view state building processes—an insight they shared in the context of a prior research project focused on "Cultural Politics of Governance in Nepal" (SSHRC International Opportunities Fund grant no 861-2008-1010); Andrea Nightingale collaborated as a Co-Investigator in that project and offered her expertise on socio-natures in forest governance as we developed an approach to studying infrastructure development. Pushpa offered his direct ties and reflections in Mugu, his home district, and interjected healthy criticism about power dynamics surrounding collaborative ethnographic research. Tulasi shared his expertise and connections with the civil service based on his appointment as Senior Director of Studies at Nepal Administrative Staff College. Lagan Rai and Shyam Kunwar brought formal ethnographic training, experience, and admirable enthusiasm for fieldwork to our collective endeavor. Lagan contributed an adaptation and translation into Nepali of "Everyone Can Do Research: A Plain Language Guide on How to Do Research," prepared by Yogendra Shakya at Access Alliance,[1] and interjected a steady stream of insightful reflections (and good humor) throughout the book-writing process. Shyam shared his encyclopedic knowledge of relevant English- and Nepali-language scholarship, and innovated consistently in obtaining and sharing archival sources such as DDC meeting minutes and local news media. We could not be more grateful to have collaborated for so long with such a generous, caring, and brilliant group of colleagues.

[1] The Access Alliance toolkit is available at https://accessalliance.ca/wp-content/uploads/2020/07/CBR-toolkit_2_May-2013.pdf; accessed May 30, 2025; and Lagan's translation/adaptation is available on the IOD project website at https://infrastructuresofdemocracy.geog.utoronto.ca/; accessed May 30, 2025.

Abbreviations

ADB	Asian Development Bank
APM	All-Party Mechanism
APP	Agricultural Perspective Plan
ASI	Assistant Sub-Inspector
CBO	Community-based Organization
CDF	Constituency Development Fund
CDO	Chief District Officer
CFUG	Community Forestry User Group
CIAA	Commission for Investigation of Abuse of Authority
CPN-UML	Communist Party of Nepal–Unified Marxist Leninist
DCC	District Coordination Committee
DDC	District Development Committee
DfID	Department for International Development, UK
DoLI	Department of Local Infrastructure
DoLID	Department of Local Infrastructure Development
DoLIDAR	Department of Local Infrastructure Development and Agricultural Roads
DoR	Department of Roads
DoTM	Department of Transportation Management
DRILIP	Decentralized Rural Infrastructure and Livelihood Project
DRSP	District Road Support Program
DTMP	District Transportation Master Plan
DTO	District Technical Office or Officer

FAO	Food and Agriculture Organization of the UN
FfW	Food for Work
FNCCI	Federation of Nepalese Chambers of Commerce and Industry
FNNTE	Federation of Nepalese National Transport Entrepreneurs
GoN	Government of Nepal
GTZ	German Technical Cooperation Agency
HMG	His Majesty's Government
IBRD	International Bank for Reconstruction and Development
ICB	International Competitive Bidding
ICIMOD	International Centre for Integrated Mountain Development
IHDP	Integrated Hill Development Project
INGO	International Non-Governmental Organization
IRD	Integrated Rural Development
JMDP	Jiri Multipurpose Development Project
JV	Joint Venture
KEP	Karnali Employment Program
LDO	Local Development Officer
LEP	Labor-based, Environmentally-friendly and Participatory
LJRP	Lamosangu-Jiri Road Project
LRN	Local Road Network
LSGA	Local Self-Government Act
MP	Member of Parliament
NCB	National Competitive Bidding
NGO	Non-Governmental Organization
NGR	Nepal Government Railway
PC	Personal Commission
RAP	Rural Access Program
RAP3	Rural Access Program, Phase 3
RBG	Road Building Group
RCC	Reinforced Cement Concrete
RCDC	Rural Community Development Center

RCIW	Rural Community Infrastructure Works
RDO	Road Division Office
RoW	Right-of-Way
RTO	Regional Transportation Office
SAP	Structural Adjustment Program
SDC	Swiss Agency for Development and Cooperation
TAR	Tibet Autonomous Region
UNODC	United Nations Office on Drugs and Crime
v.s.	*Vikram Samvat*
VDC	Village Development Committee
WTO	World Trade Organization

INTRODUCTION

Road Building, the State, and Everyday Practice in Rural Nepal

KATHARINE N. RANKIN, SARA SHNEIDERMAN AND MUKTA S. TAMANG

This book on road building in rural Nepal takes its impetus from the political transitions of the early-mid 2000s. All of the editors and authors in some way were engaged in exploratory research on the meaning and practices of "democracy" in rural areas following the decade-long civil conflict between Maoist and state forces, and the subsequent establishment of a federal democratic republic, and found that roads were continuously articulated as key sites of protest, claims-making, profit and territorial control. Post-conflict, these colliding claims manifested in a frenzy of rural road building: widely reported in the media, increasingly attracting the interest of academics, sometimes dubbed a form of "dozer terrorism" (Nepali Times 2018; Paudel and Rankin 2022). From conflict to disaster, and in the aftermath of both forms of rupture, we observed road building continue apace.

This conjuncture compelled us to ask about how roads and state restructuring are related. It also required regarding roads as agentive forces in their own right, not just as a backdrop for numerous essential activities like travel, trade, protest, moving militaries, drying grains, rushing to the hospital, or holding a wedding. Given their centrality to all kinds of governmental practices and so many facets of everyday life, we ask how roads play a central role in constituting various state projects (as well as donor agendas), and in shaping social, political, economic and environmental relations.

Given also the dramatic imprint on the landscape unfolding before our eyes in rural Nepal, it was tempting to marvel at the novelty of roads everywhere, at times going nowhere, scaling impossible terrain, suspended in time, transforming the landscape. These are by now common refrains in the literature and media. And yet as scholars, we also had to consider the durable relations and dynamics—how the current attention to roads is in fact not so new or extraordinary, how the motorable road must have always figured historically and geographically in the making of the Nepali state and in the everyday lives of its citizens. Thus our first task was to locate the present flourishing of road building in relation to various historical periods of state building in Nepal, which we characterized as managing coloniality (1846–1950), integrating the nation (1951–1970) and building economy (1970–1990) [Rankin *et al.* 2017]. In order to underscore how road building produces specific contemporary geographies, we opted to take a comparative approach, conducting ethnographic research over several years in three districts: Morang, Dolakha, and Mugu. We selected these locations for their distinctive physical and social geographies, as well as their different historical positioning in national trajectories of road building. The comparative orientation points to distinctive conjunctures in which road building articulates specific local social relations and political economies. It also allows for an overarching reckoning with geopolitical dynamics and governmental rationalities of the state. By focusing on distinct sites of rural road building within Nepal, we can appreciate how geopolitics and state projects not only direct road building but are also shaped by it.

Another emergent impetus for our work is the so-called "infrastructure turn" in the social sciences and humanities that furnishes compelling theoretical resources as well as extensive empirical scholarship on road building in Nepal and the Himalayas (Campbell 2010; Appel, Anand and Gupta 2019; Joniak-Lüthi 2020; Murton and Lord 2020; Gurung 2021; Heslop and Murton 2021; Oakes 2019; Rankin and Simpson 2021). Thinking infrastructurally, as Jessica DiCarlo and Tim Oakes (2022) recently put it, allows us to approach roads as a relational methodology as well as an object of inquiry through which to observe how socio-political processes, competing political imaginaries and ecological vulnerabilities interact on the terrain of development and planning (see also Larkin 2013 on infrastructure as things and relations among things). Roads have impacts: they shape dynamics of political and environmental change, and those dynamics in turn bring roads into being in specific ways in particular times and places.

If there is any one consistent finding from all the scholarship on roads that has come out of our own research and that of other colleagues working in the Himalayas and wider Asian contexts, it is the imperative to investigate how the actual implementation and lived outcomes of infrastructure development—even grandiose projects like China's Belt and Road Initiative—remains locally determined (Joniak-Lüthi 2020; Murton and Lord 2020; Gurung 2021; Oakes 2021). In that sense, our work joins with other ethnographic projects on road development. We present grounded, place-based ethnographic research highlighting the situated politics and processes through which roads are built in relation to diverse governmental projects. The expression, "infrastructures of democracy," is meant to signal both the contested physical infrastructures underpinning state construction and reconstruction, as well as the social and political infrastructures governing everyday life and meting out access to opportunity.

What makes our work distinctive on this terrain of scholarship? Our emphasis on roads in rapidly ruralizing areas characterized by often spontaneous construction, uneven quality and Nepali state-led development expands the scope of existing inquiry, with an emphasis on rural-urban relationality (Gillen, Bunnell and Rigg 2022). Much of the scholarship on roads in Nepal has focused on megaprojects and geopolitics. Our approach centers everyday life in relation to the rural roads and local polities that account for the preponderance of construction activity and expansion of the road network in Nepal today. In so doing we also draw heavily on local vernacular—language, concepts and idioms—as a means for expressing sensibilities, making theory, and troubling some conventional analytical frames commonly associated with infrastructure development, such as corruption, which tend to overlook local knowledge and dynamics of power. As indicated in the cover photo, we emphasize the everyday life of rural road building, which brings practices of labor, social reproduction, business, and planning into relation.

The intersection of roads, state building and political imaginaries offers a powerful vantage point from which to understand transformations of political subjectivity. After the civil conflict of 1996–2006 and throughout post-2006 processes of state restructuring, the revolutionary achievements of the Maoist movement were at once lauded and duly questioned in public discourse. Rather than engaging in political debate, we sought to look carefully at how roads research can shed light on how social aspirations are made and articulated, contributing to constituting political subjects and polities in such contexts of rapid change. When people make claims on infrastructure—donate their land, refuse to volunteer their labor, attend a public meeting to challenge construction delay—they create publics that become visible as "demanding subjects of state care," as Hannah Appel, Nikhil Anand and Akhil Gupta (2019) have highlighted. This kind of activity seemed to be happening all around us in rural Nepal—the building of polities and political consciousness in relation to the building of roads.

Finally, our work on roads seeks to engage planning and development as a normative terrain, where competing visions are put forward about what is a good and just society. We see roads not just as informing a critique of planning but also as a grounds for considering its political possibilities.

At the same time, roads may have unintended consequences. They may reinforce existing patterns of inequality and injustice, along lines of gender, caste, ethnicity, region and class. They may offer new forms of access and connectivity to some while rendering others' lives and livelihoods newly remote. These contradictions are at the heart of our inquiry, and while we cannot provide a comprehensive assessment of differential social outcomes, our ethnographic material takes readers into many experiential settings to consider some of the many ways that people on the ground in a range of subject positions have engaged with the changes that roads bring.

This Introduction proceeds by introducing six key arguments that unfold across the book's chapters. We then provide contextual background in sections on Nepal's recent political transformations and the infrastructural turn in the social sciences and humanities. Our methodology section details the research and writing process, with special attention to ethical considerations and power dynamics. Finally, we turn to a chronology of key periods in the history of Nepal's road building. We conclude by turning to the terrain of planning practice to consider the ever-relevant question, "What is to be done?" Taken together, these sections offer readers an entrée into the complex scholarly, political, and historical considerations that shape the core chapters, each of which explores the issues introduced here in a unique, geographically situated manner, driven by both the research interests and expertise of each author, and the specifics of circumstances on the ground in the locality at hand.

KEY ARGUMENTS

This book as a whole makes several interrelated arguments that emerge out of our empirical research in Morang, Dolakha and Mugu. The specific histories and political formations of each context highlight a wide range of possibilities, while also suggesting some shared domains of experience across Nepal. Here, we highlight key points of convergence as the basis for the book's critical arguments.

First, we argue that roads reveal connectivity and remoteness as a relational set of values, which must be understood in both spatial and sociocultural terms (see also Shneiderman 2014; Saxer 2017, 2023). Our chapters show in rich ethnographic detail how new roads bring connectivity for some but create new forms of remoteness for others, across variegated terrains and locations, reorienting notions of "center," "periphery," and the relationships between. This insight challenges the idea that roads necessarily beget progress, development, or better market integration. Rather, the path that they take matters, and delivers uneven experiences of accessibility and inaccessibility for different people, depending upon where they are located geographically as well as within local, regional, and national hierarchies of power. Although in Himalayan contexts we may often think of remoteness in terms of mountainous terrain, here we expand this concept to consider rivers as environmental actors that may create conditions of remoteness on a seasonal basis across the Tarai plains as well.

A second argument centers on the common expectation that the road constitutes a public good, insofar as it enhances connectivity and requires centrally coordinated investments of land, budgets, expertise, and labor. Our attention to place-based perspectives underscores the imperative to ask finer-grained questions: what is a good, and for which publics? We find that, in a material sense, roads certainly do not conform to the conventional criteria for a public good: they are not available equally to all, and the benefits that accrue to some can directly diminish the benefits roads deliver to others. The chapters probe these dynamics. To pose "good" in a more aspirational sense as benefit or value, we find similarly that the harms and benefits of road building are not distributed equally, and moreover that patterns of harm and benefit vary over time and space (see also Heslop and Murton 2021). These patterns are particularly evident in conflicts surrounding land, labor, economic development, and access to markets and services, as has been documented since the 1970s when some of Nepal's major highways were being completed

(Blaikie, Cameron and Seddon 1977). Roads also convey critical insights about contestations over publicness and the multiplicity of publics (Rankin *et al.* 2024; Shneiderman 2024). Specifically, they convey different understandings of who is responsible for contributing to infrastructure development, what forms of private gain from public road budgets are justifiable, and shifting sensibilities about the relationship between citizens and the state. The competing values that become evident through exploring these contestations provide a corrective against the gloss of corruption that commonly infuses analyses of infrastructure development. They also help us to specify locally situated logics of ethical judgment that might furnish alternative conceptions of the public good.

Third, we argue that roads generate political capital in both symbolic and material forms. Symbolically, roads are a promise that political party candidates and elected officials can offer to constituents. Such promises carry their own aspirations—for security, mobility, order, aesthetics—which can be generative in mobilizing individual political participation as well as shaping party alliances. The resulting political capital must eventually be invested in the material implementation of road building: terrain surveyed, labor and machinery secured, contracts tendered. Once the abstract promise of the road is materialized in such ways, unanticipated consequences invariably arise, even in the best-managed and well-resourced projects. These material complexities can in turn shift political alignments, as political actors become entangled in the messy, multiscalar arrangements required to realize their promises in concrete infrastructural form. Political fortunes may rise and fall in relation to the disaggregated and contested notions of "publics" and "goods," as discussed above. In these ways, the symbolic and material are relational elements of the political valence of "the road" as a whole.

We argue, fourth, that building roads forges individual and collective political subjectivity, as differently positioned people make claims, exercise agency and imagine different futures. The sheer scale of road development across rural Nepal, combined with the pace and scope of political transformation associated with the Maoist-state conflict and subsequent state restructuring, have essentially conjoined roads and politics in every corner of the country. And yet, how people formulate ideas of themselves as political actors varies in relation to specific local histories of road building. The chapters explore roads as sites of claims making, protest, and getting by. They trace how through involvement in road building, people navigate multiple scales of state and development institutions; and how pursuing their own objectives requires a trade-off between aligning with and subverting governmental regimes. The chapter arguments hinge around specifying variegated and emotionally uneven relationships with the state and notions of development writ large, as well as modes of critical consciousness and locally situated knowledge that come into view through the contradictions of the road. A key insight that emerges across the chapters is that "local knowledge" encompasses relational, tactical understanding of how specific places are situated within wider political economies.

We argue, fifth, that rural roads constitute conjuncturally specific environmental transformations. Maintaining environmental well-being is often seen as a secondary value in relation to economic development. Too often, awareness of the fragility of the landscape only increases after it may be too late to change the course of road development. "Green roads" planned around the "locally-based, environmentally-friendly, participatory" model have become conceptually important in Nepal's rural road imaginaries, but these projects do not always bear out their promise, and may instead cut tracks into unsettled terrain that is at ever greater risk of flood- and landslide-induced disasters as climate change accelerates. Throughout this book's chapters, we see variously positioned actors coming to terms with the fact that building motorable roads necessarily changes the landscape—as well as people's knowledge of how to navigate it. For example, when buses along a wide two-lane road replace narrow footpaths through the forest as a primary mode of mobility, people's relationship with their landscape shifts. Yet the nature of these changes is specific to the modality of road building that is adopted in each locale, with community members articulating nuanced analyses, and sometimes critique, of how different modalities affect their environment.

Finally, we argue that planning must be engaged both as an object of inquiry (what is the role of planning and planners at different spatial scales in shaping specific conjunctures of road building?) and as a terrain of practice (how could our research inform a planning practice committed to justice and sustainability?). The chapters identify three modalities of planning action. One focuses on technical and administrative functions associated with implementing a specific plan or program, such as a District Transportation Master Plan (DTMP), from issuing contract tenders to undertaking various quality assessments throughout the construction process. A second modality of planning action, associated with green roads, situates road building within a community-development framework involving various training programs and social protections like vegetable cultivation and savings and credit groups. In such cases the planning function encompasses local NGOs contracted to provide "social mobilizers" to coordinate the wider community development dimensions of road development. A third modality is constituted by informal planning action led by local residents, whether in the form of traditional labor exchanges being mobilized for infrastructure development or instances of labor migrants returning to their natal village to coordinate a particular infrastructure development project. We show that all of these modalities, including those with technical and administrative functions, are deeply inflected with political dynamics—in the senses of imbrication with political party politics, the operation of power within planning bureaucracies, how planners interface with communities, and perceptions of planners by community members.

These arguments and the empirical material which articulates them throughout this book seek to unsettle what are often presented as binaries between "local" versus "external" forces, "the community" versus "the state" and/or "the donor." Instead, we argue that locally situated perspectives constitute powerful expert knowledge of local dynamics, as well as of multiscalar relations among intersecting political economies. We recognize these as situated critical analyses of the field of road development, rather than as a "local point of view" that is limited to a narrow geographical and conceptual domain. These situated critical analyses convey important insights about relations of power, cultural politics, socio-spatial difference, and, crucially, techniques for controlling the terms of integration into wider political economies. Such insights can have a key role to play in imbuing official modalities of planning with explicit commitments to justice and sustainability. By the same token, this foundation of knowledge can also be the basis of collusion: mobilizing insider information for personal gain. In other words, the "local" is not inherently aligned with the common good; it too needs to be understood as a site of proactive knowledge production within dynamics of power, and not merely a site of reactive practice. The devil is in the details, and throughout the ensuing ethnographic chapters we see a diverse range of actors engaging in multiple forms of planning, practice, and protest informed by locally-grounded knowledge and expertise.

POLITICAL TRANSITION IN NEPAL

The research presented in the core chapters of this book was conducted between 2016–2019, a time of radical political and environmental transformation in Nepal. The decade-long civil conflict between the Maoist People's Liberation Army and state forces ended in 2006 with a Comprehensive Peace Agreement that promised a restructured federal state (von Einsiedel, Malone and Pradhan 2012; Kharel 2022; Tamang 2023b). This resolution was in part forged through the 2006 *Jana Andolan* II, or Second People's Movement, which continued the mobilization for a return to multi-party democracy that began in 1990. The practices and processes of road building have intertwined with these movements towards democracy over the last several decades.

The country's first ever Constituent Assembly (CA) was elected in 2008, but completed its tenure in 2012 without promulgating a new constitution as expected. Political actors continued to debate the country's future through the tenure of a second CA elected in 2013, but the devastating earthquakes of April and May 2015 hit before they could complete their work. Our research began during this critical period of post-conflict state restructuring, and continued through the parallel experience of post-disaster reconstruction.

Whether constructed by the then Royal Nepal Army to achieve better access to remote Maoist encampments, or by the Nepal government with international support to deliver development to rural communities in the hopes of tempering support for the Maoists (Leve 2009; Paudel 2016), the conflict period saw an expansion rather than contraction of road building. This only accelerated further in the post-conflict, pre-disaster period from 2006–2015, as international agencies returned to Nepal or increased their engagement, and state actors seeking to influence the shape of the future polity curried constituent favor by promising (and sometimes delivering) new infrastructure (The Asia Foundation 2017).

The new constitution was finally promulgated in September 2015. Although it delivered a federal state as promised, the boundaries of the seven new provinces fell short of expectations for many who had been mobilizing around ethnicity and regional identities, and did not see their agendas acknowledged in the new map (Shneiderman and Tillin 2015; Adhikari and Gellner 2016). This included both Adivasi Janajati and Madheshi activists, who had led movements demanding Indigenous and regional rights for those along Nepal's southern borders respectively. Although there was some protest at the federal map as implemented, many activists were sidelined by the earthquakes of April and May 2015, which disproportionately affected Indigenous communities in the 14 districts of central Nepal that suffered most (Ghale 2015; Amnesty International 2017).

The constitutional promulgation set in motion the process of administrative restructuring, with local elections occurring in late 2017 for the first time in 20 years. These elections established a new system of local governance, which incorporated erstwhile Village Development Committees (VDC, or *GaViSa* in Nepali to abbreviate *Gau Vikas Samiti*) into several larger rural municipalities, or *Gaupalika*. Much of our research occurred during this period from 2015–2017, where road building became a critical site for aspiring local leaders to position themselves for electoral success. This period introduced several important questions of jurisdiction. With a new provincial system, as well as newly formed local governments, who would be responsible for road building? How would budgets be allocated? Whose responsibility was it to ensure technical rigor and safety?

Many of these questions remain open at the time of writing in early 2025. Since the administrative restructuring of 2017, local governments have established new forms of authority and influence, and new provincial legislatures have been established. At the same time, unelected chief district officers (CDOs) have continued to be appointed by the federal government. These overlapping vectors of state power have resulted in ongoing ambiguities surrounding jurisdiction and responsibility for service provision across sectors and scales. The federal government, provincial governments, local governments, and district offices have each held authority over some dimensions of road building during our research. Much of our most recent phase of research has focused on understanding such jurisdictional complexities as both the administrative structures and material infrastructure of the roads beneath our feet continue to evolve. In this, we build upon an excellent body of scholarship that explores the lived experience of federal restructuring (e.g., Tamang 2023a, 2023b, 2023c; Johnson 2023a; Nightingale *et al.* 2023).

Throughout the time period of our research, we have heard overlapping narratives of "crisis," "transition," "emergency," and "transformation" to describe what Nepal is experiencing. We want to point out that this sensibility is not new, and that for much of the past half century both Nepali and foreign observers have used such terminology to evoke a sense of the radical change that Nepalis have continually experienced. For instance, in the 1970s, Piers Blaikie, John Cameron, and David Seddon published the first major, public critical commentary on road building in Nepal, in the form of a multi-volume report on *The Effects of Roads in West Central Nepal* (1977). This and a subsequent book titled *Nepal in Crisis* (1980) argued that expansion of foreign aid and the state apparatus in general, and highway construction in the Western Development Region in particular, had exacerbated Nepal's crisis of under-development. The authors' position profoundly contradicted prevailing accounts that regarded the presence of roads as an indicator of rural areas' accession to modernity, with territorial connectivity imagined to bring communities into connection with global flows of capital and ideology—or lack of roads seen to indicate "remoteness" as a problem of underdevelopment (e.g., Schroeder and Sisler 1971). In all cases, however, roads have been commonly implicated in accounts of crisis.

In our view, these perpetual narratives of crisis can mask transformations of political subjectivity and agency that people across Nepal have experienced over the last several decades. Although this is a broader statement substantiated by our and other research on related themes (Shneiderman 2009; Nightingale *et al.* 2018), here we offer a close reading of shifting subjectivities on the ground through our in-depth empirical material about experiences of road building in three different districts. Certainly individuals, families, and communities have experienced moments of crisis—whether in relation to the conflict, the earthquake, or other forms of uncertainty due to infrastructural development, large-scale migration, or climate change, for instance—but people have also asserted themselves as citizens in new ways, to make claims for themselves on the ever-evolving polity. One of the terrains on which such participatory citizenship unfolds is that of road building, as we hope the subsequent chapters will show. It is in this sense that roads can be understood as a contested "infrastructure of democracy."

THE "INFRASTRUCTURE TURN" AND LITERATURES ON ROADS AND MOBILITY

Our research focus on roads emerged foremost out of contemporary socio-political conditions in Nepal. And yet, its selection also coincides with the flourishing of social science scholarship taking up infrastructure as an object of inquiry in the late 20th/early 21st centuries. Infrastructure has certainly captured the interest of anthropologists and human geographers working in regions like the Himalayas that have historically lacked motorable road access and more generally modern construction techniques and materials needed for transportation and communications infrastructures. The decay of infrastructure in industrialized settings, on a scale that overwhelms capacity to address it in many cases, no doubt has also contributed to the wider scale interest in infrastructure as an object of inquiry. Anthropologists and geographers have, moreover, made the case that infrastructure presents a compelling focus for research that requires ethnographic methodologies (e.g., Star 1999; Harvey and Knox 2015; Appel, Anand and Gupta 2019; Lewison and Murton 2020; Rankin and Simpson 2021). We are inspired by this body of literature in several ways.

First, infrastructural thinking requires a commitment to exploring ethnographically the often-invisible grounds upon which socio-political life unfolds, and upon which states, cultures, markets, and various other institutions and artefacts of modern life, operate. Those grounds can include phenomena like train tracks and roads (objects), engineering expertise (knowledge) and engineers (people). Together they comprise specific material and socio-technical configurations, or systems, that play key roles in contouring everyday life—as much as more overt and visible practices of government do (Larkin 2013; Star 1999).

Second, and related, the study of infrastructure points not just to the study of material objects and associated socio-technical configurations, but also to the relations forged by those materialities (DiCarlo and Oakes 2022). For example, in communities throughout the Himalayas, peoples' interaction with the state derives largely from their interaction with infrastructure. They may qualify for a post-earthquake house reconstruction grant, or provide labor for a district road, or compete for tenders issued by the District Development Committee (DDC)—and through those processes constitute themselves as publics with common experiences as citizen-subjects, and potentially collective claims (Appel, Anand and Gupta 2019). The state in turn builds its power through infrastructural projects. Infrastructure furnishes a pathway through which states manage markets, govern populations, and pursue geopolitical and geoeconomic ambitions. The notion of the "infrastructural state," for example, underscores the significance of infrastructure development for state ambitions to enhance transnational connectivity—and, in the case of small states like Nepal, often considered "weak policy takers," to leverage competition among more powerful regional actors in pursuit of their own spatial projects, like post-earthquake reconstruction (DiCarlo and Schindler 2022; Paudel and Rankin 2022). Infrastructure thus, as Brian Larkin (2013) put it, has an important "political address;" how that address articulates across scales of practice is a matter for investigation. The call for an "infrastructural turn" in social science scholarship reflects this commitment to relational, systemic thinking, and asserts that infrastructure is a particularly generative object upon which to build such an epistemological project, which also has effects beyond its temporally and spatially bound materially form (Boyle and Shneiderman 2020).

How, in the context of the "infrastructure turn," has infrastructure been defined? Needless to say, the question has been vigorously debated. We extrapolate from these debates to touch on a few key points and to clarify our own interpretations. Infrastructure denotes dynamics going on beneath the surface that operate as systems—

systems of substrates, as Star (1999: 380) puts it. Roads can be viewed as infrastructure in this sense; they are objects territorialized on the land, deriving from specific logics and visions of development, upon which things move or are otherwise ordered.

The emphasis on infrastructures as systems points to an understanding that centers their materiality, but also encompasses the socio-political relations, governmental rationalities, and other forms of knowledge that are integral to their physical construction. Since infrastructure is relational—always constituted in relation to specific socio-political and socio-natural contexts—it can generate unexpected and unintended political outcomes, which in turn inform subsequent ideas, discourses, and practices of development (Oakes 2021). Research on roads thus requires, as Pushpa Hamal (2021) puts it, investigating both, "What brings the road and what does the road bring?"[1]

For our purposes, "infrastructures of democracy" points to the relationship between post-conflict state building and the massive roll-out of road construction across Nepal. Roads manifest a range of commitments at the intersection of "New Nepal" and neoliberalism—a state-led push for universal mobility, market opportunity, and access in all directions. They also express demands for state accountability, responsibility, and opportunities for local self-governance emboldened through decades of social and political movements demanding democracy, inclusion, and equality.

It is critical to note that some variation in epistemological orientation can be detected within the infrastructure turn. Conceptualizing infrastructure as an assemblage comprised of things, knowledges and people, helps to specify and trouble the range of agentive forces involved in the co-production of physical

[1] The quotation comes from the doctoral dissertation of Pushpa Hamal on the politics of roads and community learning in Mugu, research for which was conducted in conjunction with the IOD project. The dissertation informs the analysis in the Mugu chapter as well as the orientation in the book toward road development as social justice praxis. Thanks go to Pushpa Hamal for sharing parts of the dissertation that have enriched these elements of the book.

infrastructures. Science and Technology Studies (STS) serves as a key theoretical resource for studies of infrastructure concerned with drawing out this complexity and challenging the centrality of forces typically attributed with having causal impacts—like capital and the state (Star 1999; Barker 2005). Instead STS emphasizes how multiple actors intersect in the constitution of infrastructure, including, as Galen Murton (2013: 610) puts it, "highland populations, topographic landscapes, government officials, international traders, development agencies, environmental policies, economic interests, foreign capital, construction technologies and border systems"—even underscoring the agency of physical infrastructure itself to catalyze unintended consequences. While appreciating the insights afforded through such perspectives about dispersed agency, we also share the caution expressed by Murton (2013) about the risks of decentering power and "flatten[ing] the actor field."

Our approach is rooted more explicitly in political economy and cultural politics, with an emphasis on dynamics of domination, critical consciousness and resistance. It thus foregrounds the political-economic conditions of possibility for infrastructure development to take place, and the key terrains of conflict and struggle introduced or deepened with the arrival of roads in Nepal's agrarian districts. Within "conditions of possibility" we encompass not only materialities such as uneven development, but also rationalities, such as modernization, neoliberalism, environmental sustainability or local self-governance, and conjunctural forces that shape such rationalities and materialities in specific space-time configurations. We are also concerned with how road building projects articulate place-based social relations, modes of domination, and ideologies of caste, gender, ethnicity, region and class. Along with Appel, Anand and Gupta (2018: 17), we foreground the matter of political subjectivity—how infrastructure galvanizes people's sense of their political positioning and world view, and under what conditions they go on to make collective claims as "demanding subjects of state care." We ask: what new modes of critical political consciousness and public sphere politics emerge on the terrain of infrastructure development?

Scholarship on roads in particular has also consolidated within Anthropology, Geography and related disciplines, and furnishes rich conceptual resources. One cluster of critical roads scholarship chronicles how roads have been historically instrumental in the formation of colonial regimes and knowledge systems (e.g., Mrázek 2002; Ahuja 2004). In the case of non-colonized states like Nepal, roads have also been mobilized to thwart colonial incursion through selective development of the interior combined with deliberate lack of development at state borders (Whelpton 1983; Liechty 1997).

Ethnographers have emphasized roads as potent sites of meaning at the interface of culture and politics, where conceptions of modernity and nationalism, corruption and graft, hope and desire, fear and danger, spirituality and witchcraft collide and come into view (Rankin and Simpson 2021: 199). Our work falls within this tradition of grounded, place-based research that centers how local cultural politics, institutional histories, socio-natures and everyday life-worlds shape and are shaped by wider-scale processes and political economies evidenced through road building.

Three ethnographic accounts are particularly worth noting due to the insights they offer for our work. With a focus on Peru, Penny Harvey and Hannah Knox's *Roads: An Anthropology of Infrastructure and Expertise* (2015) underscores how roads furnish a crucial site for understanding politics and state formation; it is based on the premise, which we share, that socio-politics and roads are mutually constituted. In so doing, this book makes three analytical moves that have shaped our scholarship as well as the critical theorization of infrastructure. First, it takes up the perspective and life-worlds of those who live next to the new roads steamrolling into and through Peruvian communities, challenging the presumption that communities are blank slates onto which development interventions can be delivered. In particular, *Roads* conveys a compelling sensitivity to people's awareness of corruption and the public secrets of land acquisition and construction contracts, as well as to how people's time is excessively leveraged in various modes of "participation" across development projects. Second, Harvey and Knox develop an epistemological orientation rooted in the perspective of engineers, which is imperative for our interest in the governmental rationalities and political subjectivities forged through rural road building. Their insights about engineering consciousness afford a key perspective on socio-nature as a terrain for modernist control of unruly nature, which is a crucial element of the road assemblage. Third, they organize each chapter of the book around specific paradoxes that arise out of the interplay of those historical forces and entangled rationalities. The road allures and induces dread. It manifests grandiose ambitions and disappointing shortcomings. The road produces both connectivity and disconnection; mobility and stasis; inclusion and marginality. Raising these paradoxes helps to show how the road might be different things to different people at different times. It also helps to dismantle certain binaries that tend to accompany development discourse and practice, which also include corruption and its imagined antithesis as open markets. In sum, Harvey and Knox's ethnography in the Peruvian context highlights how road building is a deeply political act, shaped by considerable historical forces, across complex ideological terrain. These themes arise in our work as well.

A recent volume edited by Luke Heslop and Galen Murton, *Highways and Hierarchies: Ethnographies of Mobility from the Himalayas to the Indian Ocean,* centers the theme of uneven experience in road development, to argue that "roads [in fact] accelerate and compound class division and social division" (Heslop and Murton 2021: 24). The book thus features patterns of hierarchization forged by and deepened through road development. These include the differential access to opportunities and exposure to risks afforded by the road; consolidation of elite power; accumulation of power; state surveillance and borders; and reproduction of marginality and precarity. The attention here to differential impacts reflects our own insistence on tracking the political economy of outcomes in rural road development through ethnographic means. Our added emphasis on cultural politics aims to highlight dimensions of social justice relating to a politics of recognition, as well as existing cultural resources for positing alternative modes of thought and conceptions of being that could interrogate and challenge prevailing hierarchies associated with highways.

Edward Simpson's *Highways to the End of the World: Roads, Roadmen and Power in South Asia* (2022) takes readers on a narrative journey along India's State Highway 31 in Madhya Pradesh that reveals the historical and contemporary entanglements between road building and political power writ large. Beginning and ending along this particular road, the chapters in between explore the role of roads in state-building processes broadly conceived in both India and Pakistan. This book offers much inspiration both in terms of method and argument. Simpson's blend of archival and ethnographic research connects past and present to highlight the road as a multidimensional object that transcends time and space to shape political subjectivities. Our research follows a similar approach to move beyond the temptation to see road building as a recent rupture, but rather situates it within the long durée of infrastructural and political transformation in a holistic sense. Simpson also critiques the modernist promise of roads as the panacea to development woes by showing how they often advance the agendas of those already in power, rather than offering democratic access to new publics as development proposals might have us believe. In all of these ways, Simpson's analysis sets the stage for the ethnographies that unfold throughout our chapters.

In recent years, the Himalayan region has become a particularly fertile site for ethnographic accounts of road building. The Chinese Belt and Road Initiative (BRI) has appropriately attracted a great deal of interest, including several large, international research projects rooted in ethnographic methodologies (e.g., China Made, Belt &

Road in Global Perspective, Roadwork).[2] These projects all in some way address how BRI extends throughout the Himalaya. They have also challenged conventional interpretations of BRI as evidencing China's growing hegemonic, if not imperialist, status in the region. They point rather to how a seemingly coherent, hegemonic state project manifests as an "assemblage of distinctive projects that prompt *situated* struggles" (Murton and Lord 2020: 11, italics in original), as local state actors, contractors, residents and others vie for influence over infrastructural futures (see also Joniak-Lüthi 2020; Gurung 2021; Oakes 2021). This work contributes to wider geographies and anthropologies of infrastructure by emphasizing the "contingencies of social relations on which the feat of infrastructure depends," in order to underscore how even massive state-led projects are co-constructed through conjuncturally specific socio-political and socio-natural dynamics (Joniak-Lüthi 2020: 2).

Our work shares these epistemological commitments, while attending specifically to the surge of rural road construction in hard-to-reach places, managed primarily by local state bodies and premised often on participation of non-expert local populations. We include within this ambit, "district roads" whose purpose is to link up villages to district centers, and which entail complex arrangements of local contractors and local labor constituted in relation to wider regional and sometimes national procurement markets. We also include "local" or "agricultural" roads, which fall under the jurisdiction of various scales of local governments (VDCs, municipalities, districts) sometimes in collaboration with donor "green roads" projects discussed below. Characterized as "labor-based, environmentally friendly, and participatory" (LEP), green roads were conceived as an "alternative paradigm" to market-oriented and bureaucratically managed systems of procurement and contracting that have been criticized for propelling corruption, deforestation and

[2] The websites are as follows: https://chinamadeproject.net/; https://munkschool.utoronto.ca/belt-road; https://roadworkasia.com/. See also Schatz and Silvey (2025).

erosion in fragile Himalayan environments (Rankin *et al.* 2024). These more locally scaled roads, including their modes of organizing local participation in particular, have not featured extensively in anthropological accounts of road building, despite their significance for everyday life in Himalayan villages, as well as for the logics of international development agendas (Rankin *et al.* 2024; Shneiderman 2024).[3] For us they furnish a critical site for exploring the paradoxes and contradictions arising when social relations of the poor are explicitly harnessed in the provision of public infrastructure.

To think about roads is to think about mobility. Our work is therefore also in dialogue with mobility studies, a related thread of scholarship, burgeoning particularly in Geography (Creswell 2006; Shuller and Urry 2006; Urry 2007; Butz and Cook 2011). Mobility studies focus on how things move, as a key lens on social life and organization. The distinctive contribution for our purposes is the emphasis on a processual orientation toward the road, rooted in an understanding of movement itself, including the infrastructures that sustain movement; the experiences, meanings, and representation of movement; as well as types of movement and movers. We thus consider how mobility is implicated in relations of domination, in contradistinction to prevailing associations of mobility with freedom and expanded capacities. Attention to the politics of mobility requires considering how the freedom and capacity to move may be inequitably distributed and also how mobility can be a site for the curtailment of freedom—as in sex trafficking. It also points toward struggles for mobility justice attending to equity in access to the means of mobility. In this book, our analysis is not limited to road building, but encompasses road development more broadly,

[3] As a corollary, Seira Tamang (2023a: 24) similarly urges careful attention to how "multidimensional networks ... contour the political landscape at the local level" as an antidote to the emphasis on the federal scale in accounts of political restructuring. A key argument of the book is that rural road building and local state building are mutually constituted, and any effort to understand the limits and possibilities for democracy in Nepal must entail an understanding of this relationship.

including systems for the management of transportation, which are equally prone to entanglements with political and power dynamics.

AUTHORSHIP

The arguments of the book unfold through three chapters chronicling long-term ethnographic research in three districts. Those chapters are authored by the lead researcher(s) within each district: Lagan Rai in Morang, Shyam Kunwar in Dolakha, and Pushpa Hamal and Tulasi Sharan Sigdel in Mugu. The authors also collaborated with community-based researchers (CBRs): Durga Hansda and Yaman Sardar in Morang, Shanta Thapa in Dolakha, and Samjhana Nepali in Mugu. The book's introduction is authored by Canada-based Co-Investigators of the project, Katharine N. Rankin (Principal Investigator) and Sara Shneiderman (Co-Investigator), and Nepal-based Collaborator[4] Mukta S. Tamang. Collaborator Seira Tamang assisted in convening the research team and was a key touchpoint at the research design stage. Collaborator Stacy Pigg inspired the images and facilitated the connection with artist Shushank Shrestha, as part of an affiliated graphic ethnography project involving Shyam Kunwar (Pigg and Kunwar 2021, 2023).[5] Collaborator Galen Murton coordinated lead researchers' participation in the Roadology Conference in Shenzhen in 2017 and workshopped themes for the book with the core team in 2022. Collaborators Seira Tamang and Mukta S. Tamang contributed significantly in establishing the project team and affiliations with Martin Chautari and Tribhuvan University.[6] The Afterword is authored by former doctoral student

[4] Collaborator is an official designation in Canadian government granting parlance, denoting in our case an individual who contributes significantly to the intellectual direction of the research but does not play a significant role in its conduct.

[5] In this and other collaborations, Stacy Pigg has pioneered in experimenting with the ethnographic form by exploring how graphic narrative can convey ethnographers' stories as well as offer alternative framings for contemporary social problems (Pigg 2019, 2022).

[6] Martin Chautari served as our home base, most notably in the office space provided to Shyam Kunwar and occasional team meetings, and colleagues in

and collaborator, Elsie Lewison, who served in a project coordinator role through 2021. In that capacity she developed deep relationships with the researchers and provided ongoing synthetic vision. All researchers, book editors, and the project manager worked together as a "team" under the auspices of a research grant funded by the Social Sciences and Humanities Research Council of Canada, from 2014–2024.[7] The "core team" was comprised of Co-Investigators, lead researchers, and project manager.

Together we convened three workshops to foster collaboration at different stages of the research process. The workshops addressed research design (Balthali, Nepal, 2016), research analysis (Balthali and Kathmandu, Nepal, 2018), and research dissemination (Toronto, Canada, 2022), and through them we built what we termed an "IOD commons:" an archive of resources, instruments, notes, images, conference presentations, and paper drafts accessible to all core team members on a Sharepoint drive. Community-based researchers participated in the research design workshop; for that purpose, Lagan Rai translated a handbook on community-based action research into Nepali and developed a guide to doing ethnography, which was posted on the project website.[8] All research instruments were prepared in both English and Nepali so their content could be deliberated and refined at the research design workshop. Plans to involve community-based researchers in an analysis workshop for 2020 were disturbed by the COVID-19 pandemic. As an alternative, the lead researchers collaborated and/or supported community-based researchers in publishing research findings (Kunwar and Thapa 2020; Nepali 2018). Through these collaborations our aim has been to ensure data quality, generate rich theorizations, share research instruments and outputs,

---

the Central Department of Anthropology of TU offered guidance in the set-up stages.

[7] Proposal title: Landscapes of Democracy: Post-conflict Transition in Nepal's Agrarian Districts; grant number 435-2014-1883. The original grant end date was 2019, but was extended for an initial year as is commonplace, then extended incrementally until March 2025 due to the COVID-19 pandemic.

[8] https://infrastructuresofdemocracy.geog.utoronto.ca/

ensure practical significance to local communities, and contribute to the burgeoning discourse about roads and infrastructure in the Nepali public sphere.[9]

Throughout this collaborative process we sought to grapple directly with power relationships, an aspect of joint research that rarely receives explicit attention in academia. Shneiderman (PI) and Rankin (Co-I) also collaborated on a SSHRC-funded Partnership Development Grant, "Expertise, Labour and Mobility in Nepal's Post-Conflict, Post-Disaster Reconstruction."[10] This project yielded an article on "The Ethnography of Collaboration: Navigating Power Relationships in Joint Research" (Aijazi *et al.* 2021), published in *Collaborative Anthropology* and led by two Canada-based doctoral students involved as research assistants. We draw upon many of the learnings from that experience here, to consider "what collaboration may mean in settings of incommensurable inequality" (Aijazi *et al.* 2021: 56).

In the present project, two key points of tension arose that required hashing out. First, the location of our first full-team retreat, held at Balthali Village Resort in Kavrepalanchok District, July 10–13, 2018. The resort, designed in a Newar architectural style typical of tourist- and high-end venues throughout the Kathmandu Valley, is situated on a ridgetop near Panauti and offers indoor and outdoor meeting spaces. Some core team members felt Balthali was ideally suited to the needs of our retreat—to both generously host the community-based researchers in a facility that felt "special" and to convene for three days as a full team undistracted from the demands of daily life. Others advocated a public sector venue more aligned with the values of democracy espoused by the project, such as Tribhuvan University. At times deliberations became heated, framed as a conflict

[9] Publications from the research project are cited throughout and most are co-authored. Those that are not cited in the book but deserve mention are Rankin *et al.* (2016, which makes the case for researching roads in post-conflict Nepal) and Sigdel (2016a, 2016b, 2016c, a series of opinion articles in the online site, https://baahrakhari.com/).

[10] Project website: https://elmnr.arts.ubc.ca/

between the values of hospitality versus an ethics of supporting public institutions and refraining from conspicuous consumption. Pragmatics proved decisive, with those involved in the day-to-day planning being apprised of the issues, but also given the leeway to make a judgment in favor of Balthali. Community-based researchers were supported to travel from the districts and both Canadian Co-Is as well as two Canadian graduate students attended, along with the lead researchers.

Second, two stressors arose related to data sharing and authorship. In both cases the Co-Is "approved" a collaboration extending beyond the core research team without consulting the full team of lead researchers. Both collaborations involved a lead researcher in publishing data and analysis from the project, as a co-author with colleagues named as Collaborators. In both cases the Co-Is directly gave consent—in order to promote the scholarship of the lead researcher and in the broader spirit of collaboration across a wider field of inquiry about infrastructure in Nepal. As the other lead researchers learned about these initiatives only after they were well underway, all core team members agreed subsequently that these arrangements too did not conform to a value of democratic governance of the project. While the outcome likely would have remained unchanged, these experiences prompted us to develop a policy governing research dissemination. In so doing we discussed the inequities, tensions, and emotional labor inherent in collaborative work. The policy emphasized communicative and deliberative processes within the team, and the principle of balancing wider collaborations with protecting the integrity of our own collaborative process and research results. A key purpose of this volume is to feature scholarship of lead researchers in published form so that it is duly cited in forthcoming scholarship related to the Infrastructures of Democracy project.

The book is organized into three chapters corresponding to three research sites centered in three districts, which could be characterized as "agrarian" in the sense that agricultural production factors significantly in household livelihood strategies and takes a persistently smallholder form. In order to achieve coherence and advance the arguments of the book, we have organized the chapters around a set of common themes broadly related to the cultural politics of development, which appear as chapter sub-titles, namely road history and remoteness; organization of road development; land, landscape and borders; environment and sustainability; transport and markets; and politics, polity and planning. Some of the themes correspond directly to the book's arguments (e.g., about relational remoteness, environmental transformation, and planning as a terrain of practice and object of inquiry), with all five arguments of the book traceable across the shared themes of the chapters. A short conclusion consolidates findings.

As in other stages of the research, editorship of the book also has collective dimensions. The team of lead researchers, Co-I's and project manager met regularly over the year and a half of preparation, to deliberate the themes for inclusion in each chapter and to offer feedback on drafted sections. The themes maintain some continuity with the original research questions, but are shaped by the ethnographic process. The editors then drafted the Introduction and worked with a professional editor, Kathryn S. White, who herself has worked and conducted research in Nepal, to consolidate and edit the chapters. The Introduction was workshopped with the full team. The Afterword by Elsie Lewison offers further insight into these processes through a critical reflection about positionality and methods, raising questions for all of us to keep thinking with. A conclusion was drafted as we brought the book to publication in order to summarize the contributions and reflect on their implications for planning practice and envisioning just road development.

METHODOLOGY

We characterize our methodology as collaborative, relational ethnography. "Collaborative" denotes the commitment to collaboration across the research team at every stage of the research process, iteratively from research design, to fieldwork, to writing, as noted above (and as elaborated in Lassiter 2005). Commentary from community-based researchers was built into the research design and promoted through single- and co-authored publications.

"Relational" denotes a commitment to moving beyond an "impact study" modality that tends to treat localities as passive recipients of infrastructure development (Hart 2016; Miraftab 2016). Relational ethnography rather manifests a commitment to approaching places as sites of "connected yet distinctively different nodes in globally interconnected historical geographies [as well as] in the production of global processes in specific spatio-historical conjunctures" (Hart 2016: 3). It suggests both spatial and temporal dimensions of analysis. The analytical task is to trace how places are constituted through relations both within and beyond, and "how interconnected forces at play at multiple ... spatial scales come together to create new conditions with worldwide implications and reverberations." (Hart 2020: 242). Relational ethnography undertakes this kind of "conjunctural analysis"—to draw on Marxist political philosopher Antonio Gramsci—from the ground up, from the perspective of people living in communities undergoing infrastructure development. From this perspective, a focus on everyday lived experience is essential to analysis of larger processes. And, conversely, the macro-political-economic dimensions of conjunctural formations—the state, global capital, development—themselves take on relational qualities, intertwined and mutually co-constituted as they are with everyday life (e.g., see Anavarapu and Levenson 2021; Fuller and Benei 2010; Pradhan and Valentin 2019). Finally, relational ethnography has a praxis orientation—it considers hidden cracks and contradictions in prevailing ideas and structures with an eye toward imagining alternatives and the conditions of possibility for their realization (Hart 2018). We maintain this orientation to praxis through our focus on planning, not only as an object of inquiry, but also as a terrain of practice through which to pursue progressive social change.

Our research design is comparative in the sense that it involves examination of common processes of road building in three agrarian districts as a means for exploring various themes related to the cultural politics of development. We regard the district as a locality that is co-constituted through its relationships with other localities; with wider scales of policy, institutions and political-economic forces; and with everyday practices of planners, policy makers, businesses, community-based organizations and residents. Thus the districts are not treated as self-contained entities that are representative of distinctive regions of Nepal or that comprise comparative "case" variants of infrastructure development. They are presented rather as vantage points through which to generate rich and textured analysis of how infrastructure development articulates local social relations and political economies, state projects and wider geopolitical dynamics. A "relational comparative approach" thus enables insights on how specific localities that are the focus of ethnographic research "feed into and shape broader processes, rather than just reflecting or implementing them" (Hart 2018: 390). It also allows for questioning normative thinking: How has and could change be catalyzed? Under what conditions could rural roads be planned with an orientation to sustainability and social justice?

Key threads of relationality that come into view through this approach include how physical and social geographies interact (in regions where roads must navigate rivers and mountains); how situated histories of regional planning inflect contemporary road building processes; how roads relate to other infrastructures like airports, irrigation canals, and train tracks; how the dynamics of center-periphery and accessibility-remoteness become reshuffled in relation to road building; and the significance of the rural in relation to processes of municipalization.

Relational ethnography entails multiple research methods. All researchers participated in a workshop through which methods were developed and refined, and research instruments were prepared in both English and Nepali, with interviews as the core method. Each researcher worked from an interview protocol organized around the following themes: organization of road development, personal experience, road imaginaries, roads and markets, details of road building processes, transportation management, politics and conflict, locality context, and visions for the future. The interviews were semi-structured: researchers asked a consistent set of questions, while also allowing for open discussion. Most questions were designed to be general so they could be asked of any research participant; a few questions were directed to specific kinds of research participants, such as donors.

We sought to assess the perspective and experience of a wide range of participants in road building and management operating at multiple spatial scales, as follows: 1) politicians (5–10 in each district—e.g., party leaders, elected local officials, members of parliament); 2) bureaucrats (5–10—e.g., civil servants both from the district and posted from outside); 3) donors (5–10, senior and junior staff of donor agencies and/or their local NGO collaborators; 4) local residents (15–20; e.g., road users' group members, leaders of caste and ethnic associations as well as protest movements, laborers involved with road building, members of relevant road- and transportation-related committees); 5) private sector actors (5–10—e.g., contractors of various kinds, their professional associations, transportation association members, vehicle owners and operators, owners of shops located on the roadside; 6) key informants (5–10—members of local professional class, e.g., journalists, teachers, lawyers; ex-politicians and bureaucrats; and others with knowledge of road building histories. As much as possible two researchers attended each interview—one to lead the interview questions and discussion and the other to concentrate on note taking. Some interviews were conducted in Kathmandu with politicians, contractor association leaders, bureaucrats, and key informants. All interviews were recorded if permission was granted, and transcribed to support subsequent analysis. Lead researchers developed their own coding systems based both in the research design (e.g., themes organizing the interview questions noted above) and in themes and issues arriving from the research process. The coding process in turn informed the organization of the book chapters.

Observations and informal conversation supplemented interviews, in order to develop wider contextual understandings of local cultural politics, political economies and specifically sensitive topics related to road building, such as corruption. During the research period, lead researchers resided in the research sites, collaborating with community-based researchers who were long-time residents. Together, they could observe, photograph and participate in key local "road events," and they kept descriptive and analytical field notes. Some examples of road events include users' group selection processes, protests, accidents, conflicts among transportation associations, everyday practices in road work sites and roadside markets, riding on local bus routes, and contract tendering at DDC offices. Fieldnotes were also coded by the lead researchers and contributed to the project's research database, while also being treated as their own intellectual property (with protocols for referencing by other team members).

Archival research also furnished contextual and historical framings. Sources included English-language national newspapers, Nepali language media specific to the districts, Nepali-language scholarly work, and gray literature at national and local scales, with a focus on government policy, donor mission, and NGO/CBO practice, as well as specific infrastructure projects of interest. The Dolakha chapter in particular makes innovative use of DDC minutes as an archival source. Researchers reviewed the materials for content related to the research themes, created annotated bibliographies, and wrote reflective summaries addressing particular themes of interest. These then became a resource for future publications including the forthcoming chapters themselves.

SITE SELECTION

The research focuses on rural roads, which account for much of the growth in road development in Nepal today. This focus distinguishes our research from other inspiring roads scholarship in Nepal that feature mega-projects like Kathmandu's Ring Road (e.g., Khanal, Gurung and Chand 2017), Himalayan highways (e.g., Murton,

Lord and Beazley 2016; Heslop and Murton 2021; Saxer 2023), or the Belt and Road Initiative (e.g., Murton and Lord 2020). In so doing, it aims to contest the "urbanization of everything" flavor of much of the literature on infrastructure (see particularly Brenner and Schmidt 2018) and to reflect the endurance of agrarian subsistence economies in Nepal—a mode of economic organization that has become increasingly recognized as critical for sustainability in the face of climate change (Kuokkanen 2011; Fraser 2022).

While the frenzy of rural road building in Nepal correlates with current processes of "municipalization" associated with political restructuring and the redistricting of local jurisdictions, we underscore that municipalization is not the same thing as urbanization (Ruszczyk 2021; Bhattarai, Adhikairi and Gautam 2023). Municipalization is administratively created. After federal restructuring was mandated by the 2015 Constitution, VDCs were amalgamated into larger units called rural municipalities (*gaupalika*) or merged with existing municipalities (*nagarpalika*). Urbanization typically refers to both 1) population shift from rural to urban locations with a corresponding transition out of agrarian livelihoods and 2) transformation of a landscape to align with urban activities, especially through construction of roads and buildings, and with a corresponding decline in arable land, which can lead to new forms of vulnerability (Rusk *et al.* 2022). Geographers Neil Brenner and Andre Schmid (2018: 451) have made the compelling case that in the 21st century, urbanization is a planetary phenomenon, insofar as "even spaces that lie well beyond the traditional city cores and suburban peripheries"—including rural areas that furnish migrant labor, agricultural produce and natural resources—"have become integral parts of the worldwide urban fabric." "Planetary urbanization" thus refers, among other things, to processes of global interconnectedness, a blurring of the division between "rural" and "urban," and the disappearance of "wild zones" of which the Himalaya would be an iconic example.

In our emphasis on the rural we do not wish to contest these points, however we would persist, along with numerous critics (Roy 2011; Jazeel 2018; Mould 2023), in making the case for the rural as one among many constitutive "outsides." Rural areas have roads, and their residents migrate to cities for work, but they also have qualities that contest "the urban," such as the persistence of subsistence livelihoods in conjunction with wage labor, even as they engage in their own forms of infrastructural development. In fact, we might consider how those very qualities furnish critical political capacities to "remake the urban" for more sustainable planetary futures (Ruddick *et al.* 2018). At the same time, we challenge easy divisions between urban and rural, by noting that what defines urban and rural differs across the districts. For example, in inner-montaine Mugu, the urban is associated more with interconnections and hubs along new zones of mobility, while in flatland Morang, it is associated more with agglomeration in relation to the Biratnagar metropolitan area. Urban-rural, too, constitutes a relational continuum.

The three districts in which we conducted research are: 1) Mugu in the inner-montaine region of Northwest Nepal, part of Karnali Province and formerly of the Karnali Zone; 2) Dolakha in the middle hill/mountainous region of central Nepal, part of Bagmati Province and formerly of the Janakpur Zone; and 3) Morang in the southeast Tarai (flatland) belt, part of Koshi Province and formerly of the Koshi Zone. All three districts have an international border with either China's Tibetan Autonomous Region (TAR) to the north in the case of Mugu and Dolakha, or India to the south in the case of Morang. In our selection we sought to include a wide range of political-ecological, cultural-political and geopolitical contexts in which road building takes place. Mugu is commonly characterized as "remote," and was only recently connected by a strategic or trunk road (Karnali Rajmarga). It is characterized by a massive expansion of "track opening" throughout the district—which refers to excavation and bulldozing making possible the passage of motorable transport. Mugu's district center, Gamgadhi, is the zero point for a trunk road currently being constructed (with numerous delays) to the TAR border. Dolakha has seen intensive donor investment in infrastructure development, including the Lamosangu-Jiri Road, since the 1970s. In recent decades, rural road construction has experienced a significant boost in relation to two other massive infrastructure projects, namely the 456-megawatt Upper Tamakoshi hydroelectric dam in its northern region, and post-earthquake housing reconstruction since 2015. Dolakha's aspirational border project is a dry port near the dam, which also has yet to materialize. Morang boasts Biratnagar, one of Nepal's major metropolitan and industrial areas; has historically had significant influence in national politics as well as notable ethnic and Madheshi mobilizations contesting the dominance of caste Hindu hill elites; shares a relatively "open border" with India; and contains three long-time, major strategic roads—the Hulaki Rajmarga, the Koshi Highway and the East-West Highway.

Of course, districts are not homogeneous; our rural perspective helps to underscore the diversity even from one valley to the next. Districts have urban/rural, north/south, industrial/agrarian differences within themselves. Within each district, the lead researchers sought to identify two roads—one "strategic" and one "local"—as a starting point from which to build a relational ethnography of road development. In our parlance, road development encompasses both road building and construction, as well as the transportation systems and other domains of governance that transpire on the road. In the parlance of the Nepal government, as elaborated below, "strategic" refers to main highways and feeder roads providing linkages from the national highways to smaller district headquarters, while "local" refers to district feeder, rural, agricultural (connecting market centers and agriculture pocket areas), and urban roads. The roads were selected for their relevance in relation to the overarching research questions: 1) What are the political economic relations within which road building and transportation management take place?; 2) What competing governmental rationalities and practices are evidenced in road development processes?; and 3) How are prevailing cultural politics reproduced or transformed in people's everyday engagements with road building and management processes? While it proved difficult to choose particular roads, given the vast options within each district, we construed this dimension of site selection loosely, to allow the researchers to follow ethnographically relevant threads in the spirit of relational comparison.

NARRATIVE STYLE

This book has multiple audiences. We hope it will be accessible to planners and policy makers, as well as students and scholars of road building, infrastructure, and political transformation. Our analysis is based on ethnographic storytelling: first-person documentation based on observations of what researchers saw and experienced. This narrative style distinguishes our book from other forms of writing about roads, such as impact studies, which use indicators to assess outcomes in an evaluative sense.

For this reason, readers will encounter multiple voices and perspectives, some of which may seem contradictory. Rather than distilling one "true" or "right" argument, our goal is to capture contradiction by avoiding monolithic narratives about the impact of roads. Each chapter provides an affective sense of the social, material, and political messiness that researchers encountered along the roads we studied. We recognize that this is an explicitly political field of practice, which we highlight by describing empirically how different actors and interest groups articulate and negotiate with each other across space and scale, rather than aligning ourselves with a singular political position.

We regard "local" and "community" as relative concepts, signaling commitments to place-based research, while also committing to recognizing how particular places are constituted in large part by their relations with a wider spatial field. We therefore deploy widely used terms such as "local-level," "community-based," and "grassroots" with caution, since these fields are constituted in relation to other places and scales of practice, such as the district, province, nation-state, and wider spheres of development thought and action.

Due to the administrative transformations which unfolded during the course of this research, we cannot use administrative units as easy proxies for "local." The smaller unit of VDCs which were the operative administrative unit when we began the project were consolidated into larger rural municipalities or *gaupalika* in 2017. Even within the smaller erstwhile VDCs and certainly within current *gaupalika*, there are many different "localities," which may have specific community configurations. The unit of "Ward" as the smallest unit of administration is often invoked by interlocutors as a relevant anchor for political subjectivities, but in many cases not the primary way in which people think about their own identification to place. Wards also shifted meaning in 2017, from a sub-unit of a VDC to a sub-unit of the *palika*, which in many cases maintained boundaries similar to the previous VDCs. Given all these shifting boundaries, we emphasize place-based names of settlements as used by interlocutors to describe local contexts, as they have for the most part remained constant even as administrative lines have shifted around them. When relevant, particularly following such usage by our interlocutors, we occasionally reference the Ward, VDC, *palika*, provincial administrative unit, or zones within which settlements are situated.

We prefer to use the concept of "place" as much as possible, noting that it is often taken for granted as homogeneous in a way that does not reflect the realities we document in our research. Each chapter shows how every place-based community has multiple perspectives. It is that texture and diversity we hope to bring out, while also recognizing that the situated nature of place defines community in relation to the materiality of each specific road.

In the scholarship of Nepal, "community" is often presumed to refer to a group distinguished by caste or ethnicity. Along with gender, these have been focal points for much research since the 1990s, and in relation to state restructuring after 2006. In this book, an identity-based notion of community is not our entry point—as we are looking at roads as the primary object of analysis, we are concerned with all the people whose lives they transect—not only specific identity-based groups or sub-groups. Nonetheless, we are mindful of caste, ethnicity, and gender to the extent that they shape the positionality of participants in the research. The chapters accordingly note specific circumstances when identity-based dynamics are relevant to our analysis.

Much contemporary scholarship in Nepal and beyond approaches questions of identity through the frame of Indigeneity. Many communities who both self-identify and are identified by the state as Adivasi Janajati, or Indigenous Nationalities, live within the sphere of influence of the roads described here. However, we did not define our inquiry as "Indigenous research" due to the mixed residential patterns of most settlements along the roads we followed, which require an inclusive approach attentive to Indigenous as well as other positionalities. As described above, our focus is on the "local" as determined by the road's pathway, which in most cases is a multiethnic, multicultural space.

In order to denote specific communities encountered along the road, we decided to use the terms below as general descriptions when needed. These are aligned with terminology used to refer to populations in Nepal's census data and other demographic materials. Together, our chapters discuss experiences of people from across these varied populations:[11]

> ***Hill castes*** *(Brahman, Chhetri, Thakuri)*
> ***Hill Adivasi/Janajati*** *(Newar, Thangmi/Thami, Tamang, Sherpa, Mugal, Kumal, Karmarong)*
> ***Hill Dalit*** *(Bishwokarma, Nepali, Pariyar)*
> ***Madheshi castes*** *(Shah, Nuniya, Rajbhar, Yadav)*

[11] We follow the Central Bureau of Statistics census reports for this categorization (NSO 2021: 49). See https://censusnepal.cbs.gov.np/results/files/result-folder/Final_Population_compostion_12_2.pdf. See also *Social Inclusion Atlas of Nepal: Volume I* (Tamang and Gurung 2014).

Tarai Adivasi/Janajati *(Tharu, Santhal, Gangai)*
Madheshi Dalit *(Rishidev)*
Muslims

We acknowledge that many of these groups speak their own languages. Our research was conducted primarily in Nepali, the lingua franca across all our field sites. In many cases, interlocutors were bilingual, speaking their own languages such as Tharu and Tamang, but also spoke fluent Nepali. Some elders did not speak the language themselves, but all at least understood the language. We have therefore selected to use a series of vernacular Nepali language terms which emerged as important conceptual anchors for our analysis across all field sites.

Rather than relying upon theoretical language from elsewhere, our theorization is grounded in part through a series of key Nepali terms that manifest how things work in practice. We engage the vernacular as part of our analytical apparatus and theoretical framing. As we workshopped themes for the book, it became clear that several ideas belonged in Nepali as critical theoretical concepts, rather than translated into English.[12] These include:

Sugam/durgam: accessible/remote; central/peripheral. This pair of terms has been used to classify regions of the country in binary relation to one another since at least the 1960s. In addition to being descriptive terms that invoke an affective sense of connectivity to the national and global order or its lack, these are administrative terms used by the Nepali civil service to determine salaries for officials as well as priority lists for development investment. Whether deployed by government representatives or community members, these "relational categories" (Harms *et al.* 2014: 372–374) played a prominent role in interlocutors' articulations of why roads were needed where.

[12] We represent Nepali language terms in simple transliteration. We have opted not to employ diacritics in the interest of remaining as accessible as possible to a wide range of readers, and to align with Martin Chautari house style.

Milaunu/milemato: to arrange by negotiating among different parties. This expression describes what needs to be done in order to surmount bureaucratic challenges, or to bring conflicting parties into alignment. It also has the connotation of "fixing the papers" (*kagaj milaune*) and accommodating different interests to align with formal requirements. It is a critical practice for actors at all nodes of the network that brings road planners, builders, and users into connection.

Yojana, budget: plan, budget (often used in English). These words name intertwined elements of the process of future-thinking necessary to propose a project, in material, financial, and temporal terms. *Yojana* refers to the workplan and timeline to accomplish a given project, while budget (as in English) indicates the associated expenses. Budget also describes the block grants disbursed to local governments from federal, provincial or international organization coffers, which often need to be used by stipulated deadlines. Taken together, *yojana* and budget name a relation between time, resources, and labor that is often at the forefront of road building calculations.

Khane/khuwaune: eating/being fed. These terms refer to different practices that are both often glossed as "corruption" in English: *khane*/eating refers to accepting cash or kickbacks as part of road building contracts, while *khuwaune*/feeding instead points to offering respect and hospitality to those in positions of power. The former is seen as negative while the latter may be understood as not only necessary, but desirable within local logics of ethical judgment (Rankin *et al.* 2024).

As discussed further in the Conclusion to this book, we find these vernacular terms an especially effective means to trouble the term, "*bhrashtachar*,"[13] which pervades official accounts of road

[13] The Nepali for "corruption" is *bhrastachar*. We do not use the Nepali term in our analysis as it was not used colloquially in our research sites. The term circulates in national discourses of corruption and has been "used" as a weapon amongst political parties often in relation to investigations by the CIAA. On

development. They help to provide nuance and point to local registers of moral judgment against which road building practices can be analyzed at a finer grain than the English-language, "corruption," "bribe," "collusion."

HISTORIES, GEOPOLITICS, REGULATORY FRAMEWORKS AND INSTITUTIONAL ACTORS

BRIEF HISTORY AND GEOPOLITICAL CONTEXT[14]

To provide historical, geopolitical and policy context for road building we draw on an article published in *Studies in Nepali History and Society* referenced earlier (Rankin *et al.* 2017), which reviews English-language archival and secondary sources on road building beginning from the construction of motorable roads in the early 1900s to the People's Movement of 1990. In that piece, we develop a typology for periodizing motorable road development in Nepal, in relation to wider geopolitical and political-economic dynamics. Another key resource on road history introduces rural roads in relation to strategic roads, showing how the latter was the preliminary planning focus on a national scale from the 1950s, while objectives of environmental planning and decentralization concentrated on the former from the mid 1970s (Shrestha 2002). A chronology of road development can thus be articulated as follows.

1846–1950

Building on the work of historians Mahesh Chandra Regmi (1977, 1988), John Whelpton (1983) and Mark Liechty (1997), we characterize the role of roads in the period 1846–1950 as *Managing Coloniality* (in relation to both British and Gorkha rule). This was a period of national consolidation under the Shah monarchy, through

the weaponization of "corruption talk," see Ranganathan, Pike and Doshi 2023; Gellner and Adhikari 2020.

[14] Thanks to Lagan Rai for sharing parts of his dissertation that have enriched this section, especially the comparison of Shrestha's (2002) periodization of road history with our own.

to the end of the hereditary Rana prime ministerships (1950). On the one hand Nepal's rulers refrained from building motorable roads between India and Kathmandu, in order to limit access of foreigners and stem the tide of British colonization. On the other hand, they built a postal (*hulaki*), non-motorized road network within the newly constituted country as a means of issuing orders, collecting revenues, controlling the population, and generally "strengthen[ing] internal security over large swathes of the country that still bore only nominal allegiance to Kathmandu" (Nickson 1992: 10). One such *hulaki* road runs through the southern part of Morang District and is discussed in that chapter. Villagers were required to provide forced labor for constructing and maintaining tracks, arranging ferry boats and improvising temporary bridges for river crossings, as well as porterage for state services (Regmi 1988).

Rana rulers developed transportation infrastructure in the 1920s, with the first motorable roads being constructed in the Kathmandu Valley in 1924. Incredibly, luxury cars were transported by porters over the Chure Hills (also known as the Siwalik Range) into the Kathmandu Valley, where they plied roads built to service rulers in Kathmandu as a form of conspicuous consumption. Passenger travel into the Kathmandu Valley was deliberately discouraged by an explicit state policy of keeping the track over the steep passes of the Chure Hills in a poor condition, impossible even for a horse to navigate. The transport of commercial goods, meanwhile, was facilitated by a 23-km ropeway with a capacity of 8 tons per hour, constructed in 1925 and connecting Matatirtha in the Kathmandu Valley to Bhimphedi (Makwanpur District) at the base of the Mahabharat Range to the south (Landon 1928: 208, cited in Liechty 1997: 51). The ropeway began regular operations in 1927 after the launch of the Nepal Government Railway (NGR) service between Raxaul (India) and Amlekhganj (Bara District), 42 km south of Bhimphedi in the Tarai (Edwards 2023). The Rana government constructed an all-weather gravel road from Bhimphedi to Amlekhganj in 1929—completing the complex link to Kathmandu for commercial transport. Goods from India were transferred from the meter-gauge railroad at Raxaul to the NGR railroad in Nepal and moved to Amlekhganj; trucks then transported the loads to Bhimphedi, which finally reached Kathmandu via the ropeway (NPC 1956; Edward 2023). This arrangement persisted until the completion of the Tribhuvan Highway in 1956 (Edwards 2023).

1951–1970

We characterize the 1951–1970 period, corresponding roughly with Indian independence and the end of direct colonial rule in South Asia, as *Integrating the Nation.* This is more or less consistent with Shrestha's (2002) 1950–1975 periodization, which emphasizes the rapidly developing Strategic Road Network.[15] Building strategic highways was central to consolidating the modern bureaucratic state, forging national unity and navigating Cold War politics. The Ranas had lost their ruling status and a series of democratically elected governments operating alongside the restored Shah monarchy sought to establish the country's modern government bureaucracy. Transport and road building were the top priority of the Ministry of Planning and Development and the predominant budget item in the first three Five-Year Plans, a system implemented by a National Planning Commission that still determines the allocation of resources and priorities for development. Roads were also the focus of early diplomatic relations. The Tribhuvan Rajpath, launched in 1953 and completed in 1956, was built with Indian assistance to link Thankot in Kathmandu with Bhainse in present-day Makwanpur District,

[15] As per the Second Plan (1962–1965), at the beginning of this period in the early 1950s, the country had a total of 628 km of roads, including 160 km within the Kathmandu Valley, 39 km from Bhimphedi to Amlekhganj, Dharan to Biratnagar (built by the British Army seeking to recruit Gorkha soldiers), Birganj to Kalaiya, Janakpur to Jaleshwor, and tracks in Nepalganj. In addition to roads, there were 74 km of narrow-gauge railway, the section from Amlekhganj to Raxaul and one from Jayanagar to Janakpur, as well as the ropeway from Bhimphedi to Matatirtha. Air transport commenced in 1950, with an all-weather airport in Kathmandu, and fair-weather airports in Biratnagar, Simara, Bhairahawa and Pokhara being launched as part of the Second Plan.

finally providing motorized connection between Kathmandu and India. The United States Operations Mission (USOM) subsequently widened and paved a 60-km road from Raxaul to Amlekhganj, displacing the former NGR rail link (Skerry, Moran and Calavan 1991). A Regional Transportation Office was established in 1958 to coordinate the involvement of the USA and India in road building in Nepal. The RTO was a Cold War institution aimed at mitigating the perceived threat of Russian and Chinese influence through a massive investment in 1,441 km of north-south roads in Nepal (Rose 1971). This initiative soon stalled and was superseded in the early 1960s by a Department of Roads (DoR), which has since led planning of major highway construction projects (strategic roads).

An impressive record of road building was achieved during the regime of the Shah King Mahendra (1955–1972), covering the period of the first three Five-Year Plans, and entailing a coup in 1960 leading to direct rule by the monarchy through the Panchayat political system. Mahendra considered road building critical to "integrating the nation"—or, as he put it in one of the earliest reports issued by the Panchayat regime (HMG 1967),[16] to national unity, *rashtriya ekata*. The East-West Highway, which runs the breadth of Nepal across the northern edge of the Tarai, was the major road construction initiative during Mahendra's rule, and, as he put it in a treatise issued by the Ministry of Panchayat, "the primary aim of my life" (HMG 1964: 7–8, quoted in Rankin *et al.* 2017: 57).[17] The history of the East-West Highway has two significant implications for our concern with contemporary rural road building: 1) the mobilization of Nepali publics and 2) strategic management of regional geopolitics. At

[16] "V.s." refers to *vikram samvat*, which is the official calendar of Nepal. It is usually 57 years ahead of the Gregorian calendar, except during January to April, when it is ahead by 56 years. V.s. combines monthly lunar cycles with the solar year, using 12 to 13 lunar months for each solar sidereal orbital period, so the months do not correlate across the two calendars.

[17] Siting the East-West Highway across the northern Tarai favored migrant hill populations and marginalized Indigenous and Madheshi populations in the Tarai's southern belt.

the time, it was not possible to traverse Nepal on its east-west axis without going through India, leaving Nepal vulnerable to foreign control over transit routes critical for national integration (Isaacson *et al.* 2001). Mahendra's appeals for the massive labor mobilization required to complete the earthworks for the East-West Highway rested on a patriotic appeal to connect Nepalis geographically and emotionally—"to interconnect the hearts of peoples from Mechi to Mahakali" (HMG 1964: 12)—and to showcase "the potency and collective strength of the people" (HMG 1964: 11). "The government will provide the required scientists and technicians," he declared, "[a]ll I need is the labour and cooperation of every Nepali for this effort" (Shah 1961: 111, quoted in Rankin *et al.* 2017: 58). The Morang chapter particularly grapples with the legacies of labor mobilization in state-led infrastructure development.

At that time, it must also be recalled, Nepal lacked the technical capacity and funding to undertake such a massive infrastructure project, as the RTO had dissolved and the USSR had denied an initial request for funding. Mahendra nonetheless managed to turn "a dearth of funding into a surplus by strategically balancing geopolitical interests of donors engaged in Cold War politics" (Rankin *et al.* 2017: 59). A well-documented example concerns the Araniko Highway running to Kathmandu from the China/TAR border at Kodari, which is featured in this book's Dolakha chapter (Rose 1971; Muni 1973; Laskar 2017). Under pressure from India and the US following the Tibetan Uprising against Chinese occupation and India's granting of asylum to the Dalai Lama in 1959, Prime Minister B.P. Koirala had in 1960 declined assistance from Communist China to improve access to Nepal's capital city from the north. Upon imposing direct rule that same year, Mahendra, by contrast, agreed to Chinese construction of the Araniko Highway, in a strategic bid to reduce Nepal's dependence on India. Three years later when China signed up for the Janakpur-Biratnagar section of the East-West Highway (the US, India, and the USSR had all declined assistance), Mahendra leveraged India's objection to Chinese engineers working so close to the Indian border, into an opportunity to secure expanded assistance from *both* China and India.[18] India offered to construct most of the remaining sections, amounting to more than two-thirds of the highway, provided that Nepal extricate China from construction work on it (Shaha 1975: 158). In view of the risks Mahendra had taken vis-à-vis India in allowing China to build the Araniko Highway, China meanwhile agreed to redirect its assistance to constructing the Pokhara-Naubise Road through the less geopolitically contentious mid-western hills, rather than withdraw it entirely.[19] The Lamosangu-Jiri Road (1974–1986), also featured in the Dolakha chapter, illustrates how another round of bilateral assistance a decade later has continued to shape contemporary road politics.

A second impactful initiative related to strategic roads came when in 1965 His Majesty's Government under Mahendra invited the International Bank for Reconstruction and Development (IBRD) to evaluate Nepal's transport system and develop a Five-Year Transport Sector Plan for the third periodic plan (1965/66–1969/70). The mission in fact opted to create a longer-term 20-year Master Plan for Transport Development (IBRD 1965), which in turn informed the Third Five-Year Plan. Featuring roads as the most efficient and cost-effective transport modality for Nepal, the master transport plan recommended developing national highways along traditional north-south trade routes following river valleys, to complement the existing emphasis on the East-West Highway. It also introduced the distinction between strategic and local roads by proposing two separate road systems: a National Highway System for major, all-weather roads in

[18] British support was also secured (Narayanghat to Butwal) as part of the threat perceived by Western donors posed by Communist China "on India's 'vulnerable' northern flank." Nickson 1992:10, which also details how the British Overseas Development Agency (ODA) specifically was also motivated by the objective of "strengthening the lines of communication to the Gurkha recruitment camps at Dharan and Pokhara.

[19] In addition to the publications cited above, an interview with Bhekh Bahadur Thapa (November 26, 2016) contributed significantly to our understanding of this geopolitical scenario.

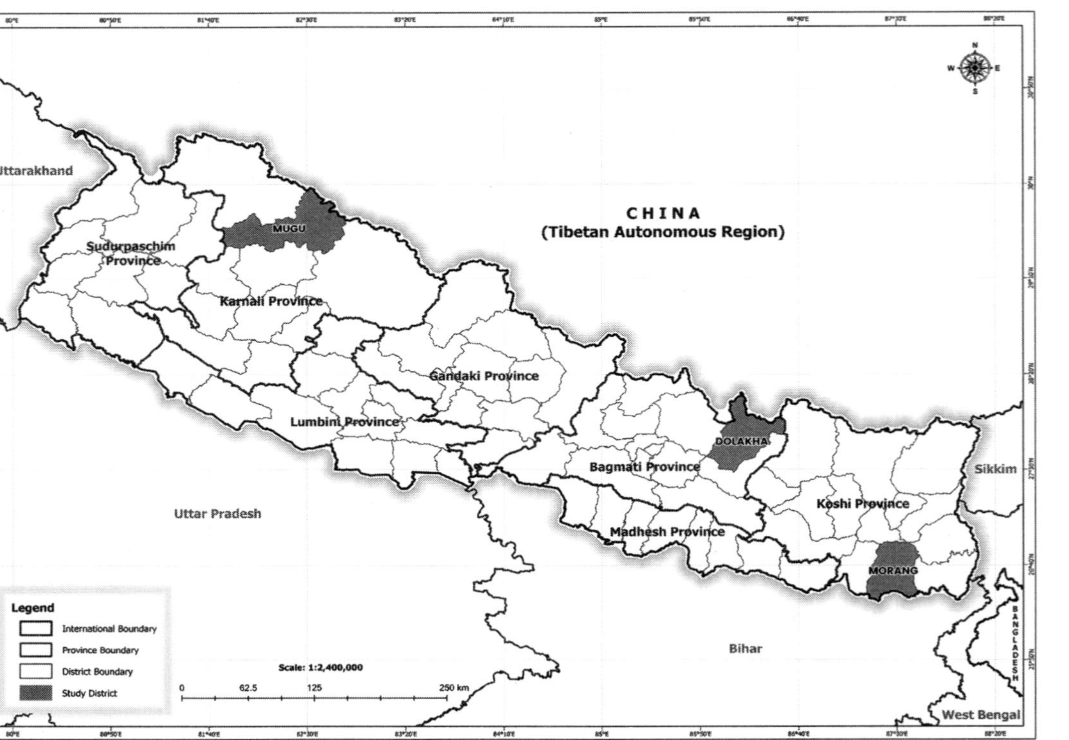

Map I: Map of Nepal including field research sites: Morang, Dolakha, and Mugu Districts (map by Naxa.com).

populated areas, managed by a centralized road authority, and local roads managed by Panchayats. Consequently, local Panchayats began overseeing the construction of tracks and trails, and mobilized local residents to carry out construction. This marked the inception of formal local governance of local participation in building rural roads.

1970–1990

If the history of road construction from the 1950s to the 1970s was marked by the state's ambition to integrate the nation through the development of strategic roads, starting in the mid-1970s, the government shifted its focus to prioritizing construction of rural roads to achieve development outcomes.[20] This transition reflected a global trend toward rural development and increasing concerns about the effectiveness of highways alone in alleviating rural poverty.[21] We term the period 1970–1990, *Building the Economy* (1970–1990), in order to reference the predominant role of regional planning; again, this periodization correlates well with Shrestha's (2002) "environmentally friendly road construction in a regional context (1975–1990)."

[20] Note, however, that in 1975, the construction of the East-West Highway, which had begun as a national pride project in 1962, was still underway and would not be completed until1982. The national per capita average then was only 1 km of road per 4,000 people—low relative to other "least developed countries" at the time (Skerry, Moran and Calavan 1991).

[21] A key vector of critique came from the multi-volume report, *The Effects of Roads in West Central Nepal* (Blaikie *et al.* 1977, which was consolidated into the 1980 book, *Nepal in Crisis* by Blaikie, Cameron and Seddon), based on field studies across hill and Tarai regions of three major highways in west-central Nepal with a methodology rooted in political economy. Together these publications, deriving from the Overseas Development Group at the University of East Anglia, revealed how roads build relations of dependency between the rural periphery and urbanizing centers that subsume Indigenous modes of production and aggravate socioeconomic inequality within and between regions. Unlike the World Bank 20-year Master Plan and the Keynesian thrust of the rural development orthodoxy that consolidated globally in the 1970s, however, this critical intervention did not have much direct traction in the national planning process at the time, which continued to make assumptions about the imperative of roads in poverty alleviation.

Mahendra appointed Harka Gurung, who had graduated with a PhD in Geography from the University of Edinburgh in 1965, to serve as Vice Chair of the National Planning Commission in 1968. Consistent with the IRDB 20-year Master Plan, Gurung pursued a comprehensive, long-term approach, and in so doing introduced Nepal to the concept of regional planning through the Fourth Five-Year Plan (1970–1975). The Plan aimed to mobilize the comparative advantages of the country's different regions by establishing five development regions, each of which was defined by a major north-south river basin. Regions were to be linked by strong east-west connections, resulting in overall national integration across mountains, hills and Tarai in a manner that would address wealth and population disparities—and, as Gurung (1969: 3) put it, "incorporat[ing] a spatial dimension in national development." Roads, of course, played a key role in realizing this vision, by connecting all districts in the country through a "fish-bone" pattern of road development entailing north-south corridors linked by the East-West Highway (Thapa 2016, cited in Rankin *et al.* 2016: 66). Each region would be served by a backbone north-south arterial road connecting a series of growth centers, from which further road linkages to regional populations would fan out. This vision was expected to promote agricultural transformation, trade, and industry across the country, and, crucially, to link food-deficit hills to food-and-land-surplus Tarai—through both migration from hills to Tarai and the emergence of new centers for production and trade.[22] Morang was particularly shaped by these dimensions of regional planning. Dolakha and Mugu were not in river basins identified for north-south corridors, a key reason why they have long been classified as "remote," or *durgam*.

Regional planning lent itself well to the emerging global orthodoxy of integrated rural development (IRD), being galvanized

[22] For a contemporaneous critique of "regionalism and national unity" emphasizing dominance of hill high-caste over Madhesh/Tarai groups, see Gaige (1975). An updated analysis of these dynamics can be found in Gautam (2008).

by prominent development actors led by the World Bank. The Food and Agriculture Organization (FAO) conference in 1971 on Agricultural Institutions for Integrated Rural Development, and the 1973 speech by the World Bank President Robert MacNamara pledging to fight world poverty through IRD, concretized an orientation to development focused foremost on alleviating poverty through human development supports combined with rural (primarily agricultural) production and incomes. Access to roads was to play a key role, but investment in infrastructure was recalibrated in relation to health, education, and agricultural extension to achieve "synergy across sectors" in "unprecedented ... disbursements in rural development" over the 1970s (Masset 2018).

These orthodoxies showed up extensively in Nepal. A 1972 World Bank report advised the Nepal government to incorporate secondary roads linking hills and Tarai into rural development programs focused on production, rather than treating them as separate projects (Skerry, Moran and Calavan 1991; see also Nickson 1992 on British involvement). From the Fifth Plan (1975–1980), greater attention was given to ensuring rural populations benefited from economic development, and spending on transportation relative to health and education began to decline.[23] The Sixth Plan (1980–1985) established a Ministry of Local Development and appointed local development officers (LDOs) to administer Integrated Rural Development Programs across the country, while the Seventh Plan (1985–1990) prioritized alleviating poverty and meeting "Basic Needs," with foreign aid assuming 66 percent of the development budget and explicit emphasis on local government participation (Khadka 1988).

Dolakha was a key district for initiatives supporting small farmers and promoting agricultural production through IRD, and its Lamosangu-Jiri Road was the first iconic road project associated with place-based rural development. The Swiss Agency for Development

[23] Gurung (2005: 7) in fact stepped down from the National Planning Commission in 1975, and noted retrospectively that he considered rural development a "diversion in focus" from the primary need of regional development.

and Cooperation (SDC) supported the construction of this road branching east from the Araniko Highway, in collaboration with the UN World Food Programme and as part of the Integrated Hill Development Project in Dolakha and Sindhupalchok Districts (B. Pradhan 1985; Schaffner 1987).[24]

Designed based on experience in the Alps, the Lamosangu-Jiri Road entailed bio-engineering techniques for mountain terrains aiming to reduce landslides and erosion. For certain parts of the Dolakha District, "agricultural extension allowed farmers to grow value-added crops and the road became a backbone to take the produce to market and increase family income. ... Dolakha was no more a food deficit area, the road opened up markets for the region's produce which included cheese, herbs, potatoes and vegetables" (Shrestha 2005). Another key characteristic of the Lamosangu-Jiri Road was its emphasis on local resources and local labor, compensated in kind through food distribution by the World Food Programme, with the aim of minimizing costs and environmental impact (however see Schaffner 1987 as well as the Dolakha chapter of this book on the complications in practice).

1990–present

IRD succumbed in the 1980s to an emerging neoliberal orthodoxy and its associated Structural Adjustment Programs (SAPs)—dubbed "the Washington Consensus" to denote the centrality of the DC-based institutions, especially the World Bank and the International Monetary Fund (IMF) [Williamson 2003]. With respect to road development, however, IRD has an enduring legacy in the "Green

[24] IHDP was the first Integrated Rural Development Project in Nepal, followed by the Rasuwa/Nuwakot IRDP (funded by the World Bank from 1976) in the late 1970s and early 1980s, by the Sagarmatha IRDP, Mahakali IRDP, Karnali-Bheri IRDP (K-BIRD)—there were ultimately eight IRDPs, funded by various bilateral and multilateral sources (B. Pradhan 1985). As has been widely documented (e.g., B. Pradhan 1985; Masset 2018), IRDPs encountered difficulties achieving their objectives of poverty alleviation because patron-client relationships and elite control over local institutions resulted in exclusion of the most impoverished individuals from development opportunities.

Roads Concept"—elaborated in a fourth periodization that we term *Restructuring the Polity,* which aligns with Shrestha's (2002) "decentralization in road development" (1990 onwards). Taking inspiration from the Lamosangu-Jiri Road, two pilot projects pioneered low-cost and low-volume rural road construction, with the participation of local labor as an off-farm employment opportunity and a focus on conservation of delicate mountain ecologies—namely the Palpa Development Project (1986–1996) in Palpa District and the Dhading Development Project (1987–1997) in Dhading District, with funding from SDC and the German Technical Cooperation Agency (GTZ). Subsequently a wide range of rural infrastructure development programs supported the construction of "green roads" through the "labor-based, environmentally friendly, and participatory" (LEP) approach. The primary funders have been SDC, GTZ, the World Bank, the Asian Development Bank (ADB), the World Food Programme (WFP) and the UK Department for International Development (DfID). The latter funds the third phase of the Rural Access Program (2014–2019), which is featured in the Mugu chapter.

Two key enabling conditions have supported the evolution of the green roads concept in Nepal, which has also traveled widely as climate change deepens imperatives for ecological design (Goldfarb 2023). First, Nepal's legendary community forestry programs had already challenged the Malthusian frameworks of environmental conservation ascribing environmental crisis and degradation to overpopulation and mismanagement in the hills of the Himalayas (e.g., Eckholm 1976)—and had generated optimism about the viability of local governance institutions to revive "traditional" systems of forest management (Ojha 2009). The "road users' groups" deployed to build green roads took inspiration from community forest users' groups (CFUGs) that had been empowered to manage Nepal's community forests. This concept has also traveled from Nepal to other global locations through aid circuits, as a model of best practice for blending social and environmental sustainability (Lewison and Murton 2020).

Second, this emphasis on participatory modalities of development coincided with the growing strength of the Communist Party of Nepal–Unified Marxist Leninist (CPN-UML), with its famous 1994 decentralization campaign dubbed "Build Our Village Ourself" (*Aphno Gau Aphai Banau*). The campaign was accompanied by reforms to empower and grant legal status to community-based organizations, like cooperatives and users' groups, as well as to empower local government bodies to undertake development. A Decentralization Act had been endorsed in 1982 to promote development activities by utilizing local resources, but financial resources remained under the control of the central government. The *Aphno Gau* campaign allocated budgets directly to VDCs annually. A Nepali Congress coalition government subsequently issued the Local Self-Governance Act (LSGA) in 1999, which formally empowered local bodies with formulating plans, policies and programs.

During this period, it must also be noted, a "Post-Washington Consensus" was consolidating in response to the grave social costs incurred by the 2008 Asian Financial Crisis and before that the 1980s Structural Adjustment Programs. The Post-Washington Consensus refers to a widespread re-evaluation of neoliberal orthodoxy and its primary emphasis on austerity and economic growth. It also encompasses additional objectives of environmental and social sustainability, to be achieved through promoting empowerment and local self-reliance of marginalized communities, as well as decentralization, transparency and accountability in governance (de Soto 2002)—without disturbing the underlying framework of capitalist development (Sheppard and Leitner 2010). While these conditions within and beyond Nepal have contributed to broader processes of political restructuring detailed above, as well as the specific form of decentralization entailed in green roads, as the Mugu chapter shows, local participation in infrastructure development bumps up against other logics that complicate expectations of "good governance."

REGULATORY FRAMEWORKS AND INSTITUTIONAL ACTORS FOR RURAL ROAD DEVELOPMENT

The LSGA, along with the more recent Local Infrastructure Development Policy (2004) and Local Government Operation Act (2074 v.s. [2017]), specifically tasks local bodies with the responsibility to undertake local infrastructure development, including rural roads, through participatory planning processes and engagement of users' groups. The Department of Local Infrastructure Development and Agricultural Roads (DoLIDAR) was established in 1998 under the Ministry of Local Development, to "provide engineering and other technical support to District Development Committees (DDCs), the main district-scale governing body, in planning and implementing rural infrastructure projects" (The World Bank 2000: 29). DoLIDAR was repositioned as the Department of Local Infrastructure (DoLI), under the Ministry of Urban Development in 2018, and has since been renamed Department of Local Infrastructure Development (DoLID), in 2024. The Department of Roads (DoR) continues to oversee the Strategic Road Network (main highways and feeder roads providing linkages from the national highways to smaller district headquarters), while the Local Road Network (comprised of district feeder, rural, agricultural, and urban roads) falls under the purview of provincial and local governments with technical and administrative support from DoLID.

Due to the absence of elected local governments during the Maoist-state conflict from 1996–2006, local governance was managed by an interim, ad-hoc arrangement known as the all-party mechanism (APM, from 2008), whereby local political parties were authorized to serve as a consultative apparatus for local government officials (Neelakantan 2015). As detailed in the Mugu and Dolakha chapters, the remnants of this negotiated and usually consensual mode of local governance have persisted in some jurisdictions even after local elections were held in 2017. The amount of funds transferred to local government bodies has increased significantly since local elections resumed in 2017 and the APM was officially banned in 2012 (as directed by the Commission for Investigation of Abuse of Authority [CIAA] on the grounds that it was not a legal entity).

Of course, not all rural roads are green roads built by users' groups. A Public Procurement Act was promulgated in 2007, which specifies the process of open bidding when road projects are tendered for contract in the private market. The Act specifies a procurement process whereby contract bids are awarded to the lowest bidder among eligible contractors within a minimum quality standard. The World Bank facilitated the introduction of e-bidding at the district scale in 2017, which was intended to make the procurement process more competitive by allowing contractors to bid online as well as in person.[25] Although e-bidding was just being rolled out at the time of our research, in practice procurement for local road development was still being undertaken through in-person bidding. A provision in the Procurement Act allowed for users' groups to directly procure the services of contractors for infrastructure development projects under NRs. 3.5 million, without undergoing competitive bidding procedures through the District Development Committee office. This ceiling has been gradually increased, making it easier for users' groups to hire contractors to use heavy equipment, and blurring the lines between the green roads and contracting modalities as discussed extensively in the Dolakha and Mugu chapters. In the fifth amendment to the Public Procurement Regulation, 2017 (GoN 2017), the Government of Nepal increased the maximum amount of money for earthwork carried out by users' groups from NRs. 6 million to NRs. 10 million.

Finally, Transportation Management Directives were issued in 2004 to coordinate local management of vehicle route permits, as buses

[25] E-bidding was initiated as a pilot project in 2007 through the Road Sector Development Project (RSDP), supported by the World Bank. The e-GP (electronic government procurement) system was launched by the Public Procurement Monitoring Office (PPMO) in January 2017.

and other transportation providers started to ply local and district roads. Through these directives, the Department of Transportation Management (DoTM) manages transportation on a particular route by granting permits and providing services to vehicle owners, as well as coordinating the flow of vehicles. However, even after obtaining permits, transport entrepreneurs often face operational obstructions from already established district and national transportation associations, which force them to join these "syndicates" in order to maintain monopolies, as described particularly in the Dolakha chapter. As a result, the Government of Nepal sought in 2018 to scrap the associations by requiring transport operators to register as private companies, vesting DoTM with the authority to grant route permits. However the Federation of Transportation Management Associations filed a case that went to the Supreme Court, which in 2024 re-established the associations' right to exist. Currently vehicle owners can register either as private companies or as operators within a transportation association. Accordingly, the challenges of "syndicate" monopolies persist, as widely reported in the media (e.g., Mandal 2018; The Kathmandu Post 2018a). Taken together, these regulations create the labyrinthine legal context which all actors must navigate to bring roads into being and use. These often conflicting yet simultaneously enacted policies enable road development led by both contractors and users' groups. Our chapters detail these contradictory experiences and outcomes in practice.

TWO PREVAILING MODES OF ROAD BUILDING

Rural roads in Nepal are built through two distinctive and sometimes integrated modalities—users' groups and contractors. Users' groups denotes an association of local beneficiaries based on shared use of a common pool resource, and a mode of participatory development initiated in the community forest sector.[26] Community forestry

[26] We use the terms "users' groups" and "users' committees" interchangeably throughout this book to reflect local parlance in each district as well as prevailing donor discourse.

legislation first gave legal status to CFUGs as "state-sponsored community-based resource management organizations, specifically authorized to manage local forests" (Biggs and Messerschmidt 2003). The model proved sustainable during the Maoist conflict because of its populist orientation, and has now transferred to almost every other rural development sector, including infrastructure. In keeping with principles of decentralization, DoLIDAR promoted the users' group modality as a key dimension of rural road construction and local income generation. Donors have also played a role, with DfID in particular funding the Rural Access Program (RAP), featured in the Mugu chapter, which pursued an approach to users' groups more rigorously wedded to a commitment to LEP green roads; the nomenclature within RAP is "Road Building Groups" (RBGs), which are facilitated through the involvement of local NGOs serving as "social mobilizers."

Contractors bid for contracts in the open bidding system specified by the Procurement Act. At the local scale, most contractors are classed level "D," which is the lowest level in terms of bid eligibility and is administered at the provincial and municipal level (or district level prior to 2017), as opposed to national scale. Class D contractors are limited to projects costing up to NRs. 3 million; they are authorized to work without prior contracting experience or heavy equipment (GoN 1999). As the Mugu chapter illustrates, at the local scale, bidding is deeply inflected with local conventions and cultural politics.

User's groups are associated with green roads and ideologies of decentralization. The green road concept was introduced in the 1980s as an ecologically sensitive method of road building that would also restore some measure of control to communities (Acharya *et al.* 1999; Shrestha 2010). It rejects the conventional "cut and throw" method of road construction involving excavation with heavy machines and explosives that contributes to the instability of mountain slopes and in turn to loss of soil and agricultural land, potentially exacerbating landslide risk (Shrestha 2010; Rosser *et al.* 2021; Pradhan *et al.* 2022). Ultimately, the central claim of the green roads approach is that by engaging local labor and resources it is possible to build roads in a way that is both environmentally and socially sustainable (e.g., Banskota 1997; Robinson and Stiedl 2001; Shrestha 2010).

The green roads approach adopts phased construction, in which the road is widened gradually through multiple phases, from a trail, to a simple motorable track, to a sustainable motorway with proper drainage. Bioengineering techniques are engaged to protect slopes against erosion, and to promote the use of local construction materials and skills, thus providing livelihood benefits (SDC 2008). The green road concept also encompasses key social protections, like minimum wage, equal pay for men and women, transparency in accounting, proper maintenance over time, land compensation, and public hearings for social audits (Klatzel 2000). Users' groups are given responsibility for manually building specific sections of a rural road, furnished with hand-held, non-motorized tools, and remunerated at just higher than local daily wage rates. The claim is that green roads control outmigration, increase local incomes, and involve women and other marginalized groups in participatory processes. As construction is less intrusive environmentally, maintenance requirements are also presumably reduced (Shrestha 2010). Local people may also benefit from income generating opportunities, which in turn build a "sense of ownership" of the road, helping ensure that roads are maintained, not just constructed. This model has had a significant impact in Dolakha and Mugu since the late 1990s.

So confident have donors been in the capacity and accountability of users' groups and local governments, that they have advocated channeling funds for road building in the form of grants to local governments, who then transfer the funds to users' groups. In response, the central government dramatically increased the funding for users' groups to engage in LEP construction (The World Bank 2011), to the point that by 2013, 70 percent of the Local Road Network (LRN) construction was carried out through direct transfers to users' groups.

The key function of DoLIDAR was to promote and manage the LEP-green roads-LRN nexus. Specifically, DoLIDAR worked through a new layer of district technical units called District Technical Offices whose role was to "to serve as focal points to provide technical expertise for local infrastructure development" (The World Bank 2000: 30). The DTOs were empowered with planning, procurement, management and oversight, including oversight of work contracted to users' groups. The DTO was also charged with developing District Transportation Master Plans (DTMPs) intended to inventory and plan for rural road networks at the district scale.

More recently there has been a turn away from extreme decentralization of road development through users' groups because of donors' perceptions that the funds have been misused. Both the ADB (2011) and the World Bank (2013) published reports documenting inappropriate use of heavy equipment in roads allocated to users' committees. The reports found that heavy equipment was contributing to exactly the kind of environmental destruction that was intended to be mitigated through green roads/LEP construction, as well as enriching a burgeoning local contracting sector. This finding harkens back to the report of researchers from Overseas Development Group at the University of East Anglia who found as early as 1976 that roads create enhanced opportunity for those with capital to invest, but can lead to loss of livelihood for those who do not (see Blaikie, Cameron and Seddon 1980). The 2013 World Bank report also detailed the infiltration of political parties into users' groups, "instead of actual users" (The World Bank 2013: 26). Contracting in rural road construction was identified as a frontier of corruption in Nepal, involving both private sector (contractors) and public sector actors (overseers and monitors). Rather than following an "objective" DTMP, small road projects were found to be "sprinkled" across districts:

> The result has been an explosive expansion of the LRN during the past decade, by far exceeding the targets set for the LRN in the Rural Infrastructure Development Strategic Action Plan (2007). The technical standard of these roads has been poor,

however, resulting in half the network currently being considered inoperable. (The World Bank 2013: 17)

The multilateral donors in particular now understand the solution as a turn toward market efficiencies overseen by strong state management, and scaling back on the role of users' groups. A key element of this turn involves a growing acceptance of heavy equipment in rural road construction, in recognition that such equipment is already being used and is less expensive than when the green roads approach was conceived. Along with heavy equipment comes contractors who are increasingly regarded as preferable to users' groups—as long as the local state plays a role in creating a "greater market for local contractors" and accountable tendering processes (The World Bank 2013: 44). The completion report for phase two of the UK-led Rural Access Program (RAP2, which was active in Mugu) makes a similar recommendation to "[p]rocure more works through contractors and the public procurement process rather than users' committees," a strategy that is being implemented in RAP3 (IMC Worldwide 2013: 33). This transition is evident in the Mugu chapter, in which RAP3 was engaging two different modalities: RBGs with compulsory women's participation, and "special RBGs" working in difficult, rocky terrain, which exclude women and allow for use of heavy equipment. The rationale given was timely completion of the Mugu-Humla Road. The Government of Nepal also exhibits shifting orthodoxies in road development, most recently in the 2024 Auditor General's Report, which indicates that quality standards should be assured in construction works implemented through user committees, and advocates use of "modern technology and materials" to achieve cost effectiveness (GoN 2024: 6).

Thus, road development has been subject to oscillating orthodoxies—most recently transitioning from an emphasis on decentralization, participation and labor-based construction (rooted in the Post-Washington Consensus, global and national movements for environmental sustainability, as well as populist impulses across all political parties), to a more market-focused ethos oriented to expanding private contracting and involving a robust state in managing procurement. This configuration is now widely understood among donors, the Nepal government, and the public sphere to be the best guard against corruption, a more realistic reflection of on-the-ground practice—in other words use of heavy equipment—and the best way to ensure that road building contributes to economic growth with the widest social base possible.

STRUCTURE OF THIS BOOK

Following this Introduction, we present three chapters focusing on Morang, Dolakha and Mugu, authored by Lagan Rai, Shyam Kunwar, Pushpa Hamal and Tulasi Sharan Sigdel, respectively. This order mirrors the chronology of road building across the country, with each district's entrée into road building occurring in a different period, as detailed above. Morang was the first of our research sites to encounter large-scale infrastructural development with the construction of the East-West Highway as a national pride project beginning in the 1960s; Dolakha experienced a later phase of donor-led road building as part of broader "integrated rural development" visions in the 1970s–1980s; while Mugu exemplifies the post-1990s emphasis on green roads. Each chapter engages with the arguments outlined in this Introduction in different ways, contributing rich empirical material to our overall understanding of the politics and practices of road building in Nepal.

The chapters are followed by an Afterword authored by project coordinator Elsie Lewison, which reflects upon the relational nature of the project that generated this book. Finally, a Conclusion by Katharine N. Rankin returns to the perennial question animating planning praxis, "What is to be done?," and offers a summary of key insights that emerge from the chapters. Readers will also find a Glossary and Appendix at the end of the book, along with a comprehensive Bibiliography. We hope that these resources may prove useful for the wide range of actors engaged in contemporary road planning and policy, in Nepal and beyond.

MORANG

Illustration by Shushank Shrestha

CHAPTER 1

The Politics and Practice of Road Building in Morang: A Paradox of Remoteness and Accessibility

LAGAN RAI[1]

INTRODUCTION

This chapter emphasizes the contradictions and paradoxes of road building in Morang District. Remoteness and accessibility emerge as relational concepts that trouble assumptions about the flatlands as more (easily) developed than hills and mountains. It also challenges established expectations that road development is experienced as progress and an improved quality of life. Rather, I address road building as a fundamentally political endeavor that generates unintended consequences, including environmental degradation, inequality and injustice among local populations (Rankin *et al.* 2017; Sudmeier-Rieux *et al.* 2019; Gurung 2021; Hamal 2021).

[1] Lagan Rai had conducted research on religious conversion, social inclusion, Indigeneity, and sand-mining in several communities of southern Morang for over a decade prior to our research on road development. His ethnographic access and insights benefited greatly from the prior relationships he had established, especially with Santhal and Tharu interlocutors. As a resident of Dharan and an instructor at the Degree Campus Biratnagar of Tribhuvan University, he also has extensive knowledge of the eastern Taerai and its relationships with eastern hill districts.

Located in the eastern Tarai, Morang is commonly considered to be one of the more developed and accessible districts in Nepal. It has been at the forefront of infrastructure development, including industry and transportation, since the mid-20th century (HMG 1975), and remains a leading industrial and commercial center in eastern Nepal (DCC 2017). It is cross-cut by three significant highways: the East-West Highway (also Mahendra Highway), the Koshi Highway (running north-south), and the Hulaki Rajmarga. The East-West Highway and the Koshi Highway are outcomes of significant investment from the government and donor agencies to foster national integration and balanced regional development, making them better maintained than the older Hulaki Rajmarga dating from the Rana era. Based on indicators of agricultural productivity, Morang is also commonly considered a "grain house" for Nepal, as well as a hotspot destination for migration from both neighboring India and the hills of Nepal.

However, several factors contribute to the perhaps surprising reality that rural areas of Morang experience significant challenges of inaccessibility, despite the overall relatively "developed" nature of the district. The legacies of regional planning in Nepal have some role to play, with their emphasis on opening up north-south corridors to help address perceived problems of overpopulation, resource scarcity, and food shortages in the hills and mountains by connecting these areas with the Tarai. Rural roads, which are crucial to the daily lives of most people, only started to receive attention for development after the democratic reforms of 1990 (Paudyal 1998). They remain in poor condition (98 percent lack blacktop surfaces) and in need of immediate upgrades, rehabilitation, and proper maintenance (DDC Morang 2013). The annual monsoon flooding of rivers and streams across Morang introduce an additional challenge for accessibility; for the most part, rural road building has not entailed rural bridge building. Political patronage has a role to play in distorting the development process, and long-term processes of transitioning from subsistence to market economies have left marginalized sectors of the population vulnerable and landless, while also creating environmental harms. This chapter explores the lived paradox of isolation and remoteness in a geographical region marked by highways and industrial development.

The research findings are presented in seven sections. The introduction presents the socio-political and environmental context, provides an overview of field sites, and outlines key arguments. The second section describes the history of roads in the district and discusses the paradox of remoteness and accessibility within the plains. The third section highlights evolving labor relations between the state and citizens, with a specific focus on the decline in voluntary labor contributions by members of road users' committees after 1990. The fourth section focuses on the encroachment of traditional public spaces designated for roads, and local peoples' resistance to land appropriation during road upgrading.

The fifth section discusses the challenges posed by rivers and floods. Additionally, it raises questions about the sustainability of river basins due to sand-mining, driven by the rising demand for sand and other materials derived from rivers in the construction of roads and other infrastructures. The sixth section focuses on the transition of labor from subsistence agriculture to emerging labor markets as an outcome of rural road extension. In conclusion, section seven highlights the impact of planning limitations, discrepancies between policies and practices, and how power relations compromise democratization processes and the sustainability of rural roads. It also delves into issues of corruption and the cultural politics of road building.

GEOGRAPHICAL AND HISTORICAL BACKGROUND OF MORANG DISTRICT

Morang District is bordered by Jhapa and Ilam Districts in the east, Sunsari District in the west, Dhankuta and Panchthar Districts to the north, and India's Bihar Province to the south.[2] It is located

[2] The boundary of Morang District has changed over time. The current administrative boundary was established in 1962 during the restructuring of Nepal into 75 districts and 14 zones (HMG 1975).

between 26°20' N and 26°53' N latitude and 87°11' E and 87°41' E longitude, covering 1,855 square kilometer (km). The district has an average east-west length of 46 km and a north-south width of 54 km (DCC 2017).

The district has diverse topography, ranging from 74 to 2,409 meters in altitude from the Tarai plains in the south to the Siwalik (Chure) range in the north. The plains have fertile soil and a higher population density compared to the Siwalik range (Pradhan 1997). Numerous perennial and seasonal rivers and streams, particularly active during the rainy season, intersect the district flowing from north to south. Major rivers in Morang include Ratuwa, Singhiya, Bakraha, Lohandra, Budhi and Dans. These rivers often flood during the rainy season, causing agricultural erosion and hindering mobility (HMG 1975).

The district's geographical location, in particular its southern border with India and access to India's railway networks, greatly influenced its administrative structure and infrastructure development, including transportation, industry, electricity, and urbanization. This impact is particularly evident in the city of Biratnagar, which currently serves as the headquarters of Koshi Province.

Morang was an independent principality governed by Kirati and Sen rulers before being annexed to the Kingdom of Nepal in 1774, during the unification campaign of the Gorkha King, Prithvi Narayan Shah (1723–1775). Initially, Morang's territory encompassed the current Sunsari, Morang, and Jhapa Districts of Nepal, and some territories of India's contemporary states of Bihar and Bengal, but it gradually shrank due to the expansion of the Mughal empires and the British Raj (Dahal 1997). Following the unification of Nepal, the Tarai region was split into the eastern, western, and far-western regions. Morang was designated as one of the eastern Tarai districts (Adhikari 1984; Regmi 1988).

The development of railway infrastructure along the northern border region of Bihar, India, during the 19th and 20th centuries had a profound effect on the establishment of administrative centers, growth of market centers, and infrastructure in Morang (see Regmi 1988; Tiwary 2008; Dahal *et al.* 2019). Bijayapur, once the capital of Morang, remained the administrative headquarters after the unification of Nepal. In 1870, the government relocated the capital from Bijaypur to Rangeli, a small town near the Nepal-India border. This move was made to enhance connectivity with the transportation infrastructure in Forbesganj, a municipality of Araria District in the state of Bihar (Dahal 1997). Forbesganj held historical significance during British rule in India and became even more important for Nepal's trade and connectivity with Indian markets after the Assam-Bihar State Railway opened the Purnea section from Kusba to Forbesganj in 1890 (Regmi 1988; Dahal 1997; Tiwary 2008). In 1916, the headquarters of Morang was again relocated from Rangeli to Biratnagar, located 20 km west. This decision was influenced by the newly extended railway networks from Forbesganj to Jogbani, a neighboring town at the Nepal-India border.

As a result, Rangeli became marginalized while Biratnagar developed into a leading industrial town and trade hub in eastern Nepal. The Biratnagar Jute Mills, Nepal's first industry, was established in Morang in 1936, alongside other factories such as Morang Chemicals Ltd., Morang Cotton Mills Ltd., and Morang Sugar Mills Ltd. Morang Hydropower Electric Company was founded in 1939 to provide industrial electricity. In 1942, a 677-kilowatt hydroelectric plant was installed at Sikarbas, Letang, to supply power to Biratnagar and its neighboring areas, marking Nepal's first plant established outside the Kathmandu Valley. Regrettably, the plant was destroyed by a landslide in 1961 and was never rebuilt (Dixit and Basnet 2005). In 1947, the Biratnagar Jute Mills witnessed the first labor strike in Nepal, subsequently sparking a historic nationwide civil disobedience movement against the Rana regime (Singh 2004). This heightened political consciousness had lasting effects on national politics, with prominent leaders originating from Biratnagar—including several prime ministers—establishing the town as a crucial political center.

The population started to grow after 1950 and saw a significant influx of migrants from the hills and India to Morang, as elsewhere in the Tarai, following a successful malaria eradication program in the 1960s (Roberston 2018; Johnson 2023b). This rapid population growth put pressure on natural resources, particularly leading to deforestation for agricultural purposes (Subedi and Gurung 1997). Prior to this, Morang was considered inhospitable, mostly covered in dense forests, earning it the reputation of *kalapani* (black water) or place of exile. Civil servants saw their assignment in Morang as a punishment, and people were reluctant to settle there due to the harsh climate and endemic malaria, despite the government's efforts to resettle people after the unification process of Nepal (Ojha 1983; Regmi 1988; Pathak 1997; Rai 2015).

Morang is densely populated and home to various caste and ethnic groups, including hill migrants; Adivasi Janajati; and Tarai Indigenous Nationalities, such as Tharu, Rajbanshi, Dhimal, Gangai, Santhal; and migrants from India (Dahal 1997). The East-West Highway in the north and the Rangeli-Biratnagar Hulaki Rajmarga in the south are important vectors of population distribution within the district. Hill people mainly live in newer towns and economic centers along the East-West Highway and north of it, in the foothills and hills. The middle part of the district, south of the East-West Highway to north of the Hulaki Rajmarga, is inhabited by both hill and Tarai people.[3] The southern part of the district, south of the Rangeli-Biratnagar Hulaki Rajmarga, consists of relatively homogeneous communities of Indigenous Tarai Janajati and Madheshi migrants from India.

[3] The terms Tarai and Madhesh are often used interchangeably. People residing in this region are commonly referred to as Madheshi (of the "Madhesh," or "plains"), in contrast to Pahadi or Pahadiya "of the Pahad," or "hills." Madhesh as a geographic community is diverse, encompassing caste Hindu communities, Tarai Indigenous Nationalities, business migrants of Indian origin, and Muslims. Historically, Madheshi have faced marginalization and exclusion from the political process, policy-making, and nearly all aspects of national life (Mishra 2006). Madhesh as a cultural community, however, only includes Madheshi caste communities, including Madheshi Dalit.

FIELD SITE

This study was conducted in Gramthan, Katahari, and Jahada Rural Municipalities, which are adjacent to Biratnagar Metropolitan City, the historical industrial town which is now the headquarters of Koshi Province. When selecting field sites, we considered geographic and sociopolitical factors; e.g., areas proximate to Biratnagar City and the Indian border with a dominant population of Tarai Janajati and Madheshi that were familiar and accessible to the co-researchers—including myself as well as community-based researchers (CBR) Durga Hansda and Yaman Sardar—for daily observation and engagement. Consequently, fieldwork was concentrated in the localities of Pidarbani in Gramthan Rural Municipality and Badi Tola in Jahada Rural Municipality, along with their neighboring locations, where co-researchers resided. Despite being close to Biratnagar, these areas are comparatively lacking in infrastructure such as rural roads, service centers, and markets. Local residents depend on Biratnagar and its surrounding areas for employment, economic activities, health services, and education.

The major roads in this cluster include the Ghinaghat-Biratchok feeder road (in Gramthan Rural Municipality), the Postal Highway from Biratnagar to Rangeli (in Katahari Rural Municipality), and the Katahari-Tarigama Road, a district road from Tarigama (in Jahada Rural Municipality) at the Nepal-India border to Katahari. Ghinaghat-Biratchok is a crucial feeder road in the western part of Morang District, connecting Biratnagar and the East-West Highway. The construction of this road began during the Panchayat regime (1960–1990), but progress was slow until the 1990s, when a bridge was built over the Singhiya River at Ghinaghat. After federal restructuring in 2017, the importance of the feeder road increased as Biratnagar was declared the provincial headquarters. Consequently, the road was upgraded to four lanes.

Tarigama-Katahari is a district road that stretches toward the southern part of Morang, connecting the Hulaki Rajmarga at Katahari (Katahari Rural Municipality) and Tarigama (Jahada Rural Municipality), a settlement located on the Nepal-India border. The

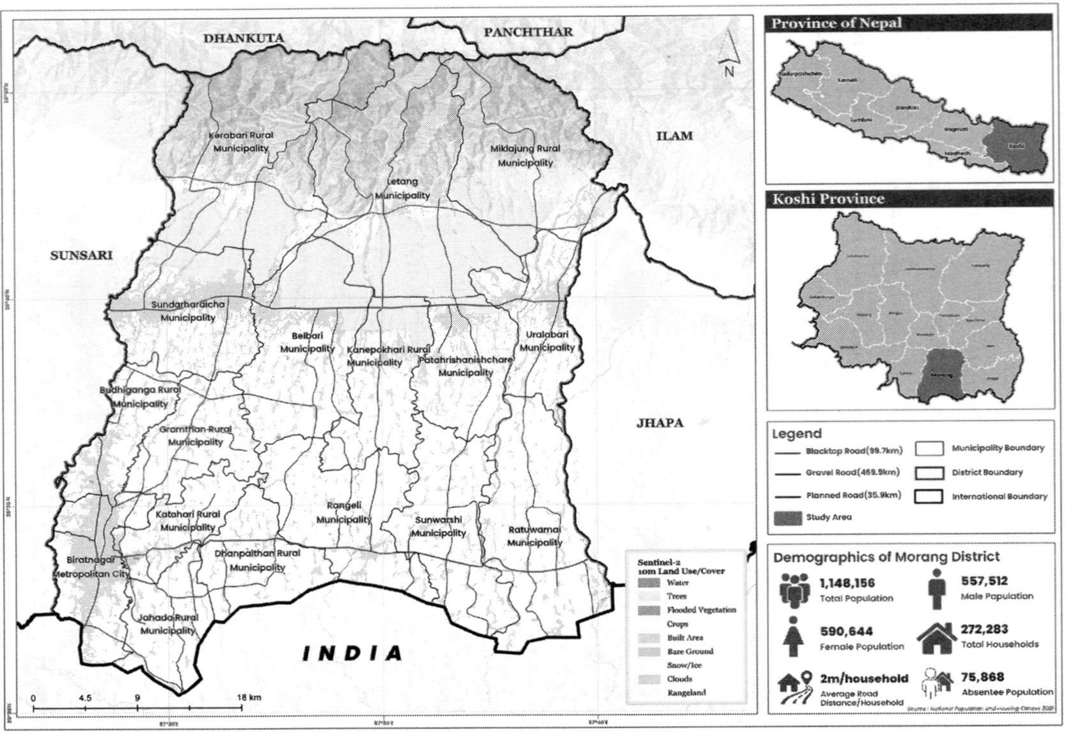

Map 1.1: Location map of Morang District (map by Naxa.com).

track, originally around three meters wide, was upgraded and widened to 18.2 meters wide during our fieldwork. However, the track was interrupted by the Lohandra River in the south. Construction of a bridge to connect Tarigama was underway during our field work.

ROAD HISTORY AND REMOTENESS

This section first summarizes the history of early road development in Morang District, highlighting the district's pioneering status for highway construction in Nepal since the 1960s. These highways, however, were impractical with respect to everyday mobility of local residents, and rural roads had yet to receive consistent public funding. As a result, rural inhabitants lived in isolation until the recent past, experiencing the contradictory situation of having regional highways without accessibility between local areas.

I then delve into the concept of remoteness in regional development planning. I argue that seasonality, rather than physical distance, is a more appropriate indicator for understanding remoteness in the plains of Morang District. Highlighting the constraints imposed by rivers and floods on road building and mobility challenges common perceptions—shaped by regional development planning discourses—that geographical distances determine remoteness, and that the Tarai landscape is easily accessible.

OVERVIEW OF ROAD HISTORY IN THE DISTRICT

Nepal opened up to the outside world after the restoration of democracy in the 1950s, leading the government to embark on modern development plans, including infrastructure projects. However, Biratnagar had already established industrial infrastructures, influenced by the expansion of railway networks along the Nepal-India border in the northern regions of Bihar (Dahal 1997; Tiwary 2008). Morang thus became an early focus of road infrastructure in the district: the Koshi Project, Jogbani-Dharan Road, and the East-West Highway. In 1954, Nepal and India reached a historic agreement to construct a barrage along the Koshi River. Known as the Koshi

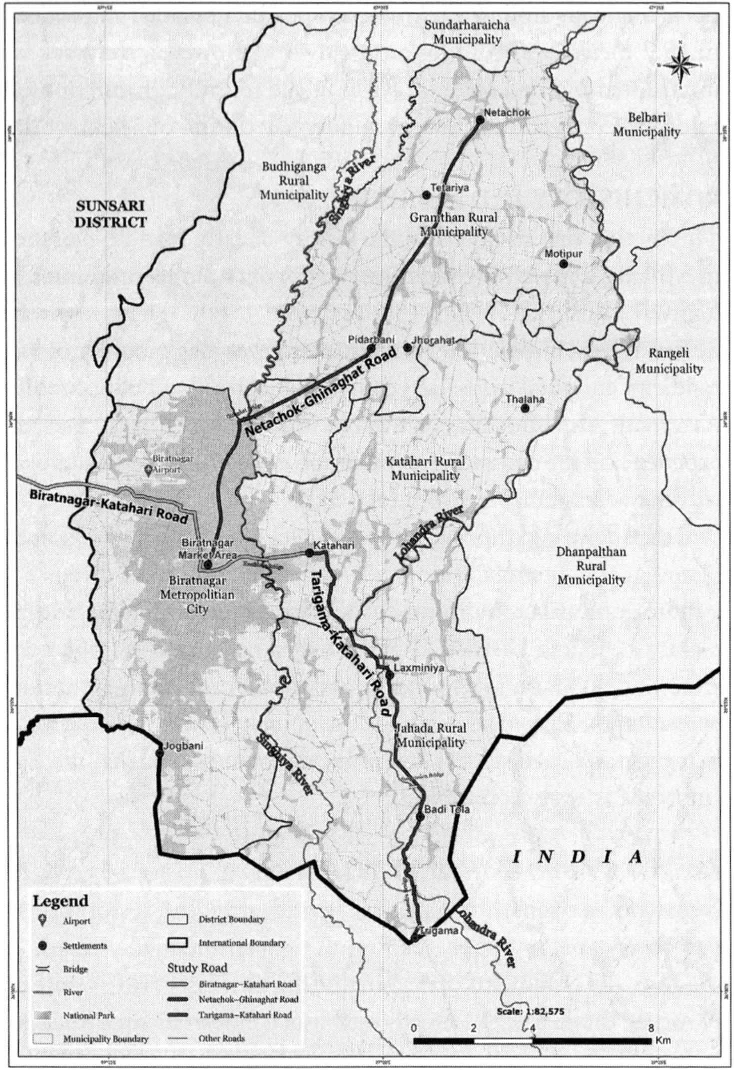

Map 1.2: Road Map of Morang District (map by Naxa.com).

Project, it aimed to control floods, develop hydropower, and improve irrigation facilities in both countries. As part of this agreement, the government of India extended the irrigation canal from Chatara on the Koshi River to the districts of Sunsari and Morang. The canal was handed over to the Government of Nepal in 1975. It was upgraded and expanded in three stages from 1978 to 2002 (NPC 2012). This expansion led to the creation of new tracks along the sides of the canal, which greatly improved mobility for local people in the inner parts of Sunsari and Morang Districts. Additionally, the Koshi Project expanded the railway network in 1957, including a cargo rail route from Bathnaha, India, to Dharan, now part of Dharan Sub-metropolitan City. This railway transported gravel, stone, construction materials, and machinery for the construction of the barrage at Bhimnagar. The place where the railway station was located in Dharan still retains its name, "Railway." The Jogbani-Dharan Road, a section of the Koshi Highway extending from the Rani Custom Office in Biratnagar, was among the earliest roads built in Nepal during the 1950s, alongside the Hetauda-Bharatpur Road and Tribhuvan Rajpath. Constructed by the British army in 1959, the road aimed to connect India to the British Gorkha cantonment, known as Ghopa Camp, located in the present-day Dharan Sub-metropolitan area of Sunsari District. Historically, this road was also referred to as the "Malaya" road, as it served as a gateway to the British Gorkha cantonment in Malaysia.

In 1961, King Mahendra initiated the construction of the East-West Highway, a section of which passed through the dense forest of Morang District.[4] Prior to the East-West Highway's completion, Nepali citizens had to traverse the Indian border to access transportation when traveling from east to west across Nepal (Skerry, Moran and Calavan 1991). The East-West Highway, later renamed Mahendra Rajmarga in honor of the king, was an important strategic road aimed at reducing the necessity of crossing the Indian border.

By the 1970s, the transportation network in Morang District relied on several key roads, including Mahendra Rajmarga, Jogbani-Dharan Road, Rangeli Road, Kanepokhari-Rangeli Road, and

[4] During the years 1963–1965 (2020–2022 v.s.), Panchayat local administrative units mobilized local villagers to contribute their labor voluntarily as *shramdan* (labor donations) to open the track. The coercive involvement of locals will be discussed in section three.

Kanepokhari-Letang Road. The Kanepokhari-Rangeli Road and Kanepokhari-Letang Roads were accessible year-round, connecting market centers, such as Letang Bazaar in the hilly region, to Rangeli in the south. Rangeli Road, a historic postal highway, linked Rangeli to Biratangar in the west and Jhapa in the east but was not functional during the rainy season due to a lack of bridges over the Lohandra, Bakraha, and Chisang Rivers. Travelers had to detour via the Kanepokhari-Rangeli Road to reach Rangeli from Biratnagar during the rainy season (HMG 1975).

In the 1970s, the government introduced a policy aimed at balancing regional development and integrating the economy across different regions. This had a significant impact on road development in Nepal and continues to shape policy and planning decisions (Gurung 1969, 2005; Paudyal 1998; Sharma 2004). The policy focused on constructing national highways in the north-south direction, spanning various ecological regions to connect growth centers across regions.[5] In eastern Nepal, the emphasis was on developing Biratnagar and Dharan in the Tarai, Dhankuta in the hills, and Hedangna in the mountains as growth centers (Gurung 1969).

In the early 1980s, the traditional road from Jogbani to Dharan was extended to Dhankuta, as the Dharan-Dhankuta Road, and later to Basantapur, as the Dhankuta-Hile Road. Collectively known as the Koshi Highway, these roads connect the hills and plains of eastern Nepal, and continue to the border of India. This highway became a lifeline for the hill districts of the Koshi Zone, opening up access to services in the region and markets in India.[6]

The hills of Koshi Zone have received significant development funds from government, donors, and private sector since the 1970s. This support has led to improvements in the economy, livelihoods,

[5] This decision was based on the recommendation of the World Bank's 20-year Master Plan for Transport Development (The World Bank 1965).

[6] Koshi Zone was one of Nepal's 14 zones until 2015 when the country adopted a federal system and replaced zones and development regions with provinces. The districts of Bhojpur, Dhankuta, Sankhuwasabha, Morang, and Sunsari, which once comprised Koshi Zone, are now part of Koshi Province.

and access to services compared to neighboring hill districts and the plains of Koshi Zone (NPC and DfID 2013). This was partly due to the implementation of regional policies, which overlooked infrastructure and development projects in the plains of Morang.

It was only after the restoration of democracy in 1990 that planners and donors finally started to focus on rural roads (Paudyal 1998). However, even two decades later, there were no significant improvements in the condition of rural roads in Morang, as was revealed in the 2013 district transport plan (DDC Morang 2013), which highlighted the poor condition of rural roads and their urgent need for improvement and maintenance, particularly when compared to highways.

In recent years, there has been some improvement in rural roads in the plains of Morang. However, as we move away from the highways and into the rural areas, particularly along the southern part of the Biratnagar-Rangeli Hulaki Rajmarga, conditions worsen. Villagers in this southern region still do not have access to well-maintained village roads and affordable public transportation. Many people rely on bicycles as their main mode of transportation, while others from Jahada Rural Muncipality have to walk for at least an hour or two to reach nearby market centers, such as Biratnagar.

QUESTIONING GEOGRAPHIC PROXIMITY: ASSESSING REMOTENESS AND UNDERSTANDING SEASONALITY

The Nepali government officially adopted regional planning as the basis of development after the 1970s, emphasizing road development as a key strategy to address remoteness and enhance connectivity (The World Bank 1965; Gurung 1969, 2005). This conception has led to a focus on developing the hills and mountains, which are seen as remote compared to the Tarai region. Consequently, the construction of roads in the Tarai region is frequently overlooked, with the argument that the existing network of roads and tracks is sufficient and transportation is accessible to most areas (Paudyal 1998). It is crucial to note that remoteness and connectivity are not mutually exclusive; one does not eliminate the other. Instead, they are interconnected concepts that influence each other across space and time in a non-uniform manner (Saxer and Andersson 2019). Remoteness is actively constructed and reconstructed across political, material, and historical scales.

Intergovernmental organizations and scholars have recently expressed concerns about a characterization of remoteness that privileges the impact of physical distance. The United Nations Conference on Trade and Development's (UNCTAD) annual report (2022), focusing on the 2030 Agenda for Sustainable Development and Sustainable Development Goals (SDGs), advocates attention to the multidimensional nature of remoteness. Similarly, scholars argue that remoteness is dynamic, relational, and has socio-political implications. The significance of remoteness as a descriptor for a specific location, thus, can vary depending on the speaker's perspective and the context (Harms *et al.* 2014). Furthermore, despite the expectation of greater equality due to advancing technology and connectivity through globalization, the world has seen increased inequality, leading to a concentration of power in certain centers and the marginalization of others. This unevenness has raised the need to reconsider the concept of remoteness and the political implications of its use in different settings (Saxer and Andersson 2019).

In the Nepal context, remote areas are commonly referred to as *durgam*, a term that literally means inaccessible, in contrast to *sugam*, meaning easily accessible (Harms *et al.* 2014). Additionally, this categorization serves as an administrative scale for civil servants; working in a "remote" area can confer additional benefits—or it may be imposed as a punishment to those who fall out of favor within the civil service. Besides the physical distance from goods and services, other factors associated with the category *durgam*, such as lower population density, higher transportation costs, elevated cost of goods, limited livelihood opportunities and agricultural production, and a lower human development index—all serve as characteristics of remote areas that become the foundation for planning and development (Regmi *et al.* 2013).

It is important to underscore that as Thomas *et al.* (2012) note, conceptions of physical distance can be subjective and dependent on the situation. Distance, for example, impacts access to health services, with factors such as terrain, travel time, and limited transportation options influencing how people perceive physical distance in the hills, while means of transportation and seasonal variation primarily affect distance perception in the Tarai. Historically, Nepal's rulers, planners, and policymakers have defined remoteness according to their own particular interests. There is not always a consistent relationship between geographical distance and socio-political connectivity. For example, despite being geographically distant from Kathmandu (as well as cut off by topography and disease), particular hill and Tarai regions have long maintained strong cultural, political and economic connections with the Nepali state and British Empire (see with regard to the Tarai, Gaige 1975; Ojha 1983; Regmi 1988). The remoteness of rural regions was a political strategy to defend the country's sovereignty from an expanding British Empire. This strategy was implemented at the time of Nepal's unification in the 18th century and continued until the end of the Rana regime in the mid-20th century. Rulers deliberately kept the hills isolated from the Kathmandu Valley in order to limit access by the British Empire (Regmi 1988). Meanwhile, they adopted policies to colonize the Tarai region internally for expropriation of resources. Tarai rivers were used as waterways to transport timber, jute, and other resources to India before the establishment of railways during the 19th century (Ojha 1983; Regmi 1988).

Despite the perceived accessibility of the Tarai, the presence of rivers and streams creates challenges, including the financial and technical burden of constructing bridges, underscoring the region's remoteness. Official publications like *Mechi dekhi Mahakali* (Mechi to Mahakali) in the early 1970s (HMG 1975) acknowledged transportation challenges in rural areas of Morang District, particularly during the rainy season. Navigating the district from east to west was virtually impossible due to the north-south flowing rivers and streams during the rainy season, despite the extension of highways making it seem accessible. Locals commonly depended on bullock carts for regular transport of goods during the dry season, and only wealthier individuals used elephants to cross rivers during the rainy season.

Photo 1.1: Rivers and streams often hinder the mobilities of residents during the rainy season (photo by Durga Hansda, 2018).

During my fieldwork from 2016–2018, locals frequently offered similar insights about the paradox of remoteness and accessibility, expressing sentiments present in the district since at least the publication of *Mechi dekhi Mahakali*. Local villagers in Gramthan Gaupalika, situated approximately 20 km from Biratnagar, indicated that highways do not necessarily help meet daily transportation needs; it is often faster to walk or cycle through non-motorized tracks than travel the distance to and from highways to reach relatives, markets, and paddy fields in nearby areas. Additionally, they highlighted how rivers, streams and thick, sticky mud hindered mobility during the rainy season. Rural road networks from east to west are completely disrupted by the lack of bridges over local rivers and streams, which flow in a north-south direction. It becomes necessary to follow north-south tracks to and from major East-West Highways, in sometimes long and inconvenient detours under these conditions.

When asked about their recent experiences with rural roads, villagers would immediately point to their knees and assert, "*Yati, yati hilo hunthyo*!" (The mud was up to our knees!). The phrase was commonly used to describe the poor condition of rural roads. During monsoon season, it was nearly impossible to walk, let alone drive, on village roads. This posed significant challenges during medical emergencies, such as snake bites or complications in childbirth, as patients had to be transported on stretchers to reach hospitals. Unfortunately, many villagers lost their lives due to lack of access to emergency health services.

Locals' narratives often reflect their strong feelings of remoteness and isolation, which sometimes serve as a motivation for them to enhance the condition of village roads. Take, for instance, Nitesh Chaudhari, an educated man in his early 40s, from Gramthan Rural Municipality.[7] He shared his reasons for wanting to improve the village road, located approximately 500 meters from his village, which connected to the feeder road linking the East-West Highway and Biratnagar.

> Our village is located so close to the highway, yet we were forced to remove our shoes and roll up our pants to navigate through muddy roads just to enter the village. During the rainy seasons, it became impossible to ride bicycles or motorcycles. We were unable to access essential services such as the fire brigade, ambulance, and even buses [for transporting the groom's party] during wedding ceremonies. This situation

[7] All personal names used in this chapter are pseudonyms.

> brought great shame upon us. A well-maintained road is a source of pride for any village.

Nitesh had worked in Qatar for many years before deciding to improve the village road. Each time he returned home on vacation, he noticed no progress had been made. Realizing he needed to take action, he made the bold choice to quit his job in Qatar and permanently return to the village to engage in social work. He successfully motivated other young people in the village to join him in the collective effort to improve the road. To his surprise, Nitesh discovered that the road had not been upgraded in almost 50 years. Some elders mentioned that the villagers had once repaired the road during the reign of King Mahendra (1955–1972).

During my fieldwork in Pidarbani, a small village along the Biratchok-Ghinaghat feeder road, I often had conversations with the head of my host family, Shiva Sardar *dai* (older brother), after dinner. He was a well-known social worker and had influence in one of the major political parties. He was familiar with the details of my research project and would frequently ask about my fieldwork. During one of our evening conversations, I mentioned my trip to Thalaha, which used to be a separate Village Development Committee (VDC) before the 2017 federal restructuring. After listening to me, he became intrigued and recounted a story to communicate the meaning of Thalaha as a muddy wetland in the Tharu language. He mentioned that Thalaha was often cut off during the rainy season, making it hard to reach. His family owned a paddy field in Thalaha, but the journey from Pidarbani to Thalaha was impassable on foot during the rainy season. Only elephants could traverse the muddy terrain to reach their field. They would occasionally visit their field by borrowing an elephant from a *jimidar*, a local landlord, who was a close relative. Eventually, they sold the field due to its remoteness.[8]

[8] *Jimidar* was a government-appointed official responsible for revenue collection in the Tarai region (Regmi 1988). In colloquial language, the term also refers to landlords associated with *jimidar* families.

As an outsider, it was hard for me to believe this common account because now Thalaha was well connected to the Biratchok-Biratnagar feeder road with a gravel road. I only realized the true remoteness of Thalaha after hearing stories from locals about a caravan that, before the 1990s, used to make the journey from Pidarbani to Biratnagar to sell paddy around the time of the Dashain festival in October/November. The narrative goes like this:

> Traveling alone was impossible in this village. The villagers would plan ahead and decide on a date to begin their journey, allowing time to prepare their bullock carts. It would take two to three days to reach Biratnagar, but the path was filled with rough potholes caused by rain and floods. The most challenging part of the journey was crossing the Singhiya River at Ghinaghat. The bullocks struggled to pull the carts with their full loads, so the villagers would unload sacks and carry them on their backs while crossing the river. To make things easier, they would tie the bullock carts together and help each other by pushing the carts through the water. This process was tiring and time-consuming, often taking hours to complete. The name Ghinaghat, meaning "dirty ghat" in the Tharu language, reflected the hardships faced by travelers while crossing the river.

Initially, I doubted these narratives, but after hearing consistent accounts from multiple respondents, I realized that construction of a bridge over the river at Ghinaghat during the early 1990s had significantly improved local access to Biratnagar. Currently, Pidarbani and Ghinaghat are connected by a well-paved feeder road from Biratchok to Ghinaghat, which is often congested with traffic. The journey from Pidarbani to Biratnagar in a private vehicle, which used to take days, has now been reduced to half an hour.

The main point I want to make is that it is difficult for researchers like me, as well as planners and policymakers who are not familiar with the area, to fully understand the impact of seasonality on remoteness. This is because we are often influenced by the prevailing discourse of development politics, which portrays hills as "remote," "inaccessible," and needing road expansion for development. This view also idealizes the Tarai region as a valuable source of revenue, a buffer zone, and a "grain storehouse" (see Gurung 1969; Tylor 1969; Eckholm 1976; Gaige 1975; NPC 1985; Ives 1987; Sharma 2004)—and certainly not a focus for road development. As a result, the plains of Morang District may appear "accessible" due to the history of infrastructure development and existing road networks. However, remoteness and accessibility in the plains of Morang District have been paradoxically intertwined for a long time.

ORGANIZATION OF ROAD DEVELOPMENT

My focus in this section is on the role of labor relations in organizing road development, while the other chapters emphasize how contracting and users' committees differ and intertwine. The dynamics of labor relations between the state and its citizens in the road building process have evolved over time in Nepal. Forced labor was predominant from the unification of modern Nepal in the late 18th century until the end of Rana hereditary rule in the mid-20th century. Following the establishment of democracy in 1951, the government promptly prohibited the practice of forced labor, recognizing it as a violation of the right to freedom from exploitation (Interim Government of Nepal Act, 1951; Constitution of Nepal 2015). Concurrently, however, the government has retained the authority to mandate citizens to provide "voluntary services" for public initiatives. During the autocratic Panchayat regime following the coup of 1960, there was a strong push toward enforcing voluntary labor for local infrastructural development, effectively resembling forced labor in practice.

Following the restoration of democracy in 1990, the Government of Nepal, planners, and donors continued the policy of fostering public participation in local infrastructure as an intrinsic aspect of local self-governance. Accordingly, local governments enlisted road users' committees for rural road building. These groups operate under the supervision of the local authority and are required to supplement the government budget through voluntary contributions of cash, labor, or other in-kind contributions such as machinery. In practice, however, a disconnect between the policies and practices of public participation in road building is emerging, raising significant questions about the effectiveness of users' groups and the sustainability of roads (N. Rai 2020).

Against this backdrop, this section critically examines local community experiences with past forced labor and the changing dynamics of voluntary labor contributions popularly known as *jana shramdan* after 1990. I argue that people's reluctance to contribute voluntary labor for road building is significantly influenced by a critical awareness of the role of voluntary labor in a democratic setting and the cultural politics surrounding budget considerations and planning, which fosters the perception of corruption.[9]

CHANGING LABOR RELATIONS: EVOLVING DYNAMICS BETWEEN THE STATE AND ITS CITIZENS

For roughly two centuries, spanning the early stages of modern Nepal's unification to the end of the autocratic Rana regime (1773–1951), forced labor dominated the construction of local infrastructure, including village paths, animal tracks, and *hulaki* (postal) tracks. Social historian Mahesh Chandra Regmi (1988) has documented instances of labor exploitation, referred to as *jhara* and *rakam*, used to maintain traditional transport and communication networks in the hills and Tarai before the advent of motorable roads. Ethnographic accounts obtained during fieldwork shed light on the involvement of the local Tharu community in building local infrastructure, such as village roads in Morang District. This participation was traditionally

[9] See Rankin *et al.* (2024) and Shneiderman (2024) on the dynamics of voluntary contribution and perceived corruption in the administration of everyday life in Nepal.

facilitated through a specific form of forced unpaid labor called *begari, beth,* or *begar*, provided by locals to *jimidar* and other authorities.[10]

Begari was a communal labor system widely practiced by the Tharu community, particularly in the western Tarai. It involved voluntary contributions of labor to village heads and community projects. However, the system was exploited by both the state and hill migrants, who treated it as forced labor through taxation and resettlement policies after the unification of Nepal (Rankin 1999; Dhakal *et al.* 2000; Fujikura 2001; Guneratne 2002). Today, the practice of *begari* has become obsolete. However, its historical legacy has significantly shaped the subjectivities of local people. During our fieldwork, elderly individuals often referenced the term when recounting their experiences of forced labor, with their tone and facial expressions conveying suffering and disgust. In discussions about voluntary labor contributions in Tharu communities today, elderly residents who had previously engaged in voluntary work would often remark, "*Aba ko janchha begari?*" (Who would go for unpaid labor now?). This phrase suggests that voluntary labor is associated with their past experience of *begari*, which they understand as a metaphor for dominance and exploitation.

In the following sections, I will present the accounts of two elderly gentlemen from Gramthan Rural Municipality, Krishna Das Tharu and Poltu Tharu. They shared their experiences of forced labor extracted to repair village tracks for Rana official visits in the 1940s, and later for the construction of the East-West Highway.

On June 13, 2018, we visited a road that was being upgraded from Tetariya to Duhabi, west of Tetariya Chok in Gramthan Rural Municipality. The road appeared wide and clear, and villagers chatted under a concrete shed nearby. As we approached, an elderly man sitting inside the shed expressed interest in us. We introduced ourselves and discussed our research, then asked to chat with him. It was exciting to meet such an enthusiastic person willing to share

[10] *Beth* and *begar* are used interchangeably with *begari*; I use the term *begari* hereafter.

his experiences. As our conversation proceeded, Krishna Das Tharu explained that the track had been built during the Rana regime and was an important route from Biratnagar to Letang, a prominent market center in the foothills north of the East-West Highway. However, it remained unfinished after the fall of the Rana regime. The District Panchayat, a unit of the Panchayat government, surveyed another road from Tetariya to Ghinaghat, which was later developed into the feeder road to connect the East-West Highway and Biratnagar.

Krishna Das Tharu shared a fascinating story about the official visit of a Rana prime minister in the late 1940s, which took place along that very road. He was filled with excitement as he recalled the procession:

> It was such a magnificent sight. We don't see such processions nowadays. The prime minister was riding in a motor vehicle at the front of the procession. Behind him were big elephants with huge tusks. *Baphre* (Oh my goodness)! The wealthy villagers had adorned the road in front of their houses with *kalash* (bronze pots) to welcome the officials. The sides of the road were crowded with villagers. Rana officials even threw coins to the crowd for amusement. I saw all of this with my own eyes.

He mentioned that the villagers were compelled to prepare the roads for these visits. They had to fill the roadbed with mud from both sides and upgrade it into a wide, smooth earthen road. They leveled and hardened the surface of the village track with wooden beams. Once the track was ready, they covered it with paddy straw, and local villagers were not allowed to use bullock carts on these roads to keep the track in good condition for the Rana officials' visits. Local authorities imposed physical punishment on those who were unwilling to work.

A week later, I had the opportunity to meet another gentleman, Poltu Tharu, who was in his 80s and lived in Lakhantari Village. He was a quiet, reserved person, and his old age had brought about some hearing difficulties. Initially, he was hesitant to participate in the interview. My co-researcher, Yaman Sardar, who was also from the Tharu community, convinced him by explaining the purpose of our research and the value of his information for telling the history of road building in Morang.

I began by asking about his experiences with the construction of the East-West Highway. He, along with other villagers, had worked for weeks in the dense forest to clear the path. I was intrigued when he used the word *begari* in connection to opening the track, so I interrupted and asked him to explain what *begari* meant. His answer was simple: "work." I had heard people using the term *begari* colloquially before, but thought it was slang with a negative connotation, referring to individuals who were idle or lazy. It was at this point that the gentleman clarified, saying, "You are not given money for work." This made it clear to me that he was referring to a forced labor relationship.

When I asked about his memories of the Rana regime, he also recalled the Ranas' official visits, with processions featuring motor vehicles, elephants, horses, and policemen. He mentioned that these visits were typically scheduled from February to March. The processions followed the track from Biratnagar along the western side of the Singhiya River and crossed the river at Ghinaghat before passing through the village. However, when I asked how the tracks were repaired to facilitate these visits, he appeared annoyed and raised his voice, asserting, "I've been mentioning repeatedly that we had to do *begari* [as he had mentioned when talking about the East-West Highway]. The authorities ordered the *gachhadar*[11] from each village to gather the villagers for *begari*. We, the villagers, had to repair the road, and we weren't paid for it." He went on to mention that villagers

[11] Head of the local Tharu community responsible for managing village affairs and serving as a liaison between government authorities and residents.

were also required to provide *begari* to set up sophisticated camps for Rana visitors at Haraicha. These visitors would stay at Haraicha, which is currently located in Sundar Haraicha Municipality in the west-central part of the district, for weeks, then move on to the next camp in Bayarban and Rajghat. Bayarban is now part of Kanepokhari Rural Municipality in the central region, while Rajghat is in Urlabari Municipality in the west-central region of the district. During their stay, Rana officials enjoyed hunting. The *gachhadar* had to mobilize villagers throughout their visit to assist with logistics.

After the fall of the Rana regime in 1951, the government took swift action to abolish practices like human trafficking, slavery, *begari*, and other forms of forced labor as part of democratic reforms. They achieved this by enacting the Interim Government Act of 1951, which explicitly defined *begar* as a type of forced labor, as mentioned in the Constitution of India. Following this, King Mahendra's autocratic Panchayat regime redefined labor relations between the state and the people by making public participation the cornerstone of their decentralization policy. Through a strategy of "public participation," or *jana sahabhagita*, the government mobilized local resources and labor for local development. The adjacent strategy of *jana shramdan*, or "labor donation," was experienced as a de facto form of forced labor in various local development projects, including road construction. This resonates with practices in Dolakha, as documented in the next chapter of this book.

A significant example of *jana shramdan* in road building was King Mahendra's call for local peoples' "voluntary" participation in constructing the East-West Highway. In the early 1960s, when the government began surveying land, individuals like Krishna Das Tharu and others were initially perplexed when they saw surveyors working in the forest. The surveyors explained the government's plan to build a highway, but the villagers were skeptical. They couldn't believe that it was possible to construct a road through such dense forest with numerous rivers and streams cutting across it.

Later, villagers were taken aback when the government issued an order for every household in Morang District to send one person to help clear the path for the highway. Krishna Das Tharu, along with other villagers, responded to this call and ventured into the forest for weeks. He recounted his experience:

> The forest was filled with people from all the panchayats (pre-VDC administrative unit) of Morang. Villagers had to arrange their own food and supplies. They stayed in the jungle until their work was complete. Their tasks included filling soil, clearing shrubs, and leveling the path through the dense forest. The villagers couldn't return home until they had finished their assigned portion of the work, so they toiled late into the night. The *gachhadar* (headman) of each village were responsible for mobilizing the villagers, and the authorities closely monitored the progress. If any villagers were absent, the authorities would promptly send the *gachhadar* to bring them back to the site.

Despite the Panchayat regime's attempts to glorify *jana shramdan* as a voluntary labor contribution, local people were well aware that it was essentially a veiled form of forced labor. Krishna Das Tharu felt a strong sense of deception and expressed his disappointment, saying:

> The government was very clever. It named the highway after King Mahendra. But when did the king come to work? In reality we built it. Now it's called Mahendra Rajmarga. It should be named the People's Highway because it was built by the people. "Mahendra Rajmarga built with the cooperation of India and Nepal" is still engraved on the side of the road. The people received nothing. They weren't provided with food while working, and their contribution went unrecognized. The government has never offered a single day of free transportation. The government could have organized a tour or some form of celebration for all those who worked, but it simply used us for our labor.

Locals became skeptical about the development of the East-West Highway because the arrival of this significant national road did not align with their aspirations. I frequently heard a sense of disappointment from elderly individuals like Krishna Das Tharu, who had participated in opening the track of the East-West Highway.

The construction of the East-West Highway in Nepal was a nationalistic project primarily aimed at bypassing the need to traverse through India when traveling from east to west (HMG 1964). The road's design prioritized technical feasibility and administrative considerations, rather than facilitating local mobility, often leading it to bypass traditional settlements (The World Bank 1965). The government stated that the primary purpose of the East-West Highway was to integrate the nation, but it also served to consolidate territorial control. Contrary to the government's claim that the East-West Highway represents national unity, the people of the Tarai often felt excluded. Critics like Jha (1993) argue that the government intentionally designed the East-West Highway to sideline a traditional *hulaki* road, also known as Padma Road, which ran through southern settlements, a decision that led to marginalization of many Tarai people.

The construction of highways, including the East-West Highway, in fact, did not effectively meet the everyday mobility needs of long-standing residents in rural areas, leaving them without essential road connectivity and transportation until only recently. Highways facilitated the establishment of new settlements along their routes, predominantly composed of residential areas for hill migrants, factories, service centers, and markets, which remained ironically "off the beaten track" for long-time residents living in interior villages. Over time, the highways traced a clear disparity in the district's landscape by creating a noticeable division between developed and underdeveloped areas.

A SORE POINT: NAVIGATING PUBLIC PARTICIPATION, BUDGET SUBJECTIVITY, AND CORRUPTION

After the federal restructuring of 2017, upgrading local roads became a top priority for newly formed rural municipalities, and local road work gained momentum in the field site area. Individuals frequently expressed curiosity about local budgets and speculated about the allocations their rural municipalities had received. I characterize the intense curiosity, diverse perspectives, speculation, judgment, and political considerations among the local population regarding budgets as "budget subjectivity." This mode of political subjectivity also manifests in a lack of public participation, *jana sahabhagita,* via voluntary labor contributions in road users' committees, which contravenes the requirement of public participation in rural road building and budget allocations.[12]

Road construction sites were often bustling with children, men, and women of all ages from the local community who were part of the road users' committee. Many would gather around the excavator machine, either as spectators for amusement or to safeguard their property during road upgrades. While there was the mandatory provision for members of the road users' committees to contribute in cash, kind, or labor to the road construction process, only a few of the executive members typically took part in a voluntary capacity, though they too refrained from contributing manual labor. Despite government policies emphasizing the use of manual labor in rural road construction and discouraging the use of heavy machinery (DoLIDAR 1999; Meyer *et al.* 1999; MoLD 2004), machines have generally replaced human labor during the construction of rural roads in Morang. Executive members of road users' committees who actively participated in road building argued that they were compelled to use excavator machines, commonly referred to as "dozers," due

[12] It is mandatory for local beneficiaries who are members of users' committees to contribute to budget allocations for road building, either in cash, kind, or through volunteer labor. Government authorities typically prefer voluntary labor contributions over cash or kind to alleviate the financial burden on rural communities (PPO 2007).

to a lack of voluntary labor contributions and increased wages for manual labor. Using machines is considered relatively cheaper than hiring labor.

Photo 1.2: Locals gathered around excavators as spectators, near Pidarbani, on way to Sidharaha (photo by Lagan Rai, 2018).

Daya Ram Majhi, who was among the first generation of educated individuals from the village and the principal at a local high school in Pidarbani, shared his perspective:

> Voluntary labor was a well-established practice during my childhood. An individual from each household used to willingly contribute labor when asked by a village leader. Villagers would come together to repair roads and irrigation canals through cooperative efforts. In the later years of the Panchayat system, the government occasionally distributed wheat and other grains to villagers as compensation for their labor. This led villagers to become more calculating, and they

> began to participate expecting cash or grains in return. As the government started providing more budget after 1990, the practice of *jana shramdan* also began to decline.

As argued by Daya Ram, the gradual rise in budget allocations after 1990 (associated with decentralization and the expansion of participatory modes of development) had a paradoxical impact on local communities' willingness to contribute labor voluntarily in road building. Like him, other informed individuals similarly acknowledged how diminishing voluntary labor contributions correlate with escalating budget allocations for rural road building. Amit Shah, a former chair of the local panchayat, confirmed that voluntary labor contributions, a well-established practice during the Panchayat era for maintaining and repairing local infrastructure, had decreased after budgets were allocated for local infrastructure development. He explained:

> Everyone is aware of the provision for *jana shramdan* in government policy, but participation has become a mere phrase in documents. People find it unjust to be expected to contribute their labor freely when there is a budget available. Villagers now expect that development work should be funded with the development budget. In the past, villagers contributed their labor freely because there were no budgets, and they had an urgent need for local tracks.

Kabindra Majhi, a senior citizen, had significant experience in mobilizing villagers voluntarily to maintain local tracks and small seasonal bridges when he was *pradhan pancha*, chair of the local panchayat. In his analysis, *jana shramdan* had been effectively mandatory for locals when the local panchayats were deprived of development budgets. Villagers were compelled to contribute their labor due to practical needs. He emphasized that the practice of voluntary labor contribution appeared strange to the younger generation, and even those individuals who had worked voluntarily in the past were now reluctant to contribute labor freely due to budget provisions after 1990. These accounts of past experiences with voluntary labor contributions suggest that a crucial transformation in public awareness of budgeting and planning occurred in the transition between the Panchayat regime and democratic government after 1990. In other words, new forms of budget subjectivity emerged.

The Local Self-Governance Act (LSGA) of 1999, and subsequent policies institutionalized labor-based, local resource-oriented, environment-friendly techniques, public participation, involvement of users' groups, and collaboration with non-governmental organizations in rural road construction (Rankin *et al.* 2017; N. Rai 2020). Mobilizing local communities through road users' committees became the primary approach for rural road construction in Nepal.

The democratic reforms of the 1990s marked a significant shift and liberation for the people who had endured an autocratic regime for three decades. It was understandable for people to have high hopes for fairness and justice in the new democratic system, but their frustration grew as the government failed to provide economic relief and equitable development. National governments were often paralyzed as they encountered challenges from opposition parties in the parliament, an inefficient and politicized bureaucracy, inter-party conflicts, and significant socioeconomic inequalities (Khadka 1993). Moreover, Nepal experienced a paradoxical phenomenon known as "exclusionary democratization," (Lawoti 2008) whereby the restoration of democracy allowed marginalized groups more political space but also increased their exclusion from influential governance arenas. A culture of impunity was heightened among ruling leaders, leading to a crisis of governance and governmental instability, which had immense impact on the social psychology of the public (Lawoti 2008).

While the government continued to stress the importance of voluntary contributions as a sign of public involvement, with the goal of promoting a feeling of ownership and responsibility, it also failed to adequately empower local communities in local development and planning. The decrease in voluntary labor participation thus started well before we began field work in 2017. The decrease can be attributed to the discrepancy between government strategy and local people's expectations. Residents hoped that the need for voluntary labor contributions would diminish once budgets became available. The government's failure to alter the existing power dynamics and guarantee transparency and accountability in budget planning also contributed to local peoples' skepticism about willingly participating in local road building. The lack of transparency raises questions, such as why they should work for free when there is a budget, and suspicions that executive members of users' committees were pocketing funds instead of using them for projects.

Many locals strongly believe that corruption is rampant. When discussing corruption, local residents rarely use the formal term *bhrashtachar*, which literally means a deviation from moral integrity. Instead, corruption is often metaphorically described using the concepts of *khanu* (eating), *milaunu* (arranging) and *chalkhel* (scheming). For example, the phrase "commission *khane*" (seeking a commission in exchange for service) is prevalent. The Prevention of Corruption Act, 2002 explicitly states that accepting a commission on public contracts, remuneration, brokerage fees, or any other benefit is considered corruption (GoN 2002).[13] Ironically, the English "commission" has become a popular slang word for corruption, deriving from commissions in business transactions, fees paid for facilitating a deal or providing services. On the one hand, the association between "commission" and corruption is based on the societal view of market economies as prioritizing financial gain and how these priorities can infiltrate the public sector too. On the other hand, referring to corrupt behavior as "commission" can also serve to normalize and rationalize such actions as legitimate compensation.

[13] Prevention of Corruption Act, 2002 understands corruption as the improper blending of public and private interests (NORAD 2011).

The slang term "setting *milaune*" emphasizes networking, highlighting the involvement of individuals or groups, often local elites, politicians, or political cadres, who use their connections or engage in bribery to manipulate situations in their favor. In fact, this term is similar to the term *milemato* elaborated in the Mugu chapter. Like for *milemato,* there is a positive as well as a negative valence to the term "setting *milaune*," as people in a wide range of social positions use their connections to arrange things favorably for themselves, friends, or family.

In all cases, corruption is relational, obscured yet widely recognized, and intertwined with power dynamics. After gathering input from stakeholders and authorities, it became evident that various forms of corruption can be detected amongst users' groups, local elites, contractors, service providers, government officials, and political party members engaged in road building processes. This environment enables those involved in corruption to shift blame and avoid accountability. Due to its relational and systematic nature, it is often challenging to identify or hold individuals accountable, to implement corrective measures, or to comprehend the genuine extent of corruption in rural road building.

Several villagers I spoke with expressed pessimism and a sense of helplessness, as corruption escalated severely during the absence of democratically elected local governing bodies for almost two decades, after 2002. Local elites and political party members often abused their connections when they were governing according to the all-party mechanism, which allowed for preferential selection of contractors and users' committee executives.[14] Locals often reported instances where fake users' committees were established, and community projects were only documented on paper, sarcastically referring

[14] The all-party mechanism, *sarvadaliya samyantra*, was a political body formed at various levels by representatives of major political parties in Nepal in the post-conflict period after 2006 (see Byrne and Shrestha 2014; Timalsina 2017).

to such projects as *kagaji ghoda*, meaning a "paper horse."[15] Such practices greatly affected the mindset of locals, further diminishing their confidence in participating in the road construction process. As a consequence of budget subjectivity and suspicions surrounding commission *khane,* setting *milaune*, and *kagaji ghoda*, the practice of public participation in government-funded rural road projects thus diminished over time, leading to negative effects on the sustainability of rural roads and the democratic value of participatory governance.

LAND, LANDSCAPES AND BORDERS

This section highlights how roads have functioned as public spaces serving various purposes for villagers, a function that has diminished in recent times due to resettlement and agricultural activities. The first subsection explores personal experiences and subjectivities related to the decline of public spaces, while the second subsection provides ethnographic insights into how the loss of spaces associated with traditional village roads has complicated efforts to improve local roads and entail social class conflicts. Overall the section argues that conflicting interests, perspectives, and rationales surrounding road expansion, encroachment, and resistance come to the forefront during the road building process.

VANISHING PUBLIC SPACES: CHALLENGES IN IMPROVING LOCAL ROADS

I want to begin by providing some evidence of how villagers in the southern Tarai where motorable roads are being built and improved associate these processes with a decline in public space. Interlocutors often reminisce about wide village paths and walkways once served multiple purposes, not just commuting, but also cattle grazing, agricultural processing, and recreation. Today by contrast, roads give primacy to the movement of vehicles, while livestock, piles of hay, and children's play are relegated to dusty roadsides. Because I was

[15] See also the discussions of *kagaj milaune*, as elaborated in the Mugu and Dolakha chapters.

staying in the household of Yaman Sardar, whose father had formerly been a renowned football player, some of these accounts came to me as stories of diminished space for football, and of a nostalgia for the passion for sport. One evening while waiting for dinner to be ready, I enjoyed a lengthy reminiscence from Yaman's father about his days as a popular football player—how his team used to play barefoot, and had to accept donated boots and uniforms when invited to play matches at the prestigious British Gorkha Camp in Dharan.[16] The next day while traveling from Pidarbani to Tetariya on a scooter with Yaman, we drove past the school grounds on which he used to play. He pointed out how it was about a quarter the size of a regular football field, saying "look at that field. It used to be much larger, but now [with the widened road and surrounding development] it has shrunk to this size. Nowadays, there is not much open space left for kids to play, so they tend to stay indoors more."

To me such anecdotes pointed to an important and overlooked function of roadways as providing public space. They convey a palpable sense that before road building and upgrading, these spaces sustained multiple activities, including but not limited to commuting and traveling. Now, I noticed, other activities are increasingly cast as encroachments on the primary function of roads, defined as vehicular movement. Tethered cattle and haystacks obstruct the passage of four-wheelers. Litter and grains spread out on straw mats and left to dry in the road bed are a nuisance, if not a hazard, to drivers. A key topic of deliberation in the area of Jahada Rural Municipality currently undergoing upgrading was encroachment by landless individuals, who had settled in the road right of way and were reluctant to vacate for road expansion. In the Tarai, such encroachment poses a unique challenge to determining technically appropriate road alignments, in contrast to Mugu and Dolakha where alignment conflicts are similarly pervasive, but are not driven by practices of squatting for residence.

[16] We laughed together when he told me this story. It touched me personally as I had spent part of my childhood in Ghopa Camp and vaguely remembered similar football matches with the less equipped local teams in the area.

Well-informed individuals claimed that the encroachment of public road space began after the restoration of the multi-party system in 1990. As landless individuals settled (squatted) along road spaces, local landowners with adjacent fields began to encroach upon the road in front of their properties, aiming to block further settlement and expand their holdings. This led to competition among encroachers. Over time, an increasing number of local villagers and landless hill migrants occupied road peripheries, narrowing roadbeds and posing challenges for their improvement. Road encroachment intensified during the peace agreement between the Maoist party and the government in 2006, given the Maoist party's desire to address the nationwide issue of *sukumbasi* (landless individuals). *Sukumbasi* settlers anticipated that they would obtain official ownership of encroached land once a commission for landless people was set up.

Interlocutors often expressed doubts about the feasibility of enhancing village roads without addressing encroachment, including how to resolve settlement issues for landless populations. These local perspectives indicate that road encroachment is a significant and complex issue ingrained in social stratification, and will persist in hindering road development in the future. The following sub-section explores class conflict and repercussions of these ongoing encroachments on public land using ethnographic examples.

VILLAGE ROAD CONFLICT AND RESISTANCE TO LAND EXPROPRIATION

In my fieldwork, I observed that road improvement projects frequently sparked disputes related to road alignment, displacement of landless individuals, and compensation for private land. Disputes were particularly pronounced when the executive members of road users' committees reclaimed land occupied by landowners, excavated soil to fill the road, and removed buildings or private structures belonging to landless squatters. A notable example of dispute and resistance occurred during the upgrading of a 400-meter earthen road section connecting the Katahari-Tarigama Road in the west to

Dhuran Tola in the east. The residents of Dhuran Tola were mainly landless individuals of the Santhal community who had previously moved from nearby Situng Tola and settled on public land along the road.[17] In total, there were seven households, only one of which had managed to purchase one *kattha* of land for NRs. 1 lakh.[18] They had relocated to Dhuran Tola because their families had grown, and there was not enough space for them to live in Situng Tola.

On May 21, 2018, I was driving from Biratnagar to the southern part of Jahada Rural Municipality early in the morning to meet one of our fellow co-researchers, Durga Hansda. Along the way, as I stopped to chat with some locals, I encountered Keshav Mandal, a local political leader and representative to the District Coordination Council (DCC) from the rural municipality office, who halted his motorcycle in front of me. Keshav told me he was in a hurry as some individuals were obstructing the widening of a road. I said I would like to accompany him, and turned back, following him northward on my scooter. When we arrived at Dhuran Tola, we found some locals and members of the road users' committee, whom I had met before, gathered by the side of the road.

Executive members of the road users' committee, who were waiting for Keshav, explained that the conflict started when Mahesh Shah, a landowner with an agricultural field next to the road, behaved rudely toward the excavator operator and executive members of the users' committee to stop them from excavating soil in front of his field. The executive members then filed a complaint with the ward office, which forwarded it to the chairperson of the *gaupalika* office. At a meeting held with the chairperson, Mahesh agreed to allow the

[17] The Santhals are a marginalized Indigenous people in Nepal, concentrated in the southern belt of Jhapa and Morang Districts. Their traditional homeland is Santhal Pargana in India, and some scholars believe they started migrating to eastern Nepal in the early 20th century (Dahal 1983). According to village elders, Rana rulers invited Santhal ancestors to clear forests and settle in the area.

[18] *Kattha* is a traditional unit of land measurement common in the Tarai region, covering an area of 338.63 square meters. It is larger than the *dhur* (the smallest unit) and smaller than the *bigha* (the largest unit). One *kattha* equals 20 *dhur*, and 20 *kattha* make up one *bigha*.

road users' committee to continue excavating. Later, however, he obstructed the excavation for a second time.

The dispute revolved around the issue of public land encroachment, sparking a debate on road alignment. The Santhal people had settled on the northern side of the road, while the southern side was attached to agricultural land belonging to local landowners, including Mahesh Shah. The executive members of the road users' committee sympathized with the landless settlers and planned to excavate soil for the road from the opposite side of the settlement to avoid damage to the property of settlers. Mahesh opposed this plan, claiming that the road alignment was encroaching on his private field. He suggested extracting soil from the public space on the opposite side where Santhal families had settled. The executive members of the road users' committee argued that Mahesh had also encroached upon public land, and that they were excavating soil from the land he unlawfully occupied. A heated argument between Mahesh and the committee ensued.

Keshav Mandal was visiting the site to help resolve the dispute. However, Mahesh was absent from the site at the time. Everyone eagerly awaited Mandal's opinion. He spoke loudly, emphasizing, "I am absolutely certain that obstructing road expansion is a serious public offense." Mandal and a member of the users' committee inspected the road alignment together and agreed that the issue should be resolved peacefully, following rules and the law. They also believed in allowing *sukumbasi* time for resettlement instead of subjecting them to immediate relocation.

After overhearing their conversation, Sunil Soren and Sunita Besra, close relatives of another landowner with a field adjacent to the roadside, approached members of the users' committee to discuss the matter. Sunil was dissatisfied with the sympathy shown toward the *sukumbasi* and, like Mahesh Shah, insisted that they too should have to vacate the roadside. Meanwhile, the excavator driver grew impatient and expressed his concerns to the users' group, stating, "We have stopped the dozer for the past 24 hours. Who will compensate us for this?" He then reversed his dozer and parked it at the side of the road, announcing his intention to take it to other sites.

After a while, two policemen arrived on a motorcycle. One was an assistant sub-inspector (ASI), the other a constable. The ASI had a pistol on his belt. As he got off the motorbike, he called the chair of the rural municipality and asked for the agreement paper with Mahesh Shah, expressing frustration with the comment, "We should throw that paper in his face." The chair clarified that their agreement with Mahesh had been informal and based on verbal consent. When the ASI tried to contact Mahesh, the latter's phone was switched off. The ASI suspected that Mahesh might be hiding because he was aware of the police presence at the location. The ASI suggested they meet with Mahesh and attempt to persuade him before taking any further action. If he refused to cooperate, they could charge him with a public crime because blocking the road was a serious public offense.

Executive members of the users' group had requested security from the local authorities after Mahesh had threatened them during the argument. They appeared reassured when the police arrived and instructed the excavator driver to continue digging so they could begin the road alignment. As the dozer entered the field and started digging, Sunil Soren, who had earlier challenged the users' committee, suddenly stepped in front of the excavator's bucket to stop it. He called for his family members to give him a *lathi* (a heavy wooden stick). In response, the police constable swiftly seized Sunil by the neck, pulling him onto the side of the road. At the same time, Sunita Besra and a young *sukumbasi* man named Mahendra engaged in a heated argument about road alignment. Sunita's face was flushed with anger. The police led Sunil to a nearby shed at the road junction to help him calm down, while also escorting Sunita away from the gathering crowd. The police, in particular the ASI, were angry with Sunil Soren and started to interrogate him: "Why did you ask for a *lathi* in front of the police? Do you think you're above the law? Even we, as policemen, face punishment when we break the law." The ASI asserted his authority as a custodian of the law, but also tried to persuade Sunil, who had tried to stop the excavator about the wider scope of the road. "Your sons might work in different jobs one day. The road is necessary for transportation and will increase your land value. They will only take some soil, not your entire field." Sunil, however, did not calm down and questioned the need for new roads when old ones were still not functional—evoking the same ethos underlying residents' refusal to furnish volunteer labor in the context of decentralized budgets. The police expressed their frustration, arguing that locals were stubborn and should understand the concept of future increases in land value resulting from road development. Sunil immediately replied that change should begin with leaders, but the police contended that individuals should first change themselves.

Two days later, on May 23, 2018, I returned to the site from Biratnagar. It was peak maize harvesting season, and villagers were busy in the fields. The village appeared deserted. Farmers had placed dried maize grains and cobs along the sides of the Katahari-Tarigama Road in front of their houses, making the road colorful. At Dhuran Tola, the road was quiet and empty. I stopped my scooter and reflected on the earlier incident. It was hard to believe that there had been such a dramatic dispute. The excavators had removed soil to align the road on the side opposite from the Santhal settlement, including from Mahesh Shah's field. I observed a group of men rebuilding a shed on the settler side, belonging to Birendra, which had been removed by the road users' committee during road clearing as it had been encroaching on the road. Mahendra's poverty and landlessness was related to a childhood accident at a rice mill in which he had lost an arm; he had to drop out of school because his parents couldn't afford tuition for him and his siblings. The users' group had found him rebuilding the shed encroaching on the road, and again complained, but Mahesh managed to convince them that he needed the shed because he did not have space for his cattle but would try to relocate gradually.

Clearly the executive members of the users' committee had a soft spot for Birendra. Users' committee and landless settlers often know each other personally as members of overlapping communities. They may share kin or kin-like relations, friendships or political affiliations, ties that inflect their interactions during alignment disputes with sympathy and humanity. However, the settlers on the roadside were equally aware that displacement from the side of an upgrading road was inevitable. Social media was replete with images of forceful demolitions of buildings for road upgrading in Kathmandu and Biratnagar, where they visited regularly and could observe. When I inquired about Birendra's resettlement plan, he responded that his family would wait until the road was upgraded to blacktop before relocating, and sought to delay relocation while he looked for sources of income and a place to settle.

Some time later, we interviewed Sunil Soren, who had tried to stop the excavator. When I asked why he had argued with the police, he responded:

> They were talking nonsense. This place won't become a market area right after the road is built. The price [of land] will go up eventually, but not immediately. First, the road needs to be blacktopped, and a concrete bridge must be constructed across the river.[19] This process will take 20–25 years. ... When will we actually make a profit? Even though land prices have increased, no one is buying land. Additionally, only the land next to the road has increased in value; the land in the middle, without road access, remains the same.

Next, we went to see Sunita Besra at her house near the suspension bridge over the Lohandra River. She explained that it is natural to protect one's private land. She was upset and got into an argument because some locals had accused her of encroaching on public land and the users' committee had started excavating soil from her field without her consent. She denied her land was part of the public land

[19] A bridge across the River Lohandra, joining Tarigama Village, was under construction during fieldwork.

designated for road expansion. She was worried about the trench that results from excavating soil; the trench would diminish land available for crops and would block a neighboring landowner from accessing his field with a tractor: "I don't see a way for a tractor to enter his field [with that trench in the way]."

She also expressed dissatisfaction with the alignment selected by the road users' executive committee and asked them to bring in an official surveyor. She contended that the road users' committee had shown bias in favor of the Santhal settlers on the other side of the road because they should have first reclaimed the occupied public land for road expansion before extracting soil from her private field.

When I asked her opinion on land prices following road construction, Sunita, too, expressed doubt about benefiting from an increase in value; land prices would only go up once the road was blacktopped and the area underwent comprehensive development, which she believed would take years. Meanwhile the road users' committee would likely excavate more soil from her land when upgrading to a blacktop road in the future, leaving her with such a small piece of land that she doubted she could profit from selling it. Sunita expressed dissatisfaction with government policies denying compensation for expropriation of private land during rural road construction, despite the significant impact on small-scale landowners. It infuriated her when authorities, including the police, tried to justify increased land values as compensation, a complaint we will hear from Dolakha as well in the subsequent chapter.

Despite the fact that landowners and settlers appreciated the arrival of motorable roads for the benefits of transportation and economic opportunity, several factors contributed to practices of encroachment and ongoing disputes. Unlike in Mugu where the road is a more recent arrival and the challenges of construction more formidable, in Morang landowners and settlers alike were unwilling to give up their land during the road alignment process, while blaming each other for encroaching on public lands needed for upgrading. Landowners argued that the government should employ official survey records and scientific methods to differentiate between private and public land when determining road alignment, and should compensate landowners for land expropriation. Landless individuals who had settled along the road depended on daily wage labor and questioned the necessity of wider roads. They argued that constructing wider roads primarily benefits landowners, through increases in land value, while it renders landless settlers increasingly vulnerable. I was surprised and impressed that the users' committee in this case articulated and acted upon a principle of social justice, rooted in an understanding that requiring landless settlers to move their homes and animal shelters during road expansion imposes significant burden and disruption. Even if displacement would ultimately be necessary, the committee executive argued, with support from the police, that settlers need time to adjust. Landowners themselves express reasonable critiques about the burdens they, too, face, from expropriation and the imposition of trenches that compromise accessibility to their own land, as well as a healthy skepticism about vague promises of increases in land value. The disputes, conflicts, and negotiations amongst differently positioned residents in Morang convey important critical insights about road building that could become a resource for planning.

ENVIRONMENT AND SUSTAINABILITY

This section examines a number of environmental challenges associated with road construction, specifically those related to bridges, rivers, and floods. I argue that the Local Road Network in the Morang plains is closely intertwined with the natural environment, and particularly the river drainage systems. A thorough understanding of these systems is crucial for understanding road sustainability, connectivity, mobility, and the daily lives of the people in relation to planning and development in this region.

BRIDGES, RIVERS AND FLOODS: UNRAVELING THE ENVIRONMENTAL CHALLENGES IN ROAD CONSTRUCTION

The Singhiya and Lohandra Rivers, along with numerous smaller streams, have had a significant impact on the daily lives and mobility of the local population in our study area. Section two above, Road History and Remoteness, has already discussed some of the influences of rivers and streams on mobility. Here I draw on my previous ethnographic research conducted among the Santhal community to further illustrate the point (Rai and Hansda 2018). Rivers have had profound impacts on the migration, rituals, and daily lives of the Santhal community, who are the numerically dominant ethnic group in Jahada Rural Municipality. They often recount that their ancestors settled along the Singhiya and Lohandra Rivers for sustenance and irrigation as they migrated to Morang District. Rivers are vital for both agriculture and life-cycle rituals. Funeral ceremonies, for example, involve offering coins to the river and asking permission for the deceased soul to cross.

Rivers also pose challenges to daily movement when they flood and were once a source of oppression from authorities. The Santhal ancestors were compelled to carry officials on their shoulders across rivers in the Tarai; they endured the cruel act of having their skin burned with cigarettes to expedite the crossing and provide amusement. Even today some villagers hastily conceal themselves upon spotting the arrival of state representatives to their village, such as policemen, due to haunting memories of this and other forced labor.

During my previous research among the Santhal community, conducted intermittently between 2010–2012 at Badi Tola, west of the Lohandra River, I observed that in winter, when the river was shallow, villagers would occasionally wade across when they were in a hurry to reach their fields or another village on the opposite bank.[20] Alternatively, locals from Badi Tola and surrounding villages would use a narrow bamboo bridge called *chachari*. This bridge, located

[20] Badi Tola is in the southern part of Jahada Rural Municipality.

about one km northwest of Badi Tola, was only three feet wide and had no side railings. People would carefully navigate their bicycles and motorcycles across this bridge. I had some frightening experiences when I nearly lost my balance several times crossing the bridge on a scooter. Fortunately, over time, I acquired the skills to balance the load and cope with the bridge's uneven movement.

The bridge was a part of a popular route that stretched from Dumariya, a border town in the east, to Biratnagar in the west. Each year, nearby residents would contribute bamboo and money to rebuild the bridge after the rainy season. A migrant family from India was appointed to look after the bridge and operated a small ferry. In exchange for their services, they would collect grains from villagers once a year and charge outsiders for using the bridge. The bridge was not operational during the rainy season as it could not span the entire river or withstand the water flow. During this time, the family would transport people and goods across the river on the ferry. When the river was flooded and the ferry could not cross, villagers had to detour via a concrete bridge approximately 10 km to the north.

When I returned after a year in 2013, I was surprised to see a new suspension bridge across the river in the same location. The family that had managed the temporary bamboo bridge for years had moved away. The construction of the new bridge made it easy for commuters to cross the river, even on motorcycles, and traffic had significantly increased. People from distant Indian villages also started using this bridge to access Jogbani railway station, which is near Biratnagar. This bridge greatly improved mobility for villagers, allowing them to commute throughout the year. The transformation was significant.

Precarious bamboo bridges and ferries were still used to cross the Lohandra River in different areas of the southern region of Jahada Rural Municipality during our fieldwork for Infrastructures of Democracy (2015–2018). The Lohandra River intersected the Tarigama-Katahari Road in the southern part of Jahada Rural Municipality near Tarigama, an ancient village and local market center situated on the Nepal-India border. A concrete bridge was under construction, and daily commuters had to depend on a small bamboo bridge to cross the river in the mean time. Locals also mentioned that ferries were used to transport goods and people during the rainy season. I frequently observed a procession of bullock carts transporting empty barrels along the Tarigama-Katahari route to the Nepal-India border at Tarigama. The large buffaloes struggled to pull the carts across the river with heavy loads and occasionally got stuck near the under-construction bridge. This recurring scene vividly illustrated the significance of the bridge for transportation and reflected the previously recounted narratives of locals from Pidarbani about crossing the Singhiya River to transport paddy to Biratnagar not so long ago.

The government has recognized landslides as a significant environmental concern in the context of road construction in hilly and mountainous areas and has stressed the importance of the environmentally friendly "green road" approach (Schaffner1987). The increasing problem of landslides in hilly areas, caused by the rapid expansion of rural roads without proper engineering design and expertise, has garnered attention from media, researchers, planners, and policymakers (Sudmeier-Rieux *et al.* 2019; B. Rai 2020; N. Rai 2020; Dixit *et al.* 2021). However, authorities have not adequately acknowledged the recurring and destructive impact of floods on road sustainability. During the last week of August 2017, 48 hours of non-stop rains caused flooding throughout the eastern Tarai that damaged houses, public buildings, crops, roads, and bridges. Elderly people said that they had never witnessed floods so devastating in their lifetime. After the rain stopped in my hometown of Dharan, located in Sunsari District, I immediately headed toward Pidarbani. I arrived at the Lakhantari Bridge crossing the Singhiya River, which had washed away part of the road on the eastern side of the bridge as it expanded to a 30-meter wide channel. Villagers had stacked cement bags filled with sand to form a narrow passage for bicycles and motorcycles to reach the bridge.

After arriving in Pidarbani, my co-researcher informed me that all the villages were flooded. Villagers had cut the dykes of nearby irrigation canals to prevent submergence of surrounding homes. Some were trapped in their houses, with the ground floor flooded. When the rain stopped, my co-researcher surveyed the area on his bike and took photos. He was shocked by the flood's impact on roads and houses. He shared these pictures with me, and one caught my attention, of locals reconstructing a washed-out section of the Lakhantari Bridge. The images contradicted my previous experiences of locals being reluctant to voluntarily participate in road users' committees. Here villagers came forward voluntarily and collectively to facilitate mobility in their surroundings. The bridge was the sole connection over the river for a large number of local residents who commuted daily to work in factories alongside the Koshi Highway.

Photo 1.3: Commuters using a temporary bridge after the August 2017 flood destroyed the concrete bridge over Lohandra River connecting Gramthan Rural Municipality and Belbari Municipality (photo by Yaman Sardar, 2017).

Another bridge over the Lohandra River at Kaseni had also collapsed. The bridge was on the Banigama Road, a side road next to the Chatara-Sunsari-Morang irrigation canal and a crucial link connecting the central areas of Morang District. When we arrived at the site, a woman and her children who had survived the flood were selling tea and cookies along the old broken bridge. She described how the flood had inundated her house, trapping and terrifying her the entire night. Debris brought by the flood had become wedged under the bridge, blocking water flow and creating immense pressure. The bridge finally collapsed at midnight with a loud boom.

Here too, local people had voluntarily constructed a temporary bamboo bridge on their own initiative. The bridge was frequently loaded, and at times overloaded, with commuters, bicycles, motorcycles, and animals. During our half-hour observation, more than 50 motorcycles passed over the bridge. There was no one to control traffic. Some local residents urged motorcyclists to dismount while crossing the river for safety reasons, but the majority of them declined. A young man who had helped build the temporary bamboo bridge expressed dissatisfaction with the bridge's quality. He explained that they had been forced to complete construction quickly due to heavy traffic pressure and thus could not add extra bamboo pillars for support. Observing the chaos on the bridge, he was upset: "They will realize the bridge's importance when they have to travel to Belbari to cross this river."[21] Following our conversation, a commuter who had paused on his bike for a break suggested the need for a dedicated employee to collect a 10-rupee fare from each commuter to manage traffic and bridge maintenance. Local villagers gathered around the bridge speculated about when and by whom the bridge would be repaired, but there was considerable uncertainty about its future.

These examples show how important bridges are for enhancing connectivity and everyday mobility in the plains, challenging the belief that roads are the only infrastructure needed for development. They also highlight the community's desire for bridges in any form and show their willingness to volunteer outside the formal green roads modality in order to construct temporary bridges in the event of flood damage. The lack of bridges frequently disrupts local mobility,

[21] Belbari is a town around 11 km north on the East-West Highway; crossing the Lohandra River at that location would add significant extended travel time.

especially during the rainy season when the rivers are difficult to cross. As a result, villagers are often cut off or forced to take long detours. Policymakers and planners, who are mostly outsiders, often overlook these challenges due to their limited knowledge and experience of the river systems in Morang.

SAND-MINING FROM THE LOHANDRA RIVER: THE IMPACT OF TRACTORS AND TRIPPERS ON ROAD SUSTAINABILITY

Rural roads in the study area are mainly made of earthen or gravel surfaces and designed for daily commuters, low traffic volume, and relatively lightweight vehicles. But overloaded trucks and tractors often disregard road usage guidelines. The rise in heavy vehicles, such as trucks and tractors, is closely linked not only to continuous infrastructure construction, but also to extraction activities from local riverbeds.

During the early stages of my fieldwork, particularly in Gramthan Rural Municipality, I was puzzled that villagers were blaming tractors for damaging roads. I understood the issue to be that roads were damaged when villagers used tractors for plowing and transporting agricultural produce from their fields. When I raised this concern with a local representative in Sidharaha Village, his tone shifted, indicating agitation with my question. He defended tractors as indispensable to farming and noted that rural roads were built to support agriculture by enabling farmers to use modern equipment that would reduce their workload, especially through a shift away from traditional cattle raising. His argument appeared logical to me. The consistent concerns from villagers about the damage caused by tractors prompted me to further investigate the effects of heavy vehicles on road sustainability. I discovered an increasing presence of tractors and trucks, locally known as *trippers*, involved in sand extraction from local rivers in the recent year.[22] Local tractors are

[22] Trucks used for carrying raw construction materials like sand and stone are popularly known by the English-derived word "tripper," for which the English translation would be dump truck.

used to transport sand and construction materials when they are not being used for agricultural purposes.

Illustrative of the growing traffic volume, the feeder road connecting Biratnagar to Ghinaghat, which passes through Pidarbani, was constantly busy with tractors and trippers during the day. The drivers and crew of these vehicles frequently stopped at a small restaurant in Pidarbani for snacks and meals. The restaurant was packed from early morning until late at night. Furthermore, the trucks transporting materials from the river for the expansion of the Koshi Highway into a six-lane road from Biratnagar to Duhabi operated throughout the night to avoid daytime traffic on the feeder road. Vibrations caused by passing trucks often disturbed our sleep, prompting us to adjust our sleep schedules.

The rapid expansion of road and building construction have driven an increasing demand for sand and gravel, placing immense pressure on local river basins in Morang District, as well as in other parts of Nepal. The demand for these resources continues to grow, making sand-mining a reliable source of daily income for laborers, a profitable business for contractors, and a revenue generator for local authorities. Sand and other river products from local rivers of Morang are used extensively in infrastructure projects throughout Morang, Sunsari and Jhapa Districts, and even transported to India.

In Gramthan Rural Municipality, the popularity of sand-mining in the Lohandra River has increased over the past decade due to the high quality of sand, as well as improvement of road access from the Biratchok-Ghinaghat feeder road. Authorities allow sand extraction during the dry season, which usually lasts from mid-September to mid-June, during which time local and migrant laborers collect substantial amounts of sand and gravel from different spots along the river. Trippers and tractors then transport the sand to major towns such as Biratnagar, Duhabi, Inaruwa, Itahari, and Dharan. The local employees working at the checkpost to collect tax suggested that hundreds of tractors and trippers are employed on a daily basis.

During our first visit to an important sand-mining site in Motipur, we traveled about 5 km east of Tetariya on a dusty road bustling with tractors and trippers. The riverbanks were teeming with laborers engaged in sand excavation, and tractors were constantly navigating the area to collect the sand and load it into trippers. As I endeavored to capture the scene on camera, a local resident grew suspicious and inquired whether we were journalists. We realized that he did not want us to interfere in the sand-mining business, as the locals were making a living from it. He expressed sympathy for the laborers and their challenging work, stating, "*Yo baluwa khanne bhanda roknelai pap lagchha*" (those who would halt this sand-mining would bear the burden of a sin). It has sustained the livelihoods of thousands of poor people. If it is stopped, what will people do? There will be theft, dacoits (bandits), robbery, and conflicts."

Photo 1.4: A tractor loading sand onto a truck at a mining site on the Lohandra River near Motipur, Gramthan Rural Municipality (photo by Yaman Sardar, 2018).

Sand-mining was the main source of income for local communities, especially for poor and marginalized individuals. Their living conditions had improved because of their involvement in sand-mining. Others came from neighboring districts like Sunsari. Sometimes, conflicts arose when land owning villagers wanted to stop sand-mining bordering their private fields to prevent erosion, causing tensions between landowners and sand-miners. Sand-mining from the river had both positive and negative impacts. It provided essential materials, such as sand, gravel, boulders, and stones, for construction of infrastructure, including roads, and also created jobs and income. However, sand-mining had a negative impact on subsistence farmers, especially those living along the riverside. The excessive extraction of sand and gravel has caused the Lohandra River to deepen, increasing the risk of flooding. It has also shifted the river's course so that it broaches some private fields, causing erosion and sand deposits that make the land unsuitable for agriculture. Other fields have dried up, negatively impacting subsistence agriculture farmers, who also had to deal with labor shortages and high prices for agricultural labor because workers were attracted to the more profitable sand-mining industry.

The demand for river materials to support increased urbanization and infrastructure construction has attracted contractors, business people, and authorities to the sand-mining business. Indeed, the tax on selling river materials is a major source of revenue for local governments. Residents claim that the sand-mining business is driven by corrupt connections among local contractors, political figures, and authorities. Consequently, despite knowledge of the detrimental effects of sand-mining on the environment and subsistence farmers, the industry continues to thrive, with excessive mining beyond what government regulations allow.

The roads connecting to the river are critical for the sand-mining industry as they enable transportation of river materials. However, local and feeder roads degrade over time due to pressure from heavy traffic. The per-trip tax levied by local governments on vehicles transporting sand does not appear to have underwritten meaningful road maintenance, and removes direct responsibility to take care of the rural roads that form the foundation of their business operations. Local residents helped build the roads, but they also suffer from pollution caused by vehicles and bear the brunt of road damage. Given the emphasis in the other two chapters on green roads, we can underscore the significance of rivers for both social and environmental sustainability in the Tarai and suggest that a commitment to green roads must expand to encompass bridge technology and the management of resource extraction.

TRANSPORT AND MARKET MAKING

This section focuses on how roads interact with subsistence agriculture and labor markets in the rural municipalities of Gramthan and Jahada.

ROAD EXTENSION AND THE TRANSITION OF AGRICULTURAL LABOR

As stated in the Road History section of this chapter, up to the early 1990s when the motorable road opened, residents of Pidarbani used to embark on a week-long journey with caravans to Biratnagar to trade rice and jute before the Tihar festival in October/November. Some landlords would transport substantial quantities, ranging from five to eight metric tons of rice. The middlemen, mostly Marwari (a merchant community of Indian heritage), used to pay in installments. After receiving partial payments, the traders would return home, engaging in Tihar festival shopping en route. Agricultural production, particularly paddy and jute crops, was the primary source of income for residents in our field sites at that time.

More recently, following increased road access to Biratnagar and other growing market centers, the traditional agricultural labor force has been steadily shifting toward labor markets in nearby factories and market centers, or bazaar areas. This transition from subsistence agriculture to wage labor was partly facilitated by road improvement. Marking a significant shift in road building policy, the government recognized the importance of rural roads in facilitating economic transition in rural areas after 1990. One of the primary reasons for prioritizing rural road networks was to enhance commercial agriculture by improving access to fertilizers, farm machinery, and markets, which was expected to ultimately improve the overall rural economy (APROSC and JMA 1995; Paudyal 1998).

Ongoing improvement of rural roads had positive effects, such as increased access to ambulances during medical emergencies, and to tractors for plowing and transporting products to the nearest market. However, most farmers were subsistence farmers who cultivated traditional crops and had limited interest in engaging with commercial agriculture. Moreover, the introduction of roads led to unintended consequences, including a shortage of agricultural labor and an increase in land prices. Agricultural land became more of a commodity than a means of subsistence production due to the growth of the real estate industry. Local landlords were enticed to sell land for profit rather than transitioning subsistence agriculture to commercial scale. Furthermore, roads facilitated the movement of traditional agricultural laborers into more lucrative sectors such as factories and construction sites in urban areas.

I often came across farmers who were frustrated by a lack of profitability, resulting from high wages for scarce agricultural labor during peak seasons. Farmers also relayed having to delay their wheat and maize harvesting or paddy planting because there was not enough labor available. The shortage of labor increased farmers' vulnerability to natural disasters such as wind, rain, and hail. In April 2018, unexpected rain and wind destroyed fields of ripe maize and ready-to-harvest wheat in our field sites. The sudden demand for laborers to harvest the wheat to prevent it from sprouting in the field lead to a scarcity of agricultural workers. Farmers had no choice but to rely on their own family members. A school teacher and his family, who lived in Katahari, about 15 km away from their original village in the southern part of Jahada Rural Municipality, traveled to assist with the wheat harvest. In our conversations, the teacher highlighted the challenges of farming, including untimely weather, labor shortages, and rising daily wages for workers.

In late May 2018, when I drove to the southern part of the Katahari-Tarigama Road, I noticed that villagers were rushing to harvest maize, as they needed to prepare the paddy fields. On my way to the home of co-researcher Durga Hansda, I encountered a local acquaintance from Badi Tola who was going to harvest corn with a friend. He explained that he had not finished harvesting maize on time due to a labor shortage. He mentioned that even though he had two sons, they showed no interest to work in the fields; instead, they were employed in the bazaar. Earning around NRs. 500–600 per day, their income hardly covered their own expenses, such as recharging mobiles and enjoying drinks with friends. Occasionally, they contributed some money to support their family. He chuckled after narrating the situation with a kind of dark humor that highlighted the reluctance of younger generations to work in agriculture. Other villagers similarly noted that their children had no interest in working in the village and preferred to work outside. Essentially, the younger generation lacked enthusiasm for agricultural labor, leading to challenges for farmers in turning a profit.

Locals from Pidarbani argued that the improvement of Local Road Networks and the increase in factories along highways had enticed villagers to pursue factory jobs over agriculture due to their perceived advantages and numerous amenities. Factory work offered a steady income, fixed working hours, and often a cleaner working environment compared to agriculture labor. Factory workers also enjoyed socializing and relaxing during breaks, while agricultural laborers often faced strict supervision and were expected to work diligently.

However, retired factory workers and well-informed individuals also emphasized that despite the factories creating job opportunities for locals, factory employment was often precarious and exploitative. Factory owners would often recruit laborers through a network of reliable employees within the same factory—typically local leaders or influential individuals—who would assure the owners that the workers would refrain from political activities, such as advocating for labor rights, demanding pay raises, or forming labor unions.

Suresh Mandal, a retired factory worker who claimed to be the first person from his community to join a factory after graduating from high school in Biratnagar emphasized that factory jobs had only recently gained popularity in his Tharu community. He pointed out that Tharus were initially not inclined to work in factories, and those who did were often stigmatized and seen as dependent on others. Factory workers even faced challenges finding spouses. For him, factory employment was appealing because it offered the possibility of receiving a salary to help deal with emergencies, whereas subsistence farmers had to rely on limited income from selling paddy and frequently faced liquidity problems. Factory laborers initially served as a source of cash in the village. Suresh was influenced by his friends from the Rajbanshi community, who had been working in factories since their establishment, and had relatively good savings and financial management compared to those families engaged in farming. However, Suresh pointed out that factories were unable to accommodate all workers, leading many locals to seek employment in informal sectors like construction. In these sectors workers faced even more precarious conditions compared to factories, such as temporary work arrangements and lack of safety regulations or basic labor rights.

Despite these challenges, in my research location, there were exceptionally few locals who were optimistic that road improvements would support small-scale farmers in transporting their products to markets. Pawan Sardar, a man in his early 40s from Motipur Bazaar in Gramthan Rural Municipality, was a forward-thinking farmer who advocated enhancing the village economy through commercial agriculture. With a degree in agriculture science as a technical assistant, he also managed a private agro-vet shop in Motipur Bazaar, situated 5 km east of Tetariya. He focused on producing off-season vegetables and asserted that poor road conditions posed significant obstacles to accessing markets. In addition, local roads allowed cattle, goats, and other livestock unrestricted access to fields, posing risks to crops. Consequently, farmers were often discouraged to scale up off-season vegetable production.[23]

Even in the areas which were connected to roads, urbanization and increased traffic had led residents living along busy roadsides to abandon traditional subsistence practices, such as raising cattle for manure and using animal power for plowing. This was mainly due to labor shortages and the challenges of raising animals amid road expansion. Animals also posed risks for road accidents. Farmers were fully dependent on tractors for plowing and chemical fertilizers, which were not readily available during peak agriculture season, making commercial farming costly for subsistence farmers.

Thus while the rationale behind building rural roads had been to boost the rural economy by promoting commercial agriculture (APPROSC and JMC 1995) the expansion of rural roads yielded diverse, sometimes unexpected outcomes.[24] Inadequate government policies and planning prevented subsistence farmers from transitioning to commercial farming, despite improved road accessibility. On the other hand, improved road access enabled marginalized agricultural laborers to secure non-agricultural employment, resulting in a limited workforce that posed challenges for the agricultural sector.

[23] He further asserted that the farming profession was frequently undervalued due to a lack of local government support for essential elements such as irrigation, fertilizer, and quality seeds, as well as the mechanization of farming. This lack of support and encouragement had contributed to a decline in self-esteem among farmers. In addition, land fragmentation is a common issue during property inheritance, resulting in small land parcels that are insufficient for family subsistence.

[24] The Agricultural Perspective Plan (APP) for 1995–2015, developed with technical assistance from the Asian Development Bank (ADB), was a crucial initiative in the rural road sector aimed at advancing Nepal's agriculture sector. The plan aimed to build 6,200 km of rural roads over a period of two decades to support agricultural development and foster regional balance in Nepal. This included constructing 3,400 km of roads in the Tarai region, 1,950 km in the hills, and 850 km in the mountains (APPROSC and JMC 1995).

NAVIGATING ROADS AND LABOR MARKETS: BICYCLE MOBILITY

In a recent development, battery-powered three-wheelers known as *safari*, and gasoline-powered three-wheelers, called "autos," gained popularity for local public transportation in the plains of Nepal, including Morang. This occurred particularly after India imposed an "unofficial blockade" of Nepal in 2015, resulting in a gasoline crisis throughout the country (Karki 2022). However, *safari* and "auto" services were limited to areas with good roads, and expensive for travel to remote areas. Public buses were also unreliable and inefficient, operating only on highways and feeder roads. As a result, many workers and laborers have no choice but to commute on bicycles, which remains a prevalent mode of transportation among daily commuters.

Bicycles have become popular only in recent years, following upgrades to village roads. In the past, cycling was difficult or impossible on muddy roads, and bicycles were also considered expensive luxury items. A senior citizen in his 70s from Lakhantari Village at Gramthan Rural Municipality proudly stated that he was the first person in his neighborhood to own a bicycle. He recalled purchasing it around 1975, when bicycles were a rare sight. Villagers would gather to watch him ride, amazed at his ability to balance on two wheels. He was probably 18 or 19 years old when he acquired the bicycle, and kept it for sentimental reasons. However, poor roads had made it impractical for commuting back then, as he often had to carry it across muddy sections.

A former factory worker from Lakhantari, who 25 years ago had worked at Pioneer Wire, a factory on the Koshi Highway, emphasized how cycling had enhanced the mobility of local workers. He noted that improved road access, along with bicycle services, particularly benefited women. Women can now return home safely after late factory shifts, pedaling bicycles equipped with a flashlight. This positive change would not have been possible without upgraded roads: "When there was no road, we had to run to the factory." His shift started at 6 a.m. and ended at 6 p.m., and for eight years, he ran to the factory every day, a journey that took about 25 minutes. He explained that the road was particularly difficult to navigate during the rainy season, making it impossible for bicycles to pass through Gokuwa and Nebuwa.

The number of individuals commuting primarily by bicycle to work in factories and market centers like Biratnagar has notably increased, thanks to increased road connectivity. Each morning and evening, I observed factory workers and laborers cycling to and from market centers like Duhabi, Biratnagar, and Katahari, contributing to traffic congestion at major junctions along the roads. These include feeder roads stretching from Netachok to Ghinaghat in the east, the Koshi Highway in the west, the postal highway in the south, and various others branching out to villages. Many of these individuals travel for hours from considerable distances.

However, despite the expansion of road networks, rural roads continue to be in poor condition, posing challenges for daily mobility and development of affordable public transportation in rural areas. One significant issue faced by regular commuters was road safety. Interlocutors noted that numerous bicyclists sustained serious injuries from accidents caused by poor visibility, slippery roads, and collisions with vehicles and animals. As a result, they often incurred substantial expenses for medical treatment. Laborers who commuted daily shared stories that highlighted the difficulties they faced due to poor road conditions, adverse weather, traffic jams, road accidents, and the lack of affordable public transportation. Manju Mardi, a 33-year-old factory worker from Katahari, recalled how she grew used to commuting by bicycle during her decade-long work at a jute mill in Katahari. Initially, the jute mill provided a shuttle bus, but it was unable to accommodate all the workers, so some walked to work. As time passed, the numbers of workers commuting from her village gradually decreased, as some workers quit voluntarily due to having to switch to night shifts or being fired for poor performance. The company replaced the shuttle bus with a small van, but even this service was discontinued after some rowdy drunk men attacked the van one night, seriously injuring the driver. The workers then requested advance payments from the manager to buy bicycles, as commuting on foot from far distances was not feasible. Some workers already knew how to ride, but others needed a month to learn. Initially, riding bicycles long distances was challenging.

When I asked her about the state of the roads, Manju exclaimed, "*Baphre* (Oh my goodness)! The roads were in such bad shape that it was difficult to commute on bicycles. Commuting to work was even harder than the actual work itself. After riding bicycles on the rough road for an hour, we were completely exhausted. However, the heat and light inside the factory would quickly dry our wet clothes, making us feel comfortable." She and her friend believed their lives would improve with better roads and frequently discussed their hope for this with each other while commuting. They were discouraged as neither the government nor private business owners seemed concerned about deteriorating roads. Their hope was eventually restored when a small section of the Katahari-Tarigama Road in front of a poultry farm was blacktopped.

Manju noted that worksites such as factories and construction sites maintain strict schedules. Laborers often had difficulty managing their time and were in a hurry. Sometimes they overslept, and women, in particular, had to take care of their children and other family members before leaving for work. They might have to travel long distances quickly to arrive on time, or risk not receiving their wages. Women also had to transition away from wearing saris in favor of kurta suruwal, in order to be able to cycle safely. Some declined to cycle, fearing they would face judgment, for example for being considered "too old" to learn to ride.

During a discussion about the daily lives of commuters and road conditions in Tarigama Godam, a village on the Nepal-India border, the chair of the local school committee emphasized the social disconnection that laborers frequently experienced due to poor road conditions and lack of public transportation. He expressed this concern to his neighbor, who had been commuting to work in

Biratnagar for many years: "We rarely see him because he leaves home early and doesn't return until late at night. He has been working since his children were young, and now they are all grown up. I don't think his kids even remember what he looks like anymore." This sarcastic commentary on the social life of commuting workers highlights the relation between social isolation and inadequate road conditions. It also speaks to the imperative to improve the quality of rural roads in regions that have grown dependent on industrial livelihoods.

POLITICS, POLITY AND PLANNING

This section highlights how patronage politics, inadequate planning, and power dynamics can negatively impact public participation and road sustainability. I argue that the influence of local leaders and elites, along with existing patron-client relationships, can lead to unintended consequences, such as reinforcement of the status quo, class conflict, exclusion of marginalized communities in the democratic process of public participation, and a disconnect between policies and practices that disproportionately affects members of marginalized communities and challenges the sustainability of roads. Moreover, this section highlights how narratives of development associated with road building still wield the power to stereotype Tarai/Madheshi people as an "impossible public"—a term coined by Harvey and Knox (2015) to emphasize those marginalized individuals who are often misunderstood as ignorant, skeptical, and conservative.

After the restoration of democracy in 1990, political parties and elected representatives gained increased influence in development governance and planning, including infrastructure and road construction. A significant step toward empowering local units was the endorsement of the Local Self-Governance Act (LSGA) in 1999, granting substantial rights and responsibilities at the local level. However, the spirit of LSGA did not flourish, as Nepal faced political instability and escalating tension due to the Maoist insurgency from 1996–2006. Following the conflict, local government units remained without elected representatives (Gurung 2011). As described in the Introduction to this book, the government set up the all-party mechanism to oversee local governance following the comprehensive peace agreement between the Maoists and the government in 2006. This move was heavily criticized for lack of transparency and accountability. It facilitated political patronage and perceptions of corruption at the local level (ICG 2010; NORAD 2011; USAID 2012). Even after the formation of the federal republic in 2015, the dissolution of the all-party mechanism and the re-establishment of local elections, party patronage has continued to intersect with local development.

A notable example is the government's provision for the Constituency Development Fund (CDF),[25] criticized for reinforcing political patronage by granting politicians discretionary power to select projects (Rai 2021).[26] This was clearly evident during the 2017 general election, as political leaders frequently made campaign promises of infrastructure improvements, raising voters' expectations (ITAD 2018). Local residents evaluate their elected leaders based on their ability to deliver infrastructure like roads and bridges. They also recognize how elected representatives often favor their supporters in local budget allocation, formation of road users' committees, and other planning processes. This recognition leads to suspicion of nepotism and a decline in voluntary labor contributions despite government emphasis on community involvement in local development.

[25] The CDF is a government scheme that provides federal and provincial lawmakers with a discretionary budget for small- and medium-scale development projects in their constituencies. Since its inception in 1994, the CDF has been known by different names while facing controversies regarding its transparency and accountability (Nepal Live Today 2022).

[26] A United Nations Office on Drugs and Crime (UNODC 2022) discussion paper and conference report highlights that the long-standing practice of allocating controversial CDF to federal legislators in Nepal has a significant influence on the attitudes and behaviors of local voters, who see their provincial and federal representatives as facilitators of development. Voters judge their representatives by how effective they are in securing development projects in their constituencies (UNODC 2022).

NAVIGATING THE DISCREPANCY BETWEEN POLICIES AND PRACTICES: IMPLICATIONS FOR THE SUSTAINABILITY OF RURAL ROADS

In this sub-section, I analyze the discrepancies between policies and practices related to road users' committees. These discrepancies make road building exclusive and unsustainable. Addressing these issues is crucial for genuine public participation and road sustainability. In recent years, the approach of involving road users' committees in rural road construction has faced criticism for rule violations, exclusion of minorities, and corruption (Shrestha 2007; CIAA 2019; N. Rai 2020). Indeed, road users' committees are political spaces where relationships among policies, authorities, and the community are often complex and conflicting.

To uphold the norm of public participation in the road users' committee, municipal authorities estimate the total project cost during the planning and budgeting stages. They then provide the budget on an installment basis, excluding the agreed upon expenses that will be covered by the community through contributions of labor, cash, or materials. When users' committee members are unwilling to contribute to road building projects, matching funds are denied. As a result, projects thus face a budget shortfall and must rely solely on the budget allocated by the authority. In our field sites, as previously discussed, locals were often unwilling to contribute labor voluntarily, resulting in a budget deficit. To address this issue, the executive committee of the road users' committee, as in Dolakha and Mugu, frequently chose to use excavators (dozers in local parlance), despite authorities' disapproval of heavy machinery usage. They argue that they are compelled to use dozers instead of manual labor to save time and money and manage the budget deficit.

After the establishment of rural municipalities in 2017, local authorities implemented corrective measures to prevent corruption based on past experiences. Rules stipulate that road users' committees should receive their first installment only after completing a specified portion of the road project. However, local elites often manipulate the rule by leveraging their financial capacity to cover the cost of the first installment. This kind of financial sponsorship allows them to influence the users' committees' choice of local contractors and suppliers for equipment and materials.[27] The absence of voluntary workers has thus created opportunities for individuals who own excavators and have family or political connections with executive members of the road users' committee. These individuals were often willing to provide their services on credit, which helped alleviate financial strain on the committee. Executive members of the road users' committees therefore appeared to act as intermediaries between individual entrepreneurs and authorities, rather than as agents to mobilize community participation.

Photo 1.5: An excavator demolishing a house to extend the Katahari-Tarigama Road (photo by Durga Hansda, 2017).

[27] In some cases, executive members who financed the first installment also charged interest.

Local authorities, including elected representatives and appointed government officials, are aware of these policy violations by road users' committees, but for multiple reasons, they often neglect the issue. First, they recognize the difficulties in finding voluntary labor to fulfill policies requiring local labor contributions; second, they know there will be pressure to overlook the violations from communities who want roads built quickly; and finally, the road users' committee plays a significant role in resolving community conflicts during the upgrading of village roads, which is one of the committee's strengths. This is evident from local contractors, who, while critical of the technical knowledge of the road users' committee, acknowledge that expanding village roads can be quite difficult due to the resistance of local residents who are unwilling to give up their property for road construction. Contractors and authorities understand that outsiders cannot widen the village roads without the coordinating role of users' committees in mitigating conflict.

Local authorities' tacit approval for road users' committees to use excavators has a negative impact on road sustainability. During upgrading, the users' committee typically uses excavators to widen the road and digs trenches on both sides to improve water drainage. They then elevate the road's level with mud and spread gravel to create a smooth surface. However, the road remains unpaved, which causes excessive dust in the dry season; in monsoon, mud and water-filled potholes pose visibility challenges for drivers and pedestrians, resulting in health and safety concerns. Villagers feel that roads and trenches constructed by excavators tend to be less compact than those built manually. As a result, they are more vulnerable to damage during heavy rains and floods. Elevated road surfaces that lack proper drainage channels can also obstruct the natural flow of rainwater, resulting in higher flood risks. This can cause further harm to properties, livestock, and crops.

The absence of a formal system for regular maintenance poses a significant challenge to the long-term sustainability of the roads. Once the construction of a road is finished, the road users' committee disbands, leaving the responsibility for ongoing maintenance unassigned. Recently upgraded roads are similarly left unattended. In addition to road upgrades, it is crucial for planners and policymakers in rural areas of Morang District to prioritize regular maintenance. Enhancing policies for road maintenance can help mitigate the vulnerability of rural roads to heavy rainfall and floods. To address this issue, the role of users' committees can be expanded, by granting them more authority in road maintenance and ongoing care.

CULTURAL-POLITICAL FACTORS CONTRIBUTING TO THE DETERIORATION OF ROAD CONDITIONS

Budget limitations have always been a common explanation for unsustainable road conditions, on the part of authorities and publics alike. However, both also recognize, and openly discuss, the challenge of how corruption is baked into political culture, emphasizing that budgets have increased since the restoration of democracy but are "leaking" through illicit use. A local anti-corruption mobilization points to the gender dynamics of corruption. A group of women from Lakhantari Village shared how they were motivated to take on leadership roles in a road users' committee to combat corruption, and discussed the challenges they faced, starting with the common practice of excluding women from development projects. They argued that men, who had traditionally held executive positions, were prone to misusing funds, such as by spending money lavishly on meals and drinks for themselves and excavator drivers, and on refueling their motorbikes. There were no mechanisms to hold them accountable for "eating" development budgets. To rectify the situation, during an open village meeting held to form the road users' committee, they expressed interest in participating.

Women were then exclusively selected as executive members of the road users' committee. The municipality had allocated NRs. 6 lakh to upgrade a village road in that fiscal year and NRs. 2 lakh for the same road in the previous year. Initially, the women were anxious about managing the project, as none of them had experience working in this capacity. Little by little, as they started visiting the rural municipality office, they learned about the technical and official procedures and what their roles entailed. To begin, they reached out to an excavator owner who happened to be a relative of an executive member. He oversaw all the construction tasks, including providing excavators and construction materials. The executive committee paid him in installments after receiving the necessary funds. They had no trouble receiving the first installment from the rural municipality office, but receiving the final installment was more challenging. The women claimed that the rural municipality official in charge of distributing funds constantly changed his demands, requesting different documents each time.

During the project, their relationship with villagers, especially male householders, did not go smoothly. Men who had been quiet during the initial meeting began to complain once the women started to work; they provoked other villagers to resist when the executive committee had to expropriate, or move, private properties that were blocking the road during the widening process. In an expression of budget subjectivity, when the women asked villagers for their labor contribution, the villagers insisted that it wasn't needed because the authorities had already allocated a sufficient budget. As one woman put it:

> The men were jealous [laughs]; they have a habit of eating (*khane bani chha;* laughs) ... They [males] start to "eat" [spend for personal use] as soon as the budget is delivered.[28] They work on one side and eat on the other side. They spend the budget on drinking alcohol and eating snacks [meat]. They did not get a chance to use the budget this time. They thought that we were going to eat all the money. They started to provoke other villagers, saying that we have a big budget and we want to eat that budget.

[28] Words spoken in English language are underlined in quoted passages otherwise translated from Nepali.

The women divided up the responsibilities of providing meals for laborers at their homes and monitoring work on a rotational basis, so that they could equally attend to their daily household responsibilities. They told us, "We used to eat meals in our own houses and also provided drivers and other laborers with delicious meals, especially meat, in our own kitchen throughout the entire construction period. We worked from 7 a.m. to 8 p.m. for two to three months, treating it like a full-time job for the sake of the road" (road is another word that was almost universally spoken in English). At times their family members were upset when they entertained workers in their home. But the women felt empowered working in the executive committee. After they completed the road work, they were shocked to discover that NRs. 2 lakh had been allocated for its upgrade in the previous year. They criticized the previous road users' committee for their performance, stating that the budget from the previous year had been wasted without any tangible results. The committee had simply dumped gravel in front of houses on the road, leaving piles without leveling them, which caused inconveniences for daily mobility. The women had to level the gravel themselves using spades. The women claimed that they were determined to construct the road without personal gain. As a result, they did not sacrifice the quality of the road and successfully upgraded the road through hard work and teamwork.

Another significant cultural-political dynamic in Morang relates to Harvey and Knox's (2015) notion of impossible publics, a concept they developed in relation to research on road building in Peru, to capture a kind of non-engagement with development projects that reflects how people may be already "otherwise engaged." Non-engagement can easily be read as disinterest. Users' committee executives, local elites (who commonly constitute those executives), development workers, and authorities involved in road construction all pointed to a stereotyped perception of Madheshi people as indifferent toward development. They suggest that this apathetic attitude is particularly prevalent in the southern part of the district.

This stereotype stems from implicit comparison to hill migrants, who are often perceived as cooperative, progressive, and eager to enhance infrastructure in their area. Madheshi people, especially those living in homogeneous Madheshi settlements, are on the contrary seen as individualistic, resistant to change, and arrogant. Failure of Madheshi communities to take up development opportunities is frequently cited as a factor contributing to their marginalization and the underdevelopment of roads in their settlements. Authorities, who are themselves often from hill backgrounds, value the presence of hill people in Tarai communities, believing that a heterogeneous community consisting of hill migrants, Tarai Janajati, and Madheshi people is ideal for the overall development of the plains. I heard countless narratives along these lines in district and local government offices.

In fact, migrants from hill region generally have higher expectations and more experience with development projects, like road construction, due to the government's historical emphasis on development in hilly areas. The success of hill migrant communities in improving road infrastructure in their region can be attributed at least in part to preferential treatment they receive at local and national levels due to their hill identity. This preferential treatment derives in part from the fact that influential politicians, service providers, authorities, and development agency staff are themselves often from hill communities.

Promoting coexistence with the hill community may have merits in terms of embracing cultural diversity. However, solely blaming Madheshi and Tarai Janajati communities for their own underdevelopment constitutes a form of discrimination that undermines the independent potential of Madheshi and Tarai Janajati people to achieve their own development. In order to gain a deeper understanding of the cultural politics of this prevailing local discourse, it is imperative to critically analyze how dominant ideologies operate through development politics, power dynamics, and the historical social marginalization of the Tarai people (Gaige 1975).

Historically, hill and Tarai people have had different experiences with roads. Certain political-economic and historical factors must also be acknowledged in the Tarai, where communities could not fully embrace road development due to concerns about safety from bandits and protection of crops from cattle. Rural residents in the plains were vulnerable to dacoits due to inadequate security measures and the open border with India; they recounted concerns that roads would provide easy access to undesirable elements, so communities often avoided them to maintain safety in closely-knit settlements. Additionally, local livelihoods depended on subsistence agriculture and intensive cattle rearing before mechanization. Road extensions posed a nuisance for subsistence farmers, as cattle and goats could easily access their fields via the road and destroy their crops. Thus, indifference to road building projects was rooted in place-specific considerations that were never taken into account by planners and engineers, reflecting how Tarai populations may be "otherwise engaged" with reasonable concerns and practices. Even today, subsistence farmers feel discouraged from shifting to commercial off-season farming due to the unaddressed problem that roads facilitate animals damaging their crops.

It is also worth underscoring that the discrimination has material historical roots. The people of the Tarai, who played a significant role in nation-building and developing the national economy, began to experience deliberate exclusion after the 1960s, when King Mahendra established a partyless autocratic regime by force. His Panchayat regime implemented the Citizenship Act in 1964, replacing the more lenient Citizenship Act of 1952 and imposing stricter requirements for obtaining naturalized citizenship. These restrictions were influenced by anti-India sentiment and had a significant impact on people in the Tarai. The government made citizenship a requirement for various economic activities, such as working in factories, joining public services, buying land, and participating in political activities. The citizenship application process itself was complicated for people of non-hill origin, who often lacked the ability to read and write Nepali and were socially and politically marginalized. The policy particularly affected poor villagers in the Tarai, especially in cases where they failed to secure support from influential elites or lacked the means to cover associated expenses. Additionally, many traditional tenants in the Tarai lost tenancy rights after the implementation of the Land Act of 1964, and they became landless due to their lack of citizenship (Gaige 1975). This prolonged alienation from fundamental citizenship rights and property ownership has strained the relationship between the state and its Madheshi and Tarai Janajati citizens, and has undoubtedly contributed to their cautious approach to road construction.

Tribhuvan Rajbanshi, the former chair of Bhatigachha VDC in southern Morang from 1997–2002, had experience mobilizing locals for road building during his tenure. He was quite familiar with the progress of road development after 1990 in the southern plains of Morang. He contended that locals felt they already had access to roads, even if they were just dirt roads. As a result, they were not persuaded to open new tracks even when existing ones were in poor condition and not fully utilized. Furthermore, individual Madheshi people were unwilling to give up their private lands, and insisted on compensation if a road was to be built through their property. They were generally suspicious of individuals who initiated road development. The subtle resistance from local communities and stereotyping by authorities and elites during road development clearly reflects a lack of trust and alienation between state and citizens. This situation is a consequence of the prolonged exclusion of the Madheshi and Tarai Janajati community and the escalating class conflicts and inequalities that resulted from it.

Moreover, semi-feudal land tenure structures have thrived alongside the growth of industries in the lowlands of the far eastern Tarai, including Morang. Consequently, land plays a vital role in class differentiation and political power dynamics (Sugden 2013). It is important to note that obtaining ownership of private land was challenging for people in the Tarai, and ownership of private land provided symbolic power to negotiate with the state during road construction. The discourse of development (*vikas*), meanwhile, was infused with hill-centered nationalism throughout the Panchayat regime, and did not have significant traction with the people of the Tarai. Individuals who questioned the development narrative were often labeled anti-system, anti-government, and even anti-national (Adhikary 1995). This legacy of hill nationalism persists, often acting as an anti-politics machine (Ferguson 1994), that amplifies suspicion of Madheshi people especially, and characterizes their resistance towards road building as arrogance and defiance. It is time to change this narrative.

LIMITATIONS AND UNINTENDED CONSEQUENCES OF ROAD DEVELOPMENT

Rural road building transforms public spaces into contested arenas wherein diverse stakeholders, such as the state, authorities, the community, politicians, technicians, and contractors, struggle and contest to fulfill their individual interests, both explicit and implicit. These struggles are often governed by historical forces and existing power dynamics. To ensure that road building is part of the democratization process, it is crucial to first embrace an approach that involves all stakeholders in decision-making and implementation. Second, the approach should prioritize the needs and perspectives of all stakeholders, including local communities, government agencies, and other organizations involved in road development. Third, the approach should ensure that in addition to improving mobility, the benefits of road construction are distributed equitably among different groups in society, thereby contributing to broader social justice and environmental sustainability objectives.

In specific, local authorities must enhance effective communication with road users' committees. Executive members of road users' committees in Madheshi and Tarai Janajati communities frequently express frustration with bureaucratic hassles caused by a lack of timely communication and orientation about the formal procedures for documenting invoices and standards for quality assurance.

Consequently, they doubt the authorities' intentions, assuming intentions of bribery or feeling dishonored and discouraged from engaging further in road building.

There is a class dimension to critiques of road building as well. Contrary to popular discourse suggesting that roads bring about development, the extension of roads has led to a significant increase in the valuation of adjacent land in rural areas resulting in the stratification of communities and spaces. Landless individuals, who rely on the labor market, have become increasingly skeptical about the value of constructing wider roads, from which they believe only landowners will benefit. Road upgrading often results in the displacement of landless settlers, adding uncertainty for those who are unable to afford land for resettlement if forced to move.

The expansion of dirt and gravel road networks in rural areas, along with an increase in traffic volume, and the booming sand-mining business from local rivers and streams, has raised concerns about environment and public health. Issues such as air pollution, accidents, traffic congestion, littering, and automotive waste have become prevalent in rural areas connected by roads. Children and elderly individuals face a higher risk of fatal road accidents due to the poor condition of rural roads characterized by potholes, unpaved surfaces, and a lack of street lights and traffic controllers.

Planners and policymakers must also consider the promotion of local public transportation alongside improved road conditions to facilitate everyday mobility. Despite the government's efforts to upgrade roads, road quality is often not sufficient to support reliable public transportation. The authorities and local residents who influence road building often argue for wider roads to meet future needs, which contradicts the desires of the majority of commuters who prefer smaller but well-maintained roads for their daily mobility.[29] A significant number of daily wage and factory

[29] Gramthan Rural Municipality has implemented a rule stating that rural roads must be a minimum of 20 feet wide in order to receive funding from the municipality. Consequently, villagers felt compelled to widen their traditional village paths in order to access funds.

workers, who commute daily to nearby market centers, still face hardships while traveling on their bicycles. Policymakers seem to have overlooked the economic contribution of such daily commuters to rural life. They could, at the very least, improve the daily mobility of locals by paving small tracks for cycles on rural roads leading to major market centers, installing solar street lights, and demarcating cycle lanes on major highways.

The improvement of rural roads can sometimes be a contentious issue, since the exclusive focus on enhancing the mobility of motorized vehicles clashes with traditional uses of village roads. These roads often serve as public spaces for activities such as drying crops, keeping cattle, providing resting places, and serving as settlements for landless people. Additionally, peoples' mobility is frequently impeded by rivers and streams, with bridges playing a significant role in connecting roads and facilitating daily commuting. However, the importance of bridges is often overlooked in discussions about road development and planning, and specifically conceptions of green roads. It is imperative for planners and policymakers to consider local perspectives, demands, and challenges in the Tarai where experiences have been largely overlooked.

Today, planners, policymakers, and local authorities must critically evaluate the government's emphasis on public participation in rural infrastructure building, particularly roads, as a measure of democratic governance. There is often a discrepancy between policies and practices that hinder sustainability of roads and democratic process itself. Marginalized communities are often excluded from road building processes, and "public participation" appears to be a euphemism for political pressure from local elites, the state, and authorities to contribute voluntary labor. This approach tends to inhibit transparency and accountability, and constrain the diversity of road imaginaries and aspirations that vary across geography and class structures, leading to skepticism and the replication of patron-client relationships.

DOLAKHA

CHAPTER 2

The Politics and Practice of Road Building in Dolakha: From Users' Committees to Bulldozers

SHYAM KUNWAR[1]

INTRODUCTION

This chapter investigates the politics of road development in Dolakha District, Nepal. My examination is based on an ethnographic study, conducted in 2015–2019 and July–August 2023, of the Lamosangu-Jiri Road, the Charikot-Singati-Lamabagar Road, and several rural roads in the northern region of Dolakha District. The chapter makes three primary arguments based on examining road building processes in practice: First, roads are built with a promise of future public good, but have in reality fulfilled the interests of a handful people who

[1] Shyam Kunwar has had a longstanding interest in the politics of labor in relation to infrastructure development. His MA thesis examined resistance and negotiation associated with the Jhimruk Hydropower Project in Pyuthan, and his MPhil thesis focused on changing labor relations in road development in Dolakha. This chapter is based on several extended stays in Charikot, Singati and Lamabagar in northern Dolakha. Shyam developed a close collaboration with Shanta Thapa, one of the community-based researchers who has decades of experience leading local community development projects and with whom he has published an article in Nepali on road construction in Dolakha. Shyam is from rural Pyuthan in western Nepal, another district where rural roads were being rapidly developed during the timeframe of the research.

wield political, social, and/or economic capital in the name of *vikas* (development). Second, the processes through which roads are built have contributed to environmental destruction and made everyday life more challenging for many people at the grassroots. Third, the political dynamics of development and planning contribute to the wide gap between plans and practice on the ground.

Dolakha is a mountainous district encompassing "middle hills" and inner-montaine Himalayan regions, where the landscape presents significant technical challenges for building roads. My emphasis is on how these processes intersect with everyday life in the communities through which roads pass, underscoring the challenges posed by political interests and cultural politics for people who live along and with roads.

The chapter is divided into seven sections in keeping with the shared structure elaborated in the Introduction to this book. Considerable weight is given to the history and organization of road building in Dolakha, given the significance of Dolakha for the evolution of "green roads" and hydropower development in Nepal. As an early site for the development of strategic roads through middle hill regions, Dolakha also played a pioneering and formative role in the development of transportation markets. Therefore, the section on markets focuses on bus syndicates in order to elaborate this important dimension of road development, in conversation with the material in other chapters on implications of roads for land valuation, financial institutions and the development of new roadside entrepots.

GEOGRAPHICAL AND HISTORICAL POSITIONING

Dolakha District is located in Bagmati Province, 133 km from Kathmandu in Nepal's central region. This district shares a border with the Tibetan Autonomous Region (TAR) of China to the north and the districts of Solukhumbu to the east, Ramechhap to the south, and Kavrepalanchok and Sindhupalchok to the west. The district extends from 27°47' to 28°00' northern latitudes and 85°50' to 86°32' eastern longitudes, covering a total area of 2,191 square km.

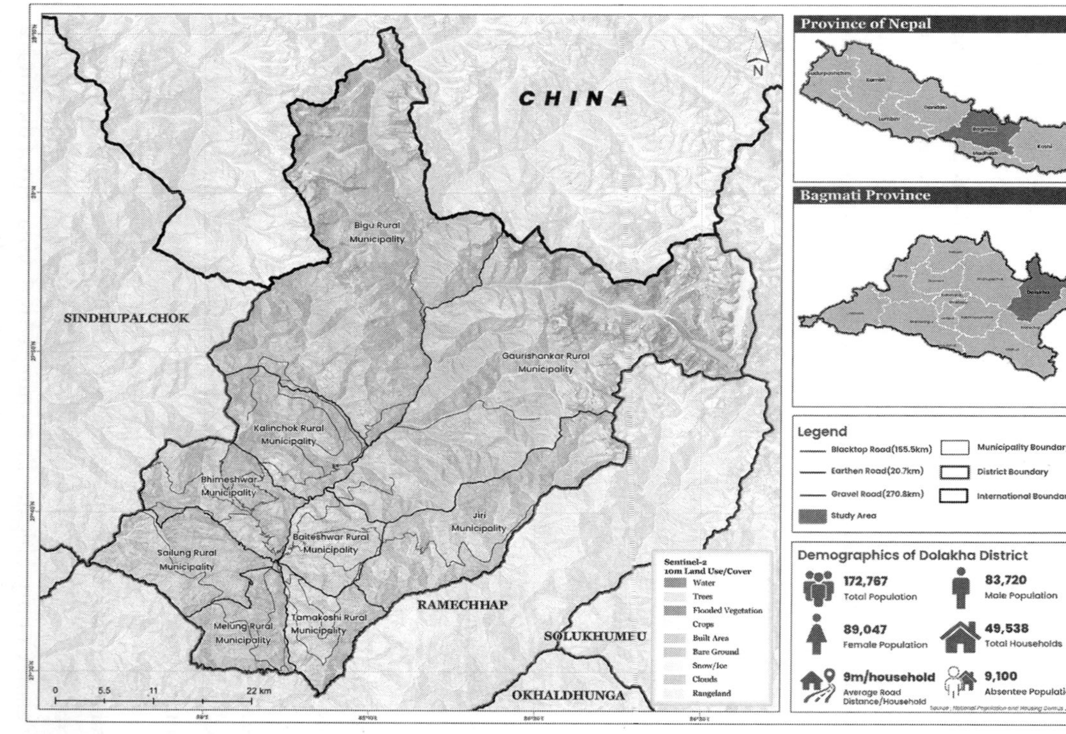

Map 2.1: Location map of Dolakha District (map by Naxa.com).

The landscape is characterized by steep terrain, high peaks, and deep ravines, making it highly susceptible to natural disasters, including landslides and flooding. The Himalayan region as a whole is subject to seismicity resulting from the collision of the Indian and Eurasian tectonic plates, with Dolakha having been an epicenter of the 2015 earthquakes. Along the river valleys, approximately 10 percent of Dolakha's terrain consists of plains, known locally as *tar* (flat land above the river stream) or *besi* (flat land on the river's edge), which are humid, hot, and fertile compared to the hilly and mountainous regions. The district headquarters, Charikot, is situated in the middle hills in the central-southwestern region of the district. Within Charikot, Dolakha Bazaar is where the district's Newar population historically settled, as well as the diverse contemporary ethnocultural mix of residents resulting from rural-town migration. Historically, Dolakha was a prime location in terms of trade, agriculture, national political influence, and transborder mobility. As historians Bajracharya and Shrestha (2059 v.s.[2031 v.s.]) note, Dolakha has a long history as a trading hub, facilitating cross-border commerce with Tibet to the north and Nepal's plains to the south. This activity predates the unification of Nepal in 1769 by King Prithvi Narayan Shah.

The Lapchi and Bigu passes cross the Himalayas from Dolakha's northern border to the TAR; their low elevation and gentle grade have long enabled transhumant livelihoods and overland trade across the border. My research focused particular attention on the Lapchi trade corridor, which passes through the Newar town of Dolakha Bazaar, to the town of Lamabagar, site of the Upper Tamakoshi hydroelectric dam in the northernmost rural municipality of Bigu, and through the settlement of Lapchi, whose monastery is also a sacred place for practitioners of Vajrayana Buddhism. The nearest Tibetan settlement across the Lapchi pass is Chupsang, a 1.5-hour walk from Lapchi, in Nyalam County, Shigatse Prefecture, TAR, China. From there it is a 3-hour bus ride to the market of Tashighang, where Lapchi residents have recently been permitted to resume trade for the first time since the COVID-19 pandemic, and where many have relatives through marriage (Shiwakoti 2023).

Despite the historical significance of the Lamabagar-Lapchi corridor for trans-Himalayan trade, currently there is not much traffic across this border. Nepali citizens residing in border regions are allowed to enter the TAR for pasture and marketing on the basis of border identity cards issued by the Chief District Officer (Shneiderman 2013), and occasionally Tibetans manage to cross out of the TAR in hopes of escaping Chinese occupation. In fact, transborder mobility along the Lamabagar-Lapchi trade route diminished to small-scale regional trading after China introduced border security after 1959. The subsequent construction of the Araniko Highway—also called the Friendship Highway—connecting Kathmandu to Kodari at the TAR border in neighboring Sindhupalchok District from 1961 to 1968, further decreased the significance of the Lamabagar corridor for commercial purposes. The 2015 earthquake halted all cross-border trade as the border was officially closed, opened briefly, and then closed again in 2019 due to the COVID-19 pandemic.

Over time, the state has continually altered administrative units and their borders within Nepal. After the unification of Nepal, Dolakha District referred to territories along the eastern side of the Sunkoshi River. During the period of Rana hereditary prime ministerships, Charikot was established in 1897 (1936 v.s.) as the administrative center of Eastern District No. 2 (which encompassed both contemporary Dolakha and Ramechhap Districts), with a district court and army camp. Subsequently, during a process of administrative restructuring under the Panchayat System in 1962, Dolakha was named a separate district, with Charikot as its district headquarters. Formerly comprised of 50 Village Development Committees (HMG 1975), as of the 2017 restructuring, Dolakha District is comprised of two urban and seven rural municipalities, and falls within Bagmati Province. Charikot is now located in Bhimeshwor Municipality. Since ethnographic research for this chapter was conducted both before and after restructuring was completed, I use administrative unit names associated with both administrative structures.

In terms of population, Dolakha is home to multiethnic and multilingual communities and caste groups, with Chhetri the largest caste group and Tamang the largest ethnic group. Other caste and ethnic groups include Brahman, Thangmi/Thami, Sherpa, Jirel, Surel, and hill Dalits.[2] Thami, Jirel, and Surel[3] are categorized as Hill Adivasi Janajati, within the category of highly marginalized Indigenous groups. The 2021 Nepal Census shows 49,538 households and a total population of 172,767 people in Dolakha, with a population density of 79/sq.km. The northern high-hill areas have lower population densities than the mid-hill and *besi* southern areas (HMG 1975; DDC Dolakha 2015b). Internal rural-urban migration has concentrated the population in Bhimeshwor Municipality, which logged 10,164 households, around 14 percent of which live in rented accommodation, mainly in Charikot, Dolakha Bazaar, and various roadhead markets.

ECONOMIC LIFE

Although historically Dolakha was a prime location for trade, many in this region experienced chronic hunger until the 2000s. Those in the northern region, in particular, have historically faced food scarcity due to limited arable land. Most households rely on agriculture for sustenance but struggle to produce enough to feed their families year-round. Labor migration, therefore, has long been a livelihood strategy, and a remittance economy has been instrumental in sustaining households and communities. Both internal and external

[2] According to the 2021 census: Chhetri 31.2 percent, Tamang 17.6 percent, Thami 10.5 percent, Newar 9.1 percent, hill-Brahman 7.5 percent, Sherpa 5.5 percent, Jirel 2.6 percent, Sunuwar 1.1 percent, Bishwokarma 4.2 percent, Mijar 2.2 percent, Pariyar 2.2 percent, and Surel 0.08 percent, with many other caste and ethnic groups at less than 1percent (NSO 2023).

[3] Surel were previously known as Sunuwar (HMG 1975; Carter 2011). Since 2021 they have been enumerated separately, and are considered a highly marginalized ethnic group (CBS 2012; NSO 2023).

labor migration continue today (see Shneiderman 2015; Kunwar, Lewison and Rankin 2021).

To characterize economic life in Dolakha, it is helpful to reference the local designations of "northern belt" and "southern belt" within the district, although these are not formal administrative divisions. Statements such as "the southern belt is more developed than the northern belt," and "the density of rural road networks is greater in the southern belt" are common. The southern belt roughly indicates the part of Dolakha District south of the Lamosangu-Jiri Road running east from the Araniko Highway, traversing the mid hills, through Charikot, to reach the entrepot town of Jiri on the eastern edge of the district. The fertile, flat *besi* lands of the district are concentrated there, allowing for a variety of crops, including paddy, maize, wheat, mustard, lentils and diverse vegetables. As a result of intensive integrated rural development projects, some "pocket areas" have developed the capacity to produce cash crops, such as the famous potatoes of Mude, which are well known in the Kathmandu Valley—even if on the whole most consumption items must be imported. Sailung is an important tourist destination in the southern belt, famous as a pilgrimage site.

The northern belt falls primarily north of the Lamosangu-Jiri Road and is generally associated with the Gaurishankar and Rolwaling Himalayan mountain ranges, their trekking routes, and sacred sites for Buddhists, Hindus, and Indigenous religions. Lapchi, for instance, has long attracted religious ascetics and increasingly tourists as a sacred Vajrayana Buddhist site where Guru Milarepa meditated and gained divine power. Bigu and Kalinchok are also key tourist destinations in the northern belt. The northern belt's rich flora and fauna and spectacular landscape received national recognition with the 2010 establishment of the Gaurishankar Conservation Area across the northern belt (extending westwards into Sindhupalchok District). Despite these assets for tourism and religious pilgrimage, the northern belt has even less capacity for food subsistence than the southern belt. Meanwhile, most of the market centers in Dolakha District developed along the Lamosangu-Jiri Road, which also passes through the district headquarters, Charikot, and neighboring Dolakha Bazaar, one of Nepal's oldest Newar settlements (Bajracharya and Shrestha 2059 v.s.[2031 v.s.]).

DEVELOPMENT CONTEXT

In the 1950s, Nepal began to establish a modern state apparatus under the rule of the Shah kings. During this time the country welcomed international aid from bilateral and multilateral donors, who considered Nepal a laboratory for development intervention given its prior inaccessibility (see, Mihaly 2009[1965]; Pigg 1992, 1993; Des Chene 1996; Fujikura 1996, 2013; Rankin 1996, 2004; Shah 2018). In this context, the Swiss Agency for Development and Cooperation (SDC) initiated small-scale development projects in Jiri, Dolakha, including a cheese factory and demonstration farm. By 1964, the Swiss scaled-up their interventions with three key regional planning projects: the Jiri Multipurpose Development Project, the Integrated Hill Development Project (IHDP), and the Lamosangu-Jiri Road Project (LJRP) [Schaffner 1987; Vajracharya *et al.* 1995]. All three have an iconic place in the history of development in Nepal, and the significant Swiss investment set Dolakha apart from other hilly and mountainous districts, in terms of its relatively advanced physical and market infrastructures throughout the Panchayat period and beyond—with opportunities concentrated in the southern belt around the Lamosangu-Jiri Road.

Budgetary decentralization, combined with significant expansion of foreign development interventions by international non-governmental organizations (INGOs), began to even out the distribution of development opportunities across and within districts in the 1990s. For Dolakha in particular, a key source of development in the northern belt has been investments in hydropower. Most significant is the Upper Tamakoshi Hydro Electric Project (UTKHEP), established in 2007, the largest in Nepal. Its intake is located at the small northern town of Lamabagar, situated in a wide highland valley at a point where the Tamakoshi River drops significantly in elevation, just 6 km south of Nepal's border with the TAR. With a capacity of 456 megawatts, the UTKHEP was the first to be capitalized by a combination of Nepali state and private-sector investors, combined with the general public and Dolakha residents—the latter hold a combined 25 percent share (UTKHEP 2024). It is also a "National Pride Project," sometimes called a National Priority Project, a designation currently given to 21 infrastructure development projects by the National Planning Commission.[4] Crucially, for my purposes, the UTKHEP project has required ongoing construction and maintenance of a 68-km motorable "access road" from Charikot, through the market town of Singati and along the Tamakoshi River, up to the dam site at Lamabagar. Numerous additional small- and medium-scale hydro projects are currently under construction or recently completed, with private sector investments leading to the expansion of road access in the northern region. Dolakha District was one of the regions hardest hit by the 2015 earthquakes in Nepal. This led to a surge of rescue, relief, and reconstruction projects focused in the northern belt, consolidating further engagement of INGOs in an extraordinary intensification of development programs (Kunwar, Lewison and Rankin 2021).

Similar to Mugu District, aspirations for development in Dolakha are powerfully rooted in imaginaries of road development. A particularly compelling narrative surrounds preparations for a tender to construct a south-north strategic road from Mahottari at the Nepal-India border, through Ramechhap and Dolakha Districts, to Lamabagar and the China border, which was underway in the aftermath of the earthquake but never materialized (Khatiwada

[4] Although ownership is exclusively Nepali, through an international competitive bidding process, the Chinese company Sino Hydro won the contract for civil engineering work, and the Indian company Texmaco Railway and Engineering Limited secured the contract for hydro-mechanical work. These companies employed Chinese and Indian skilled labor and engineers alongside local unskilled laborers (see, Kunwar, Lewison and Rankin 2021).

2019). Meanwhile, visions of Dolakha's future prosperity also hinge on exploitation of its cultural and sacred religious sites and natural resources, including medicinal herbs found in the Himalayan ranges. Of course, such imaginaries invite conflicts over resources at both community and district scales, involving local people in relation to various government agencies, infrastructure projects, and the burgeoning sand-mining business (see also the Morang chapter), which are explored in latter sections of this chapter.

ROAD HISTORY OF DOLAKHA

INTEGRATING ROADS WITH RURAL DEVELOPMENT

The road history of Dolakha tells a fascinating story of the entanglement of rural road development and integrated agriculture development in the 1970s and 1980s; the tensions between approaches requiring heavy equipment versus locally available tools and labor as rural road building became "mainstreamed" in local development budgets from the 1990s; and the way highway and other major infrastructure development relates to experiences of connectivity and remoteness in rural areas. In telling these stories, this section highlights to the book's themes of uneven development and remoteness as a relational construct.

Dolakha's traditional trade route was not a priority for the US- and India-supported Regional Transportation Organization (RTO) of the late 1950s or for the regional development plans of the newly democratizing Nepal state in the 1970s. Yet foreign aid played a major role in the development of roads in Dolakha in the early part of the Panchayat regime (1960–1990)—with bilateral Swiss assistance leading the way in an integrated rural development approach. In the 1960s, the SDC implemented the Jiri-Multipurpose Development Project (JMDP, 1964–1971). Upon handing the project over to Government of Nepal, SDC noted that the project had been compromised by a "lack of suitable communication and transportation facilities between the project area and the economic

Map 2.2: Road Map of Dolakha District (map by Naxa.com).

centers of the country" (Schaffner 1987: 1). The Swiss government thus proposed the Lamosangu-Jiri Road as an access road to provide a backbone for the success of integrated rural development activities, which it sought to continue through a simultaneously implemented Integrated Hill Development Project (Schaffner 1987: 2).

A 1987 report by the International Centre for Integrated Mountain Development (ICIMOD) identifies the Lamosangu-Jiri Road as Nepal's "first hillroad project" (Schaffner 1987: 2). Local labor using manual tools, local resources, and sustainable, labor-intensive construction models suitable for fragile hill and mountainous landscapes were deployed—and in this sense, the LJRP has been seen as an experimental precursor to the subsequently articulated "green road" model of road development. The latter later became the dominant orthodoxy of rural road building, as elaborated in the Introduction and chapter on Mugu in this book (see Bajracharya *et al.* 1995; Paudyal 1998; HMG 1999; Sharma and Maskey 1999; Mulmi 2009). Another objective of the LJRP was to enhance the skill of Nepali engineers and the capacity of administrative bodies through collaboration with Swiss engineers and technicians.[5] In both respects, then, the project aimed to support public livelihoods and institutions in conjunction with integrated rural development. Ultimately, the Lamosangu-Jiri Road was literally built by thousands of hands, with young and old, male and female coming together to labor this road into existence. As a result, Dolakha District was connected to the national Strategic Road Network in the mid-1980s, far earlier than most other agrarian hill districts.

TRANSITIONING TO HEAVY EQUIPMENT

It is difficult to convey how transformative such a development would have been for Dolakha residents. Many shared with me their

[5] One of the guiding principles for "the implementation was to give Nepali engineers a fair chance to contribute fully to the project realization," to "get maximum benefit from the applied technical knowhow and expertise," and to "strengthen and improve" the Nepali bureaucracy, where government engineers and officials actively participated in the process (Schaffner 1987: 2).

past experiences of walking along foot trails for many days and the *dukha* (hardship) entailed in transporting food and other materials for everyday life into and across the region. The Lamosangu-Jiri Road is thus viewed as a landmark for the development of the district. Although people in the southern belt closest to the roadheads benefited the most, those in the northern belt also recognized the importance of road connectivity. In the early 1980s, elected representatives and local politicians met with the prime minister and cabinet members to request allocation of a budget to build a road connecting northern Dolakha, terminating in the market town of Singati on the bank of the Tamakoshi River. However, conflicts over the alignment of the Charikot-Dolakha-Singati Road, combined with inadequate budget allocation, delayed construction for decades. During this process the use of heavy machinery launched a new, controversial modality of infrastructure development that contrasted starkly with the techniques used to build the Lamosangu-Jiri Road.

The 1992 local elections under the multi-party system led to the formation of a District Development Committee (DDC) that prioritized building a network of district trunk roads, including the Charikot-Singati Road (Kunwar 2018). SDC supported these projects under the auspices of Nepal government programs for rural infrastructure development, namely the Rural Community Infrastructure Work (RCIW) and District Road Support Program (DRSP). RCIW built 30 km of the Dolakha-Singati Road, but it was too narrow and failed to reach Singati. Later, using dozers (colloquial for bulldozer and excavator), the DDC widened and completed that track up to Singati.[6] Then the SDC, supporting the DRSP, graveled the earthen road. In 1996, DDC representatives brought an old dozer to Dolakha from the Local Development Ministry,[7] indicating a clear shift in approach from the labor-intensive practices that built

[6] The term "dozer" in fact extends beyond actual bulldozers to encompass excavators, rollers, graders, and other heavy equipment used in construction work.

[7] As per DDC meeting minutes made available to me by the former DDC chair in 2018.

the Lamosangu-Jiri Road, and the challenges became immediately apparent. The dozer then functioned just long enough to open up some road tracks in the Charikot area, but was soon grounded at the DDC office—where it remained in disrepair for decades as a powerful symbol of the interface of technology, politics and ethics in road development.

Photo 2.1: Grounded dozer at DDC office in Charikot (photo by Shyam Kunwar, 2017).

The story of this dozer not only shifted rural road construction toward more mechanization over green road practices, but also sparked political debates and controversies. Opposition parties claimed that DDC leaders had embezzled money in the name of repairing dozers. Some political leaders were formally charged, and in 1997, the Local Development Officer (LDO), who was secretary of the maintenance committee, was eventually suspended in connection with the case.

In 1997, a second team of elected DDC representatives came to power and highlighted road building in a six-year periodic plan for Dolakha. The plan, issued in 2002, revealed that Dolakha had very few rural roads; only 14 out of 51 VDCs were touched by roads at the time (DDC Dolakha 2002).[8] That periodic plan also included a grand vision to construct a ring road encircling major settlements of the entire district. As the ex-DDC chair explained in an interview,

> I sketched a circle on the district map of Dolakha ... very carefully and accurately. I pointed out the alignment of the ring road to connect market centers, special production areas, and service centers. ... After its completion, settlements will shift to the roadheads; production centers will be connected by the road. There will be communication facilities installed for the public; a drinking water scheme, education and health services will be available. ... People will gradually start to migrate near the roadheads.

What the ex-chair neglected to acknowledge was that the DDC's intention to observe environmentally friendly construction practices (especially alignments appropriate to fragile landscapes) failed to materialize; again dozers were deployed, haphazardly and excessively. The DDC once again brought a dozer to the district in 2002, which contributed to completing some unfinished road tracks, including the Dolakha-Singati Road, and other new tracks in the southern parts of Dolakha. However, the Maoist People's War was at its peak by 2002, and insurgents destroyed the DDC's dozer along with other government property (Shneiderman and Turin 2010).

During the war, road construction slowed but did not completely stop. Government could not lead the process, but at this time, ward-based users' committees (UCs), mobilized for various public work

[8] Major district roads at the time included the Lamosangu-Jiri Road (110 km), Mude-Jiri paved road (86 km), the Charikot-Dolakha section of a 22 km graveled road from Tamakoshi to Khimti (initially built for Khimti Hydro Project), and 73 km of earthen rural roads.

projects, began renting and deploying dozers for smaller-scale rural road projects. The DDC senior engineer asserted in an interview that since the Comprehensive Peace Accord (CPA) between the Government of Nepal and the Communist Party of Nepal (Maoist) in 2006, half of the development budgets each year had been spent on dozers to build rural roads on a massive scale through UCs, as will be discussed at length below.

ROADS DIVIDING GEOGRAPHIES AND CREATING REMOTENESS

Another theme that arises when considering road history in Dolakha is the relationality of remoteness associated with uneven development. Lamabagar, a market center in the northern belt and site of the UTKHEP, had once been a vibrant trade hub along the upper Tamakoshi River—along an old "silk road" connecting Tibet and China with Nepal and India (Bajracharya and Shrestha 2059 v.s.[2031 v.s.]). Long-time residents of Lamabagar recall a time when business was thriving, when Sherpa traders brought salt, wool, tea, leather, and herbs from Tibet and exchanged them for grain in the plains. Trade brought prosperity and peripheral employment; for example, Sherpa traders would hire Dolakha's Tamang as porters.

In the 1960s, with Chinese government support, the Araniko Highway was constructed along the Bhotekoshi River, the major north-south river valley west of the Tamakoshi that had been earmarked as the most desirable corridor for linking Nepal to the TAR via motorable road. As others have argued, including in relation to Nepal's Central Development Region (e.g. Campbell 2010; Shneiderman 2013), mobility can beget immobility. The Araniko Highway paralyzed the Lamabagar trade route and displaced the livelihood of its traders. Many of them moved their businesses to roadheads of the Araniko Highway, while others migrated to Kathmandu in pursuit of petty trade. Those lacking capital to support such adaptations, like many porters, lost trade-related sources of income entirely. Those remaining in Lamabagar were primarily poor and aging. The Araniko Highway had turned northern Dolakha into a remote place, an official designation that it received in the late 1970s thereafter earning central government financial transfers called "remote area development" budgets.[9] Aspiration persists for a strategic road to once again forge a significant thoroughfare through the Lamabagar corridor, leading to a revival of trade and economic activity in the region, much as for the Nakchelagna Road in Mugu. Lamabagar residents note that China has already developed necessary infrastructure, such as roads, schools, and market centers, on their side of the border, and that if the Nepali government builds the planned road up to the border, the corridor may once again prosper. The prevailing subjectivity, however, foregrounds remoteness. "*Hami kunako manchhe*" (we corner people)—people who have historically lived in a region disconnected from the road network and market—is a common expression. This sentiment was well-captured in Kesang Tseten's (2006) documentary *Hami Kunako Manchhe*, reviewed by anthropologist Stacy Pigg (2008), which documents the similarly ambivalent experience of a village in northern Rasuwa District being "connected" by a bridge. Roads play a central role in this ambivalent development imaginary. Not only the Araniko Highway, but also the Lamosangu-Jiri Road built through the southern belt, is perceived to have contributed to marginalizing northern Dolakha. The sense of remoteness derives not only from the geographic barriers of its inner-montaine Himalayan location, but crucially also from decisions made by powerful people in distant places, both within the district and beyond, starting from the 1980s when the first motorable roads were being planned for the hills of central Nepal.

ORGANIZATION OF ROAD DEVELOPMENT

There are two major models of road building in Dolakha: one is based on contract tendering, the other on a participatory approach

[9] In 1977, during the Panchayat period, the government formed a Remote Area Development Committee to run and monitor development programs in places categorized as "remote" (HMG 1977). The allocated budgets were spent mostly on making foot trails, mule trails and developing grazing lands for the benefit of those in mountainous regions.

involving UCs. In policy and planning, the models are intended to operate separately, with some roads being allocated for contract tendering and others for UCs using manual labor and local resources. This section engages ethnographic description and interview quotes to show how in practice, contractors and UCs build rural roads in a coordinated manner that results in suboptimal outcomes for users and residents. Contractors generally work in an environment where they must find illicit strategies to manage competition—*milaune*—and contend with lack of cooperation among government agencies and landowners. Meanwhile, when local rural roads are built by UCs, supported by inadequate *tukre* (piece) budgets, they become entangled in local politics with real material consequences. These dynamics are also evident in the Mugu chapter.

Both modalities result in poor quality roads. Roads whose completion is delayed that create intolerable dust in winter and mud during the rainy season. Roads subject to landslides and flooding due to insecure back-cutting, which make it difficult to even walk, threatening the safety of settlements. Public buses, ambulances, and loaded trucks get stuck for hours, increasing transportation costs, inflating prices for goods and services, and putting lives at risk. Roads that are not monitored for environmental impacts, generating secondary impacts like decreases in agricultural productivity and the spread of disease in plants and animals.

The section is divided into three parts. The first focuses on the ambiguities of the contract system that has evolved in Dolakha since the 1980s. The second section considers how UC operating with small, fragmented budgets since the 1990s end up contributing to excessive dozer use. The third section examines how contractors and UCs, in fact, build rural roads with heavy equipment in a coordinated manner despite their mutual criticism. Residents contend with significant resulting environmental hazards—dust, mud, landslides—compounded by delays in project completion and governance processes geared toward attributing blame rather than finding solutions. Based largely on ethnographic observation and repeat interviews over an extended period of time, my research also identifies additional factors challenging rural road building, and the relations among them. These include actions of homeowners, government officials and political leaders, as well as the opacity of road building processes from any given standpoint. Combined, these challenges catalyze various forms of protest and resistance.

AMBIVALENCE IN THE CONTRACT SYSTEM

I begin with the Swiss engineer, Urs Schaffner, who was involved in the construction of the Lamosangu-Jiri Road in the 1980s. His book *Road Construction in the Nepal Himalaya* (1987) details the management of road construction in Dolakha and neighboring Sindhupalchok District. Contracts were awarded by degree of technical expertise and capacity, with the larger, Kathmandu-based "A" and "B" category contractors undertaking technically difficult work, such as "water management, layer work and blacktop," while lower-class, often locally-based "C" and "D" category contractors were awarded "simple tasks like earthwork," often on a piece basis (Schaffner 1987: 27).[10] This system of contractor classification is detailed in the Introduction to this book. The LJRP made a point of hiring piece (C and D) contractors for the last 40 km of earthwork. The logic was that this would enhance local skills in infrastructure development, create employment opportunities, and "gain more direct influence and control over the work" (Schaffner 1987: 27).

Schaffner recounts that in practice, however, the contract system proved extremely difficult to manage. The project found itself enmeshed in disputes with contractors over poor quality work, delays, and associated rising costs. He attributes this to several factors. Government procurement processes create an incentive for "underbidding," that is knowingly submitting bids inadequate to the task. At the time, procurement rules stipulated that "the lowest bidder always had to get the contract," regardless of how low

[10] However, it is important to note that the main contractors delegate the execution of work to sub-contractors within their respective sections.

their bid was ("35 percent under the cost estimate in exceptional cases"). This meant that contractors were often unable to execute the work properly (Schaffner 1987: 28–29) due to the gap between budget and actual price. Schaffner attributes profit as contractors' primary motivation. The only leverage project managers had against contractors was withholding payment or refusing to approve poor-quality work. For the smaller piece contractors (including C and D), the primary challenge lay in the problem of local leaders seeking to secure preferential treatment for their own co-villagers through patronage politics (see also Mugu chapter).

Almost 40 years later, my fieldwork corroborates Schaffner's findings, although procurement requirements have changed to diminish extreme under-bidding. I earned the trust of Dolakha-based contractors with the help of community-based researcher Shanta Thapa, a Charikot resident. The contractors candidly shared, sometimes cynically, the challenges they encounter and the tactics they use to navigate the volatile market. They shared that the practice of low-bidding, as described by Schaffner (1987), actually encourages collusion in the sector. The perception that contractors are greedy and profit-driven belies the reality of having to bid low, to the point of not being able to complete the work properly. Low bidding is also facilitated by the neglect of government officials who do not enforce existing rules that could protect the quality of the outcome and the integrity of the process—especially bid security money or bank guarantee requirements that would safeguard against default.

Even in cases where government officials attempt to abide by existing regulations, contractors can use political party networks to get rid of the problem. Contractors shared how they had organized through contractor associations in each district, and how elections for leadership positions are typically driven by party affiliations and campaigning. In the 2022 federal parliamentary election many contractors secured seats in parliament, building on this nexus of parties and contractors, which is also described in the Mugu chapter. The same logic applies to elections of provincial and local governments. In Dolakha contractors were well-connected with the political parties. During my field work period, the Nepali Congress backed contractors won the major executive posts in the contractor association. Communist Party of Nepal–Unified Marxist Leninist (CPN-UML) and Communist Party of Nepal–Maoist Center (CPN-MC) backed contractors are also active. These politically-affiliated contracting associations play critical roles in helping contractors to bid for and obtain projects.

Dolakha-based contractors also shared with me that after 2006 (when the civil conflict ended) the number of contractors increased significantly, which created increased pressure for under-bidding. As a result of this competition, they acknowledge, many failed to complete contracted work on time or assure its quality. That pressure encouraged them to seek out other strategies for winning contracts, making money, and contributing to local development. Giving "commissions" to the government officials, technicians, engineers, politicians, party leaders, and their cadres to "manage" bureaucratic procedures proved more effective. The Nepali term, *milaunu*, to arrange, captures well this approach, and it does not have the same negative connotations as the English equivalent, bribe.[11] *Milaunu* is cast more as a survival strategy in a complex terrain. Contractors openly shared, even on social media, that they have to give "commissions" to different people with potential influence over the tendering process; in Mugu, "personal commission" works similarly.

Dolakha contractors began to act collectively to manipulate the bidding processes, as we also see in Mugu. Specifically, they began to bid by rotation in order to manage competition in securing bids. Tendering rules stipulate there must be at least three bidders to open the bid evaluation. Dolakha contractors discuss which contractor wants the bid, what percentage they can afford to share with other contractors who agree to put in a slightly higher "competitor" bid (2-3 percent being common), and then bid only slightly under the estimated project budget. Even after distributing commissions for

[11] The Nepali term *ghus* carries that negative connotation.

the fake competitors, the bid winner can profit well. Contractors do not consider the practice, which would translate as "collusion" in English, to be secretive or shameful; on the contrary they were frustrated with the government's failure to enforce low bid security money or the requirement for bank guarantee, which resulted in excessive underbidding and poor outcomes. The contractors also mentioned that a handful of powerful higher-class contractors, who have strong connections with political leaders based in Kathmandu, bid for multiple projects all over Nepal, and then hold many projects at a time. They are thus able to underbid local contractors. In order to survive in this competitive market, local contractors are forced to bid for these projects through joint venture (JVs) with these high-level contractors, who in practice do not work in the field. As one Dolakha-based contractor explained, "they actually do not do construction work; they give us the construction work on a piece contract basis and get margins without doing any work. ... These contractors only do documentation work." In this situation Dolakha contractors cannot bid for "good projects." It was only for their survival in the sector that Dolakha contractors began to coordinate bids for road projects.

Two specific examples illustrate issues arising through the contracting modality: 1) a short section of the Lamosangu-Jiri Road at Charikot Bazaar, the district headquarters, which had been suspended from 2013 to 2018 (Kunwar and Thapa 2020) and 2) Khadichaur-Charikot section of the Lamosangu-Jiri Road improvement project. The former involved a bidding process within Nepal called National Competitive Bidding (NCB), while the bid for the latter was awarded through International Competitive Bidding (ICB) open to companies of other countries.

Example 1: Upgrading a 1-Kilometer Road Section of the Lamosangu-Jiri Road at Charikot

In December 2012 the Road Division office in Charikot issued a tender to upgrade a 1-km section of the Lamosangu-Jiri Road in Charikot Bazaar. A joint venture of Kathmandu-based A-class contractors underbid competitors and won the bid. A contract was signed in April 2013. The work was scheduled for completion by July 2014, but was not finished until January 2018. As the deadline for completion approached, there was little progress, and contractors repeatedly abandoned the work, blaming unanticipated inflation of costs in construction materials and labor, which were exacerbated by the 2015 earthquakes (Kunwar, Lewison and Rankin 2021). Local Dolakha contractors told me that in fact the project contractor took "mobilization money" also known as a "signing amount" after signing the contract. That means that the winning contractor receives funds at the beginning—some set aside to mobilize outside contractors—and then leaves the construction site. That money is then utilized to run other projects. Such contractors prioritize profitable work by mobilizing petty contractors, for discrete tasks such as back-cutting and building supporting walls. They indicated that the contractor's ultimate goal is to expand their profit margin.

To an outside observer, it was obvious that labor had been deployed only intermittently from 2016–2018. A first group of laborers did back-cutting work to widen the narrow track (excavation and removal of soil and rock from the roadbed in order to create a level surface), but then abandoned the site. Also in 2016, other laborers installed supporting gabion and retaining walls. Before the work was completed, landslides caused by heavy rains disrupted the work; the laborers cleared the debris and then left the site. The laborers with whom I spoke explained they were working under a petty contractor, also an outsider; they did not know who the main contractor was. In January 2017, another group of laborers were installing gabion and retaining walls. They, too, were working under a petty contractor and did not know the main contractor. Work interruptions continued until January 2018 when a few hundred meters of paving completed the 1 km road upgrading project.

Local residents claimed the contractor did not work properly from the beginning. According to them, the contractor created delays by creating conflicts over the right-of-way (RoW), which was 15 meters from the center of the road according to planning specifications. Although the Road Act indicates that landowners must leave 6 meters on each side of the Lamosangu-Jiri Road when building houses or other structures, the rule was not enforced in practice. The municipality had approved their houses and was collecting taxes on the land. Landowners argued that government action gave legitimacy to their ownership rights, and refused to cooperate with contractors' efforts to clear land for upgrading—denying that their structures were encroaching on the RoW.

Photo 2.2: Road expansion works at Charikot Bazaar along the Lamosangu-Jiri Road section (photo by Shanta Thapa, 2017).

Disputes among different government agencies complicated the delays, and added another perspective on the whole process. The Road Division Office (RDO) Charikot under the Department of Roads (DoR) blamed the municipality office for not ensuring the mandated RoW when they approved house maps and allowed structures to be built on the roadside. However, an elected ward chair of Bhimeshwor Municipality asserted in an interview that the municipality had reported proposals for house construction to the RDO, and would only grant approvals with their consent. Thus conflict between the RDO and the municipality generated delays and introduced competing interpretations of blame and responsibility. Although during the project a new RDO division chief sought to enforce RoW specifications in the Road Act, another challenge arose in the layers of subcontracting. Work was being done by subcontractors unknown to the RDO, who communicated only with the main contractor—making it difficult to monitor work progress and follow the rules even if they wanted to.

Public pressure also played a role in this case. Local leaders, civil society members, journalists, and business owners collectively petitioned the RDO, Bhimeshwor Municipality, and the chief district officer (CDO) of Dolakha to address the intolerable dust and mud that resulted from indefinite delays, right at the center of the district's headquarters. The district's journalists came together across the ideological spectrum to organize a public discussion series called *Nagarik Bahas* (Public Debate) broadcasted on Kalinchok Community FM radio in Charikot from 2013 to 2017. Government offices promised in these programs and other meetings to address the issue by coordinating with the main contractor, but failed to fulfill their promise. In fact, as detailed in an interview with an official from the Charikot RDO, the government had little power in such situations. The RDO had issued numerous orders and warnings to the contractor and had extended the schedule, but the contractor simply failed to comply. The official process for finalizing the contracts was still incomplete during my last visit in 2023.

Example 2: The Lamosangu-Jiri Road Upgrading Project (from Lamosangu to Charikot)

The Lamosangu-Jiri Road Upgrading Project has been ongoing since 2014 under the auspices of the Road Improvement and Development Project Directorate of the DoR. It was intended to respond to increasing traffic volume resulting from the UTKHEP. The project fell under a third Line of Credit provided to the Government of Nepal by Exim Bank of India, a condition for which was that the work must be procured through the ICB system. The road construction work had been divided into two sections: Lamosangu-Mude and Mude-Charikot. As a result, international contractors held a 51 percent stake in a joint venture (the Indian companies Shakeel Haider and Simanchal (Shiwakoti 2021), but provided neither on-site work nor technical support; Total Management Services participated as Nepal-based consultants supervising construction; Shankarmali, Gauri Parbati, and Sunaula Khimti JV were the Nepali contractors.[12]

The upgrading project did not progress smoothly until 2018, despite a contract extension allowing for disturbances caused by the 2015 earthquakes. Significant traffic disturbances plagued the route throughout, including impinging on completion of the UTKHEP, the very national priority project the road was intended to facilitate. I met the heavy equipment supplier to UTKHEP at Singati in 2018, who had expressed extreme frustration with the project management as well as the government agencies that demonstrated no capacity to address the gridlock in traffic and work.

My purpose in selecting this example is to highlight the role of a grassroots movement that gained momentum in Dolakha and Sindhupalchok Districts, from which an alternative idea emerged. The public protested; the local government initiated dialogue with the contractors; and a mediating group formed. Jilla Samvad Samuha (District Dialogue Group) organized meetings among the project stakeholders, which included journalists, civil society members, entrepreneurs, activists, political leaders, elected representatives, and government officials. Their dialogue series (*samvad shrinkhala*) aimed to facilitate discussions among the three parties to the contract: the client (the Nepali government, including government officials, ministers, and elected MPs from Dolakha and Sindhupalchok Districts), the consultant (responsible for monitoring technical issues, ensuring that designs are followed, approving work, and preparing

[12] Sunaula Khimti was blacklisted for underperforming in 2023 by the Public Procurement Monitoring Office, operating under the Prime Minister's Office (Khabarhub 2023)

bills of finished works for approval), and the contractors. Here, I present my observations of these grassroots events.

On January 30, 2018, I attended a meeting held with all the stakeholders in Mude (a town located along a high ridge near the border between Sindhupalchok and Dolakha Districts along the Lamosangu-Jiri Road). The meeting, organized by Jilla Samvad Samuha, offered hope for a breakthrough in the interruptions to the upgrading road work. The logistical arrangements, including travel and other expenses, were funded through the Asia Foundation's Natural Resources and Conflict Resolution Center. Journalists paid close attention, capturing audio-visuals of what stakeholders were saying.

During opening remarks, the speaker, a Dolakha-based journalist and coordinator of Jilla Samvad Samuha, noted that "on behalf of the public, we organized this meeting to understand the obstacles that were hindering progress and to find ways to coordinate and create an environment that would facilitate completion of the upgrading project." He also cautioned that the public would not tolerate further delays. He then summoned the Nepali contractors as the representatives of the joint venture, who appeared angry and frustrated. They aired their grievances, to explain why the project remained incomplete. First, "the 2015 earthquakes had completely destroyed the previous survey points, which needed to be resurveyed." Second, "homeowners who had to rebuild their houses along the roadways after the earthquake were encroaching on the road by throwing soil and debris onto the road." The contractors were concerned that they would not receive payment for clearing up this debris and asked, "Who will address this problem?" Third, the contractors noted that the road design had changed after the contract agreement had been reached. Fourth, the contractors complained about a variation order that had been issued by the Department of Roads to increase the road width from 5.5 to 7 meters. This change in design required more construction materials than the contractors had budgeted. The contractors argued that they needed to install crusher machines and establish a quarry site to accommodate the increased construction materials, which also required approval from the local government; they stated, "this approval is still pending." Finally, when questioned about whether Nepali contractors were indeed responsible for 49 percent of the work, as per the contract provision, the contractors clarified that in reality Nepali contractors and engineers were responsible for all the upgrading work.

Clearly, the contractors sought to use the meeting as a platform for communicating the technical and bureaucratic hurdles that had obstructed their work. And yet they failed to address their own responsibilities regarding environmental impacts. The contract had stipulated that the contractor should minimize environmental impacts, particularly dust, mud, landslides, and traffic congestion caused by construction. These were, in fact, the public's main concern, and the project manager and consultants too were silent on these issues. Frustrated participants asked, "Who is responsible? Where do we go, when none of the contractors, the government, or the monitoring agencies were willing to take responsibility?" The meeting concluded with an agreement among the stakeholders to continue the dialogue and to arrange a meeting with the ministers, secretary, and the director general of the DoR to discuss these problems.

Despite these discussions, delays persisted. These protests took various forms including people blowing conches at the contractors, hanging their photos in public buses, and spreading slogans to shame them for leaving construction sites before completing the work. Since the government failed to properly respond to protesters' demands, protesters also hung photos of the minister, the secretary of the ministry, and the director general of the DoR. They also formed a human chain along the road at Charikot as another pressure tactic.

These cases show how stakeholders of road construction characterize the process as presenting intractable challenges from their own standpoint, and readily attribute blame to other stakeholders. We also see how difficult it is to understand the system as a whole. Laborers only see the subcontractors who hire them; government agents only see the contractors to whom they award the bid. International contractors never show up in the district. It is remarkable that the fundamental task of communication and coordination that should have been expected of professional stakeholders fell to a critically conscious public, in the form of discussion forums, radio programs and public protests. And yet, deadlines were still repeatedly missed; building rural roads through the contracting modality would seem a near-impossible undertaking.

Photo 2.3: Excavator and breaker extracting raw materials and widening the road in a landslide-prone area of Sakhine, near Charikot, as part of the Lamosangu-Jiri Road Upgrading Project under the Road Improvement and Development Project (photo by Shyam Kunwar, 2017).

USERS' COMMITTEES (UCs): THE GENESIS OF TUKRE *BUDGETS*

Since 2000, as local bodies began to receive budgets regularly, UCs became a main actor in rural road building. The concept of UCs derives from participatory development principles combined with principles of sustainability as pioneered in Nepal by the Lamosangu-

Jiri Road. It entails handing over small-scale development activities to small groups of residents who receive budgets, training, and tools to undertake "labor-based, environmentally friendly, and participatory" (LEP) modes of construction.

The allocation of budgets for road building in Dolakha increased dramatically after 2006. A senior DDC engineer noted: "In 1994 [through the roll-out of the CPN-UML decentralization campaign, *Aphno Gau Aphai Banau*], every VDC received NRs. 3 lakh [from the government], and in 2016, each VDC received NRs. 50 lakh—and nearly 80 percent of that was spent on road development." Another factor contributing to the availability of budgets for local, rural roads has come through the *Samsad Vikas Kosh* (Constituency Development Fund), instituted and expanded over the same period, as also described in the Morang chapter. The Constituency Development Fund assigns a specific budget to members of federal parliament or provincial assemblies to spend on development activities within their constituencies.[13]

Although not consistently applied (and renamed on various occasions), this fiscal resource allocated to VDCs increased from NRs. 3 lakh since its inception in FY 1996/97 to NRs. 17 million in FY 2015/16. In Dolakha, according to a senior engineer, most of that money has been spent opening or upgrading road tracks. Until 2017, there was a ceiling of NRs. 6 million on excavations and embankments of soil and rock that could be performed by UCs. The impetus for the government has been to keep this ceiling low enough to diminish the capacity of UCs to hire dozers, and enforce rules that work done in this modality must engage manual labor and not involve use of heavy machinery. And yet, even before the ceiling on earthworks was raised in 2017 as discussed below, UCs also became involved with contractors and bulldozers.

[13] However, the Supreme Court ordered a halt to the Fund due to widespread criticism and misuse and currently the fund has been discontinued (Bhattarai and Chalaune 2023; Khatiwada 2023).

A key finding from my ethnographic research is that UCs serve as an effective mechanism for political leaders and politicians to fulfill demands and secure the loyalty of political cadres, other followers, and local elites whose support they hope to cultivate. Conversations with local residents, journalists, bureaucrats, and political party leaders themselves repeatedly confirmed the practice of arranging for a UC to "open a track" that was expected to benefit these constituencies. Opening a track means doing just enough earthwork and back-cutting to make it possible for motorable vehicles to pass, and usually denotes eventual use of a bulldozer or other heavy equipment. The owner of a bulldozer explained in an interview that at the grassroots level, the trend was to allocate small budgets to address these so-called public demands, especially the demand for roads to be opened up to the villages of people whose support is needed to sustain ongoing patronage.

"*Tukre* budget" is the Nepali term for parsing local fiscal resources into small and insufficient budgets for road projects. On February 15, 2018, a senior engineer of Dolakha District explained this process to me and my community-based collaborator, Shanta Thapa:

> Our political leaders, I am not blaming them, in the name of addressing public demand, a situation has been created where only NRs. 50 thousand or NRs. 1 lakh are allocated for many rural roads. What can you do with such a small budget for a road? Nothing. That would be spent just to bring and return a machine to a remote village. The entire budget would be finished just by hiring a machine and filling up one ditch.

From an engineering perspective, "*tukre* budgets" make no sense. Donor assessments of the phenomenon similarly question the rationality by referring to the practice of spreading budgets over a large number of small projects as the "sprinkler effect" (The World Bank 2013). But in the logics of patronage politics, *tukre* budgets are intended to do just that, to extend the reach of patronage, and create opportunities for negotiation, *milaune*, among party leaders so that resources are distributed according to some locally agreed conception of fairness.

In practice, *tukre* budgets tend to be expended in a hurry at the end of the fiscal year when local budgets expire, often without following rules and engineering designs. At the same time, these small projects often run out of funds because building a road track from one settlement to another requires more money than what was allocated. Leaders of the UCs themselves admitted that when the allocated budget failed to cover expenses, they did not stop construction, because they wanted to ensure the road reached the targeted destination. Instead they promised the dozer owner that they would pay the fees out of the budget for the next fiscal year. This meant that they built roads bypassing formal processes for selecting projects, reviewing engineering designs, and approving budgets through village or municipal councils. Such roads are ultimately built on credit, *udharo*.

Of course, this is a complete perversion of the original conception of UCs as mechanisms to build roads according to LEP principles. Because they work so much faster, dozers are understood to be more manageable with *tukre* budgets. At the same time, the model requires "participation" to be fulfilled with contributions of cash when UCs engage dozers rather than manual labor. In practice, such contributions are not easy to collect, and the UCs end up documenting participation "on paper" in order to meet requirements, while in practice having to figure out other strategies to meet the budget shortfall (see also Kunwar 2020; Kunwar and Thapa 2020).

The outcome of rural road building in Dolakha through the users' committee modality has entailed an excessive use of heavy equipment, in the very district where local participation and sustainable techniques were first piloted in Nepal. With heavy equipment comes a market for petty contractors, drivers, and technicians required to operate it. A Charikot-based contractor shared his experience. In the

2000s, he said, "no one in Dolakha owned a dozer," so he had to rent one from Kathmandu to open road tracks on behalf of the UCs:

> During the insurgency period, a users' committee needed a dozer to build a road, near the Charikot area. The committee gave us NRs. 50 thousand in advance, and we had to get an additional NRs. 1 lakh on top of that. After arranging the money, I went to Kathmandu to rent the dozer [laughs]. ... We didn't have the dozer, so I had ... to rent [one] and bring it back with me.

He shared that this practice of completing earthwork essentially on credit became common. A lot of the payments are still pending, despite "visiting with" the UC leaders and VDC offices multiple times to ask for it. How did this happen? Why did he do construction work without receiving payment? He explained:

> I don't mean to say that I didn't receive payment from any of the users' committees, but some of them didn't pay. Look, while working on their behalf, I made friends and developed good relations with the [users' committee] leaders in Charikot. We knew each other well. The leaders asked me to do the work, and since we were already friends, how could I deny their request, especially as a resident of this district?

The market for local petty contracting is clearly inflected with social relations and precarious, informal financing, and we can see how it was catalyzed by UCs expending *tukre* budgets on roads. These arrangements allowed the petty contractor I interviewed to open many rural road tracks in Dolakha's southern belt and to profit from the rented dozer. He explained how other small contractors like himself began using rented equipment to build rural roads at the behest of UCs. Now many of them, including himself, own dozers.

Another outcome of such practices has been an extraordinary proliferation of low-quality rural roads. The previously mentioned senior engineer estimated that 1,500 km of rural roads have been built in Dolakha, mostly since 2000.[14] He said that most of them had not been surveyed and graded by road technicians, and lack proper drainage channels:

> Unplanned road construction is a major cause of floods, landslides, and deforestation. This is our trend in road building. ... In our district, 15 roads were selected as part of the District Road Core Network (DRCN) for upgrades, but more than 300 rural roads have been constructed. The total length of major strategic roads in our district is 314 kilometers, with an additional 1,200 kilometers of rural roads.

The reason only 15 roads were chosen for upgrades, he explained, is because maintenance costs are higher than simply opening the track. Most of the rural roads were not built properly, according to engineering designs, so they require even more money for maintenance than usual, and the available budget is not enough to upgrade all existing road tracks.

He continued to explain that most rural roads were built under the leadership of UCs hiring dozers to open the track: in fact, "dozer operators were the actual engineers in the field." This phenomenon is not limited to Dolakha; it has also been observed in other districts such as Morang and Mugu, as described in those chapters of this book. He said this with exasperation and continued:

> To be considered a road, it must be a technically sound and complete structure that meets certain standards, such as a standard grade, proper drainage channels, wide turnings,

[14] For more information, see District Development Committee publications, such as *District Development Bulletins*, and periodic plans for Dolakha District (DDC Dolakha 1999, 2002, 2005, 2013a, 2013b, 2015a, 2015b, 2016b).

> supporting walls, bridges and culverts in the streams. It should also have layers of gravel to provide a strong base, and a layer of pavement, as a cover, to sustain the road surface.

He asserted that the way rural roads are built does not meet the standard, in engineering terms, to operate vehicles. While building the road, great care should be given to technical aspects such as alignment—is there a risk of landslide, rockslide, or does the road go through a fragile or unstable landscape? Building roads haphazardly creates long-term challenges for the sustainability of the road structure and the operation of vehicles. Therefore, a detailed feasibility study is clearly needed before commencing construction. None of these requirements are met in the rushed track openings created by UCs.

CONVERGENCES OF USERS COMMITTEES AND CONTRACTORS

Explorations of the opaque worlds of contractors and UCs suggests some similar practices, even if the models are posed as distinct and sometimes conflict and tension is evident between the actors involved. In the fifth amendment to the Public Procurement Regulation, 2017 (GoN 2017), the Government of Nepal increased the maximum amount of money for earthwork that could be carried out by UCs from NRs. 6 million to NRs. 10 million. This change was significant for two reasons. First, these provisions made it easier for UCs to hire contractors with heavy equipment to undertake certain engineering tasks, rather than being strictly limited to use of manual labor. Second, contracts issued by UCs under the specified ceiling did not have to conform to standard procurement policies requiring open bidding, basic accounting, and auditing. The Federation of Contractors' Associations of Nepal protested this decision on the grounds that it would take business away from them, issuing press releases on March 29, 2017, from Kathmandu and from all district headquarters of Nepal on April 4, 2017. That same day, the contractors' association of Dolakha organized a press meet at Charikot, where the secretary of the association stated, "It is not fair to increase the amount paid for work by the users' committee from any angle. This undermines professionalism and creates a crisis for small contractors. It will increase corruption and irregularities in the users' committees' work." The claim about corruption is tied to the exemption of UCs from the same procurement standards as contractors.

The contractors' association secretary criticized the UC model, echoing concerns of other contractors we spoke with:

> There are many financial irregularities, increasing day by day, and they [the UCs] are irresponsible after construction. Instead of punishing wrong doing, he emphasized that ... the government is promoting policies that support users' committees' misconduct, which is unacceptable to us.

He also argued that increasing the ceiling on earthwork for UCs increases the monopoly of political leaders who distribute benefits to party cadres through UCs without any oversight. He stated that the decision is not in the interest of the country and poses a threat to the country's construction business, which legitimately pays taxes and submits to regulatory control.

I had heard these kinds of arguments before. In a conversation I had on May 23, 2017, in Charikot, a class D contractor who had worked on behalf of UCs shared a similar critique of how they operate in practice. First, there is political contestation around the formation of UCs, mainly a "fight for key posts." He rhetorically asked, "Why are the political cadres or their followers the only suitable candidates?" Because the main logic is *"bhagbanda,"* distributing shares among the groups, in a pejorative sense. Second, he claimed, "They have very little technical knowledge and know nothing about grading and quality materials, so how are they able to build quality roads? Third, he pointed out that collusion takes place between the committees' leaders and government technicians and monitoring committee members, who approve sub-standard work and release funds, as also described in the Mugu chapter. Fourth, he asserted that UCs work only as mediators: they hand over construction work to the contractor, and often bargain, negotiate, and receive commissions from the contractor or dozer owner. Finally, he stated that "the users' committees are not held responsible ... for doing poor quality work."

For their part, UC members insist they are compelled to use dozers due to insufficient budget and lack of volunteer labor among their members and road beneficiaries. The critiques that contractors level at UCs are widely understood to reflect the road building sector more generally. So pervasive is this common understanding that in fact a major national contractor, who was involved in road construction in Dolakha, publicly stated that when contractors win a contract, they are required to pay commissions to officials and consultants (Khatiwada 2018). Contractors with whom I spoke during the research also admitted that they must give personal commissions to various stakeholders, including officials, consultants, local gang members with affiliations to political parties, and politicians in order to secure approval for work. This raises the obvious question of how those who receive commissions could reasonably be expected to monitor the quality of the work. More than any one particular actor acting corrupt, then, the systemic collusion within the available structures for building roads facilitates the planning, conduct, and approval of poor quality work. Underbidding and negotiating shares and turns (*milaune*), *tukre* budgets and building on credit or with a commission, though widely understood to characterize the sector, are extremely difficult to trace, account for, and contest in practice. Everyone, it seems, has a stake, and only the most outrageously public and long-term harms, such as occurred with the delays on the Lamosangu-Jiri Road upgrading, seem to galvanize public protest.

LAND, LANDSCAPE AND BORDERS

Since the 1980s, disputes over land, alignment and compensation have become integral aspects of the road building process, creating borders at different scales in Dolakha District. Borders are articulated in two ways: rights-of-way, which demarcates the border between private and public land; and borders within and between administrative units, districts, provinces, and other countries, since Dolakha has an international border. These borders influence road development practices and the social imaginary. This section focuses on the first kind of border, which highlights the politics of land: its alignment, ownership and value (how it should be compensated when taken for the public purpose of building a road). These are extremely contentious issues.

In agrarian districts where roads are being built so intensively, debates over road routes, known as "alignment," are fundamental to local politics as well as environments. Road alignment debates occur at various stages, from project selection to construction, to upgrading and expansion. In relation to alignment come questions of compensation and relocation of settlements, which also create ripples in the political climate. People often contest these outcomes, leading to displacement and opposition. Marginalized people in particular face pressure to relinquish their land in the name of *vikas* or the public good for the construction of roads. This section underscores how decisions about land, alignment, and compensation are not merely technical or determined by environmental conditions; they are foremost social, political, and economic. It also shows how fundamental elements of the landscape that are now considered normal were determined not only by environmental conditions for the road, but by political ones.

ALIGNMENT DEBATES: SUSPENDED INFRASTRUCTURE

Most local alignment debates are motivated by the desires of different people for easy connectivity and access to markets; more technical criteria like economic feasibility and sustainability do not get much consideration amongst residents. To illustrate these dynamics, I give examples of alignment debates in relation to two specific roads: the Lamosangu-Jiri Road (also discussed in previous sections) and the Dolakha-Singati section of the Charikot-Dolakha-Singati-Lamabagar Road.

Example 1: Lamosangu–Jiri Road

During the mid-1970s, when the Lamosangu-Jiri Road was planned, multiple surveys were conducted to determine the alignment. There were political divisions among regional elites in Dolakha, who tried to influence the alignment for their own benefit. During the Panchayat period, two family clans, the Khadka family in the northern belt and the Upreti family in the southern belt, held political power, significantly influencing alignment decisions. I was told that the Swiss prepared three different surveys for the Lamosangu-Jiri Road in response to lobbying from these factions, in addition to opinions from engineering experts. The first alignment (favored by the Upreti clan) ran through the southern belt of the district, from Mude to Nigale, Serabasi, Kiratichhap, and Jiri, which was shorter than the existing track, but bypassed the district headquarters in Charikot (see HMG 1975). The second alignment followed walking trails through northern Dolakha, mainly targeting Dolakha Bazaar, Singati, Pikhuti, and Hanumante on the way to Jiri; this was suggested as the shortest route that would benefit the Khadka clan based in Singati. Third was the existing road track of Lamosangu-Jiri Road. The existence of these competing potential alignments itself points to the role of politics in such decisions.

A Dolakha Bazaar resident, politician, and ex-elected representative explained to me that during the planning phase, Upretis held positions at both the national and district level in the Panchayat system, and sought to "build the road along their pocket areas," meaning in their vote banks. When they were in power, Upreti politicians themselves were lobbied by Newars to build the road through Dolakha Bazaar, again by claiming this route would be shorter than the one that was eventually built. Meanwhile, the Khadka family were powerful Panchayat leaders in the Singati area, as shared by an interlocutor in that town:

> During the Panchayat period, Dhal Bahadur Khadka, the District Panchayat chair from northern Dolakha, had planned

> to build the road to connect the Singati area. However, he passed away while in office. After his death, power went to the Upreti family of Namdu [in the southern belt], and they changed the road alignment to go through Charikot to Tamakoshi Bazaar [near Namdu] and Jiri. The Upreti family was able to change the alignment because they held positions of power.

Other interlocutors from Dolakha also noted that in the 1970s and 1980s, competing factions of Panchayat leadership and Dolakha's place-based politics played a crucial role in fueling alignment politics. Both Khadkas and Upretis were able to influence road alignment decisions based on their political power.[15] In this way the alignment of the Lamosangu-Jiri Roads was determined and then changed, and changed again. The Swiss wanted to build a road, and yet it was not only environmental conditions but also the nexus of kinship and political power that directed where this major piece of infrastructure would be emplaced on the landscape. Even after the reestablishment of multi-party democracy, the influence of personal political power in decision-making processes continued to persist at the grassroots level, as evidenced by the experience of the Dolakha-Singati Road (Kunwar 2020; Kunwar and Thapa 2020).

Example 2: Dolakha–Singati Road

When the Lamosangu-Jiri Road was being built along the southern belt of Charikot, leaders from the northern belt felt left out. During a visit by the prime minister in the early 1980s, they requested a road survey up to Singati to connect the northern region with the district headquarters in Charikot. In the 1980s, the Charikot-Dolakha Bazaar section of this road was completed, but could not progress further due to conflicts over alignment in addition to lack of finances. A first alignment survey followed the old north-south trade route created

[15] For lists of elected or nominated representatives of Dolakha District during the Panchayat period, see DDC Dolakha (2016a: 118–119).

by horse trails, *ghodeto,* from Dolakha Bazaar to small settlements along the Tamakoshi River, and then upriver to Singati. This survey excluded major settlements on the hillsides on the northwest side of the river through which the currently existing Dolakha-Singati Road is routed. The rationale given for the first survey was that the route from Dolakha Bazaar directly to settlements along the Tamakoshi River was more stable, while the "hillside route," as I will call it, was a landslide-prone area.

However, Dolakha residents discerned another "rationale" for the first survey in the political interests of leaders hoping to help out their relatives living along the *ghodeto* way. Notably, the survey had the road not actually going through the land of the leaders' relatives, but only nearby and instead "eating" the agricultural land of some other residents, who naturally objected to this alignment. One such aggrieved resident told me that the proposed alignment entailed multiple unnecessary turns on his land in order to keep the road off the land of the leaders' relatives.

Other local leaders also objected to the first alignment and proposed another alignment in the late 1980s when the Swiss ambassador visited Dolakha to monitor progress of Swiss-funded development projects in the region. I interviewed the Dolakha District Panchayat representative who had proposed a second possible alignment at the ambassador's invitation. The requirement was to limit the Dolakha-Singati Road to 25 km, and so this second proposal, too, bypassed the major hillside settlements, even though the ex-elected representative had no intention of bypassing those settlements in practice. Soon after, the ambassador died. His replacement showed little interest in a Dolakha-Singati Road, and the District Panchayat was left to build the road with its own limited resources.

After 1990, when multi-party democracy was re-established, Dolakha's first elected DDC representatives again allocated a budget for the road, but alignment debates continued to cause significant delays. Archival records of the minutes from DDC meetings (1992–

1997) show that budgets were allocated but that the road still could not be built due to public protests in the major hillside settlements.[16] According to one protester:

> The vice-chair of the DDC lobbied for the road to be built along the old alignment because he controlled settlements there. But we were against this. We argued that the road should connect the major [hillside] settlements. ... We exerted a lot of pressure; we protested and stopped the road surveyors. To organize our protest and increase pressure, we called meetings of VDC representatives and village leaders ... and we all agreed that the road should pass through the major hillside settlements. We had several meetings with the DDC representatives, district administration, and other stakeholders. ... Finally, we reached an agreement to realign the road through the major settlements.

Thus the post-conflict period (after 2006) saw not only an influx of resources to local governments, but also increased mobilization of residents around matters of collective local concern, which often create collisions between those at the grassroots and those in positions of power or privilege. As the road alignment debate was going on, a major landslide occurred in Sunkhani, located almost at the half-way point of the existing Dolakha-Singati Road in July/August 1996. The landslide pushed aside the debate on alignment and the political leaders agreed to change the alignment to accommodate the major hillside settlements. Road construction work began in 1996–1997, while those in settlements above and below the hillside

[16] Minutes of the DDC meeting document alignment debates and discussions about the construction of the Dolakha-Singati Road: on November 26, 1993 (11/8/2050 v.s) decision no. 1; December 28, 1993 (13/9/2050 v.s.) decision no. 7; July 6, 1994 (22/3/2051 v.s.), decision no. 10; November 7, 1996 (22/7/2053 v.s), decision no. 3; November 25, 1996 (10/8/2053 v.s.), decision no. 1; March 14, 1997 (1/12/2053 v.s), decision no. 3. Thanks to Rudra Bahadur Khadka, the former DDC chairperson, for sharing his copy of the meeting minutes.

alignment collectively protested for the road to be built through their settlements. That contestation led to a public meeting in 2000 held at Sunkhani, which included VDC and DDC representatives, the DDC chair, and the members of parliament of Dolakha District (Kunwar 2018). The leaders were under pressure to complete the construction work as soon as possible up to Singati. In that meeting the leaders assured the protestors that they would subsequently receive a connecting road up to their respective settlements.

Inevitably, once the Dolakha-Singati Road was completed, the fears of those in settlements not on the road that local business would suffer became a reality. The Dolakha-Singati Road significantly transformed transportation in the region and concentrated market activity in Singati, while displacing markets in nearby towns like Gumukhola. This had been a vibrant *hat* open market for northern Dolakha, located on an old walking trail about an hour south of Singati along the Tamakoshi River. Some shopkeepers with whom I spoke in Singati had relocated from Gumukhola and other nearby markets. Previously their families had run retail stores in Gumukhola; most of the goods they sold were locally produced, and porters had been employed to transport them. When Singati became accessible by road, it became the commercial hub, prompting them to relocate there. Moreover, the 2015 earthquakes destroyed their houses in Gumukhola, and they did not receive priority for rebuilding as nobody lived there anymore, with the old market replaced by the new roadhead market in Singati.

After Nepal became a Federal Republic in 2008, the Charikot-Singati Road was further expanded to facilitate development of the UTKHEP. A new track was needed from Singati to Lamabagar. Again alignment politics arose. Singati interlocutors shared how hydro project managers had surveyed a road track above Singati Bazaar to the west of the market center, on the far side of the Tamakoshi River near Laduk. They did so consulting with top-level political leaders of Dolakha who had no concern for the fate of Singati Bazaar. When construction began following the survey design, the residents of Singati resisted, having learned from the experiences faced by Gumukhola residents. Singati residents, led mainly by business owners, blocked the road and warned dozer operators to stop construction work with threats of destroying their machines. The construction work stopped. After the protest, the project management team, political party leaders, and residents of Singati Bazaar held a series of meetings and resolved the alignment debate by agreeing to build the road through the existing bazaar area.

The examples I have discussed indicate that road alignment has been a persistent challenge in Dolakha, with influential individuals playing an outsized role in decision making. During the Panchayat regime, people's ability to protest was limited, but this changed after the restoration of democracy in 1990. Those directly affected by alignment decisions could now demand that their perspectives be heard.

Debates over alignment in rural road construction are common throughout Nepal. Bringing ethnographic focus to the dizzying complexity underscores how alignment becomes yet another cause for delay and sidelining technical concerns about fragile landscapes. It also highlights the opaqueness of the politics even to the studious ethnographer attempting to weave together relationships among kinship, political party affiliation, and locality to understand why the road goes where it does, and how conflicts that underlie its material manifestation on the landscape take shape.

BLURRED BOUNDARIES: LAND POSSESSION, COMPENSATION, AND RIGHT-OF-WAY

The issue of compensation is highly contested as it relates to land ownership. There is, as yet, no provision to compensate the property appropriated for road construction projects managed by UCs. However, in the case of Strategic Road Networks—feeder roads, highways, or access roads for the development of other infrastructure projects—all affected households are supposed to be compensated. In practice, however, the government often tries to avoid providing compensation, especially when upgrading rural roads to strategic roads, on the grounds that it cannot afford to.

Strategic roads in Dolakha had commonly been upgraded from the status of local, rural roads, with funding from development agencies, such as SDC, ADB, and the World Bank. An interesting trend I observed is that the implementing agency, the Department of Roads, circumvented donor expectations about mandatory compensation for landowners, by allowing a logic of *jagga dan* (land donation) to prevail over compensating landowners. The term *dan* (donation) is connected to religious faith in that making a donation is expected to purge sin or confer blessings. Local political elites promote the prospect that donating land for road construction could be considered a form of *dan*, and showcase their own generosity in the same terms, while also noting that society overall benefits from *vikas* (development) and expansion of the public good. This informal practice leaves aside what happens to those who cannot afford to donate their land, or do so at their own peril.

An official from Charikot involved in monitoring road projects explained that donor agencies have expressed concern about discrepancies between their policies regarding compensation and actual practices. For instance, after the 2015 earthquakes, some rural roads were upgraded under the Earthquake Emergency Assistance Project, with ADB funding and technical support from the Swiss government. In these cases, the government allowed political leaders to use the strategy of *jagga dan* or compensated landowners only partially for land appropriated to widen the track.

Political leaders eager to accrue symbolic and political capital seek to expedite road development by pressuring landowners to give up their land even when full compensation is not available. In some cases, this practice of land donation under socio-political pressure causes severe harm, as loss of land can lead to livelihood loss, and in some cases to displacement. During fieldwork along the Charikot-Dolakha bypass road (bypassing the longer, slower existing road from Charikot-Dolakha) built for UTKHEP, I discovered that one family lost almost all their land without receiving compensation. There had been a lengthy debate about the road alignment among settlements. While other sections of the access road for the UTKHEP provided compensation, political leaders in the area of the bypass road decided to give their land without compensation—viewing the road as an opportunity to connect their settlement and gain political support (see Kunwar 2020). They exerted extreme pressure on their neighbors to "donate" *jagga*. One poor elderly landowner was convinced to give up nearly all his land in this process, who ultimately became landless, according to a road UC leader. Political elites prioritized development at the expense of the poor and neither the project nor the government took responsibility. A similar case was reported in the Sundrawati area along the Dolakha-Singati Road. These are just a few examples of how marginalized people can be displaced in the name of development, road building and increasing accessibility.

The official from Charikot noted above attributes the displacements and hardships faced by those who are less well off to the significant socio-political pressure they find themselves under from political leaders to give up their land. In practice, they cannot refuse to do so, nor are they able to ask for compensation. He claimed that some of the families who lost land to the road were in economically disadvantaged and politically weak position, stating "no one stands up to speak in their own favor in front of the political elites." In fact, he emphasized, "this is the responsibility of the government."

Since road upgrading requires enforcement of RoW standards, it immediately implicates all the houses that have been built without observing those standards, although often with the tacit approval of the local municipality. Another occasion for displacement arises when the government enforces RoW standards to accommodate a road upgrading project. The distance landowners must leave between the road and their house varies by the road type: six meters for Lamosangu-Jiri Road and two meters for urban roads in Charikot, for example. While Dolakha may not have the same extent of landless settlers as Morang, encroachment of private homes on public RoWs for road development is certainly extensive. Enforcing these regulations can displace individuals especially in hilly and mountainous areas where flat land is scarce. Some residents, even those who received compensation, argue that these measurements should be reconsidered in regions with limited flat land.

UCs engage in similar practices of pressuring landowners to donate their land, as illustrated by the example of a road in Charikot, the district headquarters. A UC leader explained how he built this road in his area:

> We explained to the public that after this road is built, their land value will increase; we elaborated the benefits, such as the potential for their children to build houses along the road, new business opportunities, and the overall positive impacts in the future. We were convincing, and most of them supported us. However, we faced hard challenges in some places. In response, I also told them that I would build the road without encroaching on their land. I was determined to extend the road up to Deurali, regardless of any protest. ... Eventually ... an elderly couple, who had initially opposed the road, agreed to let us build through their land. We were able to convince them. In cases where elderly people or landowners were not willing to have the road built through their land, we reached out to their siblings, relatives, or children, who understood the benefits. We contacted them, whether they were overseas working or away from home, and explained the situation; and we asked them to persuade their family members in Dolakha to allow the road to be built. Despite many obstacles, we were able to open the road track by convincing those who had initially disagreed.

This narrative highlights the various techniques that UC leaders use to convince and pressure people to donate their land for the road. It shows how road building has become a hegemonic project that is almost impossible to say "no" to. And it shows the imperative for continual acquisition of land; this results in someone having to forfeit a key productive resource in the name of development or future prosperity. I explored the claim that once the road is built, land values will increase, which will in turn make it easier to get loans from banks and other financial institutions. According to local residents, this has not yet occurred in practice. Few farmers are aware of how loan processes work with formal financial institutions. Some farmers near Charikot shared their experiences, mentioning that banks only value land that is accessible by road and require borrowers to show other sources of income in order to underwrite a loan. Many farmers do not have "legitimate" multiple sources of income. They jokingly remarked that "banks only consider cash and do not take into account the amount of grain or vegetables a farmer produces." Obtaining a loan from banks is not easy, they said, "despite our leaders promoting the benefits of road access."

A final set of questions in relation to both alignment and compensation, and rooted in the politics of land, is: "Who is the public? Why do the public sometimes demand the road and sometimes protest it?" A road built in response to public demand may later be wracked by protest over the specifics of its alignment. This is another prominent contradiction that is not lost on residents of Dolakha. The definition of "public" relates to expropriation without adequate compensation. Enforcing a RoW or otherwise acquiring land for road development requires the government to redraw the border between public and private land. But for those whose private property becomes public land for the road RoW, the requirement to then pay taxes that contribute to the costs of maintaining that road is an additional injustice that oversteps the responsibility of private citizens for the public good.

This issue is compounded further by the complicity of the government (and often donors), in approving, or at least not blocking, house development especially in the new markets springing up along strategic roadways, such as Katuwachaur Bazaar, along the Charikot-Dolakha-Singati Road. Many of the buildings being constructed on these public lands are concrete buildings that are built without approval and do not follow building codes. They pose a serious challenge for implementing RoW requirements when the time comes for upgrading the roadway—which in fact we have seen was a significant cause of the years' long delay of the completion of the Charikot section of the Lamosangu-Jiri Road upgrading project. Thus the question of who is a public also demands an interrogation of responsibility and complicity in the complicated mess of land, borders, and landscapes from which the road emerges with uneven effects and benefits.

ENVIRONMENT AND SUSTAINABILITY

This section returns to the problem of excessive dozer use from the perspective of environment and sustainability. It revisits some of the ground covered in the section on Road Organization to emphasize the stakes of road building with heavy machinery. What makes Dolakha so interesting from this perspective is that the Lamosangu-Jiri Road was initially conceived as pioneering and inspiring the "green road" model of sustainable development, but that model has been continually subverted in Dolakha, resulting in extreme, ongoing environmental destruction. It is also ironic that many environmental problems derive not from large-scale earthworks, but from the massive push to expand local budgets on small-scale roads built by the very UCs designed to implement "labor-intensive, environmentally friendly" construction (this issue is discussed extensively in the Mugu chapter as well). That is because UCs in practice hire dozers, who undertake earthworks without engineering guidance or adherence to technical specifications or monitoring.

UCs hire dozers as a result of many factors. On the one hand there is money to spend at the local level after decentralization, but on the other hand, that money is split into small *tukre* budgets that are distributed widely across numerous UCs. That distribution reflects the ambitions of political leaders (connected to or part of user committee leadership) to curry favor with their cadres and voters through road building projects. The UCs have an incentive to engage dozers in part because of the lack of availability of volunteer labor expected for green roads funded by *tukre* budgets (a challenge also described in the Morang chapter), and in part because they often face time pressures trying to complete their road projects before the end of a fiscal year, and dozers are perceived to work faster at less expense. Thus we now have in Dolakha the development of a "dozer-driven" model of road development that overtly fails to meet the requirements of the green roads model (Kunwar 2020; Kunwar and Thapa 2020; Rankin *et al.* 2024). Even as the environmental impacts become evident to and debated by local residents, local leaders find a market environment where they can pursue connectivity projects aggressively without caution or control.

It is important to underscore the role of the local government and donors in this transition from green roads to donor-driven roads. In Dolakha, after the 1990s, elected DDC representatives prioritized the road sector, even as they had to contend with all the delays resulting from contestations over alignment and compensation. From 1996 when a dozer first became available in Dolakha, the DDC began constructing the Dolakha-Singati Road. In its second term (1997–2002) the DDC launched a six-year periodic plan for the district's development, with roads as the priority sector. The goal was to establish a road network that would connect village centers across the entire district.

Subsequently, according to the then (1997–2002) DDC chair, the DDC proposed to construct a "ring road" in an environmentally friendly manner, following the Swiss model used in the Lamosangu-Jiri Road in the 1980s:

> During our tenure at the DDC, we did not allow the construction of roads everywhere. We were aware that building roads everywhere could damage the environment and cause landslides in the fragile landscape. Our ring-road alignment

> design was technically sound; we had consulted with technicians, environmentalists, and other experts. In the fragile, hilly, rocky landscape, it was difficult to open the track, and there was no option to change the alignment. In those places, we had to build the road very carefully. The cutting soil was loaded on trippers [dump trucks, used to fill gaps in the road track]. We strictly followed the technical advice and only used dozers in the difficult terrain where human labor could not build the track. However, after our tenure ended, road construction started happening everywhere and became less environmentally friendly, leading to widespread environmental damage and landslides. Little consideration was given to the environment, and the damage was calculated only after the road was built.

The ring road vision was devised to request funding from SDC. The DDC chair consulted with SDC officials and made a presentation for them in pursuit of this goal. The intention was to minimize dozer use, in part because at the time they were a scarce resource. Some district-level road tracks, such as the Dolakha-Singati Road (which was part of the ring road vision) were built by mobilizing local labor through the Food for Work program, supported by the World Food Programme (WFP), the German Technical Cooperation Agency (GTZ), and SDC. However later, once the track had been opened, the DDC used a dozer to widen the road track to facilitate vehicle operation.

The pace of rural road construction in Dolakha skyrocketed after the 2006 People's Movement and peace agreement between the Government of Nepal and the Maoists, as also reported in the Morang chapter. Since then, as claimed by local government officials and corroborated by my review of DDC bulletins, each fiscal year "half of the development budget" has been spent on dozers to build rural roads, creating a boom in the dozer business. It is crucial to highlight how hazardous road construction was using this modality. As previously indicated, many roads were built by UCs on credit, before a budget had been allocated (so confident, and connected, were UC leaders), and without obtaining approval from the government office. Many of those roads were simply washed away in the next rainy season.

Our interlocutors shared that many rural road tracks were already built before the particular road project in question was budgeted by the relevant village or district council. They explained that UCs had arranged all the paperwork (*kagaj milaune*), including approval of the budget for the following fiscal year through village and district councils, and had to guarantee future payment for the dozer with the consent of political party leaders (also see Mugu and Morang chapters). Consent comes easily, as party leaders want to ensure that requests for approvals from their own cadres and associates receive easy approval from other party leaders. As a result, rural roads are built without engineering surveys, designs, or proper monitoring. A journalist based at Charikot, who was involved in the district-level monitoring team, accused the technicians and officials of not staying on top of specific technical issues of road structures and standards:

> They just managed all the requirements on paper treating them as ritual procedures of bureaucratic process; they sought commissions, estimated budgets, and approved the billing process. As a result, users' committees did not have to take technical issues seriously, such as road grading and drainage channels.

Interlocutors stated that UCs used dozers to open tracks for almost 99 percent of the existing roads in Dolakha.

Engineers had an apt term for the situation: they said cynically that dozer operators and UC leaders have become engineers. This is now common understanding, as I was involved in many informal discussions in tea shops and other public spaces where interlocutors expressed the view that dozer operators do not know or care about grade levels, nor do they understand the geological situation. They simply construct the road track and claim that vehicles can run on it. But, as a senior engineer in Dolakha put it, "construction of roads without proper planning and study in the hill region leads to soil erosion and landslides." Dozers cause vibrations, destabilizing steep slopes and increasing the risk of soil erosion and landslides.[17] Singati Bazaar has made national and international headlines since 2015 for the constant news of landslides on the hillside route of the Dolakha-Singati-Lamabagar Road, some of which I myself have observed.

CHALLENGES FOR HIMALAYAN ROADS: LANDSLIDES AND FLOODS

To address the problems of landslides and floods I begin with a story involving a conversation with a hotel owner in Singati on July 30, 2017. She shared her experience of floods and landslides in the area where she had been living for over three decades. There is "always a huge threat of landslides and floods here," she said as she described a flood that swept away her paddy fields and caused destruction to the lives of people and animals along the river. When she first arrived in Singati about 30 years earlier, it was less densely populated, with only around 10–15 houses. Prior to construction of the motor road, Singati was a small *hat* bazaar and a transit point for northern Dolakha District along the old trade route to Lamabagar and Lapchi at the Nepal-TAR border. She remembered when rumors started circulating that a road would soon be built to connect Singati with Dolakha-Charikot, and after 1993 people gradually began buying and selling land in anticipation, leading to an increase in settlements on both sides of the river. It was not until 2003 that Singati was connected by motorable road, and the hotel owner astutely noted that despite its commercial vitality, "Singati remains a vulnerable place," always at risk of natural disasters. She described an event that happened in July 1996, after heavy rains caused landslides and flooding that took many lives and destroyed millions of rupees worth of property along the river:

[17] See Pradhan *et al.* (2022) and Rosser *et al.* (2021) for further details about the interaction between road construction and landslide in Nepal.

> I was with my two small kids. ... It was a terrible situation. ... My husband wasn't at home, and we were joined by an elderly woman who was traumatized because her husband had been killed earlier that day. It was late evening, and we had to move up to the hillside as the floodwaters were entering all the houses. I only carried a bit of money and left everything else behind, with the door standing open. People were shouting that the river had been blocked by landslides. It was entirely dark; we couldn't see anything, which was very frightening. ... We had a difficult night, and the next morning we discovered that the river had been blocked at Bhorle Basi, along an old walking trail north of Singati. Our paddy field had been washed away, and our house was half destroyed. Later, we built a new house near the roadside. ... I'm amazed to see that people are still taking the risk and building houses on the river's edge.

During our conversation, the hotel owner repeatedly compared the flood and landslides to the devastating earthquakes of 2015, claiming that "Singati is not a safe place to stay." She mentioned a landslide that occurred after the earthquakes, on the opposite side of the Singati River in Bigu Rural Municipality, next to her hotel, and believed these kinds of disaster could strike again at any time.

The Charikot-Dolakha-Singati Road had become a major infrastructure development in the region, leading to the construction of many linking roads. Indeed, on September 12, 2019, landslides destroyed the road and many houses, and disrupted business in the southern part of Singati, adjacent to Kalinchok Rural Municipality, once considered the safest area of town. I went there to observe and talk with the local residents, who said that this disaster happened because of the poorly constructed linking road leading from the bazaar up to the villages of Kalinchok Rural Municipality. The residents explained that at the end of the summer season, heavy rainfall caused water to flow along a newly constructed earthen road due to the lack of a drainage channel. The accumulated water eroded the road track, leading to floods that burst just above the southwestern part of the Singati Bazaar. The flooding destroyed private properties and blocked the Singati-Lamabagar Road, and exposed a public school and health center above the market to landslide risk. Residents blamed the UCs for using a dozer to "empty the allocated budget" for widening an existing road track without constructing proper drainage channels. They reported that the monitoring team who came to check the quality of road had not questioned the poorly done work and approved the billing.

Again, on August 10, 2022, a devastating landslide destroyed Kholikhem Bazaar in the northwest part of Singati. Local residents I interviewed and subsequently talked with over the phone and accessed their Facebook wall, similarly claimed that the landslide was caused by a poorly upgraded road above the market, which lacked proper drainage channels. They shared that the local government had unnecessarily installed gabion walls in the name of upgrading the road without also constructing proper drainage channels to manage rainwater and prevent landslides. The landslide destroyed houses, businesses, public spaces, and the bus stand.

The 2015 earthquakes severely damaged Singati. Journalist interlocutors shared that a group of experts who subsequently studied the area classified Singati as a high-risk zone; the experts suggested relocating the settlement and market, but that did not happen. Singati residents criticized the government for not properly responding to the experts' report and for not allocating grant money in a timely manner. In fact, the government stopped disbursing the second tranche of house reconstruction grants to local inhabitants of Singati for some time.[18] In the space of inaction regarding relocation

[18] After the devastating earthquake in Nepal in 2015, the government provided house reconstruction grant support to nearly 1 million affected households in 14 districts, including Dolakha, one of the hardest-hit areas. The government announced that vulnerable households would receive NRs. 3 lakh in three installments for reconstruction of their houses (see Shneiderman *et al.* 2023). Singati was a focal point as the government first announced the reconstruction program there in 2016. However, an expert team recommended

of settlements, local people began building large concrete buildings despite the threat of future disasters.

Photo 2.4: Upgrading work on the Lamosangu-Jiri Road, involving widening in landslide-prone areas at the Mude-Charikot section near Sakhine, Boch (photo by Shyam Kunwar, 2017).

The landslides and flooding described in this section relate directly to the proliferation of road building following the opening of the Charikot-Dolakha-Singati Road as a major infrastructure development in the region, which also led to the construction of many small link roads. It is also clear that in addition to UCs and political leaders, the general public and government officials play significant roles in producing an environmental crisis. In general, the

---

to relocate the settlement from Singati, categorizing it as vulnerable. Instead of addressing this recommendation, the government halted the distribution of the second installment of grant money to those who had already received the first. With political lobbying, local residents and journalists recounted that the housing funds were eventually distributed.

public takes note of the environmental effects of roads, houses and other infrastructures only after construction is complete, when they personally experience dust, mud, land erosion, landslides, floods, and other hazards. Meanwhile, they tend not to question the promise of roads for economic development and future prosperity, even though poorly constructed roads continuously damage agriculture, forests, water resources, and irrigation channels. On the contrary, some homeowners contribute to the risk by building houses on vulnerable lands next to the river or in landslide-prone locations. For their part, technicians continue approving poorly constructed roads that are a leading vector of environmental degradation and crisis due to political pressure.

TRANSPORT AND MARKETS

Road development is not limited to road construction; significant developments transpire after construction, especially in relation to the organization of transportation resources. Dolakha District once again proves iconic in Nepal, both for the extent of its market in transportation services and for the conflicts associated with the syndicate system that particularly characterizes bus transportation. The influx of banks and finance companies in conjunction with road development in fact made it easy for people in Charikot to obtain loans to purchase vehicles, leading to a boom in the market for private vehicles. And yet, participating in the market for transportation services has been anything but easy. On the one hand, the government has tried to regulate transportation services in order to manage traffic pressure; on the other hand, informal and powerful bus syndicates quickly established control over the roads, thwarting government efforts as well as market competition. This section tells the story of the struggle to establish a new transportation association in Dolakha, including the contested registration process, ensuing protests against an existing monopoly, and physical fights over the right to operate public vehicles.

Public transportation services in Nepal are overseen by the Department of Transport Management (DoTM), and managed by the *yatayat samitis* (transportation committees), which were originally registered as non-profit organizations to ensure smooth operation of vehicles and welfare of transport entrepreneurs. Gradually, these associations started operating as syndicates. In 2018, the government scrapped the associations to challenge their monopolies, and required transport companies to register as private limited companies under the Company Act.

The government itself does not operate public vehicles, but the DoTM is responsible for managing the transport services sector, including vehicle registration and route permits through its branch offices at regional and district levels. Traffic police units manage traffic on the road. The transportation associations play a key role in providing transport services to the public. Transportation associations practice *alopalo pranali*, also known as *chakriya pranali*, a rotation system, amongst themselves. This means that buses and sometimes other vehicles providing transportation services can only operate as part of an association, which controls their movements on a route for which it holds a permit; when multiple associations exist on a given route they negotiate how to rotate access. Often an association seeks to establish dominance on a route, or even monopoly control, and the English word, *syndicate*, is used to characterize these dynamics. A key motivation of the associations is to ensure that their investors can recoup their investments, and thus keep the association in business.

THE PERILS OF SYNDICATES

Before delving into the processes and struggles of an association in Dolakha District, I want to share an experience that highlights how the syndicate system affects public bus services. As a passenger, my experience provides insight into how service providers operate public vehicles and raises questions about the role of transportation operators and government entities in ensuring road safety.

On April 22, 2022, I was traveling back to Kathmandu from Charikot on a bus operated by the Rolwaling Transport Association. The bus was not full due to impending local elections. The bus driver was driving slowly along the road up to Khadichaur, at the juncture of the Araniko Highway and Lamosangu-Jiri Road. Construction upgrading works were ongoing, so the road was not smooth. He was likely looking for passengers. It was late afternoon when the bus crossed Lamosangu bridge and entered the Araniko Highway. The driver then increased speed, mentioning that "a bus is following us," which I also noticed. That scared me given the narrow road.

Later, I learnt from interlocutors in Khadichaur that the Rolwaling Association is not permitted to carry passengers from Khadichaur up to Kathmandu. The Khadichaur-Kathmandu route falls on the Bahrabise route, operated by the Araniko Public Transportation Association. After crossing two hills along the Araniko Highway toward Kathmandu, my bus stopped to pick up passengers who had signaled to it. The other bus, a member of the Araniko Association, sped in front, honking aggressively and stopped in front of my bus, blocking its path. The driver and staff of the other association's bus began scolding my bus driver harshly, using derogatory words like "*radiko chhora, khana napayera marna lageko chhas*" (roughly, son of a bitch, are you dying for money, you greedy pauper!). The Rolwaling bus driver replied with a subdued voice, "*Hat diyo ta ke garnu?*" (The passenger signaled to stop, what to do?). The situation escalated. The staff of my bus who had just picked up the passengers were nearly physically attacked; they remained silent, and eventually removed the passengers in question, who were then loaded into the Araniko bus.

Both buses then continued along the route. The Araniko bus stopped in the middle of the road to pick up additional passengers in various places, making it impossible for the Rolwaling bus to pass, all the way up to Banepa, a market town in Kavrepalanchok en route to Kathmandu. The journey, which should have taken one hour normally, stretched to more than two hours. Fellow passengers mentioned that such incidents are common. Each association has its own route and does not permit other association's buses to carry passengers on their routes without an agreement in place. Clearly, such speeding, threat of violence, and fighting over picking up passengers raises serious questions about public safety.

The transport associations operate public transportation services not only on highways, but also on the newly built earthen rural roads in Dolakha. They operate vehicles according to their own internal rotation system. According to government policy for the operation of public transportation, two things are important: first, the vehicle should be registered clearly explaining its purpose to operate for public transportation services; and second, vehicles should obtain a route permit from government entities. However, in everyday practice, to avoid conflicts and confrontations, government authorities informally ask transport entrepreneurs to submit consent from a transportation association before they provide route permits. This arrangement de facto enables the transport associations to control access.

On the ground, competition among associations often turns into open contestation: efforts to block vehicles from operating on a given route can lead to physical fights, roadblocks, and vandalized vehicles. The transport associations also stage protests and demand security and compensation from government authorities. Competition becomes outright conflict that harms commuters, regional transport, infrastructure, and everyday life in general. These conflicts are ultimately resolved through negotiation among the associations' representatives, with the involvement of government entities and the Federation of Nepalese National Transport Entrepreneurs (FNNTE) which serves as an umbrella organization of transportation associations across Nepal. The FNNTE plays an influential role at all levels, intervening in everything from policy making to vehicle registration, and determining which associations can operate public vehicles on certain routes. Although it formally holds authority over the transportation sector, the DoTM has been unable to eliminate syndicate practices, regulate fares, or ensure timely services, ultimately failing to deliver goods and services to the public it advocates for.

In practice, the private sector has complete control over public transportation services.

A DOLAKHA INITIATIVE

Before exploring the story of the struggle to establish a public bus association in Dolakha, I briefly describe the public transportation associations that provide bus services in the region. One of the main service providers is *Purva Araniko Yatayat Pra. Li.* (Ex-Araniko Transportation Private Limited), which was formerly called *Araniko Yatayat Sewa Samiti* (Araniko Transportation Service Association) and which I hereafter refer to as Araniko. This organization has been operating buses on the Dolakha-Kathmandu route since the mid-1980s. It was established in 1972 in Banepa, Kavrepalanchok District, after the Araniko Highway opened. Dolakha residents recall that Banepa's bus owners, *Banepa ka sahujiharu,* were the ones who initially operated public buses on the Kathmandu-Jiri route (the Lamosangu-Jiri Road). Since then, the Araniko Association has been providing bus services throughout Dolakha.

In the past, other transportation associations have attempted to operate bus services on the Kathmandu-Jiri route, but Araniko Association obstructed them. Even Sajha Yatayat, a cooperative public transportation organization, was unable to operate buses in the region. After a long hiatus, a new transportation association began operating public buses in Dolakha. The Rolwaling Transportation Cooperative Limited, formerly known as Rolwaling Yatayat Sahakari Sanstha, hereafter referred as to Rolwaling, was established in 2001 by people from the Sunkhani area of northern Dolakha, approximately 18 km north of Charikot. Rolwaling was established after the construction of the Dolakha-Singati Road, because Araniko was not operating vehicles on this road.

After the 1990s, as rural roads were being built, local leaders—politicians, business owners and elites—collectively asked Araniko to begin operating bus services on the newly constructed Dolakha-Singati Road, but Araniko refused due to the poor condition of the road.[19] Local leaders were under intense pressure because much effort had gone into building the Dolakha-Singati Road, going back to the Panchayat period. Moreover, they had persuaded people to forfeit their land for the road by promising that transportation facilities would be available. Initially, when Araniko Association failed to provide this service, there was no other organization to turn to.

In this context, a group of people from Sunkhani decided to operate a public vehicle themselves, and went to the DoTM to register this service, but failed. They learned that according to formal policy the vehicle could only be registered under a transportation association, and for that, they needed a minimum required number of vehicles to operate public transportation services. Eventually, DoTM officials advised them that they could register a transportation cooperative under the cooperative division, which would allow them to operate public vehicles.

In an extraordinary local mobilization to improve the conditions of transportation on a base of joint ownership, members of the group sought to establish a transportation cooperative. They collected money by distributing shares to the public in Sunkhani and other areas along the Dolakha-Singati Road, and bought a bus. The idea was that all the shareholders would take ownership of the bus, which initially operated along the Charikot-Sunkhani section of the road. To expand their network, they later distributed shares to people in other areas of Dolakha District, particularly in the southern belt, where people aspired to operate public vehicles on the newly built roads in Dolakha and where Araniko had been denied the opportunity. In this way, the Rolwaling Transportation Cooperative Organization fought Araniko Association's monopoly. Of course, road conditions

[19] On January 25, 2018, a staff member of the association told me that the newly constructed road would be difficult for buses to ply due to the narrow turns. Additionally, they might not be able to make a profit operating vehicles on the earthen road, which would only increase vehicles' maintenance costs. Thus, they would not send their vehicles unless the road was paved. Therefore, they denied local leaders' request to help build the road, stating it was not technically feasible.

were challenging, with poorly built earthen roads, no bridges over streams, and vehicles frequently getting stuck in water and mud. Passengers often had to push the vehicle or use straw stacks to pull it from ditches. The bus journey from Charikot to Sunkhani could take two–three days due to these obstacles. When the road was extended to Singati, conditions remained the same, and it would take three–four days to travel the 34-km-long road from Dolakha to Singati. Local residents shared their experience of the poorly built, bumpy road. They often preferred walking the old trails along the river in the lower belt to taking the bus, despite having put their goods on it, because they could reach Singati faster that way. We can think of these arrangements as a hybrid form of mobility—where people are walking but goods are going by bus—in order to challenge the expectation that going from no road to road changes everything overnight. Rather, as this chapter has repeatedly emphasized, road building is a long-term process and so too are the ways that local people adapt and accommodate change.

Despite the poor condition of the road, several members of the cooperative brought three–four buses and operated them under the auspices of the association using a queue system. In this rotation system, all the association's buses have a scheduled departure time. They take turns based on the schedules posted by the association, and cannot ply buses outside the schedule. Association staff manage and control the schedule and sell tickets based on the time sheets. Sometimes, they add extra buses to accommodate high passenger volume, especially during festivals.

As the road was gradually upgraded, Araniko expressed their desire to operate their vehicles along this route, which raised tensions in Dolakha.[20] Rolwaling leaders asserted that Araniko would not allow them to ply their vehicles along other routes, so they attempted to

[20] Officials and entrepreneurs of Araniko in Charikot were hesitant to share details. In response to my questions they indicated that events that occurred during the contestation between them and Rolwaling were simply normal misunderstandings, and now the relationship is fine. Officials and entrepreneurs of Rolwaling were more open in sharing their stories.

negotiate with Araniko. They proposed that if Araniko wanted to operate their vehicles on the Charikot-Singati Road, then Rowaling's buses should be able to operate on the Khadichaur-Kathmandu route. But they failed to reach an agreement.

In an interview, Rolwaling's chairperson stated that they had sent a bus to Kathmandu around 2003. But when the bus reached Dolalghat, a riverside town in Sindhupalchok, "a group of hooligans mobilized by Araniko" hijacked the bus and hid it for a month. Rolwaling responded by filing a case against Araniko with the police and district administrative offices along this route to locate their missing bus, but they did not receive a response from the police. The chairperson criticized the government authorities' lack of support, saying "it was a serious disappointment of my life with the government entities." After a few days of missing their bus, Rolwaling received a call from Araniko members to retrieve their bus, but again they did not receive police support. "Without the police we would not be able to go anywhere, as anything could happen," explained the Rolwaling chair, and went on to "remind" me that Rolwaling members had been harassed, kicked off buses, and received threats of being thrown into the Koshi River during their trips to Kathmandu. He asserted that their founding chairperson and other leading members had been attacked by *gunda* (hooligans or henchmen).[21]

[21] The term *gunda* was frequently used in the election campaigns and rallies during my observations in 2017 April; I had a sense that *gunda* work in groups and can be experienced as life threatening. Given this vague understanding, two things seem crucial. One, Araniko has been operating public vehicles since the Lamosangu-Jiri Road was built in the region, so they have a stronghold—many connections along the road and many affiliated bus owners who can be mobilized as gangs to vandalize their opponents' vehicles and threaten their leaders and workers. Two, political violence can be intense in Dolakha, as is well documented during election periods—for example the killing of a local political cadre during the 2017 election was covered by national media while I was doing fieldwork there (Lohani 2018; The Kathmandu Post 2018a; Kantipur 2024). My interlocutors shared that in every election, violence occurs, including killings, looting of ballot boxes and capturing of opposition leaders or cadres. They commented that the police forces also struggle to perform well in these cases. As the Dolakha region is well-connected to Kathmandu, that also makes

Finally, after a month, they retrieved the bus, which had broken windows and was completely vandalized. The bus was repaired and operated locally on the Dolakha-Singati Road for some time.

Despite these struggles, the chairperson stated that Rolwaling added two to three buses, and attempted to obtain a route permit from the DoTM office. However, instead of a route permit, they were required to operate under the *patake* system, a temporary form of route permit that involved paying a certain amount for each round trip through the DoTM office. They also had to obtain permits from the CDO offices for operations on rural roads. This system was a temporary form of management. During this period, the chairperson and other member indicated that Rolwaling vehicles operated without route permits if the government offices did not issue the *patake* permits.

Through their continuous efforts Rolwaling increased their fleet to ten buses, even though they did not receive a route permit until 2006. When they inquired about this with the concerned offices, the officials suggested that Rolwaling needed to reach an agreement with Araniko before the FNNTE could recommend them for a route permit from the DoTM. It is interesting to note that the DoTM, a government entity, requires recommendations from the FNNTE before granting route permits, even if the applicant meets the requirements. This is clearly a political issue. If the FNNTE is the umbrella organization for all transportation associations, why wouldn't they mediate or cooperate between Araniko and Rolwaling, instead of suggesting an agreement with Araniko first, in a situation when both are fighting against each other to operate vehicles on the same route?

Additionally, why would the government entity, DoTM, which issues route permits, need the recommendation of FNNTE if all their own requirements are met? I agreed with my interlocutors in posing these questions. Rolwaling leaders thought that "it is impossible to

---

it easy to mobilize gangs against opponents and escape undetected amidst the high flow of mobility in and out of the district.

negotiate with Araniko." Then they made a plan during the 2005 Dashain festival. Rolwaling leaders with the support of local people captured a few of Araniko's buses and hid them in the bushes of Gairimudi in southeastern Dolakha, as a form of protest against Araniko domination. In response, Araniko filed a lawsuit against the Rolwaling's leaders for vandalizing their buses. Rolwaling's leaders responded that this was in retaliation for Araniko's capture of Rolwaling's bus back in 2003 and for various other troubles, such as blocking their way at Tinkune in Kathmandu or in Dolalghat on the way to Kathmandu from Dolakha.

Rolwaling also led a 19-day protest against Araniko's high bus fares at Charikot and all over the district. During the protest, they staged *banda* and *hadtal* (different forms of strike tactics), meaning they called for a halt of all public transportation services and blocked roads in the district. When Araniko ignored the strike call, protestors vandalized more than two dozen Araniko buses. FNNTE responded by coordinating a process for lowering bus fares. The Rolwaling chair could then claim that no one, including the government, could lower the high bus fares, but Rolwaling's movement succeeded in doing so.

After this protest, a meeting was held to resolve the long-standing conflict between associations, and Araniko agreed to talk with Rolwaling, but not in Dolakha. Instead, the meeting took place in Mude, a Sindhupalchok market located close to the border between the two districts. Rolwaling's chairperson doubted that "Araniko had genuinely agreed to talk with us," because he explained that, "in the past, Araniko had mobilized hooligans to disrupt our presence at a public talk program called *Sajha Sawal* (Common Questions)," which had been intended to allow the public to express their desire for healthy competition in the public transportation sector. Having learned from past events, the chairperson recounted that the Rolwaling team went to Mude with two full buses of people prepared to fight if anything went wrong. He explained:

> The meeting was arranged at a resort in Mude, where representatives from Araniko and the FNNTE were present. ... We discussed various issues, with one of the main topics being route permits. The representatives from Araniko stated that they would agree to a route permit for Rolwaling to operate the Dolakha to Kathmandu route if the FNNTE took responsibility to issue it. The FNNTE representative indicated that they would write a recommendation letter to the Department of Transport Management to grant the route permit.

After this agreement was reached, the representatives of Rolwaling went to Kathmandu and requested the recommendation letter from the FNNTE. As the chairperson elaborated, there were many twists, turns and dramatic events that unfolded that week. The first response was that "the FNNTE needed to call an executive committee meeting and agree to write a recommendation letter," but "an executive board member and vice-chairman belonging to Araniko stood against the meeting," contrary to the Mude agreement. Rolwaling representatives went to the FNNTE office to follow up and realized after a few days that the executive meeting had not yet been called, so they pressured the FNNTE to call the meeting soon. Eventually, the FNNTE did convene. The Rolwaling chairperson explained:

> During the first meeting at the FNNTE office, a fight almost broke out. The vice-president banged the table because he didn't want to give us a recommendation letter for route permits. We warned them that if they didn't give us the letter, as agreed, we would resume our strike to halt public buses in Dolakha. We questioned their intentions because they had agreed to this at the Mude meeting, but now they were backing out in Kathmandu. ... We waited two days and then gave an ultimatum of three days and returned to the office on the third day. However, they hadn't called their senior vice-president

> who was against us and the FNNTE officials, and the president kept delaying with various excuses. It was becoming late. By evening, they had shown no sign of giving us the recommendation. An FNNTE representative stated that there was no electricity, so they were thinking of postponing work until the next day. Hearing that, we were enraged. We locked the president's office from the inside and demanded they either write the recommendation letter on the spot or give us reasons why they couldn't. Our team of five–seven people continued pressuring the president. Around 9 p.m., we lit a candle so we could see, and the FNNTE president finally wrote a letter for the route permits for 12 vehicles.

All these conversations seem as much like a fairy tale to me as to my interlocutor. The Rolwaling chairperson shared his feeling of relief when they finally received a recommendation from FNNTE after these many struggles. It was like "a medicine to alleviate a long-term pain in the body." Obtaining a route permit from the DoTM office was a joyous moment despite worries about the next step. Rolwaling has been operating vehicles more confidently on the Dolakha-Kathmandu route since then.

Tensions persist, however. Araniko began using other strategies to hinder Rolwaling's bus services in Dolakha. For instance, they offered free registration to Rolwaling's bus owners in the Araniko association, which had previously charged bus owners NRs. 3 lakh per bus to operate under its auspices. The goal was to eliminate Rolwaling as a competitor. As a result, some Rolwaling buses did join Araniko.[22] Rolwaling continued expanding its fleet, adding five–seven new buses every Dashain, despite Araniko's attempts to subvert their growth. New Rolwaling owners were motivated by the greater number of operating days it offered with a registration fee that was still considered low. Now, Rolwaling operates public vehicles at

[22] During that time, Rolwaling charged a registration fee of just NRs. 10,000–20,000, because they were a new organization.

a similar scale as Araniko, although they still sometimes come into conflict with each other, as my own experience shows.

Another incident occurred in 2023, when Kathmandu Metropolitan City issued a rule requiring all long-route public vehicles to operate from the New Bus Park in Gongabu, Kathmandu. Rolwaling adhered to this rule, but Araniko Association refused to comply and established a separate bus stand at Jadibuti; it also chased Rolwaling vehicles, drivers, and staff, obstructing them from stopping for passengers in the Koteshwor area en route to the bus park. In response, Rolwaling protested against Araniko's dominating behavior by halting all public vehicles in Charikot, Dolakha. An agreement was eventually reached to stop chasing Rolwaling vehicles in Kathmandu. This incident indicates that Araniko is still attempting to enforce its monopoly in the public transportation sector.

This account of bus service in Dolakha tells another story of dysfunction in road development. Many actors are involved, each with their own account and stake. Although I did not include interviews with DoTM officials in my research, it seems reasonable to state, as have countless media reports (Kantipur 2016, 2024; The Kathmandu Post 2018b; Lohani 2018) that the state has failed to effectively manage and control public transportation and traffic. This failure extends to managing syndicates. Even if the government now charges higher taxes under the Company Act, it has failed to end syndicate control in public transportation as promised in 2015 (Kantipur 2016). Syndicates are simply continuing under the private company banner.

Meanwhile, public transportation service providers claim to offer good services, but passengers face numerous difficulties, including lack of timely services, high fares, inadequate seating, and overloaded vehicles on rural roads, leading to frequent accidents. These problems burden the public, while service providers prioritize profit over public service. What is also clear from these accounts is that road development is a gradual process that extends beyond building roads to evolving transportation systems. Again we see evidence of innovation and adaptation on the part of local residents to engage with these processes in ways that are responsive to local needs and livelihoods—whether through the extraordinary initiative to form the Rolwaling association as a cooperative to make newly opened tracks accessible to locals, or in the way residents engaged Rolwaling's services in a hybrid fashion, to transport their goods while staying safe and reaching their destination faster by opting to walk on the trails.

I end this section with a caveat that points to the subject of the concluding section. Throughout the chapter, I have refrained from attributing a role for particular political parties in road conflicts. On the one hand, the involvement of political parties is not always clearly visible. On the other hand, in my experience in Dolakha, there is no sector where political parties are not involved. Political parties' influences can be seen if we look at where their members and cadres are placed within, for example, transportation associations, or the alliances forged by their umbrella organization. I hope in the chapter I have provided a flavor of these dynamics. Given the fraught nature of the transportation sector, I have tread lightly on the dimension of party politics.

POLITICS, POLITY AND PLANNING

The concluding section considers planning both as an object of inquiry and a field for thinking about how some of the complex problems the chapter has highlighted could be viewed as opportunities for change. It discusses the contradictions with actually existing planning, how these processes are inflected with politics, the environmental harms and dangerous conditions that result, and how resources can be identified for more just and equitable planning.

PLANNING CONTRADICTIONS

Dolakha District has witnessed a transition from green road development to dozer-driven development. The Lamosangu-Jiri Road was built as an experiment serving as a precursor to the development of the "green road" model in Nepal. It aimed to mobilize local manual labor and local materials based on a principle of environmental sustainability to avoid use of destructive heavy machines. The model proliferated through rules and regulations for road construction led by UCs. Fast forward to the time of our research and we have a situation where UCs deploy dozers to open technically unsound and environmentally damaging tracks all over the landscape. Contractors criticize the diffusion of responsibility for road building to those who lack technical expertise, but they line up to do the UCs' work.

Budgets have been progressively decentralized to support planning at the local level and yet they are often divided into small pieces that allow for extensive track opening projects all over the district. UCs choose dozers to quickly clear the land and circumvent the challenges of mobilizing volunteer labor and/or the cash donations that can serve as a substitute but are difficult to raise. They often expand their budgets quickly at the end of the fiscal year or commit budgets from the subsequent fiscal year so that some tracks are effectively being opened on credit. Meanwhile, decentralized budgets also create opportunities for contract tendering, but this process is subverted by underbidding and various modes of collusion among the contractors that cause excessive delays and aborted work. In all cases the outcomes are substandard roads and significant environmental degradation, which government officials have either had a hand in approving or have been ineffective at correcting. The principle of decentralization also informs a model of transportation management that distributes responsibility for service provision to local associations. But similar patterns are evident: poor service, dangerous roads, unregulated competition, and ineffective oversight.

HOW PLANNING IS INFUSED WITH POLITICS

In Nepal "politics" often denotes political parties, and it is impossible to understand planning contradictions without considering the role of political parties. It is ironic that after the very people's movements of the 2000s that sought to secure more democratic planning processes, in fact political parties were empowered to play a greater role.

After the 2006 peace agreement, when there were no local governments for years as the transition from monarchy to federal republic was worked out, political parties agreed to establish the all-party mechanism (APM) at the DDC and VDC levels as an ad hoc means of undertaking local governance. Political parties, including Maoist local cadres, were to negotiate over the allocation of local budgets on the premise that they would be forced to reach consensus over priorities across their different perspectives. Of course such an arrangement also lent itself well to patronage politics, as it created an opportunity to use the principle of *alopalo*, taking turns, to use local budgets to reward cadres and curry favor with their constituents. In response to allegations of corruption, the Commission for Investigation of Abuse of Authority directed the government to dissolve the APM in 2010, which was executed by the Ministry of Federal Affairs and Local Development in January 2012.

As logics of *alopalo* and *milaune* are not limited to the APM, not surprisingly, political parties persisted to regard road building as a terrain for fulfilling patronage obligations. These obligations pervade not just decisions around alignment, but also relationships with transportation associations, government officials, and other stakeholders in road development. Residents of Dolakha, including political party leaders themselves, acknowledged that government budgets and resources continue to be divided among dominant political parties—in Dolakha they are primarily the CPN-UML, Nepali Congress, CPN-MC, and Rastriya Prajatantra Party—through *bhagbanda* politics or bargaining over shares. Ultimately, the phenomenon of *tukre* budgets is the product of consensus politics and budgetary decentralization policies after the 1990s. Bureaucrats, technicians, and engineers play their part by approving substandard road projects, allocating budgets to contractors and UCs known to be breaking the rules, and failing to monitor outcomes.

Another way politics also infuses road development can be seen in how existing distribution of wealth and power are reproduced. For example, when political leaders seek to persuade residents in marginal or precarious conditions to give up land for their road building projects, they are perpetuating relations of political and economic power—with real material consequences of displacement in some cases. These patterns can also be detected at a more geopolitical scale. Donors have played key roles in advancing road development in Dolakha District. But they have also, like government officials, stood by while inequitable processes repeatedly unfolded—not just road alignment conflicts, but shoddy contracting and absurd delays that saddle residents for years with inconveniences and hardships like dust and mud.

RESOURCES FOR PLANNING

At the same time, ethnographic evidence from Dolakha also points toward some interesting resources for a more equitable and just approach to planning road development. Foremost is the local knowledge about the specific ways that collaboration, collusion, embezzlement, and other illicit practices operate at different sites within the district. Understanding how things work in practice and how those processes relate to undesirable outcomes is a key first step to making change, and my research shows how Dolakha residents have such critical insights. The occasions in which they protest unjust outcomes show how such local knowledge can take a collective and public form, that pushes against the hegemonic power of established institutions like contracting, consulting, engineering, government agencies, and political parties.

Some specific examples of how local knowledge could inform more equitable planning processes include: making alignment decisions based on the capacity of landowners to absorb loss of private land without facing displacement or other harms; promoting the kinds of cooperative arrangements that allowed the Rolwaling association to initiate providing services in the face of a powerful monopoly; recognizing the hybrid nature of how people navigate transitions created by infrastructure development—such as by combining upgrades for walking paths in the transition stages when it still takes a bus longer to reach its destination than it does for a person to walk. The obstacles of course remain in entrenched local institutions and practices. However, local knowledge and experience furnish critical resources for transformation, and practices of protest suggest there is also a constituency for change.

MUGU

Illustration by Shushank Shrestha

CHAPTER 3

The Politics and Practice of Road Building in Mugu: Collusion, Consensus, and Critique in Imaginaries of a Connected Future

PUSHPA HAMAL AND TULASI SHARAN SIGDEL[1]

INTRODUCTION

Mugu District is located in the Karnali Province of northwestern Nepal, which is typically characterized as remote. In terms of topography and climate, it is mountainous and mostly arid, making agricultural production, as well as road building, a genuine challenge.

[1] Author names are in alphabetical order and both have contributed equally. Pushpa Hamal is Assistant Professor (CLTA) at the Ontario Institute of Studies in Higher Education where he teaches graduate courses on social economy and qualitative methodology. His doctoral dissertation in Adult Education and Community Development addresses road development as a terrain of community learning and activism, which is referenced extensively in the chapter. Pushpa grew up in Mugu District and maintains many relationships there, including with journalists, filmmakers and leaders in the theatre arts community, who inspire him with their critical analyses and dedicated activism. Tulasi Sharan Sigdel has strong networks in the Nepali civil service as he has worked at Nepal Administrative Staff College since 2010, now as Senior Director of Studies. In Mugu, as in virtually every other district in Nepal, he has personal ties with administrative leadership, which assisted us in accessing insights of the "local state," as well as understanding current and historical regulatory frameworks. Tulasi also publishes regularly in Nepali periodicals regarding the themes of infrastructure development and state restructuring.

The late arrival and poor quality of roads in Mugu, in turn, is often explained in terms of the challenging topography. In this chapter we argue that topography alone cannot explain the poor quality, and instead emphasize cultural politics and political-economic factors—which, we suggest, must also be addressed in order to achieve more just and sustainable development outcomes. Patronage dynamics associated with the Panchayat era, and the imposed isolation of the Karnali region vis-à-vis the center of the Nepali nation-state since its unification, have not diminished with the arrival of roads; rather, patronage dynamics have been integrated into road building processes. Roads in Mugu, like in Morang and Dolakha, are not just a physical infrastructure; they are also integral to processes of market formation, livelihood strategies and food security. Because they involve so many people and impact just about everyone, roads also play a key role in forming development imaginaries and political subjectivities—which also must be understood and engaged in any effort to make roads accessible and equitable.

This chapter makes several key arguments about how road building catalyzes not only infrastructural transformation, but shifts in economic and political subjectivity. These processes work through both modalities of contracting and user groups. Our material shows how what is imagined by donors as the field of "local governance" is in fact the domain of political parties, who exercise their influence at every stage of the road building process. These dynamics unfold through the material logics of how the road becomes territorialized on the land and embedded in social relations; we refer to these material logics as alignment, expropriation, and encroachment.

Nonetheless, compared to Morang and Dolakha, we find in Mugu a relatively more participatory process, structured by closer donor involvement, especially through the Rural Access Program, Phase 3 (RAP3), and local NGO involvement in the users' group modality. People's engagement is enhanced through well-paid work, as opposed to voluntary contributions, training in alternative technologies, and provision of necessary tools. Under these conditions people believe deeply in roads as a public good, and are willing to contribute land to their realization. Despite these desires, residents are aware of the relationships between social and environmental sustainability, and often critical of specific road building initiatives that result in greater destruction rather than the imagined development benefits. Such critical reflections constitute knowledge resources that can be mobilized in planning processes to yield more desirable outcomes, in Mugu and beyond.

DISTRICT CONTEXT

Bordering Kalikot, Jumla, Bajura, Humla and Dolpa Districts, and also the Tibet Autonomous Region (TAR) of China to the north, Mugu covers an area of 3,535 square kilometers. Mugu District in local parlance is generally categorized in four belts (*bheg*), which form the basis of the current administrative municipality designations: Gama (Chhayanath-Rara Municipality), Soru, Khatyad and Karan (Soru, Khatyad and Mugum Karmarong Rural Municipalities). Before federal restructuring in 2017, there were 24 Village Development Committees (VDCs) in Mugu, which were consolidated to form the current four administrative units. Gama, Khatyad, and Soru are populated primarily by Khas Nepali, caste Hindu groups who speak a Khas dialect known as Mugali. The district's political leaders have historically come from these three belts.

Gama is the administrative power center, encompassing the district headquarters of Gamgadhi, within the only urban municipality in the district. Connection to the Strategic Road Network via the Karnali Highway has enabled Gamgadhi to maintain its position as the primary market center for the district. Gama is densely populated compared to the other belts, and has relatively good agricultural production, including rice, barley, and other grains; apple, potato, vegetables, and beans.

Khatyad belt was divided into seven VDCs under the earlier unitary state, which have now been merged to form Khatyad Rural Municipality in the federal structure. The area of this rural municipality

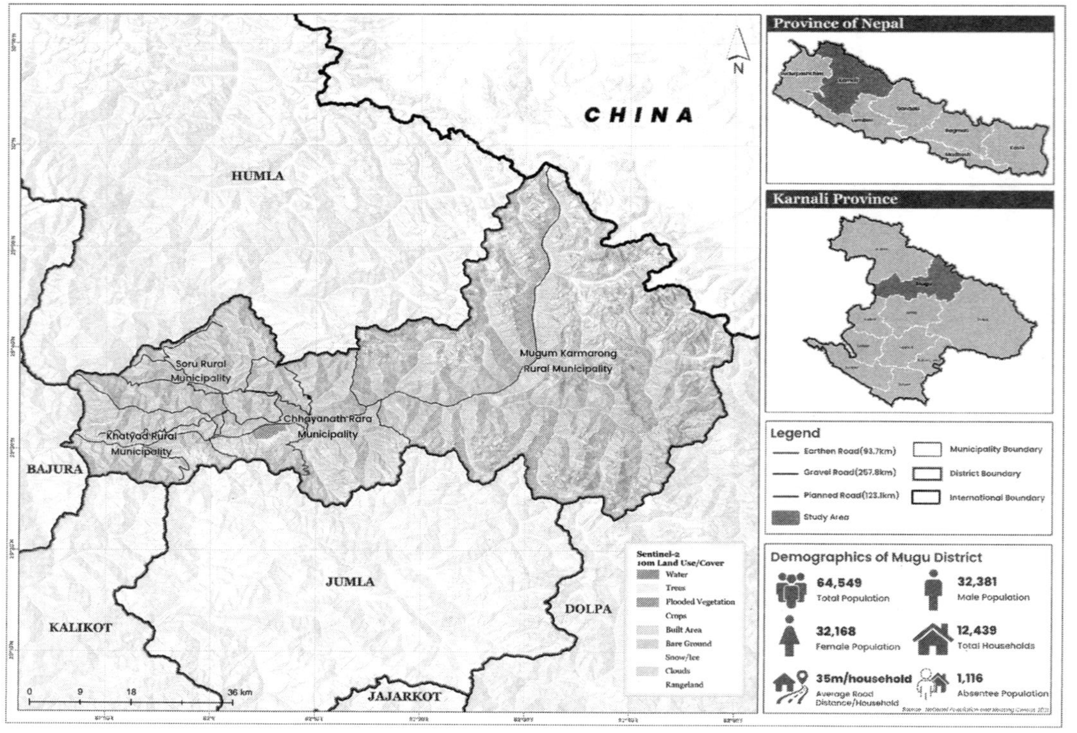

Map 3.1: Location map of Mugu District (map by Naxa.com).

is 281.12 square kilometers, and the total population is 18,832. It has put forward the developmental slogan: "Karnalima Khatyad ra Rara: Krishi, Paryatan ra Sanskritiko Sahara" (Khatyad and Rara are supports for agriculture, tourism and cultural development in Karnali). Geographically, Khatyad is situated to the southwest of Gamgadhi and is second-strongest in agricultural production, including rice, other grains, vegetables, and fruit. It aims to mobilize the agriculture and tourism opportunities for local development and has given due priority for connectivity and infrastructure development, for example, the Khatyad-Rara Tourism Corridor. This characterizes the importance of infrastructure development in the overall development of the region.

Soru lies to the Northwest of Gamgadhi; it is arid and has low agricultural productivity, concentrating more on grains and animals. While all of the Karnali Province, formerly "Region," has long been characterized as prone to food crisis (Adhikari 2024), Soru belt in particular faces regular annual food deficits between March and May when winter crops deplete and before the harvest of wheat and barley (My República 2023). The district continues to receive subsidized rice which is sold out of depots in municipality offices.

Karan/Mugum Karmarong forms the eastern part of the district, stretching northward to the border of Tibet. It is the most Himalayan belt of the district, and therefore agricultural production is largely limited to cold-region grains and potatoes. This region is popularly known for the medicinal herb *yarsagumba*, or caterpillar fungus, which attracts harvesters from all over the Karnali region, and for trade with communities in the TAR. This *bheg* is primarily settled by ethnic Mugum or Bhote people, who speak a Tibetan dialect. The development slogan of Mugum Karmarong Rural Municipality (MKRM n.d.) characterizes the area as rich in the potential for medical herbs, organic agriculture, copper mines and tourism.

The district has a total population of around 64,549 people, residing in a total of 9,600 households, and a literacy rate of 68 percent (NSO 2023). According to the 2021 National Population and Housing Census, the predominant caste and ethnic groups in Mugu District are Brahman/Chhetri (55 percent), Thakuri (14.5 percent), Tamang, Karmarong (Adivasi Janajati residing in 13 villages of Mugum Karmarong), Mugal (Adivasi Janajati residing in the village of Mugum), and Kumal (Adivasi Janajati residing in Soru and Khatyad) [9.4 percent]; and Dalit (20 percent). The Thakuri in Mugu identify as Khas Arya, a reflection of their ruling heritage in the Karnali or Khas kingdoms where the Nepali language is said to have originated.

The long-time aspiration of people in Mugu to be connected with rest of the country via the national road network became a reality in April 2007 when the Nepal Army opened the trunk Karnali Highway (running from Bangeshimal of Surkhet District to Khalanga of Jumla District, and branching north at Nagma to Gamgadhi, the district capital of Mugu).[2] However, Mugu District waited until late 2012 to be connected to the national road network, with the completion of an arm of the Karnali Highway running north from Nagma in Kalikot District to Gamgadhi in Mugu. In other words, the name Karnali Highway is given to both the earlier-constructed trunk highway and the branch that runs northwest into Mugu, as both trunk and branch are located in the Karnali Region, now Province.

Subsequently there has been a flurry of road building projects with the aim of connecting the district's former 24 VDCs to the district headquarters, and road building has consistently figured prominently in district budgets and development priorities. While the federal government is responsible for national priority projects like the Strategic Road Network, the involvement of provincial and local governments in infrastructure development reflects the devolution of these functions and the requisite budgets, beginning in the early 2000s, in response to the democracy movements of the 1990 and subsequently the institutionalization of federal governance.

[2] The former headquarters of the Karnali Zone (before federalization), Khalanga has the largest bazaar of the Karnali region.

Despite this political commitment and construction activity, Mugu is still characterized as one of the most "remote" and "backward" regions in Nepal, according to the National Planning Commission (NPC 2013; NPC and UNDP 2014). However, as we emphasize, this is not only due to challenging terrain. Rather, cultural politics and political economy also play a critical role. Roads remain for the most part narrow, unstable and rough; none in Mugu are black-topped. The danger of traveling on Mugu roads is palpable to all, evident in the reports of fatalities from vehicular accidents (e.g., Karki 2023), as much as in the landslides and associated deforestation and other visible damage to the landscape.

Related to the poor quality of motorable roads in Mugu has been its low human development indicators. According to the 2020 Human Development Report Nepal, Karnali Province has the second lowest Human Development Index in Nepal (after Madhesh Province), the highest degree of income inequality (as measured by the Gini coefficient), the highest level of gender inequality, a literacy rate below the national average for both men and women, and the highest incidence of multidimensional poverty (NPC and UNDP 2020). In 2001 and 2011, Mugu's Human Development Index was among the 5 and 10 lowest ranked districts in Nepal, and in both decades it ranked among the five districts with the highest human poverty index (NPC and UNDP 2014).[3] Food deficits have long hindered health and education. Only about 5.2 percent of the district's geographic area is available for agricultural production (DDC Mugu 2015); productivity is low and focused on subsistence. We heard many stories of severe food shortages in Mugu, and of standing in long queues for rice distribution. Mugu residents also describe having to "knock on doors of political leaders and administrative chiefs," as they put it euphemistically, to seek their favor in obtaining a few kilograms of rice. "Since the road came" (road *aye dekhi),* the food deficit crisis

[3] The Human Poverty Index measures average deprivation in three basic dimensions of human development: a long and healthy life, knowledge and a decent standard of living.

in Mugu has abated because imports have become more affordable. Yet the patronage dynamics related to uneven access to power and privilege remain—they are a key part of our story about road building.

The arrival of the road is recognized as a significant historical moment in Mugu, and much expectation is still vested in the possibility that improved transportation and mobility will also improve the quality of life in Mugu. Trade and tourism are two sectors that Mugu residents anticipate could fuel development of the district facilitated by improved road transport. Political leaders and donor organizations have sought to promote the possibility of high-value agricultural production, such as apples, beans, barley, *yarsagumba* (caterpillar fungus) and other medicinal herbs, and animal husbandry. There is also much anticipation about the possibility of expanding road connectivity and trade across the border to the north, instead of relying on more distant trade centers within Nepal like Surkhet, Nepalganj or Kathmandu. Political leaders have also promoted possibilities for tourism connected to the district's cultural and natural features, like Rara Lake National Park and the Chhayanath Temple.

Like many other districts along Nepal's northern border, Mugu was a significant trading thoroughfare with Tibet since the Khas Malla regime of the 11th–15th centuries. For Bhote communities in northern Mugu, such as Mugum Village, these trade relations remain important. Kings of Karnali used two major trade routes following the Karnali River system; the Mugu Karnali and Humla Karnali.[4] Before China occupied Tibet in the 1950s and imposed strict restrictions on movements across the borderland, people on either side of the border had large flocks of sheep and caravans of yak, and shared the high hill pastureland. Mugum village was mainly a settlement of traders having easy access to the trading depots of Tibet as well as to the grain-growing area of the Sinja Valley in Jumla District, who gained profitable positions in the salt and grain trades.

[4] After the Sinja-based Khas Malla kingdom broke up in the 14th century, Jumla itself emerged as one of 22 principalities or *Baise Rajya*, and remained intact until 1789 when it was annexed to the Gorkha Kingdom. For details, see von Fürer-Haimendorf (1975); also Mahat (2018).

After the unification of Nepal in the latter half of the 18th century, power shifted eastwards with the ascendance of the Gorkha kingdom, according distant Karnali a newly marginal status within Nepal. China's increasing restrictions on cross-border movement after 1950 disrupted Karnali's northern trade routes, and increased its dependency on Nepalganj and Surkhet. People from Mugu accordingly faced higher transportation costs associated with air travel and cargo from Nepalganj and Surkhet, and/or longer routes for porters and mules.

There is thus an important historical dimension to the aspiration for building a strategic road from Gamgadhi to the Tibetan border through Mugum, and the Gamgadhi-Nakchelagna Road, as it is called, has been imagined as a game changer for Mugu's development. The legacy of a closer relation with the TAR remains powerful in local political imaginaries, as expressed in the annual planning commitments of the Mugu District Development Committee (DDC) in 2073–74 v.s. (2016–17). The DDC undertook several initiatives to address problems in transborder trade with the TAR, including requesting the Government of Nepal to coordinate with the Government of China to promote transborder Himalayan trade and address problems of currency exchange, and establishing a "project implementation unit" in Gamgadhi to expedite building the long-stalled Gamgadhi-Nakchelagna Road.

And yet, most of these aspirations remain largely unfulfilled. The Karnali Highway has yet to be paved, and remains impassable during most of the monsoon and winter months; roads within the district are in even worse condition. Transportation services are inefficient and unreliable. The track of the Nakchelagna Road has yet to be opened after more than a decade of contracts having been issued. Food shortages continue to be experienced, especially during the rainy season when roads are blocked, and market linkages with regions to the south are tenuous for the same reasons (Adhikari 2024). Households continue to pursue strategies of labor migration (particularly to India, Surkhet, Nepalganj) to manage these difficult times. Others engage in seasonal trade of medical herbs and livestock such as sheep and *chyangra* (domesticated mountain goats), to destinations as distant as Butwal, Chitwan and Pokhara.

RESEARCH SITES

The 2013 District Transportation Master Plan (DTMP) identified 437 km of roads in its inventory—a figure that includes 194 km of strategic roads (24 km under construction and 170 km planned) and 243.18 km of local roads (19.58 km under construction and 223.6 km planned). We were not able to traverse all of them in our research, but selected four stretches of road on which to focus our attention.

The emphasis of the DTMP is to connect rural municipalities to the district headquarters, Gamgadhi. Plans to build out district and village roads (part of the Local Road Network, LRN) rely on the two modalities of road organization covered in the next section, users' groups and contracting. Typically contracted roads have been managed by the DDC, and "green roads" built by users' committees, while they fall under DDC jurisdiction, have commonly involved government and donor funding, as well as NGO oversight.

Contracting refers to roads built by contractors who win bids on the basis of technical competency and cost efficiency. We learned about the contract system first-hand by witnessing a district road tender in 2017, and through interviews with people in multiple stakeholder positions—from government officials, to major contractors, to petty contractors, to politicians. We did not focus on a specific road built by contractors, but rather sought to understand contracting as a system whenever we encountered events and knowledgeable interlocutors.

Our primary ethnographic site was the 21-km Gamgadhi-Tarapani section of the Gamgadhi-Gilaha-Dhulachaur Road (41.8 km). This was a major donor-funded project underway in the district at the time of our research—as well as the highest priority of the DDC in the DTMP. It aims to open a route to Bajura District through Khatyad belt. With construction beginning in 2014, the project constituted the third phase of the Department of International Development-UK (DfID)-funded RAP, whose aim is to increase road density in the most remote districts; improve livelihood standards and provide jobs through road building; and promote sustainability. RAP roads are "green roads" that conform to a "labor-based, environmentally friendly, and participatory" (LEP) approach to road construction. As of 2016, a local NGO that had contracted with RAP3, Rural Community Development Center (RCDC), had organized 64 groups with 20 members each, employing a total of 1,280 people from villages along the road. The work involves coordination among donors, local government offices, and local residents—and thus furnishes an ideal context for viewing road-building dynamics and relations.

The Gamgadhi-Nakchelagna Road also features in some of our interviews and observations as a strategic border-crossing, national-pride project which features prominently in Mugu road imaginaries despite, or perhaps because of, its delayed completion. Our original qualitative research about Gamgadhi-Gilaha-Dhulachaur and Gamgadhi-Nakchelagna Roads is complemented by historical material about and analysis of two other stretches: the Nagma-Gamgadhi (an extension of the Karnali Highway) and Talcha-Gamgadhi Roads.

ROAD HISTORIES AND CHANGING EXPERIENCES OF REMOTENESS

SURKHET-JUMLA ROAD

Road building in Mugu must be situated in relation to wider regional developments. Nationally, road building has been a priority for the Government of Nepal since the 1950s. However, the Karnali Zone lacked road connectivity until the Nepal Army opened up the Karnali Highway track from Surkhet to Jumla in 2007. Surkhet was at that time the regional headquarters of the Mid-Western Development Region, and Jumla was the headquarters of the Karnali Zone within it.

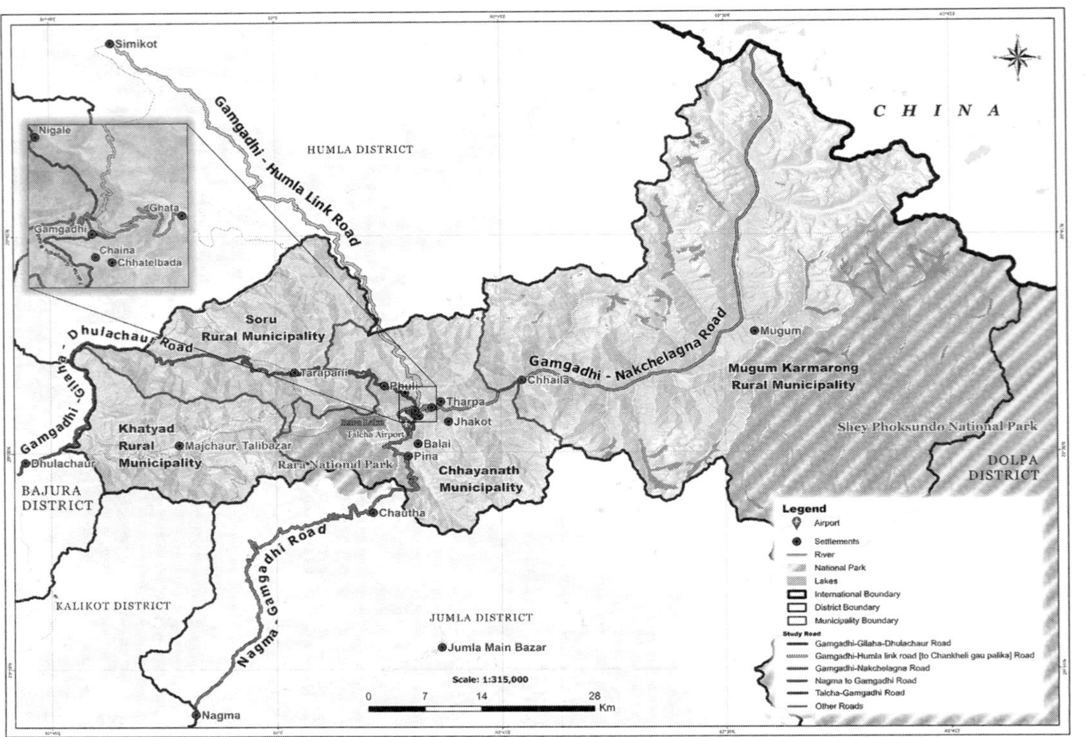

Map 3.2: Road map of Mugu District (map by Naxa.com).

The construction of the Karnali Highway was initiated under the auspices of the 20-year Master Plan for Transport Development (1965–1985) sponsored by the International Bank for Reconstruction and Development. It corresponded well with the government's contemporaneous adoption of a regional planning approach that emphasized the construction of north-south road corridors to integrate regional economies, as well as with King Mahendra's earlier (1955–1972) ambition of pursuing road development as a means of national integration (see Rankin *et al.* 2017). However, it waited for half a century to be completed. Today the Provincial planning report of Karnali Province (2020) characterizes the relatively new highway as a major contributor to Karnali's development.

NAGMA-GAMGADHI ROAD (KARNALI HIGHWAY)

Mugu would remain unconnected to the Strategic Road Network for another five years, second only to neighboring Humla District, which was the last in Nepal. The Department of Roads accomplished the track opening of an extended annex of the Karnali Highway from the village of Nagma in Jumla District to Gamgadhi, the headquarters of Mugu, in 2012. On the one hand, this road manifested an ongoing national drive to connect every district through roads, with Mugu and Humla being the most technically difficult to reach due to topography and distance from Kathmandu. On the other hand, it is significant that the Gamgadhi branch of the Karnali Highway was initiated during the conflict between Maoist and state forces, and completed in the aftermath of the conflict, during the consolidation of the new republic under Maoist government. As such, the Nagma-Gamgadhi portion of the Karnali Highway received considerable government attention and scrutiny. The difficult topography in the northern portion of the highway required heavy explosives, which the Army was brought in to handle, in order to ensure security in the post-conflict period.

The Nagma-Gamgadhi extension plays a major role in local imaginaries of development. Several hundred people gathered to mark its inauguration by Prime Minister Baburam Bhattarai in 2012, a formidable gathering in a sparsely populated district. And yet the Karnali Highway is continually under (re)construction because of the annual cycle of floods and landslides, and quality remains poor, if not dangerous. We heard many accounts of the dangers of traveling on the Karnali Highway in Mugu, with one bus traveler likening the experience to "buying a death ticket" (Hamal 2021; Murton and Sigdel 2021).

TALCHA AIRPORT

Surprisingly, before the 2012 inauguration of the Nagma-Gamgadhi branch of the Karnali Highway, a motorable road had already been constructed in Mugu, namely the 8-km Talcha-Gamgadhi Road linking the district headquarters to its nearby airport, with support from the Nepal government's Decentralized Rural Infrastructure and Livelihood Project (DRILIP), precursor to Department of Local Infrastructure Development and Agricultural Roads (DoLIDAR), both funded by the Asian Development Bank (ADB). Materials and machinery had been transported by helicopter from Jumla, revealing the urgency felt locally to advance road construction within the district, even before the strategic road was opened. The airport road was already completed, standing as a critical reminder that road building is not only driven by strategic imperatives, but also embedded in pragmatic considerations about transportation and infrastructure development writ large.

Construction of the airport had been initiated in 1975, but operations began only in 2003, with blacktopping completed in 2015. It was part of the national drive to connect remote districts that had yet to link to the Strategic Road Network. During the conflict, the airport was bombed and closed, and helicopter service was the primary mode of transportation for about ten years, from the grounds of the Gamgadhi High School. In practice, the airport did little to connect the district to the nation for any but the most elite users of transportation services.

Like elsewhere in Nepal, before motorable transport, people in Mugu traveled on foot, sometimes with the support of pack animals, mostly mules. Jumla-Surkhet requires five days to walk and Gamgadhi-Jumla requires one and a half days. The official designation of Mugu as *durgam* (remote) reflects these long walking distances. Walking trails, moreover, were not operational year-round, because of the challenges posed by winter snow and summer monsoon. People in Soru, Khatyad and Mugum Karmarong faced additional distances to reach Gamgadhi for travel south out of the district. The introduction of air transport did not significantly displace walking or use of pack animals as the primary modality, because it was out of reach cost-wise for most residents of the district.

Photo 3.1: Caravan of mules used to transport goods to villages from Gamgadhi Bazaar. Trucks are being unloaded in the distance. Women are carrying unloaded goods to the godowns in the Bazaar (photo by Tulasi Sharan Sigdel, 2017).

The key question about the political economy of transportation in Mugu therefore emerged as: who walks? The users of transit in

Mugu could essentially be divided into three groups: 1) students traveling out of Mugu for schooling, and government and I/NGO workers traveling into Mugu for their posts/work; 2) migrant workers traveling out of Mugu; and 3) traders passing through. Air travel was essentially limited to the first categories, except for the very small class of elite traders. Cost was a critical factor, but also the availability of tickets, which aside from money required connections to political leaders, local business elites, and high-level bureaucrats with power to broker access. Those lacking the financial and political capital continued to walk to Jumla for access to the Karnali Highway, reducing their walking time to two days from around five days it used to take to reach Surkhet. Mules continued to be the primary means of transit for traders wherever motorable roads have yet to reach or be completed. They have since been increasingly displaced by motorized transit after the Nagma-Gamgadhi Karnali Highway opened for destinations south of Gamgadhi, but continue to be used today from Gamgadhi north through Karmarong belt to the Tibet border. The opening of the Gamgadhi arm of the Karnali Highway, has made motorable transport far more equitable within Gama belt (if profoundly unsafe), but has created inequalities within the district as Soru, Khatyad, and Mugum-Karmarong belts remained largely inaccessible by motorable road during our research (though Soru and Khatyad have now been connected by road).

REMOTENESS

Mugu's road history powerfully illustrates the point that remoteness is experienced as a relative, not an absolute, concept in relation to the development of infrastructure. Mugu's present geographical isolation and socio-political distance from centers of power can be understood in relation to its former prominence. The Sinja Valley, currently in Jumla District, had been the center of the Khas-Malla Kingdom (1150–1390 AD) of which Mugu was a part, and which stretched at its height from Garhwal, in the contemporary Indian state of Uttarakhand to the west, the Kathmandu Valley to the east, and

Tibet to the north (Pokhrel 2023). At the end of the 14th century, the Khas Malla kingdom was dismantled through incursions of Rajput migrants from India who had in turn been displaced by "Moslims ... Slaces, Khilajis and the Tuglaques ... rulers of India" (Panday 2027 v.s.: 55). The former kingdom was parsed into feudal principalities.

During the unification of Nepal three centuries later under the Shah dynasty, Karnali principalities again became peripheral, as they were subjugated to an outside tutelage, that of the Gorkha kingdom centered in Kathmandu. The narrative of center to periphery, common all over Nepal where principalities had been their own centers before unification, contributes to what we might call "remoteness subjectivities" today—that is, the self-perception of being disadvantaged by a geographic positioning peripheral to centers of political power. Remoteness subjectivities are evident in all three districts featured in this book. With the imposition of modern bureaucratic administration, Khalanga, the market center of Jumla, became the headquarters of the Karnali Zone, and thus the site of the offices of government line agencies such as the Department of Roads, along with services growing up around those agencies like the contracting sector. Mugu was thus doubly marginalized, and rendered remote, at a regional as well as a national scale.

The Talcha Airport may have promised a technical fix for the experience of geographic and socio-political remoteness, but inequality of access only heightened the affective experience for the majority of the population. The Karnali Highway similarly recentered Gamgadhi on more equitable terms, since bus transport is far cheaper than air transport, but in turn created geographic disparities in access to motorable transportation within Mugu, as three of its rural municipalities remained largely without access to motorable transport. While the Nagma-Gangadhi branch of the Karnali Highway was celebrated for "connecting" the district, in practice a majority of the district's geography remains without motorable access. Physical distance is complicated by lack of access to power centers. When we visited Karmarong in 2017, for example, the government teachers and health workers were absent from the schools and the health posts and rarely reported to duty, according to our interlocutors. Socio-political remoteness was a variable experience, as elite households that had historically thrived from trade with Tibet had already built second homes in Kathmandu where a large proportion of the population had migrated for education and health care.

The relativeness of remoteness of Mugu can also be detected in future imaginaries. People believe that if the Gamgadhi-Nakchelagna Road to the TAR/China border comes into operation, they would be able to develop Gamgadhi as a trade route. They believe their district would be a gateway center/trade hub for China-Nepal trade relations. "Remote" Mugu would then become a lifeline of trade and commerce—connecting Nepalganj in the south with Tibet to the north, thus spatially reorganizing the district and the Karnali region.

ORGANIZATION OF ROAD DEVELOPMENT

Rural road building is achieved through two different modalities—contracting and users' groups. This section focuses on how these models articulate local practices. In so doing it contributes to the multi-scalar analysis of our project. That is, we look at how globally circulating ideologies of market-making (contracting) and participation (users' groups) relate in practice to the dynamics of patronage, "consensus making," "development nexus," and "community labor" that work to shore up longstanding patterns of uneven development on the ground.

CONTRACTING: BUILDING A PORTFOLIO, CHYANKHE KHANE, KAGAJ MILAUNE

In recent years, contracting has expanded significantly in Mugu, with the number of local contractors classified as class D having reached over 100 by the time of our research in 2017—among whom we observed only four women and no Dalit participants. As described in the Introduction to this book, class D contracts are small (up to

NRs. 3 million), and thus accessible to those who can invest modestly and want to try entering the bidding market. Nonetheless, financing is a challenge. The cost to obtain a license, which is magnified by an informal economy of license exchange and administrative delays, can be prohibitive.

At the time of our research two private banks had recently opened in Gamgadhi with active portfolios in contracting finance. Up until then, this role had been played exclusively by Rastriya Banijya Bank, one of three commercial banks in Nepal with significant government ownership, which was only authorized to issue bonds as a guarantee for road construction in 2003. Most local contractors do not have the assets to compete for a bid, even if they succeed in obtaining a license. They must thus obtain "bid bonds," through which the bank agrees to "show" the District Technical Office (DTO) that the contractor has sufficient funds for holding collateral until the bidding process is complete. Once a contractor wins a bid, another kind of financing is required, called a "performance bond," which covers the risk of default from beginning to end of the project, as installments to the contractor are paid out. A monthly interest is charged in relation to the time frame and the size of the assets being guaranteed, and again the bank holds collateral. Thus, the availability of finance underwrites the expansion of contracting, and road building itself can be understood as catalyzing not only the contracting sector, but also the private banking sector in Mugu.

For the first time, E-bidding was initiated in Mugu in 2017 for the District Road bidding process. This system aims to improve transparency, efficiency, and effectiveness of public procurement in Nepal. It is intended to simplify administrative procedures, make it easier for contractors by removing the requirement to appear physically for bidding, and improve accountability mechanisms. It also creates opportunities for local contractors to collaborate with national class A, B, and C contractors (typically from Kathmandu, Surkhet, or Nepalganj) to mutual benefit. Some projects require larger budgets and heavier machinery than class D contractors are eligible to bid for. In such cases the local class D contractors can apply jointly with bigger contractors as a way of not only establishing eligibility to bid, but also "building their portfolio" (portfolio *banaunu*). Such joint ventures also create a pathway for outside contractors who might want to break into a new market but lack reputation and standing there. They also enable those outside contractors to engage in rent seeking by taking a "personal commission," or "PC," from local contractors for the use of their licenses, logo, and bank guarantee—while not having to visit the construction site or provide mentorship or capacity building. Miyao and Chand (2023) refer to this practice as "ghost contracting" when discussing the same phenomenon at a higher scale of practice—Nepal construction entrepreneurs establishing joint ventures with international contractors (see also My República 2017). As Hamal (2021: 90), indicates, such arrangements are often made along political party lines: "Loyal party supporters in remote districts are rewarded with opportunities to build their contracting profiles through these relations with large scale contractors" belonging to the same party.[5]

One class D road contractor with whom we spoke had paid a certain percentage of the project budget simply for using the higher-class contractor's license in the bidding process. Another term used to express this arrangement is *chyankhe khane*, which translates as getting some commission for not participating in the bidding process; *chyankhe* itself gives the sense of third-person gambling. The contractor considered this a "not-good" practice, but necessary for managing the paperwork (*kagaj milaune*) required by government machineries. Additionally, local government officials are well aware of how class D contractors engage in practices of *kagaj milaune*, but have their own incentive to turn a blind eye because it is easier to put papers in order than do the harder work of inspecting the quality of work in the field (see also Mathur 2016). There is also some

[5] This chapter quotes extensively from the dissertation of Pushpa Hamal, which is based on research conducted in conjunction with this project and which particularly informs dimensions of the research related to critical consciousness and subjectivity.

fungibility in the market for procurement activities. For example, we spoke with one road contractor who was able to use his existing license for exporting medicinal herbs to declare eligibility for road contracting.

COMPETITIVE BIDDING: COMPETITION (GHATI GHATAU) *OR CONSENSUS* (MILEMATO)

Despite these opportunities to obtain financing and to build a profile, formidable challenges remain, and the contracting system tends to produce sub-optimal outcomes in terms of road quality. This is in part due to the logic of contracting: that the lowest bidder gets the contract, as long as quality is also ensured. The local expression for bidding as low as possible is *ghati ghatau.* When the value of a bid goes lower than the cost to build a quality product, either the work is not finished, or it is built to an unsustainably low standard (as also described in the Morang and Dolakha chapters). These outcomes are particularly likely if the contractors are not local, without a personal investment in local development, and are thus willing to flee the district to avoid facing consequences. Local governments are left with having to freeze project budgets, contributing to stalled development processes. People in Mugu are acutely aware of the losses caused by *ghati gatau* and the common role of outside contractors in these processes.

Contrary to the objectives of competitive bidding, local contractors coordinate bidding through the Mugu Contractors' Association (Nirman Vyavasayi Sangh, Mugu). The association manages an informal process known as *milemato* that avoids pitting contractors against one another in competition while also reducing the influence of outside contractors. *Milemato* derives from the verb *milaunu,* which means to arrange, and has a connotation of consensus. The contractors' association coordinates the bidding process by getting the contractors to agree in advance who will "win" the bid and who will instead obtain PC, personal commission, from the winning bidder. As Hamal explains (2021: 91), "In order to participate in *milemato*, a contractor has to have an up-to-date license and also to "buy" the bidding form from the district office and validate it with a bid bond from a bank."

In fact, in order to obtain a bid through *milemato*, one must have enough money to pay out the PC to other participating contractors. According to a banker we interviewed who was familiar with this process, there are only four to five contractors in this position, and others participate in bidding through *milemato*. The processes is "consensual," in the sense that the wealthier leading contractors generally take turns receiving the bid; however, it is important to underscore that only a few people ever get a "turn," and most just wait for their PC.

As we observed on the occasion of the district road tender, and as was subsequently explained, the contractor association holds a meeting before tendering takes place. Any contractor who wants to contend for "winning" the bid must actually show s/he has the cash to distribute PC. A decision is made about who will "win" the bid, based on logics discussed below, and a few others agree to put in competing "fake bids" at higher levels. The illusion of competition is thus created, even though the "winning bid" is likely higher than it would have been without collusion among contractors. The winning bidder then has to pay PC to all those who bought a bidding form, at a rate high enough to make the whole process worthwhile to them—a margin that many contractors complain is inadequate relative to costs and time.

There are many benefits of the *milemato* system for those involved. It is flexible, for one, and makes it possible for many individuals to benefit from the business of contracting, even those without experience. It allows contractors to participate in a wide range of roles, from simply joining the contracting association, negotiating PC and its distribution, to learning the ropes of DTO processes by submitting a "fake bid," to being put forward to "win" the bid and implementing a project. Contractors we spoke with indicated that they were often not "ready" or lacked "free time" to actually undertake a road building project, but appreciated being able to participate in "contracting" in all the ancillary roles of the *milemato* system. Some have never actually "won" a bid but opt to keep participating for the benefit of getting PC. Referring to the 2017 district road bid, one of the few women contractors in Mugu explained that,

> if [the larger local contractors] work together then it is actually ok because we get a little bit of money, ... [enough] money to renew the license, and we have to pay tax. ... The person who gets the contract raises the money [for distribution as PC] with about 10–15 percent of the total budget ... to the people who have filled up the tender form. (Hamal 2021: 93)

There certainly seems to be enough incentive for contractors to participate in these illicit processes. What surprised us, however, was how openly these take place, and in fact, how government officials witness and become complicit in them. The local official charged with enforcing official procurement protocols, for example, described the process with extraordinary candor:

> There are many contractors [in Mugu]. They divide different projects and take turns for [receiving] the contract. We move our process forward if they have followed our procedures, even if they come *milera* [having worked together and deciding who gets the turn]. ... What we need is proper documentation and quotation based on our process. Once they come up with that documentation then we give the contract to the lowest bidder and do the agreement. (Hamal 2021: 93)

This official is plainly stating that what matters to the state is its officials' capacity to document that rules have been followed (*kagaj milaunu*). This perspective was corroborated to us on numerous occasions in our discussions with not just government officials, but also users' group leaders, local politicians, and business owners. It also aligns with other scholarship addressing procurement processes in Nepal and South Asia more broadly (Gupta 2012; Mathur 2016; Rankin *et al.* 2024). Incredibly, in the case of the district road tender at least, negotiations within the Contractors' Association to determine who would submit the "winning bid" took place right on the grounds of the District Administrative Offices.

We were fortunate enough to observe these negotiations outside the local government office—in the presence of armed police, contractors haggling loudly, carrying bags stuffed with cash, and the same government official who spoke with us above looking on from his second-story office window. At a certain point, the contractors all departed together, walking deliberately in the same direction. The woman contractor later explained that they were headed to a local restaurant where the PC would be distributed, after which the bids could be tendered.

Photo 3.2: Contractors negotiating on the grounds of the District Development Committee Office. A government officer is looking down from the balcony. Policeman in the foreground right side is also watching (photo by Katharine N. Rankin, 2017).

The reason all this could transpire so openly, we came to understand, is that all involved, including government officials, find the *milemato* system preferable to *ghati ghatau*, which so often ends in outside contractors winning the bid and running off without completing the work. *Milemato*, by contrast, has the effect of employing local contractors and their crews, while also distributing funds throughout the local contracting sector through PC.[6] "If they go for lower bid then chances of loss are high and other [local] contractors won't get the money," explained a bank manager, "but if they all sit and decide who gets the contracts then the money is divided equally among the remaining contractors" (Hamal 2021: 97). Locals also argue that *milemato* is preferable to the use of *gunda* (hooligans or henchmen) that prevails in the *ghati ghatau* system, particularly before the introduction of e-bidding—the hiring of henchmen to intimidate and harass competitors in the hopes of discouraging bidders. The woman contractor explained that:

> If there is a big contract that is open then these boys are used to guard the process. They make sure other people do not apply for that bid. They stop others from lowering the bid. The contractor who wants to stop others from lowering the bid uses those boys ... to not let anyone else apply. (Hamal 2021: 98)

In the *milemato* system, *gunda* are not typically involved, and when attempts are made to disrupt the process with the use of force, association members work together to dissipate the threat. In *milemato*, therefore, less money is siphoned off from the tender for paying off henchmen.

Overall, *milemato* is regarded positively because it allows a way "in" to contracting through the mechanism of distributing PC and

[6] In *Taksar Magazine*, Budhathoki (2024), a journalist who writes on economic issues, has explained that PC (translated as "percentage commission") is widespread from central government to local level.

exposing new entrants to the process of obtaining a license and making bids, however "fake." And yet it also concentrates opportunity among those local contractors (men from high caste households with long-time elite status) who already have enough capital (economic as well as social and political) to distribute PC to smaller contractors. It is also important to underscore that even among those smaller contractors receiving PC, we identified only a few women and no Dalit, although their participation has likely since increased.

USERS' GROUPS: KAGAJ MILAUNE, *PATRONAGE POLITICS AND THE RAP DISTINCTION*

The other predominant modality for organizing road construction is users' groups. While the legal framework of users' groups forms a national-scale narrative and field of governance, place-specific practices emerge in relation to specific political economies, cultural politics and environmental conditions. In Mugu, users' groups predominate in building local roads because of the lack of contracting capacity and the extraordinary pace of development. Users' groups in Mugu operate within several institutional configurations. According to the Public Procurement Regulation, 2020, the District Coordination Committee (DCC) may authorize users' groups to undertake construction projects that fall within the authorized maximum of NRs. 50 million, as long as they conform to District Transportation Management Plan priorities.[7] In Mugu, some of these projects received funding from the Government of Nepal and DfID through the Karnali Employment Program (KEP), whose objective was to provide employment within a region deemed backward and disadvantaged. Two roads in particular, the Gamgadhi-Dilachaur and Gamgadhi-Humla Roads fall under the auspices of the DfID-funded RAP3, one of the most extensive bilateral programs in Nepal

[7] Since federalization in 2017, the District Development Committees (DDC) have been restructured as DCC with no executive authority, which has now been transferred to municipalities (rural and urban).

aiming to alleviate poverty in remote areas through the construction of transportation infrastructure and local income generation.

Overall, the RAP3 roads conform closely to legal frameworks requiring users' groups to refrain from using heavy machinery, while also committing separate technical staff (beyond the DTO), a budget to cover wages (unlike in Morang, Dolakha, and other green roads projects in Mugu, voluntary contributions are not expected), training and equipment for Road Building Group (RBG) members, and a partnership with a local NGO that furnishes a "social mobilizer" responsible for forming and mobilizing groups. The KEP and other users' groups by contrast, tend not to follow the standard rules of operation, instead hiring petty contractors to bring in heavy equipment rather than mobilizing local labor to build the road—as described well in the Dolakha chapter. Like the local contractors who ensure that paperwork is submitted to demonstrate compliance with the rules, users' groups similarly engage in *kagaj milaune* to document the required local contributions, to the point of submitting the fabricated attendance ledger (*dor hajir*) of laborers engaged. The sentiment is that even if rules are broken in practice, it is necessary to show respect for the rules "on paper." Doing so releases the budget that users' groups then often not so clandestinely use to contract a bulldozer.

Like with contracting, much of this *kagaj milaune* practice often takes place quite openly, with the awareness and sometimes complicity of government officials, who also have a stake through their role in monitoring and supervision. The account of a technical assistant who had been posted to Mugu on a temporary basis conveys how payments to government officials to accept and approve falsified paperwork are normalized to the point of exerting pressure on individuals in those bureaucratic positions. When we asked why he had accepted cash payments to approve users' committee paperwork, he responded:

> To be honest, sir, I am not a permanent employee. ... Previously I never took money from community people to approve a work completion report that was not up to the standard. I was honest. However, my seniors and political leaders did not appreciate my honesty because I did not have even a single rupee to share [the suggestion here is that front-line officials are expected to share cash commissions with their bosses]. They did not believe me, and suspected that I would have taken money from the users' groups when I approved their completion report. In fact, many times I did not approve the users' group's sub-standard work. But I faced huge pressure from above [referring to both political and administrative heads] to sign the work completion reports, [with the administrative and political heads] claiming that everyone is doing so and why should I be different? They denied my contract renewal, although now I have been reinstated. Community people are also not spending all the project money.[8] Everyone is compromising on the quality of the work and taking a little money. To make this work, we should maintain the paperwork. There should be perfection in paperwork.

A second common feature of users' groups (beyond the specific context of RAP3 projects discussed below) is that the space opened up for "local participation" and "local governance" of development has been well colonized by political parties. On the one hand, party leaders compete over securing the coveted executive positions on users' committees—chair, vice chair, secretary, treasurer—from which they can control processes of *kagaj milaune,* hiring dozers, and distributing the users' group budget in a manner that allows them to fulfill requirements of political patronage. These include

[8] See more below on pocketing users' group funds in the section on environment and sustainability. The users' group in question was neither KEP nor RAP.

securing votes and/or other obligations with favors, as well as fulfilling obligations incurred from receiving favors in the past, much of which operates along political party lines. On the other hand, when needed, parties engage in consensus making processes, similar to *milemato* in contracting. This practice can be illustrated with another anecdote, told from the perspective of a district bureaucrat, as follows.

One day, a group of people came to his office to form a users' group to build a road in their village in the Soru belt. They provided the required documentation, including the attendance list and minutes of a meeting held in the village and a recommendation letter from the VDC. After one or two days, however, another group of people came to the office to claim that this users' committee was phony, and that it had been formed by people from the district headquarters, in Gama belt, in order to lay claim to the development budget of the VDC in question. The second group presented a different users' group in place of the first. In fact the two users' groups had been formed by two different political parties, CPN-UML and Nepali Congress, competing for local control. Later the two groups agreed to dissolve both and formed a new group by selecting members from both. They followed all the procedures, however, they involved their party cadres in the process. A local journalist told us that in such cases the DDC usually asks parties to come to a consensus and, after debating for a few days, they form a new users' group (having dissolved the first two) and decide how to divide the executive positions between the parties. These examples demonstrate how political parties have been monopolizing the users' group modality.

RAP3, which includes the Gamgadhi-Dilachaur Road, presents a different scenario. RAP3 promotes green roads using labor-intensive, environmentally sound and climate-resilient methods "alongside complementary socio-economic interventions," as their website puts it (RAP Implementation Plan 2013). These twin objectives are pursued through a partnership with a local NGO, Rural Community Development Center (RCDC), which is tasked with mobilizing local populations to form users' groups, provide trainings and other services for members, and monitor adherence to green roads principles.

Under the auspices of RAP3, users' groups (RBGs) are formed with the help of the social mobilizer, who is tasked with ensuring that groups have 20 members and minimum 33 percent representation of women. The mobilizers encourage Dalit and members of other marginalized and disadvantaged groups to form groups, with no more than one member per household. Distribution of opportunity is also ensured as the groups are formed on the basis of households' proximity to sections of the road under construction. Depending on demographic distribution within VDCs, some groups are mixed-caste, while others are comprised entirely of Dalit. RAP's commitment to gender equality is one key reason it has earned widespread respect; social mobilizers target 50/50 representation by men and women within groups, and attempt to recruit women as *naike*, or leaders, of the users' groups, who liaise with NGO and implementing agency staff. While practice deviates marginally from these stipulations, RAP RBGs are closely monitored from the formation stage and aim to achieve inclusion criteria, as illustrated by the drawing at the beginning of the chapter.

The local implementing NGO holds public meetings annually in which grievances are heard and users' groups are reconstituted. The actual road construction happens in a phased way over several years: first the track opening, followed by a series of widenings up to 8 meters. Heavy equipment such as bulldozers and excavators are avoided in favor of manual construction with hand tools. The users' group modality implemented by RAP is highly regarded in Mugu as it provides a local source of income to those who otherwise would have to leave the district for work opportunities—as a woman group leader put it, *kam ghardhuri ma aipugeko chha* (work has reached right to our doorstep). Those who hold other full-time jobs are prohibited from joining RBGs, and pay rates and terms are considered generous.

Joining a RAP RBG also comes with training opportunities, not just for manually building a road, but also for vegetable farming, livestock raising, composting, solar power installation, as well as building other infrastructure like water mills and drinking water taps deemed desirable by the groups. In addition to the skills and income gained from participating in RBGs, people in Mugu sometimes comment on how the RAP modality of road building contributes to "social harmony" or "peace," because people develop practices of working together, rather than wasting time not getting along or doing useless things, and because the benefit that derives from this activity, the road, is shared by the whole community. RAP covers immediate costs, such as damage to personal property near the road, so conflict is mitigated. Finally, some women commented that benefits to women accrue not just from inclusion, skills, and income but also from the confidence that derives from learning new skills and working on a team. As the woman contractor cited above put it,

> After RAP leaves, we have confidence that we may get some work and we can handle all that equipment. ... People used to say that women ... should not come to work because they thought that women could not do anything except carrying stones on their back. Now we are equally competent and strong, and we compete with men. We can do all the works the men can do. For example, breaking stones. (Hamal 2021: 110)

Thus RAP's RBGs are favorably regarded for the opportunities they provide for income and training that could lead to future employment. They are also regarded as a gender equalizer. Overall, RAP is regarded as the most effective implementing agency of the users' group modality, no doubt because of its capacity to engage a local NGO to handle the micro-social dynamics of forming groups, providing training and disbursing funds.

MATERIALITY: LAND, LANDSCAPE AND BORDERS

In this section, we consider how roads constitute land, landscape, and borders, and how this materiality articulates social relations. For this purpose, we draw on Fiona Wilson's (2004) concept of the "territorializing regime" to think about roads as stretched out spaces of social relations that are etched on the landscape. "Regime" signals a political field, while "territorializing" refers to how power, conflict, and strategies of political control can be seen on the land. The section identifies three key logics of territorialization through which to explore how the material road encounters, constitutes, and is built through social relations on the ground, namely: alignment, expropriation and encroachment—themes that also arise in Dolakha and Morang. In Mugu, like in other districts, road building catalyzes and expresses significant conflicts around these three aspects of territorialization. The section ends with a brief consideration of how roads point to a national border which figures large in local imaginaries (as they do in Dolakha and Morang too). We consider what the experience of road-making thus far suggests about the possibilities for local populations to benefit from completion of a highway to the TAR/China border at Nakchelagna.

ROAD ALIGNMENT

As is common throughout areas of Nepal that have not been well served historically by motorable transport, people in Mugu generally would like any new road to pass as near as possible to their home, without actually going through it. Given the lack of systematic planning processes and the significance of personal-political relations in road building, those with some ability to influence the latter consider it their business to have an opinion on where the road should go—"alignment,"—to use the English word typically heard. Road alignment is not a matter to be left to engineers. Instead, community members look for opportunities to exert influence, through either economic or cultural-political means.

The alignment of the Karnali Highway, part of the Strategic Road Network under the purview of the Department of Roads, provided the first occasion for these dynamics to play out, and has been subject to extensive local debate. The Nagma-Gamgadhi branch climbs treacherously up the mountain range separating Mugu and Jumla Districts. The section within Mugu District, from the district border to the district headquarters, Gamgadhi, takes a mountainous route that brings the highway along a ridgeline past Talcha Airport and past the road to Rara National Park, the district's most significant tourist attraction. This existing route had the endorsement of the DOR, as well as many local constituents who wanted to align the highway with these pre-existing features, even if that meant taking a longer route. In other words, the alignment favored those who already had relatively better access to pre-existing infrastructure, and it was convenient to state actors.

Another constituency had argued in favor of a more direct route following a contour line at a lower elevation, "touching," or passing through, more villages, and thus benefiting a wider swathe of the population. This alternate route had been advocated by local leaders in the more densely settled area along that route, east of Gamgadhi. A local party leader (and RAP RBG chair), expounded at length about the dangers of the established route through Talcha airport which sits at a higher elevation and thus requires the road to traverse many "turnings and hurdles." On the lower-elevation alternate route, toppled vehicles "will just turnover," while from the established, higher-elevation roadway they are more likely to "drop off the road." The local constituency argued that the alternate route was shorter. Also, as a Gamgadhi-based businessman, whose business serves the entire district, explained, it would bring tourists from outside the district heading to Rara National Park *through* more villages as well as the district center: "If that road went through Gamgadhi then they might have stayed one day here ... they would stay in a hotel and we would benefit out of it. ... If they stay in a hotel they might need some [supplies] and come visit my store." As it is, tourists can head directly to Rara Lake from the airport, having no direct contact with the densely settled areas nearby. What is notable from our perspective is how extensively communities developed a view on the matter and have continued to engage in heated local discussions about road alignment.

In our discussions with residents, bureaucrats, donors, politicians, and others in the areas surrounding Gamgadhi, we heard these dynamics expressed repeatedly in relation to more contemporary road developments. A contractor (and local political leader) based in a village east of Gamgadhi offered a frank assessment that district roads go where political leaders need votes: "that road [referring to a branch off the Karnali Highway from Gothijyula] was built to connect Khyatad Rural Municipality because it is the area of our leader and member of parliament. A leader has to develop his area to get support from voters. ... This is the concept here in Mugu." When we asked why some powerful leaders channel more money to their area while some areas desperately needing development projects do not get any funding, a local bureaucrat working in the area of land use planning similarly commented that political leaders try to ensure that "roads pass through the areas where they have vote banks," even if they cannot easily influence decisions about which roads will be prioritized in the district. Contractors, too, are seen to have undue influence over road alignment, as the land-use planner continued, "contractors cut open the road in their own way—this is a problem that is widely evident" (as also discussed in the Dolakha chapter). Another Dalit political leader and business owner who runs a small shop in the district center described how contractors tend to adjust the alignment in order to avoid running the road through the land of "their own people." The operative logic, whether for securing votes or favors, is that those with economic and political influence can accrue political capital by managing the road building process in favor of their constituents. In return, those constituents owe votes and favors. These practices appear to be considered normal, to the point that even personally implicated contractors and political leaders shared their analysis with us in an apparently unselfconscious way. The question then becomes, from which standpoint does the analysis assume a critical flavor?

Only one case when residents banded together to demand realignment "from below" was brought to our attention during field research. It concerned the road being built from Gamgadhi to Gilaha by RAP3. Local residents demanded to realign a section of the road so that it would "touch" more villages—much as the constituency for an alternate route for the Karnali Highway had argued. An engineering survey had sited the road in a way that did not maximize possible connections with villages. Residents of the villages of Nigale and Phuli organized protests in different forms—writing a letter to the RAP3 office in Gamgadhi, lobbying the DDC and district-level political leaders, and offering to donate their own land for the purpose. The strategy reflects a savvy understanding of relationships among donors, local governments, and politicians, as well as of the expectations of "local partnership" through land donations. The pitch worked: according to a woman member of the RBG associated with the RAP3 project, in order to ensure the village was not "left out," political leaders from the seven mainstream political parties got on board. We noted in our fieldnotes (March 18, 2017) that the continued pressure from villagers essentially forced RAP and DDC to resurvey and realign the road to pass through Nigale and Phuli. While it is certainly the case that there are many pressures and voices seeking to bring a road to their "own village," examples of communities organizing together against established plans are rare in our experience. It is also important to underscore that the woman cited above shared the story of protest while lamenting that project and political leaders had not consulted with women in the first place—despite the emphasis in RAP3 on gender parity in RBGs—suggesting that local governments construe women's participation primarily in terms of labor, not governance.

EXPROPRIATION

Once the road alignment is set, there is the matter of securing the land across which the road will be built. As the other chapters suggest, this is a universally contentious process across different geographies. For the local roads that are the focus of our research, people are not usually compensated if they happen to own land that the road crosses; rather they are asked to get out of the way. Many motorable roads are built along previously existing foot trails, *goreto,* or tracks for pack animals, *ghodeto*, which are usually on public land. But making the road wide enough for vehicles to ply requires acquiring land from private or institutional owners on either side. Strategic roads involving federal agencies like the Department of Roads (e.g., Karnali Highway and DRILIP, which built the road from Talcha to Gamgadhi) do provide compensation for land, houses, fruit trees, crops, and other amenities that are destroyed in road construction.[9] In a remote area like Mugu, the rationale for not providing compensation is that homeowners will be suitably compensated over time as the road inflates land values by connecting the region to distant markets and spurring the local economy. Taking this logic farther, RAP3 in particular, undertakes "subsidiary projects" in conjunction with road building, which provide opportunities for income generation, vegetable farming, apple production, solar power, and irrigation. It also pays labor at a rate higher than the "local rate" (generally the referent is agricultural wages), calculates pay on the basis of volume rather than time (ensuring that workers remain motivated to break up rocks, carry loads, spread gravel), and provides technical training (such as how to build a gabion wall).[10]

[9] Note that compensation policy is not same across the country; it is project and agency specific.

[10] In the assessment of one local political and RBG leader, the arrangement is widely considered to be beneficial to villagers: "Now poor people are employed and have money for clothes and food because of the RAP project. ... RAP has also somehow contributed to the peace because people go to work, they get home tired and go to sleep after dinner [as opposed to staying out drinking]. The next day again they go to work ... then their bodies adapt. ... It becomes a routine."

Compared to Morang and Dolakha, our experience in Mugu suggests a relatively more consensual process, where many people are willing to "sacrifice" their land, and even their home, to facilitate road building—a sacrifice that does, by most accounts, come with an expectation of convenience and higher land values with the "arrival" of the motorable road. The sense of anticipation was evident in the village of Chaina, when people who owned houses along the roadway started building storefronts in their homes, one to two years before the motorable road was opened. Some volunteered to cut off a section of their house for widening the roadbed during the initial survey, hoping to motivate other homeowners whose houses would inevitably be "marked" for partial expropriation. A household might lose one or two rooms and have to not only rearrange sleeping accommodations but also share a *chulo* (hearth) across wider extended family members.[11] This reduction in interior space and restructuring of living arrangement poses an extraordinary inconvenience that some families accepted early on in the name of the public interest.

Why would people agree to such sacrifice? The logic of future benefit and a faith in development are certainly widespread. In addition to the higher valuation of land, those owning agricultural lands *(bari)* see an opportunity to convert that land to *ghaderi*, land for building houses, which is considerably more valuable. In some cases, as a local journalist explained, political leaders might need, "to convince the public, saying we may have to sacrifice little bit of our land for development ... and people come to consensus ... thinking that they will have more benefit than loss." A contractor from a village east of Gamgadhi similarly characterized consensus in this way:

> Mugu people understand the importance of roads. ... They have realized that without roads, no development takes place. They are ready to sacrifice their land for road building. ... They do not obstruct contractors and NGOs or INGOs if they are

[11] Sharing a *chulo* entails a significant household reorganization, as a *chulo* commonly denotes a household unit.

> there to build a road. ... They are ready to give land without compensation because they ... want the road to arrive at their doorstep.

In addition to increased land value and development, other anticipated benefits include business opportunities, increased mobility, more facilities, and concrete houses (*pakki ghar*) that are presumed to be more durable than traditional earthen houses.

The narrative of sacrifice and the perception of individual and collective benefit are not universal, however. What some characterize as "convincing" residents to give up their land for road building, others consider coercion. Samjhana Nepali, a community-based researcher with whom we collaborated, interviewed a Dalit woman who works as a laborer to load and unload trucks and carry goods from bus station to bazaar. Her notes reflect the pressure experienced by lower-income and low-status households, which often lack access to education. Samjhana paraphrased the woman's understanding of how Dalit landowners experience expropriation:

> I did not know anything in the past about road and land. People started to debate that the road is damaging their land. People asked one of our neighbors to allow the road to pass through his land. He did not agree with them. He said that it was his agricultural land. If that land is damaged due to road, how can I survive? I do not have any other source of livelihood, he said. And the villagers gave two slaps on his cheek. Later, the project overseer came and convinced him. Then he allowed a road to be built through his land.

The account clarifies how "convincing" can be a euphemism for coercion, and how for those without the means to secure multiple sources of livelihood, "sacrificing" land incurs significant hardship. A hotel owner in Gamgadhi Bazaar explained to Samjhana that in fact, as a community of smallholders, many people stand to suffer from expropriation practices. According to her fieldnotes:

> There is a debate on the land and relocation of people's houses. Those who will lose land for the road construction are against the road. Because in Mugu there are no big landlords. Everyone has a small piece of land and is dependent on agricultural production. If they lose the small piece of land what will happen to their livelihood? There is no compensation for the land in Mugu.

Some left-leaning political leaders and bureaucrats recognized how road building can territorialize inequality. One leader commented on how the expectation that land values will increase (and the associated policy of providing no compensation for expropriated land) disproportionately harms smallholders: "When the road damages the land of smallholders, they suffer a great deal; we have to think about this." In 2017, we met a local bureaucrat associated with a rural municipality in western Mugu, who similarly noted the considerable convincing required to secure smallholders' land, as well as the uneven burden.:

> When people resist [providing land for] construction of road, they [project leaders and government officials] try to convince the sufferer, like by saying that because of one or two people, the whole road building should not stop. ... However, there should be a way to provide compensation according to the economic status of the landowner. "*Gariv marne kura bhayena*"—meaning that it's not ok to inflict hardship on the poor; the state should protect poor people.

Thus in Mugu, like Dolakha and Morang, conflicts arise around land expropriation. These tend to center on compensation for those in vulnerable socioeconomic positions, or critiques of alignments skewed towards the better off. Two other Dalit women interviewed by Samjhana Nepali, both also laborers who unload trucks and porter goods to bazaar, provide an insightful assessment of these power dynamics:

> People [i.e, those with power and influence] want their land to be on the roadside. However, they do not want to donate land for road building. ... A few days back, at a discussion meeting about building the road from our village to Nyeura [place just below Tuma on the motorable road to Gamgadhi], they were arguing and fighting to save their land and take land from others for the road. At the end, those who were poor and powerless had to suffer. They decided to build the road through poor people's land. The big and powerful people save their land and fix the route to go by the side of their land.

Another Dalit woman characterized the hypocrisy this way: "When a road goes through the village, on the one hand the land value goes up and on the other hand people lose their land. Therefore, people [with influence and power] want the road go *nearby* their land but not *through* it" (see also the Dolakha chapter). Others use their influence to make, as the local journalist put it, "expensive claims." He was recounting the case of a prominent elected political leader (at the time a government health worker from an elite family) who single-handedly obstructed construction of a road through a village just south of the airport: "This obstacle started from one person who is a government employee but active in politics as well. If he had given his land, we would have buses running by now."

> Q: That person is well-educated and could have understood the consequences; why do you think he did not agree to let them construct road through his land?
>
> A: Everyone went to him and requested his cooperation but he did not agree. His demands were that he should get the

> contract to build the road through his village and that he should be compensated for the land used by the road. The policy is that if the road creates *ghaderi* (remaining land where houses can be built), compensation will not be given. ... So, it was not possible to address his expensive demands. He was the one who influenced other villagers as well. ... Everyone knows because of him that work was canceled.

We learned of several other instances in which a local road project was purportedly held up because of a single man's resistance on such grounds.

Photo 3.3: Road to nowhere, taken from Gamgadhi-Nakchelagna Road; this road branches off toward villages above the Gamgadhi-Nakchelagna Road, but the track has not been opened properly and has been abandoned for at least two years (photo by Katharine N. Rankin, 2017).

As if to answer the question about how this individual could have the courage and power to cancel a whole project, a Maoist political leader shared his analysis in a separate interview:

> There is a common disposition here—people do not want to sacrifice even a single penny of their own wealth, but they do not care if other people are losing everything. ... This kind of tendency and behavior are reflected in infrastructure development in Mugu, and I would say it is similar across the country. ... People fighting to protect their personal property and turning a deaf ear about damages to others' property—it is common.

For the Secretary of a RAP3 RBG who is involved in persuading landowners to cooperate, the challenge is incessant:

> Last year, while opening up the track of that road, there were many disturbances; when the dozer was operating, one person came, sat down on the edge of his land and stopped the work; when the problem was solved and the dozer started to operate again, the next person came and stopped the work.

Photo 3.4: People destabilizing a roadside embankment by collecting stones for construction, behind a gabion wall that had been built to prevent landslides (photo by Tulasi Sharan Sigdel, 2017).

When we first visited Mugu with the intent to develop a research project about roads, our interest was catalyzed by the dramatic expression on the landscape of these kinds of conflicts over alignment and compensation, as well as the unsettled *milemato* arrangements. Without knowing the stories, we could see the evidence of conflict and struggle in what we came to refer to as "suspended/phased out infrastructure" and "roads to nowhere" (see Turin 1997, also the Dolakha chapter). As we began our research, the road building frenzy was at its peak, with tracks being opened seemingly to connect every village across the district's precipitous mountainsides and river valleys. As we ventured off the trunk road, the Karnali Highway, to learn about the nuances of district-level infrastructure development, we would see gravel road beds ending at no meaningful destination, half way up a hillside; or people destabilizing a roadside embankment by collecting stones for construction, behind a gabion wall that had been built to prevent landslides; or simply cases where the road building work is left "half-done," as a RAP3 RBG member interviewed by Samjhana Nepali put it.

ENCROACHMENT

Gamgadhi Bazaar shows its own signs of suspended infrastructure. One notorious example came while staying at a hotel in the bazaar. Co-author Sigdel was awoken by the sound of a tractor stuck in the mud—the wheels spinning, engine racing, other construction machinery being mobilized to help. The main road through the bazaar marks the "zero point" for numerous strategic and local roads, and remains perennially under construction, including up to the present. In March 2017, mud was suspending completion of the zero point section of the Gamgadhi-Nakchelagna Road. Just the day before, Sigdel had seen a truck stuck in the mud. Though he wanted to ignore the loud noises early in the morning, he also wanted to take a picture. What he witnessed turned out to be a dramatic manifestation of the conflict underlying suspended infrastructure. Here we share excerpts from his journal entry about the events:

The tractor, which was loaded with sand, did not move ahead. The owner of the tractor arrived about an hour later. He tried to get the driver to unload the sand, but the driver and his helper convinced the owner that was unnecessary. The more they tried to move the tractor, the worse the situation got. ... After three hours of continual effort, the tractor slipped off the roadbed and tilted toward a house at the edge of the road; the big rear tire sunk into the front yard. ... I was surprised to see the anger of the woman who owned the house. Although the tractor had not damaged the house, the woman was so furious that I could not imagine how she could use those bad words in public. The owner of the tractor tried to calm her down saying he would pay any damages caused by the tractor. ... However, the woman pushed him down, saying, "How can a guy who is struggling to pay NRs. 15,000 installments on a tractor pay for damages of a house worth NRs. 20 million?" She grabbed an iron rod, and threw it at the driver, then a shovel.

In addition, she blocked the driver from getting back into the tractor and leaving the premises. ... A retired government employee arrived on the scene and tried to convince the woman that he would help ensure any damages would be paid for. ... He too was ineffective and eventually stepped aside. After another hour, the all-male police team arrived, ... and they too failed to convince the woman, who was hurling stones at the driver; they eventually restrained her to prevent further assaults on the driver, and summoned the female police, who requested her to go to the police office with the tractor owner ... to negotiate a resolution, but she refused, saying "I am the victim. My house has been damaged. Why shall I go to the police office?" The police were tired. They were just muttering, "The government is dysfunctional; the state is weak; the state can't do anything" (*kamai nalagne sarkar chha; rajya nai niriha chha*).

People who built houses on the upper side of the road were encroaching on the public land allocated for the road's improvement. They were dumping mud on the road from their own private house construction. Moreover, the municipality had not provided drainage for wastewater from those houses so the residents were pouring wastewater from their laundry and dishes directly onto the road. Given that the road had not been paved, the notorious tractor-trapping mud was the result. In fact, the aggrieved woman whose yard the tractor had breached had encroached on the roadbed herself, according to locals who had gathered. They told me that her yard was built on land that belongs to the Department of Roads, in fact on top of the gabion wall built by the DoR to prevent the road from being eroded by landslides.

Photo 3.5: An unloaded tractor stuck in the mud and sliding toward a house (photo by Tulasi Sharan Sigdel, 2017).

Clearly road expansion poses particular challenges of encroachment in the old, dense bazaar area of Gamgadhi, as in Charikot Bazaar,

Dolakha. On the one hand, as the Dalit shopkeeper cited previously aptly put it, "If the municipality tried to expand the width of the roads [in the bazaar] then half of the houses on the roadside would have to be torn down. On the other hand, those people [with houses near the road] are not going to agree to track expansion [and expropriation]." The hotel owner who discussed these dynamics with us at length shared that homeowners will often call their political party to help allay the pressure on them to relocate their houses, and "even do not hesitate to bring *gunda* to obstruct the road construction work. Meanwhile, land values are already so high in the bazaar, since the motorable road reached it back in 2012 via the Karnali Highway, how could the government afford that compensation rate?"

Photo 3.6: The homeowner had built a balcony onto the gabion wall, thus encroaching on land belonging to the DoR; the tractor hit the extended balcony (photo by Tulasi Sharan Sigdel, 2017).

INTERNATIONAL BORDER

In 2017, road improvements in Gamgadhi Bazaar were to constitute a "zero point" of a new strategic road from Gamgadhi to the

Nakchelagna border with the TAR/China. Its length is about 80 km and in three years (2014–2017), 21 km had been constructed according to the DTO. We heard many reasons about the delay in completion, among which the challenges of expropriation, encroachment, and compensation in Gamgadhi Bazaar, as described above, figured centrally. At the same time, as in Dolakha, the anticipation of an "international road" running through Mugu was palpable, and we heard numerous accounts about its desired transformative impacts ranging from facilitating development of a copper mine, to promoting tourism, to giving a major boost to trade in modern goods from China. Whether or not all would come to fruition, we can anticipate that the Nakchelagna Road, combined with the RAP3 roads being built from Gamgadhi to Dulachaur and Gamgadhi to Humla, has the potential to "redefine the spatial location of these districts" (Sigdel, fieldnotes, 3/23/2017).

In reality, the Gamgadhi-Nakchelagna Road becomes a highway once a year when thousands of aspiring traders and dealers in medicinal herbs descend on Mugu for the annual harvest of *yarsagumba* (Aidi 2023).[12] The caterpillar fungus blooms in the spring, right after the snow thaws, and has long been a staple for Mugali people to trade in Chinese and Tibetan markets north of the border as well south throughout Nepal. Local traders earn between NRs. 1.6 million and NRs. 1.8 million per kilogram (Aidi 2023), while the price in China and Singapore has been reported at 10 times that (The Kathmandu Post 2017). With the opening to vehicular transport of the Karnali Highway to Gamghadi and the first 2.5-km section north beyond the bazaar, the Mugu *yarsagumba* harvest has been made accessible to wider national and regional markets. Beyond Ghata, however, the rest of the approximately 18 km journey must be made on foot; even if a track has been opened (by KEP), most of the road is still

[12] Mugum Karmarong Rural Municipality estimated 5,000–6,000 harvesters in 2023. An extensive scholarship describes the *yarsagamba* trade elsewhere in the Himalayas—emphasizing for example its boom economies (Sulek 2019), sustainability challenges (Winkler 2009) and uneven geographies (Yeh and Lama 2013).

not motorable. Our conversations with residents of Mugum in Mugum Karmarong Rural Municipality, the northernmost village in the Karnali River Valley en route to Nakchelagna, as well as police and forest guards stationed along the road to manage the throngs of *yarsa* prospectors, suggest that little if any provision has been made to protect the local population from sudden intensive competition from itinerant traders. On the contrary, residents of Mugum appear to be treated the same as other *yarsa* pickers, in that they are required to obtain a permit and abide by the restrictions on access within a stipulated time period. We anticipate the northern landscape of the district will soon experience a different politics of encroachment, rooted in a loss of control by local populations and opportunities for rent seeking on the part of officials charged with protecting a fragile landscape.

ENVIRONMENT AND CONDITIONS FOR SUSTAINABILITY

Overall in Mugu the critique of environmental destruction accompanying road development is pervasive and well-articulated, across a range of stakeholders. We attribute this environmental consciousness to the mismatch between the intense aspiration for development through roads in one of the last districts in the country to "become connected," and the disappointing quality of the actual roads, both strategic and local. Over 10 years after the inauguration of the Karnali Highway in Gamgadhi in 2012, this strategic thoroughfare is still not blacktopped in most sections; motorable access to Mugu is still only seasonal, as the highway is often impassable during the most intensive periods of monsoon; and much of the LRN similarly remains unsuitable for motor transport for much of the year (Khatri 2023; Panday 2023). As described above, another distinctive feature of Mugu has been the role of RAP in promoting environmental consciousness through its highly scaffolded roll-out of the green roads model. Mugu residents have seen and experienced the enhanced possibilities for sustainable outcomes—socially, economically, environmentally—in a setting where "RAP roads" can be compared plainly with other local roads built through the users' group modality. At the same time development pressures and cultural-political dynamics remain.

CRITIQUES OF ROAD BUILDING

Particularly among politicians, contractors and those who stand most to benefit from development in Mugu, the environment figures centrally into road building imaginaries. A prominent politician who is also involved in contracting attributes potential development in Mugu to its abundance of natural resources and natural and religious tourist destinations. Investing in tourism by enhancing access could turn the district into a "Switzerland," he said, echoing a common refrain, while opening the Gamgadhi-Nakchelagna Road, by boosting international trade, could make Gamgadhi "like Kathmandu." Such aspirations for tourism rooted in environmental features and developing Mugu as a "trade hub" were repeated across several interviews, which also noted the draw of hot springs, biodiversity—especially the extraordinary diversity of herbs—and even the prospect of a copper mine. A leader within the district's civil society network (a loose network of civil society organizations sharing a commitment to human rights in Mugu) advocated "training courses" and "home-stay facilities" that could involve a wide base of Mugu residents in tourism promotion.

The more prominent narrative, however, concerned the critique of road building from an environmental perspective. Many Mugu residents regard the rapid proliferation of rural roads as a problem. As a business owner with district-wide distribution put it, "roads are scattered everywhere," echoing the analysis of "sprinkling" in the 2013 World Bank report mentioned in the Introduction of this book. Instead of focusing on connecting settlements to each other, as in the District Transportation Management Plan, there is a tendency to build roads to as many villages as possible. As the business owner put it, "What I have seen with my own eyes is that roads are being built on those slopes (pointing northward toward Ruga and Tharpa on the hillside facing Gamgadhi) literally one to two hundred meters apart. Of course that is going to cause environmental destruction." The RAP RBG member and political leader cited above noted that this problem is particularly exacerbated by "powerful people" who have "connections to political parties and leaders," and thus are able to bring the road to their own village.

An executive officer of a rural municipality in the region southwest of Rara Lake, who also runs a boarding school and works as a contractor described the ensuing chaos:

> There are so many landslides. For example, if the road goes to that village down there, then people from another village want the road ... as well. All the villagers will get together and demand a road. They will reach out to different offices, organizations, or projects and ask for some money. ... If the money is not enough then they will raise some funds among themselves and construct the road to their villages. When they construct the road themselves that way, it is not secure. During the monsoon season the whole village faces the danger of landslides. Look at those villages like Ruga and Tharpa—they face a huge risk of landslides. If you look at the Balai area—if you go via Chaina to Balai—you can see many landslides on the road.

As a result, a leading politician put it, "there will be natural disasters. There will be landslides and flooding. It will impact streams and sources of water. There will be more deforestation."

The rampant scattering of roads is widely understood to result from the availability of heavy machinery, such as bulldozers and excavators made possible by the opening of the Karnali Highway (The World Bank 2013). Two Mugu residents involved with administering the RAP3 green roads model used language that is also evident in the national news media to characterize the rampage of heavy machinery in fragile mountain ecosystems. A civil society and political party leader (and executive member of several local NGOs) opined that "dozer terrorism" results from collusion among contractors, political leaders and local technicians—all of whom stand to benefit from the operation of heavy machinery. A member of the RAP3 team based in Jumla, through which we sometimes transited en route to Mugu, similarly remarked on the impromptu "dozer engineering" that takes place when bulldozer operators receive guidance from politicians and contractors as opposed to "detailed engineering."

Such critiques are equally articulated by those involved on the labor side of road building. A RAP RBG member living in Chatyalbada described a road below Gamgadhi Bazaar from Chatyalbada Village, which had been built improperly with a dozer, though it had been contracted to a users' group. The group used the dozer to open the track by simply "removing a layer of soil to form the roadbed," but did not stabilize it, for example with gabion wire walls. Rather they "ate" the remaining funds from their budget by dividing amongst themselves. The roadbed "is not strong enough and just invited more damage." Such accounts were repeated over many interviews and informal discussions recounting how dozers shake the land, leaving it prone to landslides and earthquakes, and echoing the popular expression, "development begets destruction," (*vikasle vinash pani lyaunchha*).[13]

How do Mugu residents and development workers account for the destruction? They find fault with both modalities of road development—users' groups and contracting—while noting the more tightly managed RAP system falls into a different category altogether because of its commitment to sustainability. A Mugu-based journalist with a more systemic understanding of how these modalities relate to wider governance systems commented aptly on the problem that DoR bureaucrats charged with monitoring strategic road development are based in distant Jumla District headquarters. Their absence allows "dozer operators [to] ... cut the road wherever they want ...

[13] It is important to clarify that these ideas have a lineage in Nepal that goes back quite some time; see, for example, Tüting and Dixit (2018).

wherever they find an easy alignment." The same issue applies even for district-level bureaucrats supervising the Local Road Network. Career bureaucrats appointed from central ministries occupy senior positions, and Mugu is treated within the government bureaucracy as a "hardship post"—meaning that it is used either as a stepping stone for advancement to a "less remote" location, or as punishment for bad behavior (see discussion in the Introduction about *durgam/sugam*). Their offices are often left vacant during long sojourns out of the district, so that supervision of road development is in practice left to lower-level, local bureaucrats commonly embroiled in openly collusive *milemato* processes discussed above, and also characterized as a contractor-bureaucrat-business-NGO nexus of control amongst those in privileged positions vis-à-vis development works, as will be discussed further below.

BUDGET DEADLINES

Two significant explanations are offered for the poor quality of road construction undertaken by contractors, which is in turn associated with their role in environmental destruction. The most prominent relates to "*Asare budget*,"—the budget of *Asar* (last month of the Nepali fiscal calendar). This refers to the widespread tendency to expend budgets for infrastructural development toward the end of the fiscal year. When projects are rushed to completion for the sake of spending local budgets by deadlines, the standard is likely to be low, and the infrastructure falls quickly into disrepair. As the coordinator of the district's civil society network explained, the long-time absences of appointed upper-level bureaucrats noted above slows the approval process for local infrastructure development projects, contributing to the year-end pressure:

> There is always delay in agreements. ... Once the projects are brought forward to the headquarters [DDC], there is a district council meeting. The projects are passed through that council meeting in *Fagun* (mid-winter month). Those projects are

> selected from village-level proposals. ... But to pass all those projects, technically the government officers [office heads] have to sign them. If they were actually in the district then the projects would be passed in *Fagun* and ready to go [to tender or distribution] in *Baishakh–Jeth* (early spring months). But the projects remain pending while waiting for ... the head officers to approve them. And then a few months just go by and then after *Baishakh* and *Jeth* there is a rush to allocate the projects in the areas promoted by those with more access to power. And then the agreement is done quickly and the work is done during *Jeth* and *Asar*. Why are those projects even done? To not let the money allocated for the projects "freeze" [budget not expended by the end of the fiscal year must be returned to the central or provincial government]. ... That is why the work is poor in quality. Everything is done in a rush. If initiated in a timely manner then work would be completed during the winter and early spring seasons when people are not busy with other things [agriculture]. ... That would be a source of income for the public during the off season and the work would be a good quality.

While the quote attributes blame for poor quality local roads to bureaucrats, in fact, contractors and politicians are also widely understood to bear responsibility. Project selection is often delayed by conflicts among political parties. And contractors with accrued projects rush to complete them before the end of the fiscal year when they have to follow complicated procedures to renew contracts and secure committed funding. Contractors are seen to intentionally delay their work in order to create a bottleneck of work for monitoring by government technicians, and thus to get away with poor quality. Many of our interviews with a wide range of interlocutors reveal these realities. The user group modality is no guarantee against any of these dynamics. Many residents discussed the "politicization" of users' groups, whereby party leaders vie for coveted "executive" positions from which they can influence how the budget is spent. The "nexus" is at play here too, with party leaders, business owners, NGO workers and even government workers (or their family members) predominating in these roles. Under these circumstances, and in the absence of close oversight, in fact many "green" or "LEP" roads are built with bulldozers. "A users' committee is formed, and the executive committee; that main committee eats half the budget and half the remaining budget is used to pay for the dozer; the dozer comes and does construction that is not reliable, and leaves; that is how it is done here"—explained the previously cited woman active in RAP RBGs.

The political leader quoted previously, who also is a RBG member in RAP, elaborated:

> KEP is for people who are not employed here in Karnali. ... What happens is the opposite. That money is taken away from people and is given to the <u>dozer</u>. The money is actually coming from a program that is called "*Aphno Gau Aphai Banau*" [build our village ourself]. But ... the money goes ... in the mouth of ... <u>dozer</u> owners. ... The main [executive] committee keeps NRs. 2–4 lakh and gives another NRs. 2–4 lakh for the <u>dozer</u>. Karnali Employment exists only in name. People are still unemployed. ... Executive committee members and <u>dozer</u> owners work together, keeping the <u>budget</u> from the rest of the committee. ... This <u>road</u> here in [the village of] Chaina, at the beginning, NRs. 10 lakh, from zero point to the border of Karkibada VDC, was allocated. But later, it was found that NRs. 7 lakh was paid for the <u>dozer</u> and NRs. 3 lakh was eaten by the executive committee.[14]

[14] These numbers and those in subsequent interviews addressing road budget amounts should be interpreted as indicating a tendency, rather than reflecting exact figures. The KEP also acknowledged these kinds of practices in its early years and has attempted to enforce the LEP modality by arranging to pay workers directly through their personal bank account, rather than through the users' group account.

In fact, as the small business owner put it, "villagers were just happy because the road was being constructed, but all the money was taken by the dozer." An activist and a leader of Dalit community made similar comments about a dozer "taking over" on the road to Jhakot (below Gamgadhi to the southeast), as well as to Tharpa (northeast of Gamgadhi on the facing hillside). He said,

> They built roads using dozers during the nighttime; according to the rules, the users' group is supposed to call householders to do the work and use dozers only if people reject the opportunity. The users' groups rationalize the use of dozers, claiming that human labor is not available to build the road. In fact, that is not true. People have been building roads in much more difficult rocky terrains. Contractors and users' groups [executive committees] prefer to use dozers because both will profit more.

Community members do not generally protest because they also benefit from the speedy opening of a track and not having to provide labor.

Under these circumstances, the *Asare* budget logic also applies to users' groups. Another cause of delay in finalizing contracts for district roads arises in conflicts surrounding the formation of users' group executive committees (given the high demand for executive positions in a highly politicized terrain). According to a contractor-party leader (whose brother is a local government bureaucrat) from a village bordering China,

> When users' groups are not formed in time, they come to sign the contracts for road work at the end of the fiscal year, and then they ... compromise the quality of the work. ... If the contracts were signed in *Mangsir* (in winter), they would have 4-5 months to complete the work [before the end of the fiscal year]. Community people would have been involved in

> development work when they were free from agriculture work. ... When the users' group members start fighting among themselves ... they do not come to sign the contracts with the district until the end of the fiscal year ... when they have to finish the work in 8–10 days. They cannot do good work in a short time and the development budget goes to waste, like water seeping into sand. Development of Mugu has not been occurring due to this kind of development culture.

ALTERNATIVES TO "SHAKING THE LAND"

By all accounts, the closer supervision involved in the DfID-funded RAP3 mobilization of users' groups helps to contain much of this "waste," as well as employ community members and mitigate environmental damage from road construction. RAP3 has more resources to engage "social mobilizers" overseeing the formation and functioning of users' groups with elected "leaders," called *naike*, rather than an executive committee. *Naike* provide trainings in construction techniques, and phase construction over several years so that the road can settle into the landscape as it is incrementally widened. Here the track is opened to only two meters in year one, and to eight meters over time with the original bed being recovered and strengthened (Hamal 2021). RAP3 is widely considered to pay well relative to other waged labor; it pays men and women equally (in theory); and, as a woman contractor who is also a primary teacher put it,

> Even if we cut down a branch of tree, RAP gives money for that work. RAP pays for all the work we do. RAP does not make us work free whether the work is small or big in size. The work volume does not matter. We are paid for everything. (Hamal 2021: 107)

Her positive valuation is summarized in the widely circulating jingle, "*RAP3, paisa free,*" which points not only to the decent wage, but also to the decent employment conditions in which all dimensions of work are "counted."

A local bank branch manager recognized how the enhanced capacity of RAP3 is related to their larger budget and "having staff." But, he says, they also "treat the workers on the road [the RBG members] as their own staff," for example by providing insurance. Such arrangements are widely understood to be preferable than using dozers. The rush to development is certainly palpable in a district like Mugu that has long experienced access challenges. And yet, the critiques of heavy machinery are pervasive amongst those who do not stand to benefit financially from contracting heavy machinery. Why should we give our budget to the owners of a dozer? The logic goes: when we work to build the road, we can buy a new pair of shoes." A contractor, business owner, and party leader puts it this way:

> In my personal opinion, using people for manual labor is better than dozers. Dozers should only be used in areas where manual labor is not possible. ... People who do not have jobs can earn some income by building roads. ... Those who used to go to India or abroad ... are able to work ... near their homes living with their own families. I find that way better than using dozers.

He also notes that use of dozers concentrates wealth—those dozer owners are already rich. Without income, local residents don't stand to benefit much even once the road is built: "They won't get much just looking at the vehicles running through their villages; those local residents should have the capacity to earn and spend before the vehicles start running, so they can invest [in the opportunities opened up by the road]." Of course, he made these remarks without referencing his own role as a contractor engaging heavy machinery—who had, in fact, recently won the bid for building a district road.

And yet he drew frank connections between social and environmental sustainability. "The road constructed by manual labor is stable as well, while dozers shake the land around the roadbed and cause landslides." A RAP RBG member criticizing users' groups for contracting dozers in track opening, wanted us to understand clearly how RAP3 works differently. In contrast, "our user's group has been mobilizing our community members and now they have more job opportunities. Because our community is working to build the road to our own village, they are conscious about the land. They dig out the land as much as needed [with as little impact as possible]." The RAP RBG member and political leader cited above similarly explained the benefits of manual labor in environmental terms, which he argued more than justifies the longer time frame compared to dozers. Referring to the section of Karnali Highway in Mugu, he said:

> The harm from natural causes like floods and landslides is less on the road built by manual labor as compared to those built by dozers. The roads that are built by manual labor can be cleared easily after the monsoon, but we have to rebuild the whole road in the areas where a dozer was used. Last year, half of the road in Balai was destroyed and collapsed! The dozer did all that work, but it was damaged even more than it had been before the road was built. That is why RAP has a policy of not using dozers. Dozers, and the explosives that are sometimes used, shake the land. They create gaps that water can easily seep into and weaken the rocks and soil, which might lead to landslides; we might lose a whole section of the hills this way, and it will take a lot of resources to rebuild in the same place.

He also shared details about trainings that group members receive to mitigate environmental damage, like spreading excess soil and rocks on the roadbed, rather than tossing them off to the side and damaging what lies below.

RAP3 is also credited with good technical guidance in building the rock-filled gabion-wire baskets that help prevent erosion. The same RBG member continued by noting that he had learned to build gabion-wire walls and dry stone walls (without cement or mortar that can crack with the winter frost). He claimed that not a single gabion-wire or dry wall built by community people along the Gamgadhi-Dulachaur Road had fallen or collapsed, like those built by contractors along the Karnali Highway, specifically mentioning the notorious Ghuchchi turning in the very steep section just north of Ghuchchi Lek. He attributed the difference in quality to the sound training and oversight requiring RBGs to "follow the instruction of technical staff." He also echoed a common refrain in the discourse on participatory development: "people had ownership and they built the [RAP] road thinking that this is our road and we have to make it strong for ourselves; but the contractors were focused more on making profit and saving time." At the time, the RBG member was pointing to the impressive results of manual labor on the Gamgadhi-Tarapani section of the RAP road to Dulachaur. We reflected, however, that "ownership" does not result simply from "participation;" it has a material basis in the mode of remuneration—the decent wages, the gender parity, and the mode of accounting by volume of work rather than time.

To be fair, some critiques were shared with us about the RAP3 project in Mugu, suggesting in addition to the inequities in land acquisition noted earlier, that prevailing modalities of organizing work also crept into the RBGs. A female RBG chair noted that some households in her village have figured out how to circumvent the one-member-per-household rule by sending multiple household members to participate (Hamal 2021: 106). Doing so required having the influence to ensure that no one reported an objection, which allowed these households to "make a lot of money." However, overall we were struck by the consistency with which RAP3 projects are compared favorably with roads built by both contractors and community-based manual labor under less tightly structured conditions. We were therefore surprised to learn of a transition that seemed to be underway at the end of our field research in Mugu, toward increased use of heavy machinery on a new RAP road to Humla District. We documented a consensus emerging among a range of actors about the benefits of dozer use. RAP3 and political parties wanted to build the road faster; local contractors were proliferating and wanted the work; and people did not object. It remains to be seen how the commitment to sustainability will be reflected in the details of how dozers are managed and community members engaged.[15]

ROAD CONNECTIVITY AND MARKETS

As already discussed, contracting is the most immediate market associated with road building. But the principle of collusion in fact extends beyond the procedures for *milemato* in bidding, to encompass a web of relationships that concentrate access to the business of road building within a narrow group of households. The English term "nexus" is used, in otherwise Nepali public discourse, to characterize the tight ties among those occupying key roles, or multiple roles: contractor, government employee, supplier of equipment, government employee, even NGO local staff. Collusion within a nexus may take place below the official radar or in plain sight. It helps ensure the smooth functioning of *milemato* when low-level government officials, those residing in Mugu who are often left with keeping things afloat when the office heads are (commonly) out of district, are part of the nexus. As described above, there is a small informal trade in licenses, and one contractor described how he had gotten into road building by possessing a license for trade in medicinal herbs. He had purchased his license for NRs. 50 thousand from someone he refers to as "*dai,*" older brother. He recounted an absurdly time-consuming process for registering the license, which could only be finalized when a Local Development Officer associated with the same party as the contractor was deployed in Mugu. While his primary business interest lay in the *yarsagumba*

[15] Thanks to Jagannath Adhikari (personal communication 2024) for noting a corresponding promotion of mechanization in agriculture planning. See UN Food and Agriculture Organization's sustainable agricultural mechanization website (FAO 2025).

trade, this contractor also hoped to get in on the commission from the contractor designated to win the road bid in the *milemato* system.

It is extremely difficult to penetrate into the inner circle of class D contractors among whom the competitive and consensual winning bids circulate. Every one of these contractors we interviewed or knew about, in fact, had direct family ties with, or personal roles as, political party leaders. Most had direct family and/or political affiliations to businesses from whom they procured equipment. Conflict-of-interest rules prohibit occupying two stakeholder positions in infrastructure development; in such cases, the common work-around is to register the contracting license or supply business in the name of the spouse. That contractor or business owner would then in practice run the contracting or supply business and benefit from at least the inside information available to local bureaucrats, if not influence over decision making. For those seeking entry to the contracting and procurement markets but lacking these connections, the barriers are experienced as impenetrable.

Chyankhe khane, or taking PC in the context of consensual bidding, allows new entrants to build a profile on paper, which might increase their eligibility for winning a contract at some future date. But it does not enable them to accrue experience. A woman contractor, also a teacher, explained:

> Experience can only be gained by working, but they [the main local contractors] do not allow us to work and we are ineligible [not enough experience], so how can we gain experience? Our forms [bid] are just there under the pile. Yesterday, I requested them to include my application at least. I told them that even if other people get the contract, I will build my <u>portfolio</u> if my form gets included. (Hamal 2021: 100)

She described the experience of being disrespected by those able to win the bid "consensually"—those paying the PC to new entrants—who "accuse" them of being "fake contractors." "We actually want to work but they say those things and we still [do not have experience and recognition]. How are we supposed to gain experience ... (Hamal 2021: 100)?

Who is in the inner circle? According to the medicinal herb trader who also participates in petty class D contracting:

> These are the people who have better connections, and have the capacity to spend money and pay PC. And are also able to take advantage of nepotism. On top of that if you are involved in politics and have political connections. ... All the people involved in politics are contractors. To be honest these contractors are either politicians or their mobilized cadres.

Unlike the woman teacher-contractor, this petty contractor has no interest to acquire "real" experience. He is content to receive his PC, and enjoy the small margin after covering the costs of license renewal and buying the form to submit his deliberately losing bids:

> This [contracting] is for rich people. If you are *sojho* (honest) then you should not take up this job. Contracting and politics are the same. A person who is a contractor, and a person who is in politics ... they will never speak the truth. They will always lie. I do not like this profession as you have to lie and misuse [the funds and power].

This characterization of nexus and the opportunities it opens for private gain resonated with other interviews and our observations of the district bid tender. We also want to underscore that government officials have key roles to play in the nexus. When describing the construction of the Talcha-Gamgadhi Road, a Gamgadhi-based businessman (who is also an executive officer of the local transportation association), frankly asserted that the government official charged with measuring, monitoring and approving the construction work "would take 10 percent PC; if the contract is

NRs. 1 Crore, at 10 percent the PC would be NRs. 10 lakh." This demonstrates the logic and dynamics of "nexus" that enables the concentration of opportunity, wealth, and power amongst households with longtime privileged status.

The market in transportation is less well developed in Mugu than other districts, such as Dolakha, given the poor condition of Mugu's roads. The cost of travel by plane and helicopter is out of reach for most residents, and, as the businessman and executive member of the local bus transportation association explained, "It requires favor from political leaders to get a ticket." When we conducted our research in 2017, there was one established and two emergent bus transportation associations in Gamgadhi. An executive member of Rara-Chhayanath Transportation Pvt. Ltd., who is also a leader in the business sector, convinced the chair of the Federation of Nepalese Chambers of Commerce and Industry (FNCCI) to approach the Chief District Officer for support in founding a transportation association. The purpose of such associations is to provide services to vehicles providing "public" transportation, such as insurance and advocacy in the case of accident. In fact, the Ministry of Transportation also requires transportation associations to manage a route permit system in every jurisdiction. All public buses must obtain a route permit in order to offer services on a particular road. Thus Rara-Chhayanath began permitting bus owners, as did another subsequently formed association, Karnali Yatayat Samiti (Karnali Transportation Committee).

The Rara-Chhayanath executive acknowledged the prevalence of transportation syndicates throughout Nepal—as described in the Dolakha chapter—through which competition takes a coercive and sometimes violent form:

> These days, there is syndicate system in everything. The government claims that there are no syndicate systems but in practice we can mobilize *gunda* and not allow anyone to use this route except Rara-Chhayanath if we want. It is like a

> monopoly where we would only allow our vehicles to use this route. And then when we go down to Surkhet they won't allow us to use their routes, so we have to work using networks across jurisdiction.

By all accounts, this potential dynamic has not taken hold in Mugu, and the two associations function peacefully and in parallel. To the extent that we learned of conflict on the Nagma-Gamgadhi section of the Karnali Highway, it centered around taking additional charges and fierce bargaining over bus fares. While these practices are experienced as additional dangers of bus travel, beyond the poor condition of the road, they are not considered to be linked to the transportation associations. The syndicate logic does operate, however, through the networks mentioned above, through which associations in Mugu align with associations in adjacent districts (Surkhet, Jumla) for the purpose of channeling business. Similarly, transportation associations develop ties with hotels and restaurants in the key transit centers such as Gothijyula so that bus passengers are delivered to particular establishments in exchange for free food and lodging for the driver and a commission paid to the association. Despite the expectation that roads foster economic development, then, this brief look at transportation markets underscores that emerging markets are governed at multiple scales and through informal as well as formal processes.

We can also note a range of market developments associated with the opening of the Karnali Highway to Mugu. Gamgadhi Bazaar now has a direct connection to Surkhet and Nepalganj. Though the road quality is not good, mobility has increased and supported the expansion of facilities. There are now numerous hotels, computer institutes, and banks. Marketplaces and bazaars have also expanded. Gamgadhi itself, despite being on top of a ridge of fragile and sandy land, has expanded in the two decades since the opening of the Karnali Highway. The bazaar has grown not only in number of establishments but also the volume and range of imports to the district—especially white rice (not grown in arid Mugu soils) and other food products, electronics, fashionable clothing, and consumer goods considered modern and convenient. A new labor market is evident in the bustling Gamgadhi bus depot where one sees ticket counters, bus drivers and attendants hailing passengers, and porters, especially women, engaged in unloading and transporting wares to storage houses. These markets in labor and goods are made possible by the lower cost of transportation associated with road construction, and are experienced as improvement in quality of life. That being said, we routinely heard two concerns. Property values in Gamgadhi and along the roadside increase rapidly with the introduction of motorable transport; this benefits landowners, but locks others out of ownership, even if Mugu's real estate market is not as extensive as those of the market centers in Dolakha and Morang.

A commonly repeated refrain muses about the long-term dependency created as trucks arrive full of consumer goods, but leave empty, as Mugu does not produce or manufacture significant goods for export. Dalit participants in the research and those in analytical professions like journalism and experiential education also observed that poorer households have more difficulty adapting to the monetized economy, as profit is systemically concentrated amongst the merchant classes: "the road has arrived here," noted a local journalist, "but justice has not been established."

Roadside markets are also flourishing. Gothijyula, Nagma, Chaila, Phuli, and Bhubule are common examples of expanding markets. Gothijyula, for example, which sits on a river plain at the base of the mountain range forming the border between Jumla and Mugu, owes its very existence to the Karnali Highway. It grew up on the roadside because of its geographical convenience as a resting stop, and now compares to Gamgadhi as a commercial center, with dozens of restaurants and hotels (in multi-story concrete buildings), shops, and the requisite dust and pollution associated with being a bustling entrepot "on the way" along an unpaved highway. Each of the rural municipalities, too, despite their dry, barren land, now have a market center of their own upon being connected to the Strategic Road Network, and residents no longer need to come to Gamgadhi to access a market. Similarly, satellite markets have grown up around the district center, such as Chautha, Balai, Ghata, and Chaila. Expansion in both supply and demand of consumer goods has enabled residents to develop experience with starting new businesses, including assessing market demand and securing finance capital.

Just six months after the inauguration of the Karnali Highway, three new banks and two savings and credit cooperatives had already opened, leading to an expansion of financial services beyond the previous two state-owned banks and local moneylenders. While apple farming had been the primary business supported by banks in Gamgadhi, now people describe their experiences obtaining business loans from banks as a helpful and relatively easy experience. Banks actively market loans for houses, real estate, motor vehicles and commercial businesses—as well as for the contracting sector as discussed above.

Many programs led by non-governmental organizations, including RAP, KEP, and WFP, now include a savings and credit component, targeted often toward women who have established practices of saving and investing in household economies. Typically, these programs require monthly savings contributions of NRs. 250 to NRs. 500, which allow members to take out loans at lower interest rates than banks. The RBGs formed under RAP3 have such compulsory saving schemes requiring members to deposit at least 10 percent of their wages. Some of the groups provide loans to members on a rotation basis and some groups save their funds in local banks. Such schemes, in addition to promoting women's economic agency, also contribute to the overall demand for consumer goods.

POLITICS, POLITY AND PLANNING

In Mugu, roads are a powerful political imaginary and a heavily contested socio-political field, with key implications for economic development and social justice. That much is clear to all those who participated in our research. This final section considers how polity—not only in the sense of the franchise, but also the field of political subjectivities forged through a revolution, a process of federalization, and local governments restructuring—relates to planning, in the sense of both official, institutionalized processes as well as the informal mechanisms emphasized in this chapter. Both are inflected with party politics as we have underscored throughout, and we cannot talk about planning without acknowledging this reality. This section thus both reports on the politics-planning terrain as we encountered it, as well as offers some thoughts about desirable planning action.

We begin by noting that roads bring planning to the forefront of people's consciousness. There are many views about where the road should go, how to manage processes of expropriation and encroachment, and the pros and cons of using heavy equipment to open a track. The resulting poor quality of roads in Mugu is widely understood, not in terms of its challenging topography, which is taken for granted as the natural way of things, but in terms of poor planning. "Modern" reinforced concrete (RCC) houses built with iron rods and cement—locally called *pakki ghar*—in the Gamgadhi Bazaar should have been subject to planning standards in anticipation of a motorable road. Planning dictates, such as prohibitions against dumping household wastewater into a roadway, must be enforced to be effective, but instead the mire of mud and stuck vehicles in the Mugu Bazaar point to a situation where those enforcing the law have less power than other actors. The use of heavy machinery should be controlled to protect against landslides and environmental damage. In these ways, roads figure in people's everyday life and are understood to be state projects, about which people forge opinions about what should be done. The chaotic outcomes of road development have inspired in Mugu an interest in how planning might be beneficial.

At the same time, we find in Mugu, considerable critical awareness about how planning transpires in practice. Knowledge about *milemato, Asare budget,* PC, the nexus of contractors, party leaders, government officials and NGO workers, as well as other informal planning mechanisms, is widespread and discussed openly, by all involved and others who observe. These practices are against the rules, but they carry on as the normal way of things. Participants in our research had an analysis of the pros and cons. In the "pro" column, people stated that development budgets are expended, not frozen, capital stays in the district, and the benefits of contracting are distributed. On the "con" side, we heard about poor road quality, lack of maintenance, danger of travel, and environmental damage. Knowledge of local informal planning processes, moreover, is used to contradictory ends. Those within the nexus benefit in the form of bids won, PC received, a desirable road alignment, and so on. Those outside the nexus experience marginal benefit at best, as in a PC distribution to a petty contractor from a *milemato* agreement, but more often frustration, sometimes displacement.

Despite such critical consciousness, there is a sense that it is difficult to protest, that the existing informal planning processes are so imbricated in local party politics, economic histories, and dynamics of power that they are difficult to change. As the petty contractor engaged in medicinal herb trade explained, if complaint leads to canceling contracts, that means the people's money (local government budget) gets wasted; whereas if you do complain, then elites (contractors, suppliers, government officials) keep eating the money—either way, it is the poor people who get short changed. The *milemato* system subverts protest and complaint by offering opportunities to participate in the tendering process for those with limited means, but some business experience and interest. To protest would be to deny oneself such opportunity.

Our contention in concluding this chapter is that the critical consciousness evident in residents' analysis of the cultural politics of road building itself can be considered as a resource for planning. Not in the sense of people's capacity to participate in various programs run by the state or by NGOs with donor funding, or to participate in public forums staged to solicit public input on budgets and programs that have already been deliberated by government officials and political party leaders. Given the openness of informal systems of road planning, often in public places, in the presence of police, government officials, and the general public, we advocate including knowledge of how planning transpires in practice into the official record—the District Transportation Management Plan, most of all. Such knowledge resources include insights about the nature of processes that generally get glossed as "corruption" by donors and consultants, as well as the media, who similarly bring knowledge resources to bear on road development. We suggest that these local knowledge resources offer valuable commentary on what is considered locally as good or bad practice, which can be useful for informing planning practice.

Finally, we advocate increased community control over local planning processes. "Community" is as encompassing and ambiguous a term as "local knowledge." Therefore, it is also important to specify groups who are underrepresented in official and informal planning processes, as well as those professionals with an explicit praxis of critique: Dalit and members of other marginalized ethnic groups, petty class-D contractors, and local journalists, for example. Innovative proposals will likely arise when such groups inform, contribute to, and evaluate planning for infrastructure development, such as the suggestion of a petty class D contractor to introduce a mentorship system into the local contract tendering system geared toward training and supporting new entrants, or the aspirations of a Dalit-run theatre group to animate local awareness and critique of development processes. Under these conditions, local residents would not simply be engaged in road building projects, but also exercising democratic values, empowering themselves, and developing critical spaces and critical consciousness for building infrastructures of democracy.

CONCLUSION

The Politics of Roads and the Praxis of Planning

KATHARINE N. RANKIN

We conclude with a summary of arguments and a consideration of how our research could inform a planning practice committed to justice and sustainability.[1] In this book we have opted for a collaborative, relational and comparative approach to the ethnography of road development. Ethnography allows for the emphasis on road development as a contradictory and contested process, entailing multiple meanings and highly differentiated experiences and outcomes across space and time. It takes the perspective of people living in communities undergoing rapid infrastructure development as a foundation for the analysis of contemporary conjunctural formations. Relational comparison requires investigating how roads develop in relation to dynamics both within and beyond the districts chosen as our research sites, and in the vortex of the inter-connected, multi-scalar forces that constitute those sites. It also points to a praxis orientation—to the links between research and action—which we maintain through a focus on planning both as an object of inquiry and a terrain of practice.

[1] The Conclusion maintains the first-person plural in view of the collective nature of the work, but all errors and oversights can be attributed to the author.

Collaboration infuses the research. The research team was fortunate to have worked closely with colleagues based in the three districts of Morang, Dolakha, and Mugu, each of whom brought community development expertise and local knowledge to bear on the research process. Community-based researchers particularly contributed access to a wide range of participants, as well as reflections on interview findings and field observations. Chapter authors deliberated a common structure for the chapters and identified the themes of road history and remoteness; organization of road development; land, landscape and borders; environment and sustainability; transport and markets; and politics, polity and planning. The co-editors subsequently developed the book's arguments in consultation with the authors, reading across the chapters from their cross-disciplinary locations in anthropology, geography and planning.

The Conclusion returns to the key arguments of the book in sequence as outlined in the Introduction, and ends with the animating normative question for planning praxis: what is to be done? It refrains from extensive citation of the literatures reviewed in the introduction.[2]

CONNECTIVITY AND REMOTENESS

Ethnographers have consistently underscored the relational quality of connectivity and remoteness forged by road development. Our comparative approach points toward a framework that traces how roads 1) create connections for some places and new forms of remoteness for others; and 2) even within a single locality, deliver uneven experiences of accessibility and remoteness for different people, depending also on where they are located within dynamics of power. In Morang, iconically connected via Nepal's first national highway since the 1960s, remoteness persists in a southern belt lacking

[2] Thanks go to Jagannath Adhikari for advocating a conclusion in addition to an Afterword, and for sharing his reflections on some concluding points. His particular contributions are noted throughout, the first of which is to suggest a framework for interpreting remoteness, which is provided in the subsequent section.

reliable rural road connections that become impassable in monsoon mud and floods, despite being a hub of industrial and agricultural production. For subsistence farming households, connectivity begets exploitation in nearby factories, along with exhausting bicycle commutes and a resulting shortage of agricultural labor.

In Dolakha, the Araniko (Friendship) Highway in neighboring Sindhupalchok District displaced trans-Himalayan trade running through its northern belt, while integrated rural development and the iconic Lamosangu-Jiri Road concentrated on the more accessible southern belt. On the newly upgraded road to Charikot and Singati, self-regulating transportation syndicates subject passengers to conflict and associated hazards like chases, detours, and arbitrary stops.

In Mugu, remoteness has prevailed as an official designation and a political subjectivity since national unification centered political and economic development in Kathmandu and subsequently Jumla as the center of the Karnali Zone, now Province. The rapid proliferation of rural roads in a region only recently connected to the national strategic road grid has generated a flourishing of contracting opportunities—yet these are predictably controlled by a nexus of political party affiliates, government officials, and local businesses that limits access for those lacking these connections.

A framework of remoteness and connectivity can also account for different dimensions of remoteness, for which the local vernacular often serves as an apt guide. Physical distance from economic and political networks can indicate remoteness, particularly in Mugu located in the country's far northwest and lacking motorable connection to the border with the Tibetan Autonomous Region (TAR). In Dolakha, the commonly articulated expression, *hami kunako manchhe* (we corner people), evokes a spatialized hierarchy and shifting center-periphery dynamics that can marginalize places within districts and regions, themselves characterized as "central" and "accessible."[3] In Morang, critical indicators of remoteness

[3] We heard the similiar, "*hami durgamko manchhe*" in Mugu—meaning "we remote people."

are frequently articulated, defying common assumptions that the flatlands of the Tarai are uniformly accessible. To convey a seasonal dimension of remoteness, villagers use their own bodies as a gauge in expressions like *yati yati hilo hunthyo*—"the mud came up this high"—pointing to their knees. Encapsulated in this expression of remoteness in somatic terms are road closures, collapsed bridges and swollen rivers, lack of transportation, and literal fixity in the mud. The stakes are high and consequences sometimes tragic, as households lose access to basic and emergency services; navigate precarious, improvised river crossings; and struggle to reach their own fields to manage a flood's effects on agricultural production.

Thus a framework for connectivity and remoteness must encompass an element of differentiation, as roads may offer new forms of access and connectivity to some while making everyday life for others newly remote. It must also encompass a multi-dimensional register that accounts for seasonality, rivers as well as mountains, time to destination, quality of transportation facilities and other factors particular to local experience. Understanding remoteness and connectivity through such a framework underscores how differentiated experiences and factors of remoteness shift in relation to wider-scale dynamics such as climate change or regional political economies. It also underscores how any effort to support connectivity must therefore account for its relational dimensions.

PUBLIC GOOD AND PRIVATE GAIN

Roads conform to classic understandings of a public good in the sense that they are basically available and openly accessible (they generate positive externalities), while it is not immediately obvious how they can be reliably financed and produced (they generate a free-rider problem, wherein people benefit from a resource without paying their fair share). Public provision proves challenging where a reliable tax base is lacking and development assistance inconsistent. The ethos of participatory development that gained traction through the 1980s and 1990s provided a rationale that beneficiary communities should bear some responsibility for the provision of public goods like roads, through contributions in cash or kind, in order to enhance feelings of ownership and long-term accountability. Private provision, meanwhile, has generally been characterized by practices of collusion, embezzlement, and other forms of illicit extraction, facilitated by the large capital outlays and the high number of actors involved in infrastructure development, as well as well-honed patronage relationships. In Nepal and other contexts where subsistence production intertwines with market exchange, legacies of informal, collaborative provision of public goods persist, for instance through impromptu initiatives to build temporary bridges during monsoon floods.

As the chapters demonstrate, in the midst of these competing logics, road development in the aftermath of two forms of rupture—conflict and disaster—becomes a key site for deliberating the nature of publics, the appropriate relationship between citizens and the state, and what forms of private gain are justifiable in the provision of public goods. Here again local vernacular expressions such as *milemato* (consensus/collusion) prove instructive. Such concepts convey competing values that help to specify local conceptions of who is responsible for infrastructure development, as well as locally situated logics of ethical judgment that might provide a corrective against the gloss of corruption as well as furnish alternative conceptions of the public good. We draw upon empirical material from the book's chapters to highlight three examples of these dynamics in practice.

First, a remarkable feature of rural road building in Nepal is the expectation that landowners would donate their land to accommodate the alignment of the road. The official rationale is that the road creates value for landowners in the form of rising land costs and opportunities to locate housing next to a vehicle corridor. Our research suggests another calculus from the perspective of residents. Land contributions are offered willingly where construction labor is well-paid and social protections are provided to those enlisted for road building, such as in the Rural Access Program, Phase 3 (RAP3) projects in Mugu.

Social protections, combined with shared legacies of remoteness, create conditions for a positive valuation of collective development, and a willingness to offer significant material contributions to the cause. In Dolakha, however, party leaders and local elites mobilize concepts of honor and shame to coerce landowners into making land donations. They evoke the principle of *dan*, a form of gifting to priests and deities in Hindu and Buddhist frameworks that is understood to confer merit, when they promote the prospect that donating land, *jagga,* for road construction could be considered *jagga dan*. In the context of a highly competitive local political economy (with enduring elite factions and a well-articulated labor market), such invocations of religious merit are perceived as an unwelcome exercise of elite power and arrogance.

Second, our findings about consistent subversions of the rules governing rural road development likely come as no surprise to most readers. However, it is worth dwelling on various forms of breaking the rules that are routinely considered within the realm of common sense and justifiable under the present conditions. A most compelling example along these lines is the practice of *milemato,* arranging the bid to rotate amongst leading contractors affiliated with political parties, as elaborated extensively in the Mugu chapter, but also evident in Dolakha. *Milemato* entails giving PC, personal commissions to those who participate in fixing the bid by consensually submitting "fake" high bids that ensure a chosen contractor will "win." Sometimes accepting a commission would be expressed as *chyankhe khane,* which translates as taking (literally "eating") a commission for not participating in a bidding process, and denotes an ethos of gambling. These processes occur openly, under the noses of district government officials posting and awarding bids, bank managers providing bid bonds, and law enforcement officers on guard in district government headquarters—all of which are overwhelmingly male and absent Dalit representation. Participants and observers, while they may have a clear understanding of the exclusionary implications of *milemato*, also recognize some benefits: such collusive practices hold contractors from outside the district, and their *gunda,* at bay; they afford opportunities for petty contractors who would like to gain some exposure to official procurement processes; and they support power sharing among political parties.

Third, certain acts of collusion, bribery and lack of accountability do of course contravene local moral frameworks and evoke critique. *Milemato* even in Mugu is understood to manifest a "nexus" (the English word is used) of contractors, businesses, government officials and NGOs—colluding to create opportunities for private gain in a way that concentrates opportunity, wealth, and power amongst households with longtime privileged status. Much of the organized protest surrounding road upgrading in Dolakha relates to the opaque nature of these relationships in a context where capital outlays for road development are high and rooted in longer histories of road building. A key threshold for intolerance of private gain at public expense centers around *dukha,* hardship (see also Rai 2015). When citizens are subject to material hardships caused by road "upgrading"—persistent dust, unreliable transportation—roads as a shared imaginary for future progress cease to hold the public trust. When the perception that prevailing practices, like donating land without compensation or consenting to collusive *milemato* processes, creates acute hardships for those who are less well-off in Mugu, the normalcy is questioned, sometimes openly in local newspapers and popular theatre performances. In Morang, when villagers perceive that expectations of voluntary labor for road building evoke legacies of forced labor, or when people perceive that local governments have "budget"—the English word is used—to spend on local development, they act through refusal to volunteer their labor or otherwise participate. Thus we might suggest (as we have elsewhere, Rankin *et al.* 2024: 362) that from the perspective of research participants, the public good is not road development itself, but getting quality roads built in a way that honors people's dignity, relationships and demands on their time, while also mitigating against concentration of wealth and opportunity.

POLITICAL CAPITAL IN MATERIAL AND SYMBOLIC FORMS

Rural roads build political capital, we also argue. The chapters underscore the (relational) symbolic and material dimensions. The symbolic valence of roads has been duly noted by ethnographers. Everyone, almost everywhere, wants a road, despite the fact that roads notoriously flood, erode, and lose vehicles off sharp, precipitous corners. Roads furnish powerful imaginaries of a better future, a reprieve from the scourge of remoteness. And they are continuously articulated as key sites of claims-making, profit, protest, and territorial control. Key points of articulation along these lines include the aspiration of connectivity for the resumption of cross-border trade in Lamabagar, (northern) Dolakha and Mugum Karmarong, (northern) Mugu. In southern Morang, people express they want to live in a village where there is a road. The road enhances their position in a wider space. They can boast about it while marrying their sons and daughters in traditional arranged marriages. The accessibility of their village to ambulances and other emergency services carries symbolic weight. Not having a road, or having a road that becomes impassable in monsoon, is a source of shame.[4]

Such aspirations create opportunities to wield political capital. We have seen in the chapters how political leaders engage the road as a promise of reward for the loyalty of constituents—such as by advancing allies for contractor roles (Mugu and Dolakha), or by managing (*milaune*) the alignment of a road in their favor (all three districts). Similarly, in Mugu, petty contractors subscribe to a *milemato* system that inherently reproduces existing hierarchies and the existing nexus of power, in large part because they are drawn to the opportunity to symbolically "build their portfolio" by participating in official procurement procedures.

The challenge, of course, arises when elites are unable to turn the symbolic aspiration and promise of the road into a viable material reality. Roads remain unpaved, impassable in the monsoon (Morang)

[4] We are grateful to Jagannath Adhikari for sharing insights on this aspect of symbolic capital.

or the monsoon and winter (Mugu), with inefficient transportation (Dolakha being the paradigmatic example, where a syndicate system undermines material achievements of road building). Some roads remain suspended entirely, terminated abruptly half-way up a hillside, evoking sedimented conflict, perhaps over alignment, perhaps over budgets, perhaps over the terms of engaging manual labor or machine operators. Political capital, that is, must eventually be invested in concrete infrastructural forms, through which the gap between plan and aspiration for road building, on the one hand, and material outcomes on the other, become territorialized on the land for all to witness. Causes of the discrepancy between the symbolic and the material were not lost on our research participants. People understand how various forms of PC (personal commission) necessarily drain road budgets in Mugu, how *tukre budgets* (parsing local fiscal resources into small pieces) sprinkle road projects with insufficient budgets in Dolakha, how various forms of encroachment on public lands designated for road development create time-consuming conflicts over alignment and displacement in Morang, and how *Asare budget* (the practice of expending allocations at the end of the fiscal year) everywhere entail rushed and substandard work resulting from the unsupervised use of heavy equipment.

POLITICAL SUBJECTIVITY AND CLAIMS-MAKING

Political capital may disintegrate into political liability when material outcomes do not meet expectations or reflect promised plans. Political alignments can shift as protest galvanizes, contradictions are exposed, and elite beneficiaries of the contractor-party-bureaucracy-business-NGO nexus become subject to critique. Another set of arguments in the book therefore concerns the formation of individual and collective political subjectivity as people develop and articulate such analyses, make claims, and imagine different futures.

In this regard our chapters draw out how road development furnishes a critical ground on which people formulate ideas of themselves as political actors. In Mugu, although the Karnali highway was inaugurated almost a decade ago, people still harbor strong views about where the road should have gone (touching more villages, bringing tourists through the district center). In all districts, alignment, expropriation, and encroachment—by which rural roads territorialize contradiction, conflict and power—have become contentious public issues and terrains for making claims about what is right and good. Dolakha residents coping with landslides on the poorly planned Singati-Charikot Road improvised a hybrid form of mobility, whereby they sent their goods by bus but preferred to reach their destination faster by walking on the old trails along the Tamakoshi River. Morang residents assert new forms of "budget subjectivity" when they articulate that a local government with decentralized budgets should assume more responsibility for road development. The stakes are high and people living in communities where rural roads are being developed know it.

Our chapters detail how people must thus navigate multiple scales of state and other development institutions in their exercise of political agency. Budget subjectivity in Morang manifests as refusal to furnish voluntary labor for road development in official contexts of users' committees (UCs). At the same time, refusal created some space for women to take over the management of UCs and organize volunteer labor in a more collaborative manner, achieving experiences of leadership and political agency. In the absence of speedy reparative action by the state when bridges are destroyed by floods, moreover, villagers in the southern belt have coordinated informal, collaborative processes for building temporary bridges to support local mobility. The Mugu chapter provides an account of women residents organizing to shift the alignment of a road through villages slated to be bypassed on a route through the forest. They made their case collectively to the District Development Committee (DDC) office and were successful in achieving the desired re-alignment—in a rare instance of genuinely grassroots intervention in planning processes.

The chapters also convey distinctive modes of collective political consciousness and public sphere politics emerging on the terrain of infrastructure development. Journalistic reporting proved critical in Mugu and Dolakha for staking out a public sphere where contractors, party leaders, and government officials were asked to account for harmful delays, environmental destruction, and inequitable outcomes. In Dolakha, a District Dialogue Group staged public meetings and protests demanding accountability for road construction delays and clarity about opaque processes; local knowledge and critique had taken an organized, collective form. A popular theatre group formed in Mugu to communicate critical analysis of development with communities most subject to exclusion and displacement—with the politics of infrastructure as a prominent focus (Hamal 2021). In Dolakha, residents on the Charikot-Singati Road established the Rolwaling Transportation Cooperative in the absence of service by the local transportation association, in order to make newly opened tracks accessible to locals. Local knowledge had taken a collective form in these examples, pointing to the possibility that it can also serve as a resource for not only critiquing but also informing planning processes.

ENVIRONMENTAL TRANSFORMATIONS

Our chapters also grapple with how roads are bound up with environmental transformations, and how people in the communities where rural roads are being developed grapple with these changes. They convey a clear picture of the environmental costs of road building—how landslides and floods are associated with Himalayan roads, and render some places, like Singati in Dolakha, unsafe for long-term habitation. People in Singati, located on the banks of the Tamakoshi River where the Charikot-Lamabagar Road descends from the hills and veers north, have come to understand that disaster can strike at any time, and not only through seismic instability.

In the Tarai of Morang people lament the experience of remoteness created by floods, which traps them in their villages, and keeps them from fields, marketplaces, emergency services, and other critical dimensions of connectivity. They rightly note that appropriate technologies of green roads have been developed in relation to hill and mountain topographies, but have neglected to innovate approaches to sustainability in the face of seasonal flooding in the Tarai. The Tarai context also highlights secondary forms of environmental destruction resulting from road access. Sand-mining has introduced increased pressure on local and feeder roads, as "*trippers*," dump trucks, make trips back and forth from mining to collection sites, throwing up dust, "shaking the land," and making noise all night long—on top of their impact on river-bed ecologies. In the local parlance of all three districts, the common phrase, *vikasle vinash lyaunchha,* development begets destruction, is commonly referenced in relation to road development.

Residents of Morang, Dolakha, and Mugu understand the correlation between use of heavy equipment, and landslides, flooding, and unsustainable rural roads. In Morang, for example, villagers commented how excavators make roads and trenches less compact than manual approaches—and thus also vulnerable to damage during heavy rains and floods. In the hills of Dolakha, they noted how backcutting performed by "*dozers*" similarly builds an insecure roadbed—difficult even to walk on in the aftermath of inevitable floods and landslides, and threatening the safety of nearby settlements. Such problems are commonly attributed to the conflation of users' committee (UC) and contracting modalities, whereby UCs contract heavy equipment in a direct subversion of the "labor-based, environmentally friendly, and participatory" (LEP) philosophy that had in fact originated as official development doctrine in Dolakha District. While they may participate, residents also have an analysis of how such processes relate to local cultural politics and political economies—of how political patronage produces a multiplication of small road projects spread around the district to facilitate patronage dynamics, or contributes to endless delays as political leaders compete, resulting in rushed, substandard road projects at the end of the fiscal year. Under such circumstances, they understand, operators of heavy equipment acquire outsized influence over the technical aspects of road building; they become "*dozer engineers*" with unpredictable motivations.

In Mugu, it must be recognized, environmental consciousness also entails positive recognition of a donor-led green road project with provisions for both environmental and social sustainability. RAP3 was leading the construction of two rural roads during our research. Rigorous adherence to LEP principles was matched with various mechanisms for social protection, including engagement of a local NGO to provide a "social mobilizer" responsible for recruiting and managing "Road Building Groups" (RBGs, comparable to UCs) allegedly free from political interference; wages deemed reasonable in local market conditions; compensation for all labor associated with all the ancillary dimensions of road building that commonly go un-remunerated; and provision of tools, training, and supports like savings and credit groups. Many residents positively valued the emphasis in RAP3 on environmental sustainability, noting how "RAP roads" experience less flooding and landslides than other roads built by UCs that contract heavy equipment in violation of their mandate. Thus, when RBG members claim that they feel a sense of "ownership" and pride in the road sections they have built, it is not merely participation to which they are referring. Rather, "ownership" had a material basis in the respectable wages, along with social and environmental protections.

POLITICS OF PLANNING

One of the loudest "messages" that comes through in this work, is the impressive extent to which all dimensions of planning are inflected with politics, whether in the sense of implementing a specific plan or program, or organizing community participation, or informal planning action led by local residents.[5] Political conditions shape planning decisions about land (especially alignment and encroachment), labor (composition of UCs, labor management),

[5] We by no means wish to suggest that this phenomenon is limited to the three districts, or to Nepal.

building modality (specifically the tendency to blend UC and contracting modalities), and the organization of transportation.

The influence of political parties comes first to mind, given how pervasively patronage dynamics work through parties and become integrated into road development (see Hachhethu 2008 and Tamang 2023a for extensive discussions). Party leaders seek to secure legitimacy and support through the exercise of patronage—currying favor and opportunity with would-be constituents; their capacity to do so hinges around a consensus mode of local politics, institutionalized through the now-discontinued all-party mechanism (APM) but persisting in the post-conflict, post-disaster, and post-restructuring periods. Examples of exercising patronage by currying favor include distributing UC executive positions—a practice that became more lucrative during our research with the increase in the cap on allowable expenditures for heavy equipment from UC budgets—and aligning track openings in areas where party leaders wish to secure vote banks. *Milemato* (collusively arranging a bid), *chyankhe/PC, khane/khuwaune* (taking and giving commissions), *tukre budget* and *Asare budget* (spreading local budgets thinly across many small projects and expending them in a hurry at the end of the fiscal year at a pace that makes oversight difficult) all manifest a consensus mode of local politics by which opportunities to exercise patronage through infrastructure development rotate amongst political leaders (Tamang *et al.* 2023: 83–84 has a helpful discussion of such dynamics at the federal scale). Doing so requires consent and collusion from a cohort of petty contractors hoping to get a "piece of the pie" and aspiring to improve their portfolio by participating in the procurement process, even if only by taking a commission to help fix the bid.

Consensus notwithstanding, party politics are at root competitive. The capacity to compete hinges around how party leadership is embedded within a nexus of influence that encompasses social and familial connections to local government offices, contracting and other businesses, and in some cases non-governmental organizations contracted by donor agencies. The nexus consolidates opportunity and mobilizes insider information, such as in contracting and procurement; it subverts democratic management, conflict-of-interest and other rules, and codes of conduct. It facilitates *kagaj milaune* (the arrangement of documentation such as bid approvals, compliance with work protocols, or quality assurance). And it is facilitated by administrative logics, whereby bureaucrats appointed to posts categorized as *durgam* (remote) seek to maximize time spent out of their posts—leaving lower-level, local bureaucrats to act in their roles (and thus activate the nexus).

Political ambition, then, trumps not just environmental and social consciousness, but also technical rationality when it comes to planning. Those who monitor and evaluate planning processes and outcomes lack incentive to carry out these duties—due to a combination of the proliferation of small projects, the commissions they are offered to "manage the paperwork" in various ways, and their personal complicity in nexus politics.[6] The most extreme examples we found in this regard were the practice in Dolakha of completing road construction projects with budgets arranged by political leaders from the subsequent fiscal-year planning cycle, and the utter failure to manage the violence of bus syndicates. Technical rationality is also compromised by opacity amongst the institutions of government charged with planning practice. The chapters demonstrate how governmental jurisdictions—for example the Road Division and the Municipality offices in Dolakha—pursue competing interests in the project of road development. They demonstrate how planners convey bigoted misinformation about the agency of Indigenous and marginalized groups in southern Morang, while lacking basic knowledge of flooding and bridges, and overlooking support required for subsistence farming in the process of road development (as in the green roads modality advanced in the hills).

Finally, we can consider planning as an explicit terrain of critique and political consciousness. Our chapters convey extensive

[6] Tamang (2023a: 24) aptly distinguishes between "capacity" and this wider formation of the local political landscape.

awareness of how planning gets subverted by politics, and an analysis by residents of the complex networks and assemblages of actors producing environmental and socioeconomic harms associated with road development. At times this consciousness is expressed as a politics of accountability focused on attributing blame—which makes for compelling content in public forums and news reporting. In the Morang chapter, we see how sometimes planning action in fact serves to protect vulnerable residents like *sukumbasi* encroachers on public lands—and political consciousness takes the form of elite (landowner) resistance. Or it takes the form of residents taking planning into their own hands in the absence of state action—as in emergency construction of temporary bridges when faced with flooding conditions or instances of labor migrants returning to their natal village to coordinate a particular infrastructure development project. Most interesting for our purposes of broaching planning as a normative terrain, is the evidence of how people confronting the enduring logics of patronage work out ethical judgments about justice and fairness.[7] By local accounts, there is a benign dimension of *milemato, tukre budget,* and the like, for example in that it keeps capital local and keeps outside contractors away. But there is also awareness about the malign aspects—substandard or suspended projects resulting from budgets rendered inadequate through consensus politics and hasty work.

WHAT IS TO BE DONE

Implicit in these arguments are some thoughts about how to make road development more equitable and just, to which we turn in conclusion. In so doing we transition explicitly to engaging planning as a terrain of practice, to consider how our research might inform a praxis committed to justice and sustainability. Praxis denotes an iterative or dialectical relationship between knowledge and action, theory and practice—and the rejection of a false binary between them.

[7] "Normative" in planning theory refers to conceptions about what is good, especially ethical, planning praxis.

We present these thoughts as research findings that signal toward answering the pesky "What is to be done" question (to borrow the title of Lenin's 1902 political pamphlet on the ideological formation of the proletariat), which bedevils local residents as much as planners. We organize these thoughts around domains of praxis that we call procedural justice, infrastructure justice, and transportation justice.

It must first be acknowledged that our findings underscore barriers to just outcomes that have been well documented in the literature on road development in Nepal and elsewhere. These center around a political economy of uneven development within which road building is embedded, such that they create enhanced opportunity for those with capital and political power to invest, but can lead to loss of livelihood for those who do not. They encompass as well a cultural politics within which the conditions for collective political subjectivity and action are undermined by multiple factors—such as the opacity of road building processes, or the aspiration to "get in on the action" of contract bidding, which mitigates the impulse to critique or protest. Syndicates, patronage, collusion, bribery, embezzlement, collusion, dozer terrorism, dozer engineers—all addressed in the popular press, the gray literature, as well as academic literature—can be experienced as sedimented systems that are difficult to change, as a perennial trap, or even as a "common sense" about the normal way of things. These dynamics of *vinash*, destructive development outcomes, are as much informed by local knowledge as their critique and resistance.

PROCEDURAL JUSTICE

Procedural justice begins with local knowledge. Our chapters show that locally situated perspectives constitute powerful expert knowledge of local dynamics, as well as of multiscalar relations among intersecting political economies. We recognize these as situated critical analyses of the field of road planning and practice, rather than as "local points of view" limited to a narrow geographical and conceptual domain (as discussed in the Introduction). Situated critical analyses convey important insights about relations of power, socio-spatial difference, and of how things work in practice—such as how the opportunity to donate land for road building can become a terrain for coercion from the perspective of Dalit landowners in Mugu, or how practices of hybrid mobility in Dolakha convey knowledge about inadequate conditions of the road. We have also seen that critical insights rooted in local knowledge are widely accessible to those who seek them out. Just as some flagrantly break rules in pursuit of individual gain, others do not hesitate to articulate their negative judgment—not just professionals like journalists or popular educators, but also other observers of and participants in road building. Some knowledge is not explicitly critical, but can equally serve as a resource for planning, such as how bankers, politicians, government officials, and contractors all talk openly about *milemato* arrangements in Mugu and Dolakha.

The question becomes, under what conditions can critical insights have a key role to play in imbuing official modalities of planning with explicit commitments to justice and sustainability? Here our findings about local frameworks of ethical judgment are instructive. For example, *dukha*, harm, could be seen as a principle against which road development practice must be evaluated. Or the interpretation of the road as a public good encompassing basic rights to emergency services and dignified livelihoods. Or people's understanding of consensus as encompassing coercion and inequity.

"Breaking the rules" and other forms of subverting official planning processes are subject to greater scrutiny when they also contravene local ethical frameworks—and thus constitute a kind of "common ground" on which planners can beneficially focus processes of monitoring, evaluation, auditing, public disclosure, and participatory decision making. Where local frameworks for ethical judgment do not align with rules governing official planning processes, they suggest an imperative to subject those regulatory frameworks to public deliberation. Similarly, local ethical frameworks offer a corrective against narratives of corruption, which serve to pathologize local populations and justify reforms oriented to "correcting" their behavior. They offer a finer grain of analysis that can serve instead as a resource for injecting democratic values and principles into local political cultures through collaborative planning. And when local ethical frameworks are expressed as protest, they reveal an explicit constituency for change.

We advocate community control over planning processes—as distinct from participation in the labor of road building—as a second key domain of procedural justice. Innovative proposals may arise when underrepresented and marginalized constituencies, as well as those engaged in critical activism against unjust road development, are given jurisdiction to inform and evaluate planning for infrastructure development. Here we can recall the suggestion of a Mugu-based petty class D contractor to introduce a mentorship system into the local contract tendering system, geared toward training and supporting new entrants. Various social-economy models can also be considered, including cooperatives familiar in Nepal, but also social enterprises (business explicitly focused on improving wellbeing of community members and not just on private profit) and community land trusts that permanently transfer land from the speculative market to a trust controlled by a nonprofit organization for common benefit. Of course, *kagaj milaune, milemato,* and other logics of patronage and subversion can infiltrate such formations, too; but can incentives be structured to require democratic governance that does not offer inherent advantage to those with privileged access to nexuses of power? Subjecting planning to deeper modes of community review and control can slow down the process, expand the base of knowledge resources, and hold those with the greatest stores of economic, political, and social capital to account. At best, it can enroll infrastructure development in building a democratic polity where "remote" places like Mugu, northern Dolakha and southern Morang can influence the terms under which they integrate with national, regional, and geopolitical agendas.

There is a well-known, if contested, precedent in Nepal for community control over scarce resources: the community forest users' groups (CFUGs), from which UCs in the green roads model were derived. The idea of devolving planning from state bureaucracies to local users' groups in an effort to balance forest conservation and livelihoods, in fact, traveled the world as models of community-based management, and proved durable during Nepal's civil conflict because of their grassroots base and federated structure. The experience with CFUGs raises cautions in at least two respects. Indigenous movements have critiqued CFUGs as a form of elite capture, displacing Indigenous control over forest resources in the name of democratic governance.[8] CFUGs, that is, presage the challenge of political capture faced by road UCs. There are, however, key differences between forests and roads that can also be considered. CFUGs manage a valuable resource relevant to local livelihoods, from which benefits and proceeds can be equitably distributed amongst members. They are long-term, informal, community-based organizations not tied to the timeline of a particular development project. Road UCs, by contrast, operate on a short timeframe (the time it takes to build a section of a road) with respect to a not-so-public good, from which members may benefit, but over which they exercise no direct long-term control. They may thus be even more subject to "capture" by political party interests and others motivated to further shorten timelines with the use of heavy machinery, as indicated in all chapters here. The logic is participation, not community control.

We can also consider how some resources have become more accessible, and contested, as a result of road building. The harvest of *yarsagumba* (medicinal caterpillar fungus) once managed by residents of Mugum, has now, with the slow development of the Nakchelagna Road, become a destination for thousands from across the Karnali region and beyond hoping to find fortune. At the time of our research, the harvest was managed by the Nepal Army, and local residents had to engage in risky practices of evasion and subversion to

[8] Citing Mukta Tamang (2011), Sara Shneiderman (2018: 98) notes that "Indigenous scholar-activists in Nepal have called into question the caste and ethnic hierarchies of the country's much-touted CFUGs."

access a resource long sustained under their control. Sand-mining in Morang is the purview of private interests. Local residents might find employment, but they have no say over the extent of mining, or how the crushing industry plies their trippers on local roads to transport the sand.[9] In view of the experience with CFUGs and road building UCs, it is worth exploring how the management of these resources could incorporate some dimension of local control in combination of local auditing practices aimed at mitigating political capture.

INFRASTRUCTURE JUSTICE

Our chapters have numerous implications for staking out what might be called infrastructure justice. This concept has had some traction in the North American context where existing infrastructure is aging out and being massively challenged by climate change, with socio-spatially differentiated impacts. In the United States, for example, the Policy Link research and action institute ran a campaign on Infrastructure Justice as a Road to Reckoning, Repair, and Transformation. The campaign sought to seize the moment of Joe Biden's COVID-19 stimulus and infrastructure investment packages to "reframe the national discussion around infrastructure and build a bridge to an equitable recovery" (PolicyLink 2025). The Infrastructure Justice for LA (Los Angeles) Coalition similarly engages regional infrastructure development as a platform upon which to promote public health, equity, and social and community justice. We can think along these lines in relation to road development in Nepal, to consider social protections, sustainable mechanization, community control, and mitigation of harm.

To the extent that some localities opt to persist with a participatory model of road building involving UCs engaged in manual labor, we can recognize the imperative to provide social protections accounting for the wider livelihood challenges facing people enrolled in road building on a temporary basis. Based on the experience

[9] See Kumar (2022) regarding the proposal to introduce a people's partnership model for sand-mining.

in Mugu, however, we know that the donors formerly advocating green roads, not just the UCs illicitly hiring heavy equipment to undertake their labor contributions, have questioned the viability of the LEP modality.[10] They too want faster progress and, along with politicians, want to demonstrate their efficacy. Having promoted the green-roads orthodoxy, DfID (now the Foreign Commonwealth and Development Office, FCDO), the World Bank and others began bringing in consultants and researchers to evaluate green road construction, and then reversed course to endorse the contract method and mechanization (e.g., The World Bank 2013). This transition in ideologies of global sustainable development has a corollary in "sustainable agricultural mechanization," to use the FAO's (2025) terminology. The claim here is that mechanized technology can still be "environmentally friendly," while also reducing the drudgery of manual labor (especially for women, it is argued), relieving the burden of labor shortages commonly associated with outmigration, and creating new employment opportunities such as manufacturing, repair, and provision of mechanization services.

We certainly do see a flourishing of the local contracting sector in Morang, Dolakha, and Mugu. Like any market, contracting is a political terrain; thus far it has been primarily planned through quotas, limits, and unenforced quality standards. We might consider how contracting and ancillary businesses can create opportunities not just for employment, but also for forms of community control more robust (and just) than UCs. Supports could be provided to contractors and various hire services who constitute themselves as cooperatives, or, given experiences with dysfunctional and dishonest management in Nepal, as social enterprises geared toward generating community and environmental benefits.

Planning informed by local knowledge could respond to the realities of *milemato* bidding by instituting a mentorship system within local tendering processes so that aspiring entrants to the

[10] Jagannath Adhikari reports the same for Bhojpur. Personal communication, 2024.

market, especially women and Dalit, are engaged beyond *chyankhe khane,* taking commissions in exchange for high bidding. We know of instances where local leaders and charismatic returnees from abroad mobilize remittances and other resources to undertake reconstruction (Dolakha) or build temporary bridges (Morang) in emergencies. We can thus consider a role for planning in directing such spontaneous initiative toward well-supported social enterprise. Standard community development techniques that have supported such a role for planning elsewhere include mapping assets to identify where capacity lies for productive enterprise (including through local work traditions like labor exchanges or social ties linking buyers and sellers), tours to other jurisdictions where such enterprises exist, and informal feasibility studies attending to gaps in the existing market (e.g., CEC and Gibson 2009). An advantage to engaging such modes of community-controlled road development lies in the scope for also undertaking maintenance over the long term, rather than merely building roads in the present moment. Such processes will undoubtedly have to attend to the challenge posed by out-migration particularly in the hill and mountain districts where rural road construction is currently so extensive—such as by engaging the services of social enterprises or cooperatives from elsewhere or by creating incentives for outside labor to join such initiatives.

Finally, the articulation and experience of *dukha* also furnishes a critical planning resource. Our chapters show how harms fall in some areas that are not typically considered the purview of the engineers and planners tasked with overseeing road building and its models. They point, for example, to how the capacity of landowners to absorb the loss of private land must be factored into alignment decisions; how alignment can compromise livelihood; how delayed construction poses everyday headaches and obstacles to livelihood; and how ill-informed stereotypes persist, particularly about Indigenous groups in the Tarai, but also even about Dalit and women. They also point to how road building can render some places newly or more remote, indicating an imperative for redistributive action, ideally in a manner that engages local discretion. Planning infrastructure, that is, must address the harms generated by road development.

TRANSPORTATION JUSTICE

We conclude briefly with transportation justice—a concept that is flourishing in North America, Europe, and Australasia, but has generally been focused on urban contexts. An urban focus also characterizes more recent activism on transport justice in Nepal, which seems to have concentrated on environmental dimensions including air pollution/EVs and bicycle infrastructure. Our chapters prove instructive vis-à-vis rural contexts. Foremost, they indicate an imperative to exercise principles of "cause no harm" and "passenger rights" in situations where transportation syndicates carry on competitive practices that pose direct danger to passengers, as well as significant inconveniences. Simply put, people should get fair treatment when they travel.

Like infrastructure justice, transportation justice could be promoted by policies supporting social enterprises and cooperatives. We have seen some of the promises and challenges for transportation cooperatives in the experience of the Rolwaling Transportation Cooperative. Wresting transportation from already existing entrepreneurs' associations having close connections with parties appears particularly challenging. Here again we suggest that expanding the base of community control through supports for a wider range of social enterprises and cooperatives could be worth exploring; these might include initiatives providing ancillary services such as mechanics, or even restaurants and hotels in market centers cropping up along the road. Local knowledge proves instructive as well in terms of identifying dimensions of rural road transportation not typically addressed in government and donor planning processes, but which would enhance local livelihoods. These might include paved and well-maintained bicycle trails and single-lane roads involving minimal investment and resources, particularly in the southern Tarai where the terrain is flat but so often rendered remote by a combination of neglect and flooding. Or upgraded walking trails to support hybrid mobilities.

Our purpose has been to consider infrastructures of democracy, not only in the sense of how the conditions of political restructuring shape infrastructure development today, but also in the sense of how infrastructure development might deepen processes of democratization. Of course, some of the advocacy here for various forms of community control has the ring of standard participatory development, which has been criticized for reproducing prevailing power dynamics. As we have suggested, however, the devil is in the details. Our thoughts here on what is to be done to achieve equitable and just outcomes are informed by locally grounded knowledge and expertise conveyed through the foregoing ethnographic chapters. They center on addressing the vexing challenges of political capture, corruption, and monopoly power endemic to infrastructure development, not by advancing non-enforceable regulations, pathologizing discourse, and punitive frameworks—but rather by creating conditions for economic democracy and community control. Road development guided by these principles—in which harms are mitigated, local knowledge and ethical frameworks resourced, significant control vested in a wide base of residents—might serve as a training ground for building strong democratic polities rooted in the aspirations of critically conscious publics.

AFTERWORD

Reflections of a Project Coordinator

ELSIE LEWISON

I am honored to be able to leave the reader with a brief reflection on this book and the larger Infrastructures of Democracy project. The inception of the Infrastructures of Democracy project—roughly a decade ago as of writing—coincided with an emerging popularity of "infrastructure" within anglophone academic social sciences. Over the course of the research, interest in the concept boomed and infrastructure suddenly seemed to be everywhere, not just "on the ground," but also in sessions at conferences and workshops, special issues in journals and new research initiatives. South and Southeast Asian geographies were particularly prominent in this scholarship, influenced in large part by growing attention to China's Belt and Road Initiative, which was building momentum and making headlines. The Infrastructures of Democracy team was thus in good company and well positioned to contribute to, and learn from, this "infrastructural turn."

As noted in the Introduction to this book, the Infrastructures of Democracy project is distinctive within this scholarship on infrastructure in its focus on rural roads. While seemingly mundane in comparison to some of the large-scale infrastructural endeavors taking shape across Asia, the rich ethnographic material presented by the research team in the preceding chapters demonstrates the extent and depth of the impact of rural roads and road building on the lives of individuals and communities across Nepal. Seemingly minor concerns—whether or not an agricultural road is widened a few feet, a new road goes up along a ridge or down along the valley, a group of small-scale contractors is colluding or competing—can have real material significance for rural landscapes and household wellbeing, and prompt heated debates over development, tradition, and the public good.

Here, I want to highlight a few other distinctive features and contributions of the Infrastructures of Democracy project, particularly in relation to its approach to collaboration and relational comparison. Before proceeding, however, I want to emphasize that this reflection is based on my personal engagement with the project, which was mostly from behind a computer screen in Toronto, Canada as a graduate student (and eventually postdoctoral) research assistant and project coordinator. It is important to underscore that collaborative research across geographies of profound economic, political, and social inequity is necessarily fraught. Rather than attempting to do justice to the subject from my limited perspective in this short Afterword, I will again point readers to Aijazi *et al.* (2021), who provide thoughtful reflections on a number of the challenges and points of tension faced by the Infrastructures of Democracy team. These include divisions of labor, questions around authorship, Canadian university administrative structures, the dominant role of English in many of our outputs (including, of course, this book), and the centrality of anglophone scholarship in our citational practices, to name just a few.

I want to use this opportunity to highlight the productive tensions and contributions that came out of this collaboration, and the different analytical lenses, praxis orientations, and personal and professional interests that it brought together. These tensions and "encounters across difference" (Aijazi *et al.* 2021: 88) were not incidental to the work, or something that needed to be overcome to proceed. Rather they were central to the research process and outputs, including the unwillingness in this book to compromise inclusiveness of experiences and perspectives for the sake of providing a tidy narrative or a singular argument. Having the chance to be a part of these conversations was also, at least for me, a valuable opportunity for critical self-reflection and learning.

Interlinked with the collaborative approach was the framework of relational comparison described in the introduction. Relational comparison, across not only three districts, but also multiple roads in each district, was important for developing a robust, conjunctural understanding of rural roads and road building across distinct localities that are also part of "interconnected historical geographies" (Hart 2016: 3). As we have seen, the districts had diverse histories of roads and road building, as did different localities within these districts. Indeed, the research shows the remarkable difference that a few kilometers (or meters, when it comes to road widening) can make in a community's or an individual's experience of roads, mobility, and remoteness. These distinct experiences with roads were shaped by interconnected physical geographies, markets, economies, and cultural politics.

In Morang, for example, we find a long history of roads, including symbolically and strategically important roads like the East-West Highway. Today, the presence of regular employment opportunities in nearby towns has made daily commuting a common road use, and cycling has become a key mode of transportation on rural roads. Meanwhile, claims to land on and alongside roads, including by landless individuals and families, has raised potent debates over public space and land rights within communities.

Dolakha also has a relatively long history of road development, particularly given its hilly and mountainous terrain, in which international development agencies played a central role. The development of large-scale hydropower projects has also shaped expectations and experiences of roads, while the particular contingencies of mobility and market dynamics in the district has given rise to tense stand offs between transportation syndicates.

In Mugu, the arrival of roads, along with their promises of future prosperity, has been relatively recent. Mugu offers a window into new iterations of labor-based, environmentally friendly road construction administered by international development agencies, alongside contracting and users' committee-based road building modalities. We find growing anxieties about trucks that arrive loaded with goods and leave the district empty, as well as concerns about how these new roads will impact the high value *yarsagumba* trade and the ecologically fragile landscape along the northern border.

Across these diverse localities, the team also encountered a range of shared and interconnected processes and concerns, many of which are captured in the arguments outlined in the book's introduction. The preceding chapters explored the relative and contingent nature of connectivity and remoteness, with localities experiencing remoteness in a variety of different ways—through official categorizations, a washed-out bridge, a new road constructed the next valley over, or lack of access to a vehicle. Across the sites, roads are also transforming environments by, for example, destabilizing hillsides and altering drainage patterns. These processes lead to increased risk of landslides and flooding. There are also indirect impacts, through the expansion of markets for sand, for instance, or shifts toward more chemical-intensive agriculture in response to declining labor availability.

We similarly saw how roads and road building have become key sites of contestation over the public good across the districts, including in heated debates over land "donations" for rural roads, and critical analyses of the uneven distribution of harms and benefits arising from new or wider roads. Across the chapters, roads are closely linked to the operation of symbolic and material political capital, contributing to the intensity of battles over alignment and control of users' committee budgets. The ethnographic accounts in this book also demonstrate how political subjectivities emerge and transform through these varied engagements, with important implications for planning and advocating for more just alternatives.

Reflecting on the collaborative nature of this relational ethnography, the lead researchers in each district also brought their own unique perspectives to each field site. Thus, for example, where the Morang chapter presents richly detailed oral histories of the experiences of laborers working on the first roads in the area, the Dolakha chapter provides a thorough and insightful account of the politics of road alignment in the district, and the Mugu chapter offers a nuanced account of the complex cultural politics of contracting markets and bidding practices. Each of these in-depth explorations followed from the particular interests of the lead researcher(s), as well as the opportunities and contingencies encountered over the course of fieldwork.

The ethnographic accounts and analyses offered across all of the chapters were also shaped by the contributions of multiple project members and extensive collaborative engagements within the research team, through significant time dedicated to sharing, dialogue, and reflection. Collaborations with community-based researchers in each district were particularly critical to the research process. These collaborations took different forms; while all teams conducted joint interviews, community-based researchers also conducted interviews independently (particularly where uneven power dynamics might impact the comfort of interlocutors), documented local road stories through field notes and photography, and authored or co-authored articles for the local media and academic journals (Nepali 2018; Kunwar and Thapa 2020). Across all of the field sites community-based researchers contributed key analytical insights and perspectives that would have otherwise been overlooked or remained inaccessible. These included insights into the often intentionally impenetrable operations of contractors and users' groups, as well as candid views of road building from individuals whose perspectives and interests were among the most marginalized within local power structures.

The district leads also joined each other for visits to one or more of the other districts as time and other commitments permitted. The project PI, Katharine N. Rankin, spent significant time at each site with the district leads and community-based researchers over the course of multiple trips. Co-PI, Sara Shneiderman, brought decades of experience conducting ethnographic research in one of the focus districts, and joined team members on several research trips. Other members of the project, including myself, also had a chance to join research teams at field sites. Stacy Pigg's graphic ethnographic project entailed several visits to Dolakha in particular with Shyam Kunwar and Shanta Thapa. This time walking and riding along roads, observing, and conducting interviews together were critical to the research process. They allowed different members of the team to develop and contribute their own ethnographic insights, work together to untangle the complexities of different modalities of road building, and gain a shared understanding of the affective and embodied experiences of rural roads.

The multi-day workshop held in 2018 in Balthali, Nepal offered an important chance for the project team to gather together in person. A number of the core themes and arguments structuring this book emerged from discussions at this workshop. A good portion of the time was devoted to storytelling, with the researchers providing richly detailed (and sometimes very funny) accounts of encounters on the road or the experiences of a particular road building project or interlocutor. While many of these stories and narratives did not make it into the book, they offered important context for the group as we began the collaborative processes of reviewing and analyzing the fieldnotes and interview transcripts that made up the core data of the project. Alongside these opportunities to gather in-person, we also remained in regular communication over the course of the project through online and in-person meetings, emails, messages, and a variety of joint writing projects. This ongoing communication was a chance to share updates, seek clarification, and discuss emerging themes and divergent interpretations.

Another important feature of relational ethnography, as noted in the introduction, is its praxis orientation and the impetus to imagine and propose alternatives (Hart 2018). The Infrastructures of Democracy team was firmly united around a common concern for justice and equity, and we had many shared points of reference for what a more equitable and just world could and should look like. However, our interpretive lenses and praxis orientations were also shaped by our distinct positionalities. My own positioning, for example, was as a Canadian graduate student who had recently graduated from an international development studies program feeling disillusioned and searching for an alternative career path. As a graduate student, my political and theoretical leanings were strongly influenced by an anglophone critical development studies literature centered in North America and the UK. My politics were thus closely bound up with material and professional interests, including aspirations to contribute to this literature in publications viewed as important by the types of institutions where I might one day look for employment.

Given this positioning, my scope of praxis and critical lens tended to focus, often simplistically, on international development agencies and institutions—a myopic tendency that was productively challenged over the course of the research. For example, I approached the Rural Access Program (RAP) described in the Mugu chapter with cynical skepticism, looking for opportunities to apply theories from my critical development studies toolbox. This skepticism, however, ran up against the consistently positive reviews of the project from the researchers and their interlocutors. Conversations within the team about this program were productive, and insights from interviews and field observations of the RAP bolstered an emerging argument for sustainable, labor-based, road building methods that provide fair compensation for labor and adequate resources for construction. The RAP program still, of course, raises important questions about whether the agent of a powerful foreign state should have the power to make important decisions about who gets roads and when. However, our discussions remained an important opportunity for me to interrogate my biases and predispositions.

My colleagues on the project team brought nuanced analyses of the interconnected operation of power across scales. Their different positionalities across the district sites offered a rich diversity of standpoints and praxis orientations that informed the project's critical engagements with power. This included engagements with an array of practices broadly glossed as corruption—from labor contributions made "on paper" only and the improper use of users' group funds for entertaining—to collusion among small-scale contractors, to the outright pocketing of road funds. A key contribution of the project's relational ethnographic approach is its ability to situate "corrupt" practices within interconnected, multiscalar, historical geographies, cultural politics, and uneven relations of power. The collaborative and comparative methodology provides nuanced insight into locally situated registers of moral judgment that can offer a basis for alternative conceptions of the public good in the planning and development of road infrastructure.

Overall, the collaborative research documented in this book underscores the point that everyday experiences of roads defy reductive narratives of either *vikas* or *vinash*—of positive development and progress, or the negative destruction of nature and traditional ways of life. Elements of both were present in many of the road stories that the team encountered. The dominant modalities of road building—market-based contracting systems and community-led mobilization—similarly blurred together and defied straightforward narratives of success and failure. The collaborative nature of the project, as well as the structure of this book, allowed room to explore and highlight these ambiguities, contradictions, and conjunctural experiences of rural roads and road building. It has also allowed the research team to address different audiences and speak to our diverse concerns and imperatives.

As the authors argue, bringing about more just approaches to planning, constructing, and maintaining roads and other pathways for mobility in rural Nepal requires recognizing and grappling with this on-the-ground complexity through messy and variegated democratic processes. Attention to the political subjectivities forged in these everyday interactions is critical to understanding the landscape of state building and political imaginaries in contemporary Nepal, as well as the conditions of possibility for more just and equitable infrastructures.

Bibliography

Acharya, Bed Nath, Rajendra Aryal, Bijaya Bahadur Karmacharya and Werner Paul Meyer. 1999. *Green Roads in Nepal: Best Practices Report.* Kathmandu: German Technical Cooperation Agency (GTZ) and Swiss Agency for Developent and Cooperation (SDC).

Adikhari, Jagannath. 2024. *Food Crisis in Karnali: A Historical and Politico-economic Perspective.* Kathmandu: Martin Chautari.

Adhikari, Krishna Kanta. 1984. *Nepal Under Jang Bahadur: 1846–1877.* Kathmandu: Buku.

Adhikari, Krishna P. and David N. Gellner. 2016. New Identity Politics and the 2012 Collapse of Nepal's Constituent Assembly: When the Dominant Becomes 'Other.' *Modern Asian Studies* 50(6): 2009–2040.

Adhikary, Kamal R. 1995. The Fruits of Panchayat Development. *HIMALAYA: The Journal of the Association for Nepal and Himalayan Studies* 15(2). Available at https://digitalcommons.macalester.edu/himalaya/vol15/iss2/6; accessed August 10, 2025.

Ahuja, Ravi. 2004. "Opening Up the Country"? Patterns of Circulation and Politics of Communication in Early Colonial Orissa. *Studies in History* 20(1): 73–130.

Aidi, Hari Krishna. 2023. Yarsagumba Collection Begins in Mugu. *The Rising Nepal,* May 25. Available at https://risingnepaldaily.com/news/27214; accessed January 12, 2025.

Aijazi, Omer, Emily Amburgey, Bina Limbu, Manoj Suji, James Binks, Courtney Balaz-Munn, Katharine Rankin and Sara

Shneiderman. 2021. The Ethnography of Collaboration: Navigating Power Relationships in Joint Research. *Collaborative Anthropologies* 13(2): 56–99.

Amnesty International. 2017. "Building Inequality": The Failure of the Nepali Government to Protect the Marginalized in Post-earthquake Reconstruction Efforts. Available at https://www.amnesty.ie/wp-content/uploads/2017/04/ASA3160712017ENGLISH.pdf; accessed January 12, 2025.

Annavarapu, Sneha and Zachary Levenson. 2021. The Social Life of the State: Relational Ethnography and Political Sociology. *Qualitative Sociology* 44(3): 337–348.

Appel, Hannah, Nikhil Anand and Akhil Gupta. 2019. Introduction: Temporality, Politics, and the Promise of Infrastructure. In *The Promise of Infrastructure.* Nikhil Anand, Akhil Gupta and Hannah Appel, eds., pp. 1–40. Durham: Duke University Press.

APROSC (Agricultural Projects Service Centre) and JMA (John Miller Associates). 1995. *Nepal Agriculture Perspective Plan (Final Report). Main Document.* Kathmandu: APROSCand JMA.

Bajracharya, Dhanavajra and Tek Bahadur Shrestha. 2059 v.s. [2031 v.s.]. *Dolakhako Aitihasik Ruprekha*. Dolakha: District Development Committee (DDC).

Bajracharya, Sushma, Debendra Manandhar, Regula Meierhofer, Shambhu Lama, Othmar Schwank and Dieter Zürcher. 1995. Development Trends in Dolakha and Sindhupalchok, Nepal (1975–1995). INFRAS for Swiss Development Cooperation (SDC), Zurich/Kathmandu. Available at www.infras.ch/media/filer_public/4b/c4/4bc466c3-4125-441e-9f70-301ae14eeb3f/dholaka-development_status_report_1995.pdf; accessed December 2, 2024.

Banskota, Mahesh. 1997. *Mountain Accessibility and Rural Roads: Innovations and Experiences from Nepal.* Issues in Mountain Development 97/5. Kathmandu: ICIMOD.

Barker, Joshua. 2005. Engineers and Political Dreams: Indonesia in the Satellite Age. *Current Anthropology* 46(5): 703–727.

Bhattarai, Ishwori and Ankalal Chalaune. 2023. Samsad Vikas Koshko Marma Loktantra. *Kantipur*, June 12, p. 7.

Bhattarai, Keshav, Ambika P. Adhikari and Shiva P. Gautam. 2023. State of Urbanization in Nepal: The Official Definition and Reality. *Environmental Challenges* 13. https://doi.org/10.1016/j.envc.2023.100776

Biggs, Stephen and Don Messerschmidt. 2003. The Culture of Access to Mountain Natural Resources: Policy, Processes and Practices. Livelihood Support Programme Working Paper 7. Available at https://openknowledge.fao.org/server/api/core/bitstreams/ff8b2d96-7c86-48e5-a66e-2a30483ed322/content; accessed August 20, 2024.

Blaikie, Piers M., John Cameron and David Seddon. 1977. *The Effects of Roads in West Central Nepal: A Summary*. Norwich: University of East Anglia.

Blaikie, Piers M., John Cameron and David Seddon. 1980. *Nepal in Crisis: Growth and Stagnation at the Periphery*. Oxford: Oxford University Press.

Boyle, Edward and Sara Shneiderman. 2020. Redundancy, Resilience, Repair: Infrastructural Effects in Borderland Spaces. *Verge: Studies in Global Asias* 6(2): 112–138.

Brenner, Neil and Christian Schmid. 2018. Planetary Urbanization: from Urban Constellations (2011). In *The Globalizing Cities Reader*. Second edition. Xuefei Ren and Roger Keil, eds., pp. 449–452. Oxon: Routledge.

Budhathoki, Gajendra. 2024. Sansthagat Baneko PCko Jalo. *Taksar* 4(2): 20–25.

Butz, David and Nancy Cook. 2011. Accessibility Interrupted: The Shimshal Road, Gilgit-Baltistan, Pakistan. *The Canadian Geographer* 55(3): 354–364.

Byrne, Sarah and Gitta Shrestha. 2014. A Compromising Consensus? Legitimizing Local Government in Post-conflict Nepal. *International Development Planning Review* 36(4): 434–453.

Campbell, Ben. 2010. Rhetorical Routes for Development: A Road Project in Nepal. *Contemporary South Asia* 18(3): 267–279.

Carter, Jane. 2011. *Suriko Kura: Development and Social Change in a Nepali Village*. Lalitpur: Helvetas Swiss Intercorporation Nepal.

CBS (Central Bureau of Statistics). 2012. *National Population and Housing Census 2011: National Report.* Volume 01. Kathmandu: CBS, GoN.

CEC (Community Economies Collective) and Katherine Gibson. 2009. Building Community-based Social Enterprises in the Philippines: Diverse Development Pathways. In *The Social Economy: International Perspectives on Economic Solidarity*. Ash Amin, ed., pp. 116–138. New York: Zed Books.

CIAA (Commission for Investigation of Abuse of Authority). 2019 (2076 v.s.). Sthaniya Tahama Hune Bhrashtachar Sambandhi Adhyayan. Available at https://ciaa.gov.np/uploads/publicationsAndReports/I4X3xF.pdf; accessed January 5, 2025.

Cresswell, Tim. 2006. *On the Move: Mobility in the Modern Western World*. Abingdon: Routledge.

Dahal, Dilli R. 1983. Economic Development through Indigenous Means: A Case of Indian Migration in the Nepal Tarai. *Contributions to Nepalese Studies* 11(1): 1–20.

Dahal, Pesal. 1997. Morangko Aitihasik Ruprekha. In *Morang: Ek Parichaya*. Raghunath Adhikari, Yadav Lamichhane, Anil Paudel and Hari Phuyal, eds., pp. 29–36. Kathmandu: Morang Kathmandu Samparka Manch.

Dahal, Pesal, Ghanashyam Bhattarai, Shyam Prasad Dahal and Kularaj Jnawali. 2019. *History of Nepal Customs*. Kathmandu: Department of Custom, Ministry of Finance, GoN.

DDC (District Development Committee) Dolakha. 1999. *Jilla Vikas Yojana: Arthik Varsha 2056/057 v.s.* Dolakha: DDC, Dolakha.

DDC Dolakha. 2002. *Dolakha Jillako 6 Varshe Avadhik Jilla Vikas Yojana: Arthik Varsha 2057/058–2063/064 v.s.* Dolakha: DDC, Dolakha.

DDC Dolakha. 2005. *Jilla Vikas Yojana: Arthik Varsha 2062/063 v.s.* Dolakha: DDC, Dolakha.

DDC Dolakha. 2013a. *Dolakha Vikas Bulletin.* No. 9. Dolakha: DDC, Dolakha.

DDC Dolakha. 2013b. *Dolakha Vikas Bulletin.* No. 10. Dolakha: DDC, Dolakha.

DDC Dolakha. 2015a. *Varshik Jilla Vikas Yojana: Arthik Varsha 2073/074 v.s.* Dolakha: DDC, Dolakha.

DDC Dolakha. 2015b. *Dolakha Vikas Bulletin.* No. 12. Dolakha: DDC, Dolakha.

DDC Dolakha. 2016a. *District Profile of Dolakha-2072.* Dolakha: DDC, Dolakha.

DDC Dolakha. 2016b. *Dolakha Vikas Bulletin.* No. 13. Dolakha: DDC, Dolakha.

DDC Morang. 2013. *District Transport Master Plan.* Biratnagar: DDC, Morang.

DDC Morang. 2017. Brief Introduction of Morang. Available at https://dccmorang.gov.np/brief-introduction; accessed January 5, 2025.

DDC Mugu. 2015. *Varshik Jilla Vikas Yojana 2071 v.s.* Mugu: DDC, Mugu.

De Soto, Hernando. 2002. *The Other Path: The Economic Answer to Terrorism.* New York: Basic Books

Des Chene, Mary. 1996. Editorial: In the Name of Bikas. *Studies in Nepali History and Society* 1(2): 259–270.

Dhakal, Suresh, Janak Rai, Dambar Chemjong, Dhruba Maharjan, Pranita Pradhan, Jagat Maharjan and Shreeram Chaudhary. 2000. *Issues and Experiences: Kamaiya System, Kanara Andolan, and Tharus in Bardiya.* Kathmandu: Society for Participatory Cultural Education (SPACE).

DiCarlo, Jessica and Seth Schindler. 2022. Introduction. In *The Rise of the Infrastructure State: How US-China Rivalry Shapes Politics and Place Worldwide.* Seth Schindler and Jessica DiCarlo, eds., pp. 1–10. Bristol: Bristol University Press.

DiCarlo, Jessica and Tim Oakes. 2022. Fourth ChinaMade Workshop: From China Model to Global China. ChinaMade Brief No. 14. Available at https://chinamadeproject.net/chinamade-brief-14/; accessed November 25, 2024.

Dixit, Ajay and Shreshna Basnet. 2005. *Recognising Entitlements and Sharing Benefits: Emerging Trends in Nepal's Hydropower Terrain*. Kathmandu: IUCN Nepal.

Dixit, Ajaya, Sanchita Neupane, Dinanath Bhandari and Bamshi Kumar Aacharya. 2021. Political Economy of 2020 Landslides, Road Construction and Disaster Risk Reduction in Nepal. Oxford Policy Management. Available at https://www.preventionweb.net/publication/political-economy-2020-landslides-road-construction-and-disaster-risk-reduction-nepal; accessed December 10, 2024.

DoLIDAR (Department of Local Infrastructure and Agricultural Roads). 1999. *Approach for the Development of Agricultural and Rural Roads: A Manual for the Preparation of District Transport Master Plan and for the Implementation of Rural Road Sub-project*. Kathmandu: DoLIDAR.

Eckholm, Erik P. 1976. *Losing Ground: Environmental Stress and World Food Prospects*. New York: Norton.

Edwards, Daniel W. 2023. Rust in Peace. *Nepali Times*. March 18. Available at https://nepalitimes.com/news/rust-in-peace; accessed January 2, 2025.

FAO (Food and Agriculture Organization). 2025. Sustainable Agricultural Mechanization. Available at https://www.fao.org/sustainable-agricultural-mechanization/en/; accessed January 12, 2025.

Ferguson, James. 1994. *The Anti-politics Machine: Development, Depoliticization, and Bureaucratic Power in Lesotho*. Minneapolis: University of Minnesota Press

Fraser, Nancy. 2022. *Cannibal Capitalism: How Our System is Devouring Democracy, Care and the Planet, and What We Can Do about It*. New York: Verso.

Fujikura, Tatsuro. 1996. Technologies of Improvement, Locations of Culture: American Discourse of Democracy and 'Community Development' in Nepal. *Studies in Nepali History and Society* 1(2): 271–311.

Fujikura, Tatsuro. 2001. Emancipation of Kamaiyas: Development, Social Movement, and Youth Activism in Post-Jana Andolan Nepal. *Himalayan Research Bulletin* 21(1): 29–35.

Fujikura, Tatsuro. 2013. *Discourses of Awareness: Development, Social Movements and the Practices of Freedom in Nepal.* Kathmandu: Martin Chautari.

Fuller, C.J. and Véronique Benei, eds. 2010. *The Everyday State and Society in Modern India.* New Delhi: Orient Blackswan.

Gaige, Frederick H. 1975. *Regionalism and National Unity in Nepal.* New Delhi: Vikash Publishing House.

Gautam, Bhaskar. 2008. *Madhesh Vidrohako Nalibeli.* Kathmandu: Martin Chautari.

Gellner, David N. and Krishna Adhikari. 2020. Guarding the Guards: Education, Corruption, and Nepal's Commission for the Investigation of Abuse of Authority (CIAA). *Public Anthropologist* 2(2): 177–200.

Ghale, Shradha. 2015. The Heart of the Matter. *The Record.* Available at https://www.recordnepal.com/the-heart-of-the-matter; accessed January 12, 2025.

Gillen, Jamie, Tim Bunnell and Jonathan Rigg. 2022. Geographies of Ruralization. *Dialogues in Human Geography* 12(2): 186–203.

Goldfarb, Ben. 2023. 'Green Roads' are Plowing Ahead: Buffering Drought and Floods. *Yale Environment 360.* Available at https://e360.yale.edu/features/green-roads; accessed January 11, 2025.

GoN (Government of Nepal). 1999. *Construction Business Act, 2055.* Available at https://repository.lawcommission.gov.np/np/wp-content/uploads/2020/12/निर्माण-व्यवसाय-ऐन-२०५५.pdf; accessed May 30, 2025.

GoN. 2002. *Prevention of Corruption Act, 2059*. Available at https://ciaa.gov.np/uploads/publications AndReports/1403179654anti_corruption_2002.doc; accessed August 18, 2024.

GoN. 2015. *Constitution of Nepal*. Available at https://lawcommission.gov.np/content/13437/nepal-s-constitution/; accessed January 12, 2025.

GoN. 2017. *The Public Procurement (Fifth Amendment) Regulation, 2017*. Kathmandu: GoN.

GoN. 2024. *The Auditor General's Sixty-First Annual Report: Summary*. Kathmandu: Office of the Auditor General.

Guneratne, Arjun. 2002. *Many Tongues, One People: The Making of Tharu Identity in Nepal*. Ithaca: Cornell University Press.

Gupta, Akhil. 2012. *Red Tape: Bureaucracy, Structural Violence, and Poverty in India*. Durham: Duke University Press.

Gurung, Harka. 1969. *Regional Development Planning for Nepal*. Kathmandu: National Planning Commission (NPC).

Gurung, Harka. 2005. *Nepal: Regional Strategy for Development*. Kathmandu: Asian Development Bank.

Gurung, Niru 2011. Local Democracy in the Political Transition of Nepal. Available at https://sias-southasia.org/local-democracy-in-the-political-transition-of-nepal/; accessed January 11, 2025.

Gurung, Phurwa. 2021. Challenging Infrastructural Orthodoxies: Political and Economic Geographies of a Himalayan Road. *Geoforum* 120: 103–112.

Hachhethu, Krishna. 2008. Nepali Politics: People-Parties Interface. In *Resistance and the State: Nepalese Experiences*. David Gellner, ed., pp. 133–176. New Delhi: Social Sciences Press.

Hamal, Pushpa. 2021. Political Economy of Road Building in Nepal: Limits of Transformative Change. PhD diss., University of Toronto.

Harms, Erik, Shafqat Hussain, Sasha Newell, Charles Piot, Louisa Schein, Sara Shneiderman, Terence Turner and Juan Zhang. 2014. Remote and Edgy: New Takes on Old Anthropological Themes. *HAU: Journal of Ethnographic Theory* 4(1): 361–381.

Hart, Gillian. 2016. Relational Comparison Revisited: Marxist Postcolonial Geographies in Practice. *Progress in Human Geography* 42(3): 1–24.

Hart, Gillian. 2018. Relational Comparison Revisited: Marxist Postcolonial Geographies in Practice. *Progress in Human Geography* 42(3): 371–394.

Hart, Gillian. 2020. Why Did It Take so Long? Trump-Bannonism in a Global Conjunctural Frame. *Geografiska Annaler. Series B, Human Geography* 102(3): 239–266.

Harvey, Penny and Hannah Knox. 2015. *Roads: An Anthropology of Infrastructure and Expertise*. Ithaca: Cornell University Press.

Heslop, Luke and Galen Murton. 2021. Why Highways Remake Hierarchies. In *Highways and Hierarchies: Ethnographies of Mobility from the Himalaya to the Indian Ocean*. Luke Heslop and Galen Murton, eds., pp. 21–37. Amsterdam: Amsterdam University.

HMG (His Majesty's Government). 1964. *Purva Pashchim Rajmarga ra Hamro Kartavya*. Kathmandu: Ministry of Panchayat, HMG.

HMG. 1967. *Vikas Rekha: 2017 Aghi ra Pachhi*. Kathmandu: HMG.

HMG. 1975. *Mechi Dekhi Mahakali* Kathmandu: Ministry of Communication, HMG.

HMG. 1977. Shri 5 ko Sarkar Griha Panchayat Mantralayako Suchana: Durgam Kshetra Vikas Samiti (Gathan) Adesh, 2033 v.s. *Nepal Rajpatra,* Part 3, Section 26, pp. 1–4. Kathmandu: HMG.

HMG. 1999. *Local Self-Governance Regulations, 2056 v.s.* Kathmandu: GoN.

ICG (International Crisis Group). 2010. Nepal's Political Rites of Passage: Asia Report No.194. Available at https://www.crisisgroup.org/asia/south-asia/nepal/nepal-s-political-rites-passage; accessed August 15, 2024.

IMC Worldwide, with Helvetas Nepal. 2013. Rural Access Programme Phase 2: Progress Completion Report. Kathmandu, IMC Worldwide, with Helvetas Nepal.

Isaacson, Joel M., Christa A. Skerry, Kerry Moran and Kay M. Kalavan. 2001. *Half-a-Century of Development: The History of U.S. Assistance to Nepal, 1951–2001*. Kathmandu: United States Agency for International Development (USAID).

ITAD (Information, Training and Development). 2018. Management of the Local Roads Network in Federal Nepal, Policy Brief. Available at www.itad.com/knowledge-product/management-local-roads-network-federal-nepal-policy-brief/; accessed August 24, 2024.

Ives, Jack D. 1987. The Theory of Himalayan Environmental Degradation: Its Validity and Application Challenged by Recent Research. *Mountain Research and Development* 7(3): 189–199.

Jazeel, Tariq. 2018. Urban Theory with an Outside. *Environment and Planning D: Society and Space* 36(3): 405–419.

Jha, Hari Bansh.1993. *Tarai Community and National Integration in Nepal*. Kathmandu: Centre for Economics and Technical Studies (CETS).

Johnson, Amy. 2023a. Negotiating Federal Governance: Mapping Local Federalism in Nepal: An Exercise in Constitutional Cartography. In *Nepal's Federal Conundrum: Negotiating a Strong Federal System on Weak Democratic Foundations*. Seira Tamang, ed., pp. 173–226. Kathmandu: Martin Chautari.

Johnson, Amy. 2023b. Settler Sensibilities and Environmental Change: Unmaking Malarial Landscapes in Nepal. *Journal of Asian Studies* 82(4): 639–662.

Joniak-Lüthi, Agnieszka. 2020. A Road, a Disappearing River and Fragile Connectivity in Sino-Inner Asian Borderlands. *Political Geography* 78: 102–122.

Kantipur. 2016. Yatayat Syndicate Toda. February 19, p. 6.

Kantipur. 2024. Yatayat Syndicate Pharkaune Ulto Yatra Tayarima Sarkar. April 23, p. 4.

Karki, Shristi. 2023. Highway Accidents are No Accident in Nepal. *Nepali Times*. September 9. Available at https://nepalitimes.com/

here-now/highway-accidents-are-no-accident-in-nepal; accessed August 20, 2024.

Karki, Tej. 2022. Political Blackmailing: A Case Study of India's Unofficial Blockade on Nepal. Available https://ssrn.com/abstract=4197326; accessed January 11, 2025.

Khabarhub. 2023. Govt Blacklists 20 Underperforming Companies. October 3. Available at https://english.khabarhub.com/2023/03/320818/; accessed October 15, 2024.

Khadka, Narayan. 1988. Nepal's Seventh Five-Year Plan. *Asian Survey* 28(5): 555–572.

Khadka, Narayan. 1993. Democracy and Development in Nepal: Prospects and Challenges. *Pacific Affairs* 66(1): 44–71.

Khanal, Prashanta, Anobha Gurung and Priyankar Bahadur Chand. 2017. Road Expansion and Urban Highways: Consequences Outweigh Benefits in Kathmandu. *HIMALAYA: The Journal of the Association for Nepal and Himalayan Studies* 37(1): 107–116.

Kharel, Pranab, ed. 2022. *Reading Nepali Transition (2006–2015)*. Kathmandu: Martin Chautari.

Khatiwada, Naresh. 2023. MPs Criticize Court Order on Constituency Development Fund. *The Kathmandu Post*, August 25, p. 3.

Khatiwada, Ramesh. 2019. Govt Prepares to Open Bid for Roads to Lamabagar Boarder. Available at https://myrepublica.nagariknetwork.com/news/govt-prepares-to-open-bid-for-roads-to-lamabagar-border/; accessed October 10, 2024.

Khatiwada, Shyam. 2018. Nirman Vyavasayile Kam Liyepachhi Sarkar ra Paramarshadatalai Dam Nachadai Hudaina: Lamichhane. *Gaurishankar Post*, April 3.

Khatri, Yagya. 2023. Karnali Highway Proves a Death Trap for Travellers Even After 20 Years in Operation. *Onlinekhabar*. August 30. Available at https://english.onlinekhabar.com/karnali-highway-death-trap-travellers.html; accessed August 20, 2024.

Klatzel, Frances. 2000. Green Roads: Building Environmentally Friendly, Low Maintenance Rural Roads Through Local

Participation. GTZ Food for Work, Nepal. Available at https://lib.icimod.org/record/10516/files/355.pdf; accessed October 12, 2024.

Kumar, Ramesh. 2022. A Nation Built on Sand. *Nepali Times.* September 3. Available at https://nepalitimes.com/banner/a-nation-built-on-sand; accessed March 1, 2025:

Kunwar, Shyam B. 2018. Anthropology of Road: Imagination, Building Practices and Changing Labour Relations in Dolakha, Central Nepal. MPhil Thesis, Central Department of Anthropology, Tribhuvan University (TU).

Kunwar, Shyam. 2020. Bhuin Tahama Nagarik Samaj: Sadak Nirman Upabhokta Samiti ra Nagarik Sahabhagitako Prashna. In *Loktantrama Nagarik Samaj: 25 Varshako Samiksha.* Harsha Man Maharjan, Devraj Humagain, Pratyoush Onta, Lokranjan Parajuli and Devendra Uprety, eds., pp. 361–388. Kathmandu: Martin Chautari.

Kunwar, Shyam and Shanta Thapa. 2020. Dolakhama Sadak Nirman: Abhyas ra Jatilata. *Samaj Adhyayan* 15: 59–84.

Kunwar, Shyam, Elsie Lewison and Katharine Rankin 2021. Labour and the Humanitarian Present: Thinking through the 2015 Nepal Earthquakes. In *Epicenter to Aftermath.* Michael Hutt, Mark Liechty and Stefanie Lotter, eds., pp. 87–109. Cambridge: Cambridge University Press.

Kuokkanen, Rauna. 2011. Indigenous Economies, Theories of Subsistence, and Women: Exploring the Social Economy Model for Indigenous Governance. *American Indian Quarterly* 35(2): 215–240.

Landon, Percival. 1928. *Nepal.* London: Constable.

Larkin, Brian. 2013. The Politics and Poetics of Infrastructure. *Annual Review of Anthropology* 42: 327–343.

Laskar, Rezaul H. 2017. After 1962 War, CIA Feared China Could Attack India through Nepal, Myanmar. *The Hindustan Times.* Available at www.hindustantimes.com/india-news/after-1962-war-cia-feared-china-could-attack-india-through-neaplmyanmar/story-nlXqFNgFzyFx0gI1YLg8wM.html; accessed January 11, 2025.

Lassiter, Luke Erik. 2005. *The Chicago Guide to Collaborative Ethnography*. Chicago: The University of Chicago Press.

Lawoti, Mahendra. 2008. Exclusionary Democratization in Nepal, 1990–2002. *Democratization* 15(2): 363–385.

Leve, Lauren. 2009. Women's Empowerment and Rural Revolution: "Rethinking Failed Development." *Dialectical Anthropology* 33(3): 345–363.

Lewison, Elsie and Galen Murton. 2020. Geographical Scholarship in Nepal: Sustainability, Infrastructure, Disaster and Power. 25(1): 15–58.

Liechty, Mark. 1997. Selective Exclusion: Foreigners, Foreign Goods and Foreignness in Modern Nepali History. *Studies in Nepali History and Society* 2(1): 5–68.

Lohani, Monika. 2018. Explainer: What is the 'Syndicate' Controversy All About? *Onlinekhabar*, May 4. Available at https://english.onlinekhabar.com/explainer-what-is-the-syndicate-controversy-all-about.html; accessed November 24, 2024.

Mahat, Jaya Jung. 2018. Karnali 2.0. *The Kathmandu Post*, August 31. Available at https://kathmandupost.com/opinion/2018/01/28/karnali-20; accessed August 20, 2024.

Mandal, Chandan Kumar. 2018. 282 Transport Firms Listed After End to Syndicate. *The Kathmandu Post*. Available at https://kathmandupost.com/valley/2018/07/21/282-transport-firms-listed-after-end-to-syndicate; accessed September 15, 2025.

Masset, Edoardo. 2018. Integrated Development: Past and Present. *IDS Bulletin* 49(4): 17–31. Available at https://www.researchgate.net/publication/330610397_Integrated_Development_Past_and_Present; accessed September 15, 2025.

Mathur, Nayanika. 2016. *Paper Tiger: Law, Bureaucracy and the Developmental State in Himalayan India*. New Delhi: Cambridge University Press.

Meyer, Werner Paul, Bed Nath Acharya, Rajendra Aryal and Bijaya Bahadur Karmacharya. 1999. *Green Roads in Nepal: Best Practices Report.* Kathmandu: German Technical Cooperation Agency (GTZ)/Swiss Agency for Development and Co-operation (SDC). Available at https://www.scribd.com/document/485571772/GREEN-ROAD-IN-NEPAL-BEST-PRACTICES; accessed March 1, 2025.

Mihaly, Eugene Bramer. 2009[1965]. *Foreign Aid and Politics in Nepal: A Case Study*. Lalitpur: Himal Books.

Miraftab, Faranak. (2016). *Global Heartland: Displaced Labor, Transnational Lives, and Local Placemaking*. Bloomington: Indiana University Press.

Mishra, Ratneshwar. 2006. Ethnicity and National Unification: The Madheshis of Nepal. *Proceedings of the Indian History Congress* 67: 802–833.

MKRM (Mugum Karmarong Rural Municipality). n.d. Bahumulya Jadibuti, Organic Kheti, Tamakhani, Chhayakshetra, Paryatan Purvadhar Samriddha Samunnat Mugum Karmarongka Adhar. Available at https://mugumkarmarongmun.gov.np/; accessed May 15, 2024.

MoLD (Ministry of Local Development). 2004. *Local Infrastructure Development Policy, 2061*. Lalitpur: MoLD, HMG.

Mould, Oli. 2023. Intervention – What Are the Limits of the Planet in Planetary Urbanisation? An Exploration of the Final Frontier to the City. *Antipode.* Available at https://antipodeonline.org/2023/12/18/the-limits-of-the-planet-in-planetary-urbanisation/; accessed July 1, 2024.

Mrázek, Rudolf. 2002. *Engineers of Happy Land: Technology and Nationalism in a Colony.* Princeton, NJ: Princeton University Press.

Mulmi, Abhiman Das. 2009. Green Road Approach in Rural Road Construction for the Sustainable Development of Nepal. *Journal of Sustainable Development* 2(3): 149–165.

Muni, Sukh Deo. 1973. *Foreign Policy of Nepal*. New Delhi: National Publishing House.

Murton, Galen. 2013. Himalayan Highways: STS, the Spatial Fix, and Socio-cultural Shifts in the Land of Zomia. *Perspectives on Global Development and Technology* 12(5–6): 609–621.

Murton, Galen and Austin Lord. 2020. Trans-Himalayan Power Corridors: Infrastructural Politics and China's Belt and Road Initiative in Nepal. *Political Geography* 77. https://doi.org/10.1016/J.POLGEO.2019.102100.

Murton, Galen and Tulasi Sharan Sigdel. 2021. Stuck on the Side of the Road: Mobility, Marginality, and Neoliberal Governmentality in Nepal. In *Highways and Hierarchies: Ethnographies of Mobility from the Himalaya to the Indian Ocean*. Luke Heslop and Galen Murton, eds., pp. 39–69. Amsterdam: Amsterdam University Press.

Murton, Galen, Austin Lord and Robert Beazley. 2016. "A Handshake Across the Himalayas:" Chinese Investment, Hydropower Development, and State Formation in Nepal. *Eurasian Geography and Economics* 57(3): 403–432.

My República. 2017. Ghost Contractors a Serious Problem in Project Execution in Nepal, Says ADB. February 28. Available at www.myrepublica.nagariknetwork.com/news/ghost-contractors-a-serious-problem-in-project-execution-in-nepal-says-adb; accessed September 15, 2025.

My República. 2023. Mugu Villages Reeling Under Food Shortage. May 21. Available at https://myrepublica.nagariknetwork.com/news/mugu-villages-reeling-under-food-shortage/; accessed August 20, 2024.

Neelakantan, Anagha. 2015. Nepal's Political Faultlines. *Daily Maverick*, May 27. Available at www.dailymaverick.co.za/article/2015-05-27-op-ed-nepals-political-faultlines/; accessed January 11, 2025.

Nepal Live Today. 2022. Everything You Need to Know about the Controversial Constituency Development Fund. November 18.

Available at www.nepallivetoday.com/2022/11/18/everything-you-need-to-know-about-the-controversial-constituency-development-fund/; accessed August 10, 2024.

Nepali Times. 2018. Bulldozing Democracy. No. 917, July 6–12, p. 2. Available at https://nepalitimes.com/editorial/bulldozing-democracy-axxp121z; accessed September 11, 2024.

Nepali, Samjhana. 2018. Vikasma Badhdaichha Durupayog. *Rara Sandesh*, July 25, p. 3.

Nickson, R. Andrew. 1992. Foreign Aid and Foreign Policy: The Case of British Aid to Nepal. Papers in the Administration of Development, No. 48. Development Administration Group, University of Birmingham.

Nightingale, Andrea J., Anil Bhattarai, Hemant Ojha, Tulasi Sigdel and Katharine N. Rankin. 2018. Fragmented Public Authority and State Un/making in the 'New' Republic of Nepal. *Modern Asian Studies* 52(3): 849–882.

Nightingale, Andrea J., Lutgart Lenaerts, Ankita Shrestha, Pema Norbu Lama 'Tsumpa' and Hemant R. Ojha. 2023. The Material Politics of Citizenship: Struggles over Resources, Authority and Belonging in the New Federal Republic of Nepal. In *Nepal's Federal Conundrum: Negotiating a Strong Federal System on Weak Democratic Foundations*. Seira Tamang, ed., pp. 279–308. Kathmandu: Martin Chautari.

NORAD (Norwegian Agency for Development Cooperation). 2011. Corruption and Anti-corruption in Nepal: Lessons Learned and Possible Future Initiatives. Available at https://www.norad.no/en/toolspublications/publications/2011/corruption-and-anti-corruption-in-nepal.--lessons-learned-and-possible-future-initiatives/; accessed May 15, 2024.

NPC (National Planning Commission). 1956. *First Five Year Plan*. Kathmandu: NPC, HMG.

NPC. 1985. *Seventh Five Year Plan (1985–1990)*. Kathmandu: NPC, HMG.

NPC. 2012. Impact Evaluation of Sunsari-Morang Irrigation Project. Available at https://npc.gov.np/images/category/sunsari_morang.pdf; accessed May 15, 2024.

NPC. 2013. *National Priority Projects' Short Introduction and Progress.* Kathmandu: NPC.

NPC and DfID (Department for International Development). 2013. Research into the Long Term Impact of Development Interventions in the Koshi Hills of Nepal. Kathmandu: NPC/DfID, Nepal. Available at https://assets.publishing.service.gov.uk/media/5a7c62aeed915d6969f44819/Long-Term-Impact-Dev-Study-Report-Koshi-Hills-Nepal.pdf; accessed June 10, 2024.

NPC and UNDP (United Nations Development Programme). 2014. *Nepal Human Development Report 2014: Beyond Geography, Unlocking Human Potential.* Kathmandu: NPC and UNDP. Available at https://www.npc.gov.np/images/category/NHDR_Report_2014.pdf; accessed August 20, 2024.

NPC and UNDP. 2020. *Nepal Human Development Report 2020.* Kathmandu: NPC and UNDP. Available at https://hdr.undp.org/system/files/documents/nhdr2020nepal.pdf; accessed August 20, 2024.

NSO (National Statistics Office). 2021. *National Population and Housing Census 2021: Population Composition of Nepal.* Available at https://censusnepal.cbs.gov.np/results/files/result-folder/Final_Population_compostion_12_2.pdf; accessed December 14, 2024.

NSO. 2023. *Nepal Population and Housing Census 2021.* Available at https://censusnepal.cbs.gov.np/results; accessed August 20, 2024.

Oakes, Tim. 2019. China Made: Infrastructural Thinking in a Chinese Register. *Made in China* 4(2): 66–71.

Oakes, Tim. 2021. The BRI as an Exercise in Infrastructural Thinking. Chinamade Brief No. 8. Available at https://chinamadeproject.net/china-made-brief-8/; accessed June 10, 2024.

Ojha, Durga P. 1983. History of Land Settlement in Nepal Tarai. *Contributions to Nepalese Studies* 11(1): 21–44.

Ojha, Hemant. 2009. Civic Engagement and Deliberative Governance: The Case of Community Forest Users' Federation, Nepal. *Studies in Nepali History and Society* 14(2): 303–334.

Panday, Ram Niwas. 2027 v.s. The Ancient and Medieval History of Western Nepal. *Ancient Nepal* 11: 45–60.

Panday, Tularam. 2023. State Neglect Leaves Surkhet-Jumla Section of Karnali Highway in Dire Condition. *The Kathmandu Post,* June 6. Available at https://kathmandupost.com/karnali-province/2023/06/06/state-neglect-leaves-surkhet-jumla-section-of-karnali-highway-in-dire-condition; accessed August 20, 2024.

Pathak, Laxmi. 1997. Morangma Adhikaran tatha Punarvash Karyakram ra Tyasko Asarharu. In *Morang: Ek Parichaya*. Raghunath Adhikari, Yadav Lamichhane, Anil Paudel and Hari Phuyal, eds., pp. 37–42. Kathmandu: Morang Kathmandu Samparka Manch.

Paudel, Dinesh. 2016. The Double Life of Development: Empowerment, USAID and the Maoist Uprising in Nepal. *Development and Change* 47(5): 1025–1050.

Paudel, Dinesh and Katharine Rankin. 2022. Himalayan Geopolitical Competition and the Agency of the Infrastructure State in Nepal. In *The Rise of the Infrastructure State: How US-China Rivalry Shapes Politics and Place Worldwide.* Seth Schindler and Jessica DiCarlo, eds., pp. 213–226. Bristol: Bristol University Press.

Paudyal, Durga P. 1998. *Access Improvement and Sustainable Development: Rural Road Development in Nepal.* Kathmandu: ICIMOD.

Pigg, Stacy Leigh. 1992. Inventing Social Categories Through Place: Social Representations and Development in Nepal. *Comparative Studies in Society and History* 34(3): 491–513.

Pigg, Stacy Leigh. 1993. Unintended Consequences: The Ideological Impact of Development in Nepal. *South Asian Bulletin* 13(1–2): 45–58.

Pigg, Stacy Leigh. 2008. We Corner People. *Visual Anthropology* 21(3): 273–275.

Pigg, Stacy Leigh. 2019. The Penstocks. *Roadsides* 002: Labor. Available at https://roadsides.net/pigg-002/; accessed May 30, 2025.

Pigg, Stacy Leigh. 2022. Collaboration as Wayfinding: Fieldsites, Editors' Forum on Graphic Ethnography on the Rise. Available at https://culanth.org/fieldsights/collaboration-as-a-way-of-finding; accessed May 15, 2025.

Pigg, Stacy L. and Shyam Kunwar. 2021. On the Roadside: Pangs of Memory, Tastes of Futures. *Multimodality and Society* 1(3): 350–365.

Pigg, Stacy L. and Shyam Kunwar. 2023. Nepal, Roads, Mobility, Graphic Ethnography, 2018. In *Naked Fieldnotes: A Rough Guide to Ethnographic Writing*. Danielle Elliott and Matthew J. Wolf-Meyer, eds., pp. 231–244. Minneapolis: University of Minnesota Press.

Pokhrel, Aupson. 2023. Khas Malla Kings of Nepal. *Itihasaa*. Available at https://itihasaa.com/khas-kings/khas-malla-kings-of-nepal/; accessed August 15, 2024.

PolicyLink. 2025. Infrastructure Justice! Building a Better Future for All. Available at www.policylink.org/infrastructure-justice; accessed May 15, 2025.

PPO (Public Procurement Office). 2007. *Public Procurement Act, 2063*. Available at https://ppmo.gov.np/content/7400/7400-public-procurement-act-2063-e/; accessed June 9, 2024.

Pradhan, Bharat B. 1985. *Integrated Rural Development Projects in Nepal: A Review*. ICIMOD Occasional Paper No 2. Kathmandu: ICIMOD. Available at https://lib.icimod.org/record/21461/files/attachment_88.pdf; accessed August 15, 2024.

Pradhan, Samprada, David G. Toll, Nick J. Rosser and Matthew J. Brain. 2022. An Investigation of the Combined Effect of Rainfall and Road Cut on Landsliding. Engineering Geology 307(5). https://doi.org/10.1016/j.enggeo.2022.106787.

Pradhan, Uma and Karen Valentin. 2019. Towards a Relational Approach to the State: Understanding Social and Political

Transformation in Nepal. *South Asia: Journal of South Asian Studies* 42(5): 880–885.

Pradhan, Upendra Man. 1997. Morangko Bhaugarbhik Banawat. In *Morang: Ek Parichaya*. Raghunath Adhikari, Yadav Lamichhane, Anil Paudel and Hari Phuyal, eds., pp. 6–9. Kathmandu: Morang Kathmandu Samparka Manch.

Rai, Bhrikuti. 2020. Across Nepal's Mid-hills: Unplanned Roads Are Leading to More Landslides and More Deaths. *The Record*, November 10. Available at www.recordnepal.com/across-nepals-mid-hills-unplanned-roads-are-leading-to-more-landslides-%E2%80%94-and-more-deaths; accessed January 10, 2025.

Rai, Janak. 2015. "Owning Land Was So Much of *Duḥkha* in the Past": Land and the State-*Ādivāsī* Relations in the Tarai, Nepal. *Studies in Nepali History and Society* 20(1): 69–98.

Rai, Jayanta. 2021. Including the Excluded? The Political Economy of the Constituency Development Fund in Post-War Nepal. *Conflict, Security & Development* 21(6): 805–830.

Rai, Lagan and Durga Hansda. 2018. *Santhal Jatiko Chinari*. Lalitpur: National Foundation for Development of Indigenous Nationalities (NFDIN).

Rai, Nirjan. 2020. *On Users' Roads: Examining the User Committee Mechanism in Developing Local Roads in Nepal*. Kathmandu: Policy Entrepreneurs Incorporated. Availabel at https://pei.center/wp-content/uploads/2024/08/15.On-Users-Roads_-Examining-User-Committee-Mechanism-in-Local-Roads.pdf; January 15, 2025.

Ranganathan, Malini, David L. Pike and Sapana Doshi. 2023. *Corruption Plots: Stories, Ethics, and Publics of the Late Capitalist City*. Ithaca: Cornell University Press.

Rankin, Katharine N. 1996. Planning for Equity: Ethical Principles from Newar Representations of Finance. *Studies in Nepali History and Society* 1(2): 365–393.

Rankin, Katharine N. 1999. The Predicament of Labour: Kamaiya Practices and the Ideology of Freedom. In *Nepal: Tharu and Tarai*

Neighbours. Bibliotheca Himalayica Series. Harald O. Skar, ed., pp. 27–45. Kathmandu: EMR Publication.

Rankin, Katharine N. 2004. *Cultural Politics of Markets: Economic Liberalization and Social Change in Nepal*. London: Pluto Press.

Rankin, Katharine and Edward Simpson. 2021. Roads and the Politics of Thought: Climate in India, Democracy in Nepal. In *Highways and Hierarchies: Ethnographies of Mobility from the Himalaya to the Indian Ocean*. Luke Heslop and Galen Murton, eds., pp. 197–220. Amsterdam: Amsterdam University Press.

Rankin, Katharine N., Andrea J. Nightingale, Pushpa Hamal and Tulasi Sigdel. 2016. Roads of Change: Political Transition and State Formation in Nepal's Agrarian Districts. *Journal of Peasant Studies* 45(2): 280–300.

Rankin, Katharine N., Tulasi S. Sigdel, Lagan Rai, Shyam Kunwar and Pushpa Hamal. 2017. Political Economies and Political Rationalities of Road Building in Nepal. *Studies in Nepali History and Society* 22(1): 43–84.

Rankin, Katharine, Shyam Kunwar, Lagan Rai and Elsie Lewison. 2024. Between Eating and Being Fed: Competing Ethics of Community-based Road Building in Nepal. *Anthropological Quarterly* 97(2): 219–251.

Regmi, Kiran, Surendra Upreti, Maureen Dar Lang, Hom Nath Subedi, Devi P. Prasai, Kapil Babu Dahal, Chhaya Jha, Shilu Aryal, Swaraj Rajbhandari, Rachel Phillipson, Stephen Keeling, Alison Dembo Rath and Deborah Thomas. 2013. A Study on Access to Maternal, Neonatal, and Child Health Services in Remote Areas of Nepal: Consolidated Report of Findings. Family Health Division and Nepal Health Sector Support Programme, Kathmandu. Available at www.nhssp.org.np/NHSSP_Archives/ehcs/Remote_areas_study_october2013.pdf; accessed May 20, 2025.

Regmi, Mahesh Chandra. 1977. *Landownership in Nepal*. New Delhi: Adroit Publishers.

Regmi, Mahesh Chandra. 1988. *An Economic History of Nepal: 1846–1901.* Varanasi: Nath Publishing House.

Robertson, Thomas B. 2018. DDT and the Cold War Jungle: American Environmental and Social Engineering in the Rapti Valley of Nepal. *Journal of American History* 104(4): 904–930.

Robinson, Richard and David Stiedl. 2001. Decentralization of Road Administration: Case Studies in Africa and Asia. *Public Administration and Development* 21(1): 53–64.

Rose, Leo E. 1971. *Nepal: Strategy for Survival.* Berkeley: University of California Press.

Rosser, Nick, Mark Kincey, Katie Oven, Alexander Densmore, Tom R. Robinson, Dammar Singh Pujara, Ram Shrestha, Jakub Smutny, Kumar Shanu Gurung, Sundup Lama and Megh Raj Dhital. 2021. Changing Significance of Landslide Hazard and Risk After the 2015 Mw 7.8 Gorkha, Nepal Earthquake. *Progress in Disaster Science* 10(9). DOI:10.1016/j.pdisas.2021.100159.

Roy, Ananya. 2011. Slumdog Cities: Rethinking Subaltern Urbanism. *International Journal of Urban and Regional Research* 35(2): 223–238.

Ruddick, Susan, Linda Peake, Gökbörü S. Tanyildiz and Darren Patrick. 2018. Planetary Urbanization: An Urban Theory for Our Time? *Environment and Planning D: Society and Space* 36(3): 387–404.

Rusk, Jack, Amina Maharjan, Prakash Tiwari, Tzu-Hsin Karen Chen, Sara Shneiderman, Mark Turin and Karen C. Seto. 2022. Multi-hazard Susceptibility and Exposure Assessment of the Hindu Kush Himalaya. *The Science of the Total Environment* 804(4). https://doi.org/10.1016/j.scitotenv.2021.150039.

Ruszczyk, Hanna A. 2021. Newly Urban Nepal. *Urban Geography* 42(2): 218–225.

Saxer, Martin. 2017. New Roads, Old Trades: Neighbouring China in Nepal. In *The Art of Neighbouring: Making Relations Across China's Borders.* Martin Saxer and Juan Zhang, eds., pp. 73–92. Amsterdam: Amsterdam University Press.

Saxer, Martin. 2023. *Places in Knots*. Ithaca: Cornell University Press.

Saxer, Martin and Ruben Andersson. 2019. The Return of Remoteness: Insecurity, Isolation and Connectivity in the New World Disorder. *Social Anthropology* 27(2): 140–155.

Schaffner, Urs. 1987. *Road Construction in the Nepal Himalaya: The Experience from the Lamosangu-Jiri Road Project*. ICIMOD Occasional Paper No. 8. Kathmandu: ICIMOD.

Schatz, Edward and Rachel Silvey, eds. 2025. *Seeing China's Belt and Road*. New York: Oxford University Press.

Schroeder, Mark Cabet Waldo and Daniel G. Sisler. 1971. *Impact of the Sonauli-Pokhara Highway on the Regional Income and Agricultural Production of Pokhara Valley, Nepal*. Ithaca: Cornell University Press.

SDC (Swiss Agency for Development and Cooperation). 2008. *Nepal: Roads to Prosperity Partnership Results*. Asia Brief. South Asia Division. Kathmandu: SDC.

Shah, Mahendra Bir Bikram.1961. *Pages of History: A Collection of Proclamations, Messages, and Addresses Delivered by His Majesty King Mahendra*. Kathmandu: Ministry of National Guidance, HMG.

Shah, Saubhagya. 2018. *A Project of Memoreality: Transnational Development and Local Activism*. Kathmandu: Himal Books.

Shaha, Rishikesh. 1975. *Nepali Politics: Retrospect and Prospect*. New York: Oxford University Press.

Sharma, Pitamber. 2004. Pahadi Vikasko Rananiti. In *Nepalma Gariviko Bahas*. Bhaskar Gautam, Jagannath Adhikari and Purna Basnet, eds., pp. 430–439. Kathmandu: Martin Chautari.

Sharma, Suresh and Madhuban Lal Maskay. 1999. Community Participation and Environmental Protection in the Construction of Mountain Roads: Promotion of the "Green Road" Approach in Nepal. *Transport and Communication Bulletin of Asia and Pacific* 69: 57–77.

Sheppard, Eric and Helga Leitner. 2010. Quo Vadis Neoliberalism? The Remaking of Global Capitalist Governance After the Washington Consensus. *Geoforum* 41(2): 185–194.

Shiwakoti, Kedar. 2021. Mude-Charikot Road Upgradation Remains Incomplete Even After Six Years. *The Kathmandu Post,* October 27. Available at https://kathmandupost.com/province-no-3/2021/10/27/mudhe-charikot-road-upgradation-remains-incomplete-even-after-six-years; accessed October 15, 2024.

Shiwakoti, Kedar. 2023. Tibet Border Reopening Provides Relief to Nepal Villagers. *The Kathmandu Post.* October 11. Available at https://kathmandupost.com/province-no-3/2023/10/11/tibet-border-reopening-provides-relief-to-nepal-villagers; accessed October 20, 2024.

Shneiderman, Sara Beth. 2009. The Formation of Political Consciousness in Rural Nepal. *Dialectical Anthropology* 33(3): 287–308.

Shneiderman, Sara B. 2013. Himalayan Border Citizens: Sovereignty and Mobility on the Nepal-Tibetan Autonomous Region (TAR) of China Border Zone. *Political Geography* 35: 25–36.

Shneiderman, Sara. 2014. Remoteness as a Relational Category. *HAU: Journal of Ethnographic Theory* 4(1): 372–374.

Shneiderman, Sara. 2015. *Rituals of Ethnicity: Thangmi Identities Between Nepal and India.* Philadelphia: University of Pennsylvania Press.

Shneiderman, Sara. 2018. Temple Building in Secularizing Nepal: Materializing Religion and Ethnicity in a State of Transformation. In *Tolerance, Secularization and Democratic Politics in South Asia.* Humeira Iqtidar and Tanika Sarkar, eds., pp. 75–107. Cambridge: Cambridge University.

Shneiderman, Sara. 2024. Equivocating Houses: Kinship, Materiality, and Bureaucratic Practice in Post-earthquake Nepal. *Anthropological Quarterly* 97(2): 253–284.

Shneiderman, Sara and Louise Tillin. 2015. Restructuring States, Restructuring Ethnicity: Looking Across Disciplinary Boundaries at Federal Futures in India and Nepal. *Modern Asian Studies* 49(1): 1–39.

Shneiderman, Sara and Mark Turin. 2010. Negotiating Nepal's Two Polities: A View from Dolakha. In *Hope and Fear: Living Through the People's War in Nepal.* Prabin Manandhar and David Seddon, eds., pp. 200–213. New Delhi: Adroit Publishers.

Shneiderman, Sara, Bina Khapunghang Limbu, Jeevan Baniya, Manoj Suji, Nabin Rawal, Prakash Chandra Subedi and Cameron David Warner. 2023. House, Household, and Home: Revisiting Anthropological and Policy Frameworks Through Postearthquake Reconstruction Experiences in Nepal. *Current Anthropology* 64(5): 498–527.

Shrestha, Chandra B. 2002. Developing and Testing a Participatory Methodology for District Road Network Planning in Nepal. PhD diss., Asian Institute of Technology, Bangkok.

Shrestha, Hare Ram. 2010. Road vs. Hill Environment: The Trend of Road Construction in Nepal. Transport in Mountains: An International Workshop, 21–27 November, Kathmandu Nepal.

Shrestha, Prayog. 2005. The Great Green Road. *Nepali Times,* 254, July 1–7. Available at https://archive.nepalitimes.com/news.php?id=496; accessed January 10, 2025.

Shrestha, Purusottam Man. 2007. *Corruption in Infrastructure Provision and Service Delivery at the Municipal Level in Nepal: A Case Study.* Leicestershire: Loughborough University. Available at https://assets.publishing.service.gov.uk/media/57a08c0ced915d622c0010bf/WEDC-Nepal-casestudy.pdf; accessed January 12, 2025.

Shuller, Mimi and John Urry. 2006. The New Mobilities Paradigm. *Environment and Planning A* 38(2): 207–226.

Sigdel, Tulasi Sharan. 2016a. Kamjor Rajya ra Baliyo Syndicate. *Baarhakhari.* Available at http://baahrakhari.com/news-details/4131/12khari; accessed November 15, 2024.

Sigdel, Tulasi Sharan. 2016b. Karnalima Sadak: Artha-rajnaitik Sambandha ra Vikas. *Baarhakhari.* Available at http://baahrakhari.com/news-details/492/12khari; accessed November 15, 2024.

Sigdel, Tulasi Sharan. 2016c. Sadak Pugdaima Karnaliko Vikas Hunchha? *Baarhakhari*. Available at http://baahrakhari.com/np/2016/06/24/18857/; accessed November 15, 2024.

Simpson, Edward. 2022. *Highways to the End of the World: Roads, Roadmen and Power in South Asia*. London: Hurst.

Singh, Chandra Prakash. 2004. Rise and Growth of Anti-Rana Movement in Nepal. *Proceedings of the Indian History Congress* 65: 992–1002.

Skerry, Christa A., Kerry Moran and Kay M. Calavan. 1991. *Four Decades of Development: The History of U.S. Assistance to Nepal 1951–1991*. Kathmandu: United States Agency for International Development (USAID).

Star, Susan Leigh. 1999. The Ethnography of Infrastructure. *American Behavioral Scientist* 43(3): 377–391.

Subedi, Govinda and Yogendra Gurung. 1997. Morang Jillako Janasankhyako Ek Chinari. In *Morang: Ek Parichaya*. Raghunath Adhikari, Yadav Lamichhane, Anil Paudel and Hari Phuyal, eds., pp. 62–74. Kathmandu: Morang Kathmandu Samparka Manch.

Sudmeier-Rieux, Karen, Brian G. McAdoo, Sanjaya Devkota, Purna Chandra Lal Rajbhandari, John Howell and Shuva Sharma. 2019. Invited Perspectives: Mountain Roads in Nepal at a New Crossroads. *Natural Hazards and Earth System Sciences* 19(3): 655–660.

Sugden, Fraser. 2013. Pre-capitalist Reproduction on the Nepal Tarai: Semi-feudal Agriculture in an Era of Globalisation *Journal of Contemporary Asia* 43(3): 519–545.

Sulek, Emilia Roza. 2019. *Trading Caterpillar Fungus in Tibet: When Economic Boom Hits Rural Area*. Amsterdam: Amsterdam University Press.

Tamang, Mukta S.L. 2011. Multi-Stakeholder Forestry Programme (MSFP) Nepal Social Appraisal. Submitted to Department for International Development (DfID), Swiss Development Cooperation (SDC), Government of Finland (GoF).

Tamang, Mukta S. and Om Gurung, eds. 2014. *Social Inclusion Atlas of Nepal Ethnic and Caste Groups.* Vol. I. Kathmandu: Central Department of Sociology/Anthropology, TU.

Tamang, Seira. 2023a. Introduction: Interrogating the Democratic Foundations for Federalism. In *Nepal's Federal Conundrum: Negotiating a Strong Federal System on Weak Democratic Foundations.* Seira Tamang, ed., pp. 1–42. Kathmandu: Martin Chautari.

Tamang, Seira, ed. 2023b. *Nepal's Federal Conundrum: Negotiating a Strong Federal System on Weak Democratic Foundations.* Kathmandu: Martin Chautari.

Tamang, Seira. 2023c. "They've Given Us the Chair, But Bound Our Hands and Feet": Embedding Elected Female Representatives in Institutions in Nepal. In *Nepal's Federal Conundrum: Negotiating a Strong Federal System on Weak Democratic Foundations.* Seira Tamang, ed., pp. 227–278. Kathmandu: Martin Chautari.

Tamang , Seira, Sumina Rai Karki, Amol Acharya and Srijana Nepal. 2023. Beyond "Capacity": Gendered Election Processes, Networks and Informality in Local Governments in Nepal. In *Nepal's Federal Conundrum: Negotiating a Strong Federal System on Weak Democratic Foundations.* Seira Tamang, ed., pp. 71–108. Kathmandu: Martin Chautari.

The Asia Foundation. 2017. *A Survey of the Nepali People in 2017.* San Francisco, CA: The Asia Foundation. Available at https://asiafoundation.org/wp-content/uploads/2018/04/Survey-of-the-Nepali-People-in-2017_revised-752018.pdf; accessed December 12, 2025.

The Kathmandu Post. 2017. Harvest Season: Yarsa Collectors Swarm Over Highlands. June 3. Available at https://kathmandupost.com/money/2017/06/02/yarsa-collectors-swarm-over-highlands; accessed January 12, 2025.

The Kathmandu Post. 2018a. Breaking the Cartels. May 7, p. 8.

The Kathmandu Post. 2018b. Interview: If Govt Breaks Some Syndicates Successfully, It Sets a Precedent for the Future.

Available at https://kathmandupost.com/interviews/2018/05/07/if-govt-breaks-some-syndicates-successfully-it-sets-aprecedent-for-the-future; accessed September 15, 2025.

The World Bank. 1965. A National Transport System for Nepal: Including an Investment Program for the Third Plan, 1965/66–1969/70. Vol. 1. Planning Framework and Principal Recommendations. Available at https://documents1.worldbank.org/curated/en/269131468291697296/pdf/multi0page.pdf; accessed January 12, 2025.

The World Bank. 2000. *Nepal: Public Expenditure Review*. Vol. IV: Transport Sector. Infrastructure Sector Unit, South Asia Region. Report No. 20211-NEP. Available at https://openknowledge.worldbank.org/server/api/core/bitstreams/857286d2-d2e0-5a35-99e4-49587393e8d3/content; accessed January 12, 2025.

The World Bank. 2011. Nepal—Public Expenditure Review – Roads. South Asia Region: The World Bank.

The World Bank. 2013. *Nepal Road Sector Assessment Study: Main Report*. Kathmandu: World Bank and GoN. Available at www.scribd.com/document/486911728/road-sector-assessment-study-main-report-final-30may2013-pdf; accessed January 12, 2025.

Thomas, Deborah, Stephen Bell, Kapil Dahal, Rachel Grellier, Chhaya Jha, Sitaram Prasai and Hom Nath Subedi. 2012. Voices from the Community: Access to Health Services. A Rapid Participatory Ethnographic Evaluation and Research (PEER) Study, Nepal. Kathmandu: MoHP (Population Division Ministry of Health and Population), GoN with support from NHSSP (Nepal Health Sector Support Programme).

Timalsina, Rajib. 2017. Consensus Modality in Nepal's Transition: Accommodating Parties and Shrinking Democratic Spaces. *Asian Journal of Peacebuilding* 5(1): 67–88.

Tiwary, Vijay K. 2008. Advent of Indian Railways: It's Expansion in the Bordering Districts of Nepal and their Impact on Indio-Nepal Trade Relations (1846–1947). *Proceedings of the Indian History Congress* 69: 635–643.

Tseten, Kesang. 2006. *We Corner People.* Available at https://www.youtube.com/watch?v=TwFa_psi2LE; accessed January 12, 2025.

Turin, Mark. 1997. Essentially a Road to Nowhere. *The Kathmandu Post,* May 3, p. 4.

Tüting, Ludmilla and Kanak Dixit, eds. 2018. *Bikas-Binas? Development-Destruction: The Change in Life and Environment of the Himalaya.* Kathmandu: Ratna Pustak Bhandar.

Tylor, Daniel C. 1969. Population Growth and Nepalese Development. *Vasudha* XII(12): 29–32.

UNCTAD (United Nations Conference on Trade and Development). 2022. SDG Pulse 2021: UNCTAD Takes the Pulse of the SDGS. Available at https://www.un-ilibrary.org/content/books/9789210058841/read; accessed January 12, 2025.

UNODC (United Nations Office on Drugs and Crime). 2022. UNODC & GOPAC Pacific Regional Conference: Constituency Development Funds Conference Discussion Paper & Report. www.unodc.org/roseap/uploads/documents/pacific/2023/CDF_conference_report.pdf; accessed January 12, 2025.

Urry, John. 2007. *Mobilities.* London: Polity.

USAID (United States Agency for International Development). 2012. Democracy, Human Rights, and Governance Assessment of Nepal: Final Report. Available at www.harrywblair.com/wp-content/uploads/2015/05/Nepal-DRG-Assessment-Report-Oct12final-1gwr9ok.pdf; accessed Janu 12, 2025.

UTKHEP (Upper Tamakoshi Hydroelectric Project). 2024. Introduction. Available at https://utkhpl.org.np/; accessed October 10, 2024.

von Einsiedel, Sebastian, David M. Malone and Sagar Pradhan, eds. 2012. *Nepal in Transition: From People's War to Fragile Peace.* Cambridge: Cambridge University Press.

von Fürer-Haimendorf, Christoph. 1975. *Himalayan Traders: Life in Highland Nepal.* London: J. Murray.

Whelpton, John. 1983. *Jang Bahadur in Europe: The First Nepalese Mission to the West.* Kathmandu: Sahayogi Press.

Williamson, John. 2003. The Washington Consensus and Beyond. *Economic and Political Weekly* 38(15): 1475–1481.

Winkler, Daniel. 2009. Caterpillar Fungus (Ophiocordyceps Sinensis) Production and Sustainability on the Tibetan Plateau and in the Himalayas. *Asian Medicine* 5(2): 291–316.

Yeh, Emily T. and Kunga T. Lama. 2013. Following the Caterpillar Fungus: Nature, Commodity Chains, and the Place of Tibet in China's Uneven Geographies. *Social & Cultural Geography* 14(3): 318–340.

Glossary

Nepali	English
alopalo	rotation system (between transport organizations)
Adivasi Janajati	Indigenous Nationalities
Aphno Gau Aphai Banau	build our village ourself – political slogan
Asare budget	end of financial year budget allocations in the Nepali month of Asar
baluwa	sand
baphre	exclamation: oh my goodness!
begar, begari	forced labor
bhagbanda	negotiated illicit distribution
bhrashtachar	corruption
chalkhel	scheming
chachari	bamboo bridge
crore	ten million
dai	older brother
dukha	suffering
durgam	remote (opposite of *sugam* – accessible)
gachhadar	headman
Gau Vikas Samiti (GaViSa)	Village Development Committee (VDC)
gaupalika	rural municipality
ghati ghatau	competition for low bidding
ghodeto	animal trail

ghus	bribe, kickback
goreto	foot trail
gunda	hooligan, henchmen
hat bazaar	occasional market
hadtal	strike
hilo	mud
hulaki	postal
jana sahabhagita	public participation
jana shramdan	people's labor donation
jadibuti	medicinal herbs
jagga dan	land donation
Jana Andolan	People's Movement
jhara	form of labor exploitation through corvee labor
Jilla Samvad Samuha	District Dialogue Group
jimidar	landlord
kagaj	paper
kagaji ghoda	paper horse
kagaj milaune	arranging the paperwork
kalapani	black water
kalash	bronze pot
kattha	traditional unit of land measurement commonly used in the Tarai
khane	to eat
khuwaune	to feed
kunako manchhe	corner person
kurta suruwal	pajama outfit
lakh	one hundred thousand
lathi	baton
Madheshi	plains people
mijar	tax collector

milaunu	to arrange
milemato	consensus/collusion
nagarik	citizen
nagarpalika	(urban) municipality
paisa	coin/money
palika	municipality
patake	temporary route permit
pradhan pancha	head of a Panchayat unit
rajmarga	highway
rakam	a system of taxation
sarvadaliya samyantra	all-party mechanism
shramdan	labor donation
safari	battery-powered three-wheeler vehicle
sojho	gullible/honest
sugam	accessible (opposite of *durgam* – remote)
sukumbasi	landless individuals
tukre	piecemeal
udharo	credit
vikas	development
vinash	destruction
yarsagumba	caterpillar fungus
yatayat	transportation
yatayat samiti	transportation committee

Appendix: Relevant Initiatives Related to Road Development in Periodic Plans of the GoN

Plan (years)	National and global context	Relevant initiatives related to road development	Relevant acts, plans, programs
First plan (1956–1961)	First five-year plan after end of the autocratic Rana regime; Shah monarchy restored; series of governments. Cold War. Modern bureaucracy established, including National Planning Commission. The plan aimed to promote economic growth and social development by increasing production and creating employment. It also aimed to establish a data system for monitoring the living conditions of the population, with foreign assistance especially from India and the US.	This plan aimed to lay the foundation for essential infrastructures such as roads, agriculture and electricity. Transportation was designated a priority sector; with projects focused on roads, ropeways, railways and airways. Priority sectors were allocated 10.4 crore out of a total budget of 33 crore.	A Regional Transportation Organization (RTO) established in 1958 with the support of India and the US, with a focus on building roads to mitigate the perceived threat of Russian and Chinese influence in Nepal. The East-West Highway was initiated (Hetauda to Narayanghat) and focus also turned to North-South roads along historical trade and travel routes. Rapti Valley Multi-purpose Project (supported by USAID Nepal) established.

Plan (years)	National and global context	Relevant initiatives related to road development	Relevant acts, plans, programs
Second Plan (1962–1965)	First three-year plan, which coincided with King Mahendra taking power from an elected Nepali Congress Government and establishing the Panchayat System (1960–1990). It aimed to establish a foundation for long-term development with a focus on economic growth, employment generation and social equality.	Lack of transportation was identified as a major obstacle to rapid economic development of the country. This plan made the transportation sector, mainly roads, a top priority. Transportation, communication and power sectors jointly received 39 percent of total estimated budget.	Major road construction programs: Raxaul-Bhaise Road, Kathmandu-Kodari Road (Araniko Highway), East-West Highway, and Sunauli-Pokhara Highway RTO dissolved. Department of Roads established, 1962, superseded the RTO. Land Reform Act passed in 1964, emphasizing administrative decentralization, and authorizing local leaders to build earthen roads.

Plan (years)	National and global context	Relevant initiatives related to road development	Relevant acts, plans, programs
Third Plan (1965–1970)	First full five-year plan after King Mahendra overthrew elected government, seized power, banned political parties, and introduced the Panchayat System in 1960. The Panchayat regime's primary objective was to achieve rapid economic growth and to increase national income and unity.	Transportation, communication, and power once again identified as priority sectors, with a focus on challenges posed by the lack of such infrastructure in the hill region. These three sectors consumed 37.2 percent of total budget expenditures.	20-year Perspective Plan initiated, a long-term development plan to build 2,500 km of road, prioritizing previously planned road projects. Assistance from International Bank for Reconstruction and Development (IBRD). Priority projects focused on major highways: East-West Highway, Araniko Highway, Siddhartha Highway, Prithvi Highway, along with many north-south roads. Regional Development Policy implemented; administrative decentralization focusing on engaging local leaders to undertake development with local resources and labor. Harka Gurung appointed Vice Chair, National Planning Commission.

Plan (years)	National and global context	Relevant initiatives related to road development	Relevant acts, plans, programs
Fourth Plan (1970–1975)	Regional planning becomes the organizing principle for national planning under Harka Gurung's leadership. Robert MacNamara speech at World Bank pledging to fight world poverty through integrated rural development—through human development supports combined with rural (primarily agricultural) production and incomes. This plan promoted the concept of balanced regional development. It prioritized increased production, infrastructure development, agriculture, and industry. Aimed to expand international trade, control inflation, and develop labor force was promoted.	Roads were envisioned as key to regional planning—connecting all districts in the country through a "fish-bone" pattern entailing north-south corridors linked by the East-West Highway. Previously promoted road projects continued to be prioritized. Transportation and communications sectors accounted for 35.4 percent of the total budget.	Aimed to connect districts and zonal headquarters by 1985. Roads classified broadly in two categories, motorable and non-motorable. Typology of motorable roads established. Lamosangu-Jiri Road initiated, 1974.

Plan (years)	National and global context	Relevant initiatives related to road development	Relevant acts, plans, programs
Fifth Plan (1975–1980)	Continued emphasis on regional planning. Four development regions were established. Greater attention was given to ensuring rural populations benefited from economic development. The government prioritized hill and Himalayan regions by classifying poverty and underdevelopment. The plan emphasized promotion of agriculture and cottage and small-scale industries to expand income opportunities for rural communities, entailing a major realignment of resource allocation.	Agriculture production and public administration were identified as priority sectors, taking precedence over transportation and communication. However, previously planned road projects were continued. The total budget share allocated to transportation and communication was reduced to 26.4 percent.	Road classification was modified. Integrated Rural Development Programs were initiated, with the support of aid agencies and multilateral financial institutions, such as the Swiss Development Cooperation, German Technical Cooperation Agency, World Bank, Asian Development Bank, and International Monetary Fund.

Plan (years)	National and global context	Relevant initiatives related to road development	Relevant acts, plans, programs
Sixth Plan (1980–1985)	Aimed to achieve rapid economic growth, create productive employment and fulfil the basic needs of the population. It emphasized agriculture, micro- and small-scale industries, export trade and tourism, conservation of natural and cultural heritage, and development of water resources. Infrastructure was considered a mechanism for improving resource utilization and economic efficiency.	Ministry of Local Development was established and appointed local district officers to administer Integrated Rural Development programs across the country. Priority given to connecting hills and mountains with Tarai to achieve national & regional integrity; as well as to connecting district headquarters with feeder roads, and to building north-south roads within regions; roads were regarded as the backbone for other sectors of development.	Decentralization Act, 1982. Continued Integrated Rural Development policies and programs. Remote Area Development Program (RADP), focused on high hill and Himalayan regions, including development of walking trails. More reclassification of roads. Far-western Development Region was further divided into two separate development regions, creating a total of five.
Seventh Plan (1985–1990)	Structural Adjustment Programs, neoliberalism and participatory approaches characterize development globally. Aimed again to increase productive employment and meet basic needs. Continued promotion of national economic integration, decentralization and development administration. Political upheavals increased during this period.	Continuation of road development in previous plan. Green roads become a prevalent approach to local road building. Emphasis on mobilizing local people and local resources at local levels, as well as on controlling environmental degradation.	North-South Highways: Mechi Highway, Koshi Highway, Sagarmatha Highway, Rapti Highway, Karnali Highway, Dhangadi-Darchula Road. Mid-Hill East-West Highway initiated. Roads promoted under Integrated Rural Development Programs (IRDPs).

Plan (years)	National and global context	Relevant initiatives related to road development	Relevant acts, plans, programs
Eighth Plan (1992–1997)	Political change: end of Panchayat regime and beginning of multi-party democracy; Nepali Congress wins majority and forms government. Maoist-state conflict, 1996–2006. First periodic plan formulated after the restoration of multi-party democracy. Focused on sustainable growth, poverty reduction, and regional disparities, aimed to enhance the role of the private sector and adopted economic liberalization policies.	Roads seen as a means for regional integration and balanced development. Royal Nepal Army enrolled in development works, including road construction. This plan also initiated road network master plans (for detailed survey design and feasibility studies) and urban road master plans. Rural roads regarded as a means to promote industrial growth and market expansion in rural areas, as well as access for agriculture and hydropower projects.	CPN-UML introduced *Aphno Gau Aphai Banau* and decentralized budget. Priority Investment Plan, 1997. Roads were reclassified again. Rural Self-reliance Program funded rural roads at the VDC level. Rural Accessibility Improvement and Decentralization Project implemented in 20 districts built rural roads and opened tracks. Remote Area Development Programs. World Food Programme, Food for Work programs supported rural road building.

Plan (years)	National and global context	Relevant initiatives related to road development	Relevant acts, plans, programs
Ninth Plan (1998–2002)	Political instability, conflict between Maoist insurgents and then Royal Nepal Army. Central goal: poverty alleviation via priority sectors, including agriculture and forestry, water resources and energy, human resources and social development, industrialization, tourism, international trade, and physical infrastructure. The plan also emphasized decentralization.	Agriculture road network as supplementary road network to increase agriculture production and productivity. Green road concept as a sustainable approach to building rural roads in the fragile hill and mountain landscapes.	A 20-year Long-Term Vision, 2002–2022; Remote Area Development Programs; Agriculture roads; Constituency Development Fund. Department of Local Infrastructure Development and Agricultural Roads (DoLIDAR) established in 1998 under the Ministry of Local Development. Integrated Rural Development Programs: Rural Community Infrastructure Work (RCIW), Rural Community Infrastructure Development Program (RIDP), Rural Infrastructure Project (RIP), District Road Support Program (DRSP), Rural Reconstruction and Rehabilitation Project (RRR), Rural Access Program (RAP) implemented in many districts, including building rural roads. Local Self-Governance Act promulgated in 1999.

Plan (years)	National and global context	Relevant initiatives related to road development	Relevant acts, plans, programs
Tenth Plan 2002–2007	Civil war intensified, People's Movement (*Jana Andolan)* in 2006, leading to peace process; King Gyanendra seized absolute power after royal massacre. The plan aimed to reduce poverty by mobilizing available resources optimally through the joint participation of the government, non-governmental sector and civil society. Millennium Development Goals (MDGs) informed poverty reduction strategy.	This plan identified the road network as a basic infrastructure essential for socio-economic development; lack of road access was identified as the main cause of rural poverty. Involvement of the private sector and users' groups were to be integrated from project formulation to implementation. Capacity of government bodies at all levels was to be promoted.	Aimed to link all the district headquarters into the national road network. Strategic and local road classification established. A vision for three parallel East-West Highways (existing East-West Highway, Mid-Hill Highway and existing Postal Highway through southern Tarai belt). North-South Highways and feeder roads; National Transport policy, 2002; Roads Board Act, 2002; Local Infrastructure Development Policy, 2004. Continued Integrated Rural Development Programs in different phases. Public Procurement Act, 2007.

Plan (years)	National and global context	Relevant initiatives related to road development	Relevant acts, plans, programs
Eleventh Plan (2007–2010)	Political transition, peace process, and first constituent assembly elections. Plan aimed to lay the foundation for economic and social transformation, prioritizing establishment of peace, promotion of social cohesion, and reconstruction of infrastructure in the aftermath of conflict.	The Build, Own, Operate and Transfer (BOOT) approach was promoted to increase private sector involvement in building physical infrastructure, including roads.	Strategic Road Network under the Department of Roads and Local Road Network under Department of Local Infrastructure Development and Agricultural Roads (DoLIDAR). 10-year Priority Investment Plan, 2007-2017. Eight North-South trade and transit corridors were initiated; Kathmandu Tarai Fast-Track project; Kathmandu Valley Road extension project. Agriculture and Rural Road Implementation Guidelines, 2007.
Twelfth Plan (2010–2013)	Political instability, followed by frequent changes of central government. Constituent Assembly was dissolved and debate on second Constituent Assembly took place; parties agreed to form an interim government under the leadership of Khila Raj Regmi, the Chief Justice.	Road was defined as development, and as the basic infrastructure for production and social services.	Continued rural road construction through Rural Infrastructure Development programs, such as DRILP, RAP, RAIDP, DRSP and RCIW.

Plan (years)	National and global context	Relevant initiatives related to road development	Relevant acts, plans, programs
Thirteenth Plan (2013–2016)	New Constitution promulgated; Madhesh Movement challenged the New Constitution; economic blockade from India and earthquake were key events in 2015. This plan aimed to elevate Nepal from its Least Developed Country (LDC) status to a developing country. It focused on improving living standards by increasing income and reducing poverty. The priority sectors were water resources, power development, agriculture productivity, governance, natural resource conservation, environment protection, and industry and tourism.	Road as synonymous with development, reducing regional imbalance, and seen as critical for effective service delivery and social integration.	Nepal Road Safety Action Plan 2013–2020. Three layers of government (Federal, Provincial and Local) were established and emphasis was given to Provincial and Local infrastructure.
Fourteenth Plan (2016–2019)	First plan after the promulgation of the New Constitution; it outlined the federal structure. It aimed to establish an independent, prosperous and socialism-oriented national economy that supports the creation of a welfare state committed to social justice; it sought to establish Nepal as a middle-income country.	Roads are a fundamental infrastructure for transportation systems, connectivity, and overall development of other infrastructure and social sectors.	National priority projects were launched, including many strategic roads. Sustainable Development Goals 2030. Disaster Risk Reduction and Management Act, 2017. E-bidding introduced at district scale.

Plan (years)	National and global context	Relevant initiatives related to road development	Relevant acts, plans, programs
Fifteenth Plan (2019/20–2023/24)	Initial years of federalism, relative political stability, resolution of power outages, and decrease in political unrest and strikes. This plan constituted the first five years of the Long-term Vision 2043, 25-year plan, and aimed to lay a foundation for prosperity. It set an ambitious growth target of 9.6 percent. The COVID-19 pandemic hit in the first year. Then the Russia-Ukraine war disrupted international supply chains, leading to price increases on such key imported commodities as petroleum products.	Concerns expressed about quality of construction materials and weaknesses in contract management. Lack of inter-agency coordination also noted, in relation to land acquisition, encroachment on national highways, disputes over road boundaries during expansion, and resistance from local communities demanding compensation. Many national priority projects, strategic road upgrades, and North-South trade routes remained incomplete relative to initial estimates. Landslides and soil erosion were noted as being on the rise due to unplanned road construction and the effects of climate change.	A 25-year Long-Term Vision 2019–2043 Plan, "Prosperous Nepal, Happy Nepali." Continued national and regional Strategic Road Networks and trade corridors and access roads. During this periodic plan all district headquarters were connected through road networks.

Source: Periodic Plans (1 to 15) published by the National Planning Commission of Nepal. Available at www.npc.gov.np/category/620/; accessed May 30, 2025. Acts and Programs listed in the third column are suggestive of trends, rather than comprehensive, as they are not provided in the published periodic plans.

Notes on Contributors

Pushpa Hamal is Assistant Professor (CLTA) at the Ontario Institute of Studies in Higher Education where he teaches graduate courses on social economy and qualitative methodology. His doctoral dissertation in Adult Education and Community Development (Ontario Institute of Studies in Education, University of Toronto) addresses road development as a terrain of community learning and activism.

Shyam Kunwar is a doctoral student in the Department of Geography and Planning at the University of Toronto. His MA thesis examined resistance and negotiation associated with the Jhimruk Hydropower Project in Pyuthan and his MPhil thesis focused on changing labor relations in road development in Dolakha, both from the Central Department of Anthropology, Tribhuvan University.

Elsie Lewison is Development Officer at the River Institute in Cornwall, Ontario. She holds a PhD in Geography from the University of Toronto and held a SSHRC Postdoctoral Fellowship in the School of Public Policy & Global Affairs at the University of British Columbia. Her dissertation addressed the politics of markets in organic apple production in Jumla, Nepal. She served as project manager for Infrastructures of Democracy, and editor of *Landmarks: The Journal of Undergraduate Geography*.

Lagan Rai is a faculty member at the Degree Campus, Biratnagar of Tribhuvan University and a doctoral candidate at the Central Department of Anthropology, Tribhuvan University. He has conducted research on religious conversion, social inclusion, indigeneity, and sand-mining in several communities of southern Morang in addition to his current research on road development.

Katharine N. Rankin is Professor in the Department of Geography and Planning at the University of Toronto. She is author of *Cultural Politics of Markets: Economic Liberalization and Social Change in Nepal* (University of Toronto Press, 2004).

Sara Shneiderman is Associate Professor cross-appointed in the Department of Anthropology and School of Public Policy & Global Affairs at the University of British Columbia. She is author of *Rituals of Ethnicity: Thangmi Identitites between Nepal and India* (University of Pennsylvania Press, 2015), co-editor of *Darjeeling Reconsidered: Histories, Politics, Environments* (Oxford, 2018), and a founding member of the Digital Himalaya Project.

Tulasi Sharan Sigdel is Senior Director at the Nepal Administrative Staff College, where he has worked for 15 years. He holds a Masters degree from the Central Department of Rural Development, Tribhuvan University, during which he investigated local development planning in Raipur VDC.

Mukta S. Tamang is an anthropologist who teaches at the Central Department of Anthropology, Tribhuvan University where he also served as Research Director. He received his PhD from Cornell University. He has been a Visiting Fellow at New School University, New York, in 2016 and a Public Policy Practitioner Fellow at the University of British Columbia, Canada in 2025.

Index

Agency 7, 13, 17, 131, 183, 244–5, 250, 280, 294, 299
Agrarian 17, 24, 26, 28, 32, 34, 150, 176
Alignment 7, 39, 97–8, 100–1, 103–5, 151, 153, 173, 175–82, 184, 186, 188–9, 210–1, 216, 246–50, 253, 257, 266, 282, 289, 292–4, 297, 307, 314–5, 357
All-party mechanism (APM) 53–4, 95, 124, 210, 298
Anthropology/ical/ists/ies 14, 18, 21–2, 155, 286
Araniko Highway 44–5, 50, 143, 145, 154–5, 197, 199, 287, 354–5
Asian Development Bank (ADB) 51, 119, 183, 228, 357
Authorship 23–7, 312
Backcutting 296
Belt and Road Initiative (BRI) 3, 20–1, 32, 311
Bicycle 75, 79, 107–8, 110, 120–3, 136, 308
Bid/bidding 44, 54, 56, 147, 157–61, 167, 173, 175, 209, 224, 233–40, 271, 274–6, 282, 290, 298–9, 301, 306–7, 315, 363
Border viii, 11, 17–9, 27, 33–4, 44, 65–7, 69, 71, 73–4, 96, 107–8, 114, 122, 132, 140, 142–3, 147, 155, 165, 175–6, 186–7, 191, 204, 219, 222–3, 225, 230, 232, 246–7, 260–2, 268–9, 279, 286–7, 292, 314
Bribe/ry 40, 95, 135, 159, 291, 301
Budget 6–7, 12, 39, 42, 49, 52, 83, 90–6, 102, 124–5, 128–30, 146, 148, 151, 154–6, 158–9, 165, 167–73, 175, 179–80, 187–90, 193, 209–10, 220, 233–5, 237, 241–3, 265–71, 281–2, 291, 293–4, 298–300, 314, 353–5, 357, 359
Business 4, 29, 68, 94, 112–5, 122, 135, 148, 154, 163, 173–4, 181–2, 185, 189, 192–3, 196, 199, 230, 236–7, 246–8, 252, 263, 266, 268–9, 271, 274–8, 280, 282, 287, 291, 293, 298, 303, 306
Caste 5, 17, 30, 34, 36–7, 48, 68, 144, 217, 220, 240, 244, 304
Citizen/ship 2, 7, 13, 15, 65, 73, 82–9, 92, 120, 132–3, 143, 186, 289, 291

Climate change 8, 13, 32, 51, 288, 305, 364
Cold War 42-44, 353
Collaboration/ive viii, x, 21, 23–7, 30–1, 50, 93, 139, 150, 169, 211, 233, 252, 285–6, 289, 294, 303, 312–6, 318
Collusion/ive 10, 40, 158, 160, 174–5, 209, 211, 215, 236, 265–6, 274, 289, 290–1, 298, 301, 318
Common sense 290, 301
Communist Party 52, 154, 159, 168, 210, 243, 359
Community 9, 16, 23–6, 28–9, 31, 35–8, 51–2, 56, 68–9, 83–4, 86, 90, 95, 99, 106, 110, 115, 118, 124–7, 131, 133–4, 139, 148, 158, 169, 215, 232, 242, 245–6, 252–3, 269–70, 272–4, 283, 286, 297, 303–9, 313, 315, 318
Community forestry 51, 55, 303
Community forestry user group (CFUG) 51, 56, 303–5
Comparison/tive vii, 2, 28–9, 35, 40, 48, 131, 285–6, 311–3, 318
Conflict 1, 4, 6, 8, 10–11, 13, 16–7, 24–5, 30–1, 39, 53, 55–6, 93, 95–105, 113–4, 123, 125, 127, 133, 148, 151, 159, 161–2, 173, 178, 180, 182, 195, 198, 207–8, 211, 227–8, 245–6, 253, 257, 267, 269, 275, 278, 287, 289, 293–4, 298–9, 304, 359, 360, 362
Connectivity 5–6, 13, 15, 19, 38, 67, 75–7, 89, 105, 110, 121, 148, 151, 167, 188, 219, 222, 225, 274–80, 286–8, 292, 295, 314, 363
Consciousness 4, 8, 17–9, 67, 234, 262, 281–3, 294, 297, 299–300
Constitution 11–2, 17, 32, 82, 87, 363
Contractor 21, 30, 54–6, 58–9, 95, 112, 114, 126–7, 134, 156–68, 170–1, 173–5, 209–10, 224, 232–41, 245, 248, 251, 263–7, 269–71, 273–6, 281–3, 290–3, 295, 298, 300, 302–3, 306, 312, 315, 318
Contradiction/s 5, 8, 22, 28, 35, 63, 186, 208–9, 293–4, 318
Cooperatives 52, 91, 131, 199–201, 208, 211, 280, 303, 306–8
Corruption 4, 7, 18–9, 21, 31, 39–40, 58, 60, 65, 83, 90–6, 124–5, 128, 174, 210, 283, 289, 302, 309, 318
Crisis 12–3, 51–2, 93, 120, 174, 194–5, 219, 221
Cultural politics x, 10, 17–8, 20, 27, 29, 31, 34–5, 56, 65, 83, 131, 140, 216, 221, 240, 282, 296, 301, 313, 315, 318
Deforestation 21, 68, 172, 221, 264
Democracy 1, 3, 10–1, 14, 16, 22, 25, 71, 75, 82, 93, 123, 128, 178–9, 220, 283, 309, 359
Department of Local Infrastructure Development and Agricultural Roads (DoLIDAR) viii, 53, 56–7, 228, 360, 362
Department of Roads (DoR) 43, 53, 162–3, 166, 183, 227, 231, 247, 250, 259–60, 265, 354, 362
Development 3–4, 6–11, 13, 15–20, 22, 27–9, 33–4, 36, 38, 40, 42, 44, 47–56, 58–60, 63–6, 71, 74–7, 82, 87, 89, 92–4, 97–8, 102, 104–5, 110, 120–1, 123–4, 128, 130–6, 139–40, 145–8, 150–2, 154–5, 157, 159, 167–8, 176, 179, 181–9, 192, 194–5, 207–8, 210–11, 215–7, 219–23, 225, 227–8, 230, 232, 235, 240,

242–3, 248, 251–2, 256–7, 261–3, 265–6, 270–1, 273, 275, 278, 280, 281–3, 285–91, 293–6, 298–309, 312–4, 317, 318, 353–63
Department for International Development (DfID) 51, 56, 225, 240, 270, 306
Disaster 1, 8, 11, 116, 142, 191–2, 194, 264, 289, 295, 298
District Development Committee (DDC) 15, 31, 53, 151–4, 168, 172, 179–81, 188–9, 210, 221, 223–4, 238, 240, 243, 249, 266, 294
District Transportation Master Plan (DTMP) 9, 58, 224, 240
District Technical Office (DTO) 58, 233, 236, 241, 261
Dolakha viii, 2, 5, 23, 31, 33–4, 44–6, 48–50, 53–5, 57, 60, 87, 96–7, 104, 125, 139–212, 216, 235, 241, 246, 248, 251, 253–4, 257, 260–1, 277, 279, 286–7, 290–6, 299, 302–3, 306–7, 313, 315–6
Donors 2, 10, 21, 30–1, 34, 44–5, 55–60, 64, 74–5, 82, 146, 169, 183, 186, 188, 211, 216, 222, 224–5, 248–9, 282, 283, 297–8, 306, 308
Dozer 1, 90, 100–1, 125, 151–4, 156, 168, 170–2, 175, 187–91, 193, 208–9, 242, 256, 265, 268–9, 271–2, 274, 296
Dozer engineer 297, 265, 301
Dozer terrorism 1, 265, 301
E-bidding 54, 233, 239, 363
East-West Highway 34, 43–5, 47–8, 60, 64, 68–9, 71, 73, 79, 84–7, 89, 110, 313, 353–6, 358, 361
Encroachment 65, 96–8, 100, 104, 184, 216, 246, 257–62, 281, 293–4, 297, 364
Engineer/ing 14, 19, 44, 50, 53, 108, 132, 147, 150, 154, 157, 159, 166, 168–70, 172–3, 177, 187, 190–1, 210–11, 246, 249, 265, 297, 301, 307
Environment/al 2–3, 6, 8–10, 17, 21–2, 27, 40, 47, 50–2, 57–9, 63, 65, 93, 95, 105–6, 108, 114–5, 117, 134–5, 140, 153, 156, 165–6, 168, 176, 178, 187–91, 194–5, 208–9, 217, 225, 240, 242–3, 262–4, 266, 270, 272, 281–2, 286, 295–7, 299–300, 306, 308, 314, 358, 363
Equity/inequity 22, 302, 305, 312, 316
Ethical frameworks 302–3, 309
Ethical judgment 7, 39, 289, 300, 302
Ethnicity 5, 11, 17, 36–7
Ethnography/ic 2–3, 5–6, 10, 14, 18–20, 23–4, 27–9, 34–5, 63, 83, 96, 98, 106, 139, 143, 156, 169, 182, 211, 224, 285, 292, 309, 311, 314–6, 318
Everyday life 2–4, 14, 18, 22, 28, 83, 140, 151, 198, 281, 288
Excavator 90–1, 99–103, 125–9, 151, 167, 244, 264, 296
Expropriation 77, 98–105, 186, 216, 246, 250–7, 260–1, 281, 294
Factory/ies 67, 89, 109, 115–8, 120–2, 132, 135, 146, 287
Five-year plans 42–3, 45, 48, 353–64
Flood/ing 8, 64–6, 71–2, 81, 105–10, 114, 127–8, 142, 156, 172, 191–5, 228, 264, 272, 287–9, 292, 294–7, 299–300, 309, 314
Forced labor 41, 82–4, 86–8, 106, 291
Freedom 22, 82
Gender 5, 17, 36–7, 128, 221, 244–5, 249, 273

Geography/ers/ies 2, 5–6, 10, 14, 18, 21–2, 28–9, 32, 44, 48, 45–6, 68–9, 71, 75, 77, 136, 140, 154–5, 219, 221, 230–1, 250, 261, 279, 286, 301, 311–3, 318
Geopolitics 2, 4, 15, 29, 33, 40, 43–5, 211, 303
German Technical Cooperation Agency (GTZ) 51, 189, 357
Government of Nepal (GoN) 54–5, 59, 73, 82, 148, 154, 163, 173, 189, 223, 225, 240
Green roads 8–9, 21, 51–2, 54, 56–60, 108, 110, 115, 136, 140, 150, 152, 187–8, 208, 224–5, 241, 243–4, 262, 264, 296–7, 299, 304, 306, 358, 360
Gurung, Harka 48, 355–6
Heavy equipment/machinery 54, 56, 58–60, 90, 125, 148, 150–1, 156, 164, 168–70, 173, 187, 209, 241, 244, 264–5, 271, 274, 281, 293, 296–8, 304, 306
Hegemony/ic 21, 185, 211
Hills 41, 45, 48–9, 51, 63–4, 68, 74–5, 77, 82–4, 119, 140, 142, 145, 155, 197, 272, 295–6, 299, 358
Himalaya/n 3, 6, 14–5, 20–2, 31–2, 51, 140, 142–3, 145, 148, 155, 191, 219, 223, 261, 287, 295, 357–8
History/ical 2, 5, 8, 14, 18-20, 27–31, 34, 40, 43, 47, 65, 67–9, 71–7, 82–4, 86, 106, 115, 131–2, 134, 140, 142–4, 146, 148, 154–5, 215, 217, 222–3, 225, 230, 232, 246, 282, 286, 291, 313, 315, 318, 353
Honor 73, 135, 290–1
Hospitality 26, 39
Identity 36–7, 131, 143
India 20, 33–4, 41–5, 64–74, 77, 87–9, 99, 107–8, 112, 115, 120, 122, 132, 142, 147–8, 154, 163–4, 223, 230–1, 271, 353, 363
Indigenous/eity 11, 37, 43, 47, 63, 68, 99, 144–5, 299, 304, 307
Industry/ial 14, 34, 48, 64–7, 69, 71, 114, 116, 123, 133, 277, 287, 305 356–60, 363
Inequality 5, 25, 47, 63, 76, 93, 133, 221, 230–1, 253
Infrastructural state 15
Infrastructural turn 5, 15, 311
Infrastructures of democracy 3, 16, 283, 309
Integrated rural development (IRD) 48-50, 60, 145, 148, 150, 287, 356-61
Interview 29-31, 45, 86, 103, 153–4, 156–7, 162–3, 169, 171, 179, 193, 202, 207, 224–5, 236, 252, 254–5, 257, 263, 265, 267–8, 275–6, 286, 315–7
Justice 9-10, 16, 20, 22, 29, 63, 93, 105, 134, 279–80, 285, 300–9, 312, 316, 363
Karnali Highway 217, 220, 223, 225, 227–8, 230–1, 247–50, 257, 260–2, 264, 272–3, 278–80, 358
Kickback 39
Labor/er 4, 6–7, 9, 15, 21, 26, 30, 32–3, 39, 41, 44, 50–1, 57, 59, 65, 67, 73, 82–4, 86–8, 90–4, 102, 105–6, 112–27, 129–30, 135–6, 139, 144–5, 147–8, 150–1, 156, 161, 166, 168, 170, 173, 175, 187–9, 209, 223, 225, 232, 241, 243, 249–50, 252, 254, 265, 269–73, 279, 287, 289–94,

296–7, 300, 303, 305–7, 312, 314–5, 317–8, 355–6
Lamosangu-Jiri Road 34, 45, 49–51, 139, 145–6, 150–3, 155, 157, 160, 162–7, 175–8, 184, 187–8, 194, 197, 199, 202, 208, 287, 356
Landscape 2, 8, 17, 22, 27, 32, 71, 89, 96, 140, 142, 145, 150, 153, 173, 175–8, 182, 187–9, 209, 221, 246, 257, 262, 270, 286, 299, 312, 314, 318, 360
Landslide 8, 50, 56, 67, 108, 142, 156, 161, 166–7, 172–3, 179–80, 188–95, 221, 228, 256–7, 259, 264–5, 272, 281, 294–7, 314, 364
Local Self-Governance Act 16, 52–3, 93, 123, 360
Life-world 18
Local road 45, 47, 54, 90, 94, 96, 118, 224, 240, 250, 255, 257, 263, 267, 305, 315, 358, 361
Local Road Network (LRN) 53, 57–8, 105, 117, 224, 262, 266, 362
Labor-based, environmentally friendly, and participatory (LEP) 8, 21, 51, 56–8, 168, 170, 225, 268, 296–7, 306
Mahendra, the King 43–5, 48, 73, 80, 87–8, 132, 227, 354–5
Maintenance 57, 64, 75, 110, 115, 127–8, 147, 152, 172, 200, 282, 307
Marginality, marginalized 19, 43, 52, 57, 64, 67–8, 76, 89, 93, 99, 114, 119, 123, 131, 133, 136, 144, 155, 176, 184, 211, 223, 231, 244, 283, 287, 299, 303, 315
Market(s) 6, 14–6, 19, 21, 27, 30–1, 34, 50, 54, 59–60, 64–5, 67, 69, 74–5, 78, 85, 89, 94, 103, 107, 115–6, 118, 120–1, 135–6, 140, 142, 144–7, 151, 153–5, 158, 160, 170–1 176, 181, 186, 188, 193, 195, 197, 204, 216–7, 223, 231–5, 250, 261, 274–80, 286, 289–90, 295, 297, 303, 306–8, 313–5, 318, 359
Materiality 16, 36, 246
Media 1–2, 31, 55, 103, 108, 159, 202, 207, 264, 283, 315
Migration 13, 48, 57, 64, 106, 142, 144–5, 223, 306–7
Mobility 7–8, 14, 16, 19, 22, 25, 33, 66, 71, 73, 79, 89, 105–7, 109–10, 120–1, 130, 134–6, 142–3, 154, 201, 203, 222, 252, 278, 294, 302, 313, 318
Mobility justice 22
Mobility studies 22
Monarchy 40, 42–3, 353
Morang 2, 5, 23, 33–4, 41, 44, 46, 48, 60, 63–136, 148, 168, 172, 184, 188–90, 216, 235, 241, 246, 251, 253, 279, 286–7, 291–6, 299–300, 303, 305–7, 313, 315
Mugu 2, 5, 16, 23, 33, 46, 48, 51–4, 56–7, 59–60, 95–7, 104, 125, 147, 150, 155–6, 158–9, 172, 174, 187, 190, 213–83, 286–7, 289–97, 302–4, 306, 314–5, 317
Municipality 12, 21, 32, 36, 56, 67, 69, 79, 84, 87, 90, 97, 99, 101, 106–7, 109, 111–3, 115–6, 118, 120, 125, 128–9, 135, 142–4, 162–3, 170, 184, 192, 217, 219, 224, 231, 240, 248, 253, 259–62, 264, 279, 299
Municipalization 29, 32

Negotiate/ion 35, 39, 53, 105, 133, 139, 170, 175, 196, 198, 202, 204, 210, 236, 238, 258
Neoliberalism 16–7, 50, 52, 358
Nepali 2–3, 13, 24–5, 29, 31, 38–9, 43–4, 73, 75, 77, 129, 132, 139, 143, 147, 150, 155, 159, 164–6, 169, 215–7, 220, 266, 274
Nepali Congress 52, 159, 210, 243, 354, 359
New Nepal 16
Nexus 57, 158, 178, 232, 266, 268, 274, 276–7, 281–2, 287, 291–3, 298–9, 303
Normative 4, 29, 286, 300
Panchayat 43, 47, 69, 73, 82, 85, 87–8, 91–3, 132, 134, 143, 146, 148, 155, 177–9, 182, 200, 216, 354–5, 359
Paradox/es 19, 22, 63, 65, 78
Participation/ory 7–8, 13, 19, 21–4, 29, 31, 47, 49, 51–3, 55, 57, 59, 82–3, 86–7, 89–90, 92–4, 96, 109, 123, 125–6, 128, 132, 136, 150, 155, 164, 167–8, 170, 195, 216, 225, 232, 234, 236–7, 240, 242, 245, 249, 273, 276, 279, 281–2, 286, 288, 290–3, 296–8, 302–5, 309, 358, 361
Periphery 6, 29, 32, 38, 47, 98, 231, 287
Personal commission (PC) 159, 175, 234–5, 290, 293
Planning 3–5, 9–10, 26–9, 40, 43, 47–8, 53, 58, 60, 64–5, 71, 74–5, 77, 83, 93–4, 105, 119, 123–5, 136, 140, 146, 156, 162, 175, 177, 191, 208–11, 217, 223, 227, 246, 248, 274, 280–3, 285–308, 314, 318, 356–7
Political capital 7, 183, 230, 248, 292–3, 314
Political economy 2, 8, 10, 17–9, 28–9, 31, 33–4, 40, 47, 132, 216, 221, 229, 240, 288, 290, 296, 301
Political transition 1, 10, 362
Polity/ics 3, 8–11, 13, 16–8, 20, 22, 27, 29–31, 34–5, 42, 44–5, 51, 56, 60, 63, 65, 67, 82, 123, 177–8, 181–2, 186, 208–10, 215–6, 221, 240, 254, 262, 276, 280–3, 123, 131, 134, 139–40, 152, 156, 158, 169, 176, 285–6, 294–301, 303, 313, 315, 317–8
Popular theatre 291, 295
Positionality 27, 37
Post-conflict 1, 11, 16, 25, 95, 180, 227, 298
Postal road 41, 69, 74, 83, 121, 361
Power 4–6, 9–10, 12, 15, 17, 19–20, 23, 25, 39, 65, 67, 72, 76, 94–5, 119, 123–4, 131, 133–4, 145, 153, 163, 177–8, 180, 210–11, 217, 222–3, 230–1, 245–6, 250, 254–5, 264, 267, 276–7, 281–2, 286, 290–2, 294, 301–3, 309, 313, 315, 317–8, 354–5, 361, 363–4
Praxis 16, 28, 60, 283, 285–309, 312, 316–7
Precarity 19
Private gain 7, 276, 288–9, 291
Procurement 21, 54, 56, 58–60, 157–8, 164, 173–4, 223, 235, 237–8, 240, 275, 291–2, 298–9
Province 11, 33, 36, 65–6, 69, 74, 140, 143, 176, 215, 219–21, 227, 287

Public good 6–7, 139, 176, 183, 186, 217, 288–91, 302, 304, 312, 314, 318
Public Procurement Act 54, 59, 164, 173, 240, 361
Public sphere 18, 25, 60, 294
Publics 4, 6–7, 15, 20, 43, 128, 130, 289, 309
Rana/s 41–2, 64, 67, 77, 82–7, 99, 143, 353
Rationality 169, 299
Refusal 102, 291, 294
Region/al 5–6, 11, 13–5, 17, 20–1, 29, 33–4, 38, 43, 47–50, 64–6, 68, 71, 74–5, 77, 80, 82, 87, 99, 105, 107, 119, 123, 131, 139–48, 151, 155, 177–9, 181, 185, 191–2, 194, 196, 198–9, 202, 216–7, 219–20, 223, 225, 227, 231–2, 240, 250, 261, 264, 287–8, 303–5, 353, 355–9, 363–4
Relational/ity 3, 6–8, 15–6, 27–9, 33–5, 38, 60, 63, 76, 95, 148, 154, 285–6, 288, 292, 312–4, 316, 318
Remoteness 6, 13, 27, 29, 63, 65, 71, 75–82, 106, 286–8, 148, 154–5, 225, 230–2, 290, 292, 295, 313–4
Repair 80, 84, 86, 91–2, 110, 152, 203, 266, 305–6
Resistance 17, 65, 96, 98, 127, 133–4, 139, 157, 255, 300–1
Responsibility 12, 16, 53, 57, 93, 115, 267, 128, 163, 166, 184, 186–7, 205, 209, 289, 294
Restructuring 12, 65, 69, 80, 90, 143–4, 217, 281, 298
Restructuring (administrative) 12, 143
Restructuring (political) 22, 32, 51–2, 309
Restructuring (state) 1, 4, 8, 11–2, 36, 65, 69, 80, 90, 215, 217
Rights 11, 118, 123, 133, 162, 263, 302, 308, 313
Route permit 54–5, 196, 198, 203, 205–6, 277
Rural 1–4, 7–8, 11, 13, 19–22, 29, 31–4, 40, 43, 47–51, 53–60, 64–5, 69, 71, 75, 77, 79, 83, 89–90, 92–3, 96, 104, 108, 111, 115–6, 119, 121, 123, 125, 128, 132, 134–6, 139, 142, 144–5, 148, 150–7, 167–73, 182–90, 198–9, 203, 207, 232, 240, 263, 287, 289–90, 292, 294–7, 307–8, 311–4, 316, 318, 356–62
Rural Access Program (RAP) 51, 56, 59, 216, 241–5, 247, 249–50, 256–7, 261–2, 264–5, 268–74, 280, 289, 297, 317, 360, 362
Rural municipality 12, 32, 36, 69, 75, 79, 84, 87, 90, 97, 99, 101, 106–7, 109, 111–3, 115–6, 118, 120, 125, 129, 135, 142–3, 192, 217, 219, 224, 231, 248, 253, 261–2, 264, 279
Sand-mining 63, 65, 111–4, 135, 148, 296, 305
Shame 80, 166, 290, 292
Sindhupalchok 50, 140, 143, 145, 157, 164–5, 202, 204, 287
Social mobilizer/s 9, 56, 241, 244, 270, 297
Strategic road/s 33–4, 40, 42–3, 45, 47, 53, 73, 140, 147, 150, 155, 172, 182–3, 186, 217, 220, 223–4, 227–8, 247, 250, 257, 260, 265, 280, 287, 361–4

Struggle 17, 21–2, 81, 108, 134, 144, 195–6, 199, 202–3, 206, 257, 288
Subjective/ity 4–5, 7, 13, 15, 17, 19–20, 36, 77, 84, 90, 93, 96, 129, 155, 216, 231, 234, 281, 287, 293–5, 301, 303–4, 314, 318
Suspended infrastructure 176, 257
Sustainability 9–10, 17, 27, 29, 32, 52, 59, 65, 83, 96, 105, 108, 111–5, 123, 125–8, 134, 136, 167, 173, 176, 187–91, 209, 217, 225, 262, 265, 271, 274, 285–6, 296–7, 300, 302
Swiss Agency for Development and Cooperation (SDC) 49–51, 146, 148, 151, 183, 189
Syndicate 55, 140, 195–9, 207, 277–8, 287, 293, 299, 301, 308, 313
Tarai 6, 33, 38, 41, 43, 48–9, 64, 66, 68–9, 71, 74–5, 77, 82–4, 89, 96–7, 106, 108, 115, 123, 131–4, 136, 288, 295–6, 307–8, 358, 361–2
Territorialize/ation 16, 216, 246, 253, 293–4
The World Bank 49–51, 54, 58, 183, 263, 306, 356–7
Tibetan Autonomous Region (TAR) 33–4, 44, 140,142–3, 147, 154, 191, 217, 219, 223, 232, 246, 261, 287
Track opening 33, 173, 209, 227, 244, 272, 298
Trans-Himalayan trade 143, 287
Translate/ion x, 24, 38, 160, 234, 290
Transportation 14, 30, 41, 43, 49, 55, 64, 66–7, 73, 75–8, 88, 102, 104, 108, 114, 120–2, 135, 140, 148, 156, 181, 195–6, 198–200, 204, 207–8, 222–3, 228–9, 231, 241, 277–8, 287–8, 291, 293, 298, 301, 308–9, 313, 353–7, 363
Transportation association 30–1, 55, 195–200, 203, 208, 210, 276–9, 295
Transportation management 23, 30, 34, 54–5, 209, 240, 263, 283
Transportation system 34, 207
Tripper 111–5, 189, 296, 305
Trust 133, 158, 291, 303
Underdevelopment 13, 131, 357
United States 305
Upper Tamakoshi Hydro Electric Project (UTKHEP) 146–7, 154, 163–4, 181, 183–4
Urbanization 32, 66, 114, 119
Users' committee/s (UC) 58, 65, 82–3, 90, 93–5, 98–105, 109, 124–8, 130, 134, 139, 153–4, 156, 167–75, 182, 184–5, 187–90, 193–4, 209–10, 224, 241–3, 268, 294, 296, 314
Users' group/s (UG) 30–1, 51–9, 83, 93, 95, 100–2, 216, 224, 232, 237, 240–5, 263, 265, 267, 269–70, 272, 303–4, 315, 318, 361
Vernacular 4, 38–9, 287, 289
Village Development Committee (VDC) 12, 21, 32, 36, 52, 80, 88, 133, 143, 153, 168, 171, 180–1, 210, 217, 220, 243–4, 268, 359
Ward 36
Washington Consensus 50, 52, 59
World Food Programme (WFP) 50–1, 189, 280, 359